Contents

CW01499104

Preface ix

Part one Profile of data processing and computing

1 Data processing and computing concepts 3

Data processing; Data; Data processing operations; The data processing model; The need for computer literacy in modern society; Social aspects of computers

2 Profile of computers 18

Nature of computer systems; Architecture of computer systems; Interfacing computer systems; User interface

3 Types of computer system 28

Mainframes; Minicomputers; Microcomputers (PCs); Conclusion

4 The processor 39

General considerations; The arithmetic/logic unit; Control unit; Buses; Processor clock; Microprocessor; Computer logic; Internal storage

5 Organisation of a data processing and management services department 61

Organisation of a data processing department: by function or activity; Organisation of a data processing department: by purpose; Organisation of a management services department

Part two   Computer input, output, data storage and retrieval, databases and backing storage and media

6   Computer input   73

Computer input media and data capture methods and techniques; Kimball tags; Magnetic input: encoding techniques; Magnetic ink characters; Optical characters; Optical marks; Terminals; Data collection systems; Workstations; Speech synthesis and analogue input

7   Computer output   101

Output devices; Printers; Magnetically encoded; Visual display unit and graph plotter; Computer output on microfilm (COM); Computer aided design (CAD)

8   Data storage and retrieval   109

Folders and directories; Storage and retrieval — use of pointers; Fields; File organisation and retrieval of records; Direct access methods; File activities; Relationship between master files, transaction files and reference files; Virtual storage; Other storages aspects; Logical records and files; Electronic document storage and retrieval

9   Databases   148

Concepts; Database structures; Summarising the advantages and disadvantages of a database; Data modelling

10   Backing storage devices and media   167

The nature of backing storage; Magnetic discs: Winchester and exchangeable; Floppy discs; Comparison of storage devices; Optical and integrated discs; Advantages and disadvantages of direct access storage

11   Data communication   182

Basic concepts; Analogue communications; Digital communications; On-line and off-line transmission; Communication equipment; Accuracy and speed factors; Telecom Datel services; Other Telecom services; Digital PABX telephone exchange; Satellite transmission; Services other than British Telecom

Data Processing

Volume 1 Principles and Practice

Data processing

Volume 1 Principles and Practice

R G Anderson
FCMA, M Inst AM(Dip), FMS

Seventh Edition

THE M & E HANDBOOK SERIES

Pitman Publishing
128 Long Acre, London WC2E 9AN

A Division of Longman Group UK Limited

First published 1974
Second edition 1978
Third edition 1979
Fourth edition 1983
Fifth edition 1984
Sixth edition (2 vols) 1987
Seventh edition 1990
Reprinted in this format 1991

International Student Edition 1987, 1990

© Macdonald & Evans Ltd 1974, 1978, 1979, 1983, 1984
© Longman Group UK Ltd 1987, 1990

British Library Cataloguing in Publication Data
Anderson, R. C.
    Data processing.—7th ed.—(The M & E handbook series)
    Vol. 1. Principles and practice
    1. Data processing
    I. Title
    004

ISBN 0 7121 1019 4
ISBN (ISE) 0 7121 0849 1

Founding Editor: P.W.D. Redmond

Typeset by FDS Ltd, Penarth
Printed in England by Clays Ltd, St Ives plc

12   Networks   196

Types of network: local area networks; Network topology: ring, star and bus networks; Value-added network (VAN) and store and forward systems; Wide area networks

Part three   Checks, controls, security and processing techniques

13   Checks, controls and privacy in computerised systems   209

Spectrum of control; Types of control; Procedural and operational controls; File security; Data Protection Act; Batch control; Auditing computerised business systems; Software (program) checks — validation; Check digit verification; Datakey and Smartcard; Systems development controls; Data processing standards and documentation

14   Processing techniques and configuration requirements   237

Batch processing; On-line processing; Interactive processing; Real-time systems; Multi-user applications; Multi-tasking; Other processing techniques; Processing aids: windows, icons, mouse and pointers (WIMP)

15   Computer bureaux and computing services   259

Computer bureaux; Computing services

Part four   Development of computer applications

16   Framework for the development of computer applications   267

Initial considerations; Education, training, communications and recruitment; Feasibility study: objectives, costs and other factors; Traditional stages of systems development; Structured systems development methodology; Prototyping; Systems analysis and duties of systems analyst; Fact-finding techniques; Recording facts

17   Systems design and implementation   291

Objectives and essentials; Forms design; System specification; System modification requests; Benchmark tests; Project management and control; Systems installation, testing and maintenance; Planning the installation; Direct changeover; Parallel running; Pilot scheme; Test data and dry running (desk checking); System monitoring and maintenance; Retraining personnel

Part five   Programming and software

18   Computer programming and decision tables   313

Nature of computer programs and programming; Program development cycle; Program structure; Structured programming; Structured English and constructs; Program documentation and standards; High-level languages; Procedural languages; Non-procedural languages; Fourth generation languages (4GLs); Aids to programming; Program dumps and restart procedures; Compile time and execution time errors; Closed and open shop programming; Closed and open sub-routines; Program maintenance; Decision tables; Decision tables and program flowcharts

19   Applications software   350

General aspects of software; Vertical market applications software; Accounting packages; The nature of integrated accounting packages; Nominal ledger packages; The sales and purchase ledgers; The sales ledger; The purchase ledger; The payroll; Arguments for and against the use of packages

20   Control software and utilities   389

General aspects of control software; Operating systems; Utility programs

Appendix 1 Examination technique   400
Appendix 2 Case study: car hire company   402

Index   409

Preface to the seventh edition

Since publication of the first edition of this M & E handbook, the subject has expanded from traditional data processing into the realms of information systems and related information technology. This has made it impossible for the subject to be covered in adequate detail in one volume and so it has been necessary to split the M & E handbook into two volumes.

This first volume deals with the fundamentals of data processing and covers the syllabuses of the following bodies:
The Chartered Association of Certified Accountants (ACCA)
The Chartered Institute of Management Accountants (CIMA)
  (Students should also read Volume 2.)
The Institute of Chartered Accountants (ICA)
The Institute of Chartered Secretaries & Administrators (ICSA)
The Society of Company & Commercial Accountants (SCCA)
  (New syllabus — Information Technology)
The Association of Accounting Technicians (AAT)
  (Students taking Analysis of Systems & Design of Systems should
  also read Volume 2.)
The Institute of Data Processing Management (IDPM)
The Business and Technician Education Council (BTEC)
The Royal Society of Arts (RSA)
The City and Guilds of London Institute (CGLI)
The British Computer Society (BCS)

This edition has been extensively revised and updated to reflect technological developments. Matters relating to hardware take into account computer architecture in respect of mainframes, minis and microcomputers. Software has been updated and revised to provide a more practical appreciation of menu-driven accounting packages and vertical market applications.

Interfacing techniques have been added, indicating the various ways in which both machines and people can be linked to the processor. Interfacing includes an appreciation of GEM interfacing software, which enables non-specialist computer personnel to use a computer in a user-friendly and simple manner. Details relating to the functions of the processor have been expanded to provide a greater understanding of the fetch–execute cycle. The use of windows, icons, menus, mouse and pointers is also considered.

Programming principles have been presented in a more practical way to provide a greater understanding of the underlying philosophy. The nature of structured programming is discussed together with the use of structured English for defining the logic of a problem before program coding is undertaken. An appreciation of prototyping and structured system development methodology is also included.

Acknowledgements. The co-operation and assistance of the following organisations, without whose help this book would not have been possible, are gratefully acknowledged.

Apple Macintosh: photograph of multi-tasking screen display.
Ashton-Tate (UK) Ltd: photograph of dBASE1V control centre and queries screen.
British Telecom: details relating to Datel and other services.
British Telecom Picture Unit: photograph of Intelsat V.
Data Card (UK) Limited: provision of details and photographs relating to Data Key.
IBM United Kingdom Limited: photographs of IBM 3090 Model 400 and AS/400 computers.
ICL: DNX-2000 digital PABX exchange.
Litton Business Systems Ltd: examples of Kimball tags.
Midlands Electricity Board: provision of meter reading sheet and details of processing procedure relating to electricity bills.
M4 Data Ltd: photograph of tape streamer.
Philips Data Systems: photograph of optical disc.
Quest Micropad Limited: photograph and details of Micropad.

Soft Numbers Limited: illustrations of screen displays of Apple Macintosh accounting applications.

System C Limited: details of program generator software.

R G Anderson
February 1990

Part one
Profile of data processing and computing

Part one

1

Data processing and computing concepts

Data processing

1. Data processing defined. Data processing consists of those activities concerned with the systematic recording, arranging, computing, updating, displaying and printing of details relating to business transactions. To be effective, data processing needs to be systematised, dynamic and directly integrated and the physical activities and processes so that the information produced assists in the efficient running of the business. A data processing system may therefore be viewed as an administrative system superimposed upon the physical business systems such as manufacturing and selling. There are many types of business: chemicals, engineering, electronics, insurance companies, building societies, banks, tour operators, breweries, stockbrokers, airlines, distributors of goods, and so on. Educational establishments and central and local government offices also have data of one type or another to process. All these different types of organisation undertake data processing activities to obtain information with which to control financial and administrative aspects of the business so that managers and administrators are always fully aware of the status of financial, production, marketing, engineering and personnel matters. In all cases data processing systems respond to events occurring in the business environment and they are therefore event-driven, that is, they record business transactions and process the relevant details to provide various types of information (*see* **2** and Figs. 1.1 and 1.2).

2. Integrative nature of data processing. Table 1A and Figs. 1.1 and 1.2 look at the integrative aspects of a data processing system in relation to the physical business activities of a manufacturing and marketing-orientated business.

Table 1A Integrative aspects of a DP system

Physical activity	Data processing activity
Prior to production	
Procure raw materials and parts	Preparation of purchase orders
Supplies received	Record on stock or job records
	Update suppliers' accounts
	Prepare remittance advice
	Remit amount owing to suppliers
	Purchase analysis
Production to commence	
Issue materials and parts to production centres	Compute value of issues
	Record issues on stock and job records for stock management and costing
Production operations carried out by employees	Record hours attended and /or units or operations performed for wages calculation purposes
	Compute wages earned
	Assess deductions and tax
	Prepare payslips and payrolls
	Analyse and record wages earned on overhead summary sheets for indirect wages and job cost sheets for direct wages
Completion of production	
Production stored in warehouse	Update warehouse stocks
or	*or*
Goods despatched direct to customer	Prepare despatch documentation
	Prepare invoices
	Update customers' accounts
	Prepare statements of account
	Record remittances from customers
	Sales analysis
End of operating period	Preparation of operating reports, profit and loss statements and balance sheets

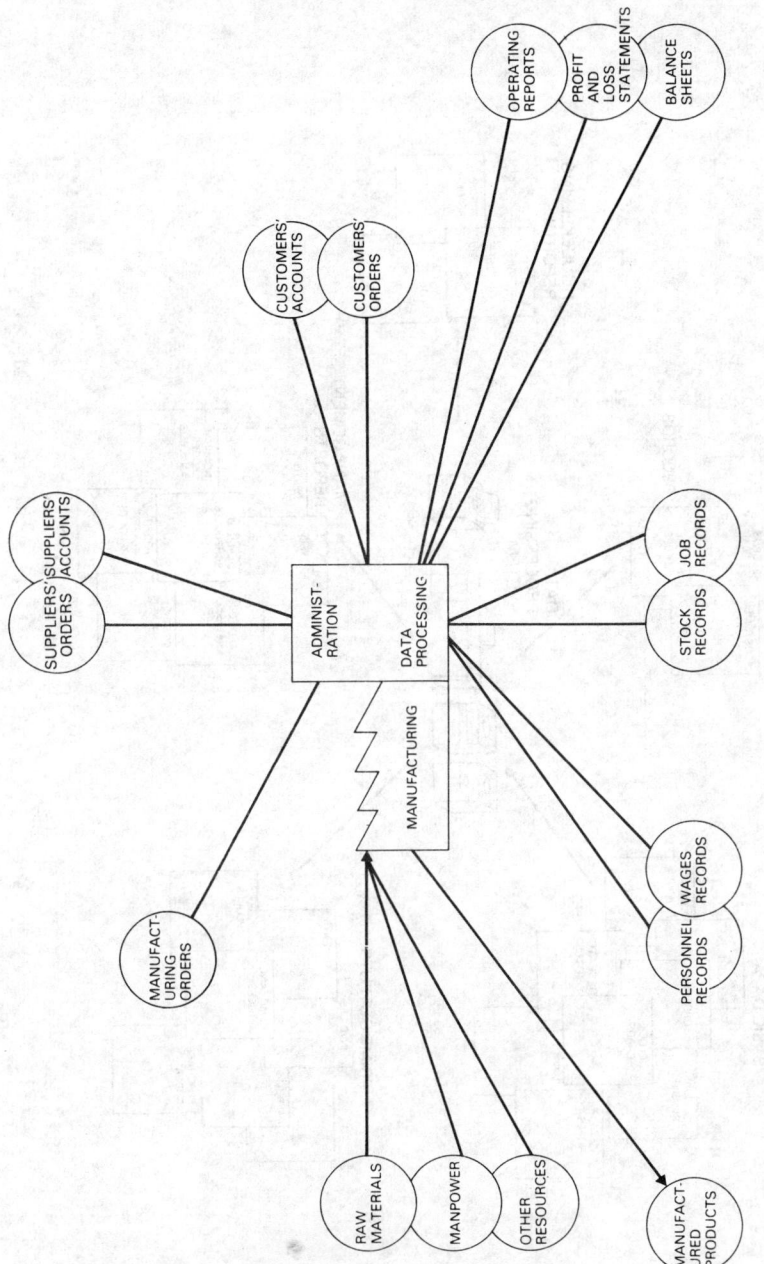

Figure 1.1   *Outline of manufacturing and related data processing activities.*

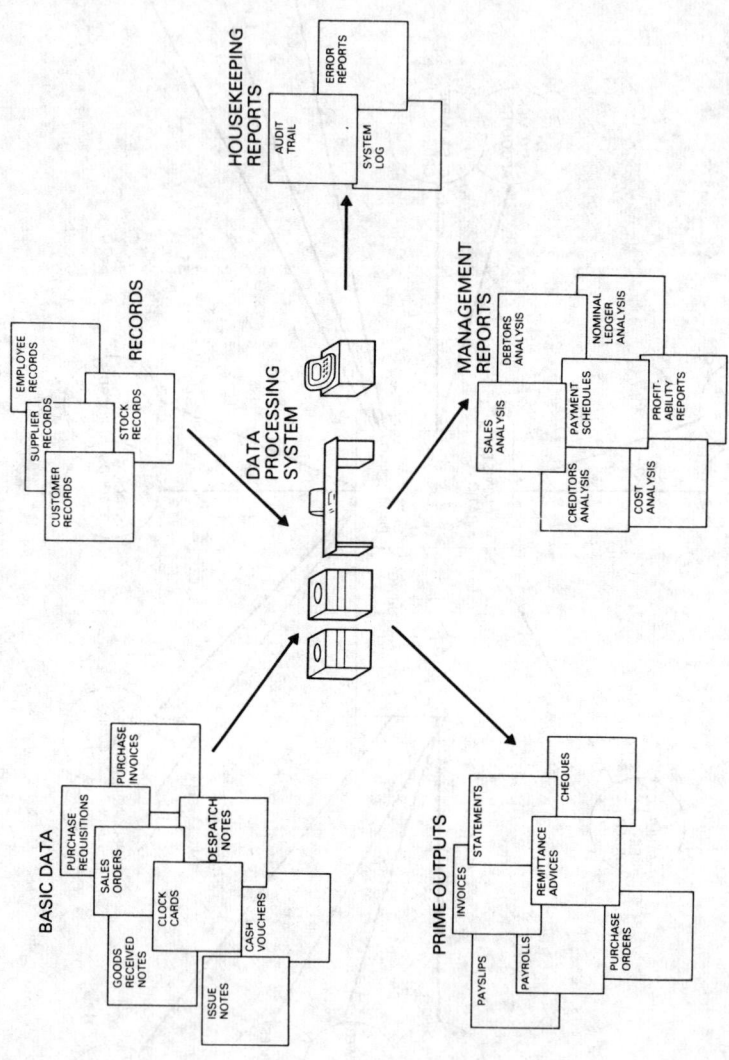

Figure 1.2   *The nature of data processing.*

3. Advance of electronic technology. In many instances, computers perform data processing tasks previously undertaken by clerks. The advance of electronic technology has enabled office tasks to be automated, increasing the level of productivity and accuracy of results compared with those attained by clerical systems (manual methods). Computers have also reduced the level of administrative overheads in many cases, by carrying out routine clerical tasks that would previously have required an army of clerks. Not only larger companies but also one-man businesses can use computers for data processing activities to their advantage: for example, by using them for specialised (as well as routine) applications, such as preparing cost estimates for jobs as a basis for providing quotations to prospective customers.

Data

4. What is data? In the strict data processing context, data may be defined as unprocessed information consisting of details relating to business transactions which are collected into homogeneous groups for input to a data/information processing system to produce information.

5. Bits and characters. The smallest unit of data is the binary digit, or bit, combinations of which represent characters on the basis of a specific binary code or in pure binary. An 8-bit character is known as a 'byte'.

6. Character set. The term 'character set' is used to define the range of characters which can be displayed by a computer, including:

    (*a*) alphabetic:
        (*i*)   Upper case (CAPITAL letters)   A B C X Y Z
        (*ii*) Lower case (small letters)   a b c x y z
    (*b*) numeric:
        0 1 2 3 4 5 6 7 8 9
    (*c*) punctuation symbols and special characters
        ; : . , - ! ? ~
    (*d*) mathematical and logic symbols (*see* Chapter 4):
        + − * % / ^

7. Fields. The smallest unit of usable data is known as a 'field,' which is identified by a field name: quantity in stock, for instance. A field stores the value of a variable — which is a quantity that can assume different values. For example, the quantity in stock varies for specific stock items but each value is stored within the same field name: quantity in stock. Fields are also referred to as 'attributes', examples of which are name of customer, address of supplier, employee number, stock code and the quantity in stock. When data processing and/or database systems are developed fields need to be precisely specified, including:

(*a*) name of the field;
(*b*) number of characters,
(*c*) type of character, whether alphabetic or numeric;
(*d*) range of values for validation purposes;
(*e*) if it is to be used for indexing;
(*f*) if it is to be used in calculations.

8. Records. Related fields combine to form a record of a specific type of entity or group of entities, for example employee record, customer record, supplier record, and so on. Each record is identified and referenced by a record key or key field. Transaction documents contain a key field which is matched with its record on the relevant master file for updating.

9. Structure of a customer record. The fields which combine to form a typical customer record are as follows:

(*a*) account number (the key field);
(*b*) name;
(*c*) address;
(*d*) credit limit;
(*e*) discount category;
(*f*) account balance;
(*g*) age analysis of account balance.

10. Structure of a employee (payroll) record.

(*a*) employee number (the primary key field);
(*b*) name;
(*c*) department code (secondary key field);

(*d*) taxable gross pay to date;
(*e*) tax to date;
(*f*) taxable gross pay from previous employment;
(*g*) tax paid in respect of previous employment;
(*h*) NHS number;
(*i*) NHS category;
(*j*) employee's National Insurance to date;.
(*k*) total National Insurance contributions to date;
(*l*) holiday credit to date;
(*m*) other deductions.

Note: The subject of files is dealt with in Chapter 8.

Data processing operations

11. The primary operations. In order to put data processing into its correct perspective, it is important to appreciate that although data processing activities are largely computerised very little actual 'computing' is performed in most business applications. No doubt this is why the activity is called 'data processing' (*see* 1) and not 'computing.' Computing is a term restricted to performing 'number crunching', i.e. arithmetical calculations including adding, multiplying, subtracting and dividing as well as exponentiation (raising numbers to specified powers) etc. The primary operations for processing business data are summarised below.

(*a*) Capture and record data.
(*b*) Collect/transmit data.
(*c*) Control data throughout all stages of processing — prepare control totals.
(*d*) Prepare data in machine sensible form when relevant.
(*e*) Verify accuracy of data preparation.
(*f*) Input data to the computer.
(*g*) Validate data and generate control totals.
(*h*) Sort data to master file sequence.
(*i*) Compute value of variables.
(*j*) Update master files.
(*k*) Print list of transactions and control totals for accounting and audit trail purposes.
(*l*) Print schedules.

(*m*) Re-input data.

(*n*) Re-sort data for analysis purposes.

(*o*) Summarise data for management information.

(*p*) Produce analyses and statistical reports.

Examples of computing operations performed by a computer for a number of business applications include those shown in Table 1B.

Table 1B Computing examples

Applications		Computations
Invoicing	Gross value	= Quantity sold x Price
	Discount	= Gross value x Discount rate
	Net value	= Gross value – Discount
	VAT	= Net value x VAT rate
	Invoice value	= Net value + VAT
Wages	Gross wages	= Standard hours x standard rate
		+
		Hours @ time and half x premium rate
		+
		Hours @ double time x premium rate
		or:
		Number of units produced x piece rate
		+
		Piecework supplement
	Net wages	= Gross wages – (income tax + standard deductions, etc.)
Stock control	New quantity in stock	= Old quantity in stock
		+
		Receipts
		+
		Returns to store
		–
		Issues
		–
		Returns to supplier
Electricity bill	Amount due	= Standing charge + Unit charge
	Unit charge	= (Present reading – Previous reading) x unit rate

The data processing model

12. Elements and characteristics of a data processing system. A

data processing system in its simplest form consists of three primary elements, i.e input, processing and output. These elements apply whether the system is manual, mechanical or electronic. Data relating to business transactions such as items sold to customers, issues to production from the stores and hours worked by employees is input for processing. The data is subjected to processing operations in order to convert it into a more meaningful form prior to being output. The output, referred to as information, consists of documents such as invoices and payslips; schedules such as payrolls and sales summaries; and reports relating to customer credit standing and stock availability.

The characteristics of a data processing system may be contrasted with those of a factory manufacturing system; they are very similar although one processes raw facts and the other raw materials. The input to the factory system consists of raw materials for conversion into finished or partly finished products, whereas the finished product of a data processing system is information.

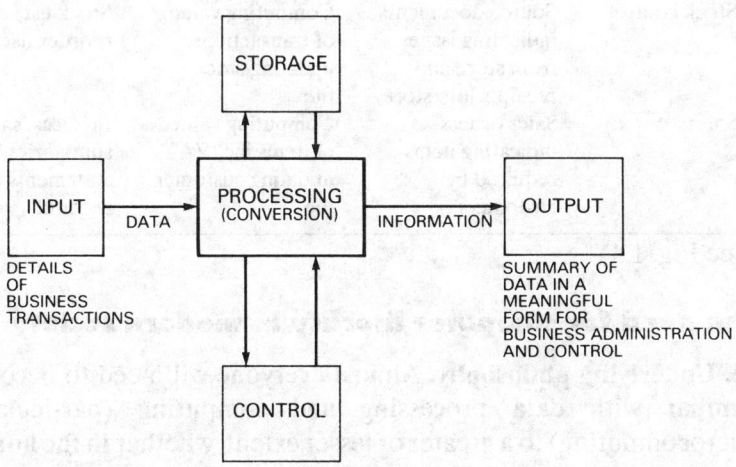

Figure 1.3 *Elements of a data processing system.*

Two secondary, but nevertheless important, elements may be added to the primary elements of a data processing system. These are storage and control. Storage is concerned with filing documents and records relating to business transactions so that the state of affairs of specific business situations is readily available; e.g. amounts owing to customers, amounts owed by suppliers and the quantity of items in stock. Control relates to the monitoring by a supervisor to ensure that activities are conducted in the prescribed manner (*see* Fig. 1.3).

13. Inputs and outputs. All applications, whether processed on a computer or performed manually, consist of inputs and outputs such as those outlined in Table 1 C.

Table 1C Relationship of input and output

Application	Input	Processing	Output
Payroll	Clock cards including hours worked and rates of pay	Computing gross to net wages, tax and standard deductions up-dating payroll file	Payslips, payrolls,tax and deduction summaries
Stock control	Source documents indicating issues from store and receipts into store	Computing value of transactions, updating stock file	Stock list, reorder list
Sales	Sales orders indicating items required by customers	Computing value of items inc. VAT, updating customer file	Invoices, sales summaries, statements of account

(See Fig. 1.4)

The need for computer literacy in modern society

14. Underlying philosophy. Almost everyone will need to become familiar with data processing and computing (particularly microcomputing) to a greater or lesser extent, whether in the home, office, school, college or factory. The microcomputer is now widely accepted as a very efficient device for performing many types of operation, such as the display of business and other information from a Prestel database and for performing computations of varying types at high speed including professional, scientific, engineering and accounting calculations, as well as mathematical calculations for the classroom and word processing in typing and secretarial departments.

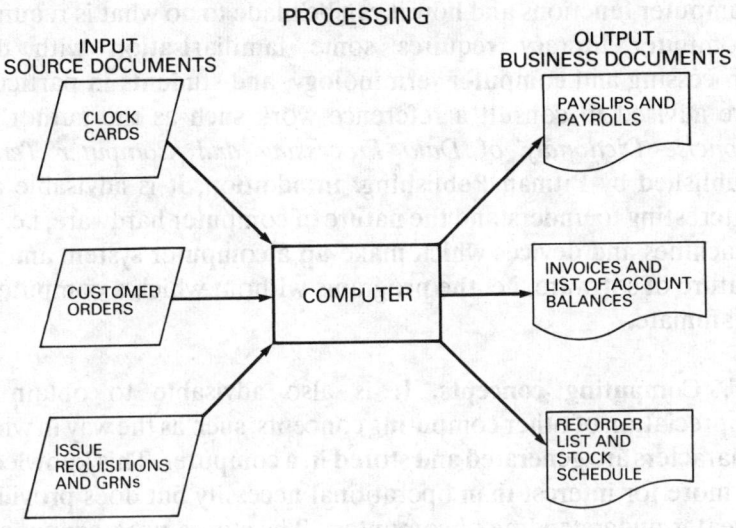

Figure 1.4 *Relationship of input and output.*

In business, the computer, whether a mainframe, mini or micro (*see* Chapter 3), is recognised as a means of increasing administrative efficiency in payroll processing, sales invoicing, order processing, stock control and production planning. Insurance renewal notices and gas and electricity bills, for example, are usually printed by computer. This means that almost everyone will need to become what may be termed 'literate' in the computer context.

The nature of clerical work is changing as jobs are restructured to take advantage of the new technology. Many clerks are being provided with workstations, instead of pens and pads of forms, for dealing with customer orders being phoned in, so that the order details can be directly input to the computer for processing. This is known as an on-line order entry system. These new roles not only provide increased administrative efficiency but also increase the level of job enrichment as clerks become more interested and feel part of the new technology. Clerks do not need to become involved with the programming of computers as this is the prerogative of the systems staff. Package programs may be used for the various applications in most instances.

It is very interesting to obtain an understanding of how a

computer functions and how it can be made to do what is required. Computer literacy requires some familiarisation with data processing and computer terminology, and students in particular are advised to consult a reference work such as the author's *A Concise Dictionary of Data Processing and Computer Terms,* published by Pitman Publishing. In addition, it is advisable and interesting to understand the nature of computer hardware, i.e. the machines and devices which make up a computer system and the nature of software, i.e. the programs without which a computer is inanimate.

15. Computing concepts. It is also advisable to obtain an appreciation of other computing concepts, such as the way in which characters are generated and stored in a computer. This knowledge is more for interest than operational necessity but does provide a greater understanding of computers. The stored program concept is of primary concern to the functioning of a computer.

Social aspects of computers

16. Primary problem. The primary problem stemming from the increasing use of computers in industry and commerce is the increasing level of unemployment as computer controlled manufacturing and administrative activities supersede the older technologies and working methods

High unemployment causes many social problems and, as world demand for goods and services has declined, even fewer people are required to satisfy this demand, creating further redundancy in addition to that attributable directly to the implementation of computers.

High unemployment places an additional burden on the working population, as they are required to pay higher levels of taxation than would otherwise be needed, to provide funds for unemployment pay and other social security payments.

Possibly the only remedy is a reduction in the world's population to the level required to satisfy world demand for goods and services and which the international economy can effectively cope with to provide a minimum standard of living for everyone.

How to overcome these problems is of paramount importance to the governments of the world. One remedy is to retrain personnel in the new technologies: in the areas of computer-aided design, design of computers, design of systems and of programming techniques. This would reduce the level of unemployment caused by the technological factor.

Higher levels of productivity attained by automated processes and the use of robotics should reduce the cost of production. If such decreases are reflected in selling prices then demand, in theory, should increase thereby reducing the level of unemployment.

The retirement age could be lowered allowing the employed people to vacate their jobs earlier, thereby providing vacancies for the unemployed. This policy creates a financial burden on the government and the working population, as funds with which to finance early retirement pensions may create additional taxation unless monies for this purpose are redeployed from some other source.

17. Leisure time. The increasing amount of leisure time available to the population, owing to increasing unemployment and the shorter hours worked by the employed because of the introduction of new technology, has created a demand for more leisure facilities (at least for those who can afford them) thus providing some additional employment to offset the unemployment caused by the increasing use of computers (discussed in **16**).

18. Changing technology. Many people, particularly the older generation, cannot and do not want to change their ways of life, although changing technology tends to force this on the population. We are now approaching the era of supermarket shopping direct from the home by the use of home computers linked to Viewdata television sets; financial transactions occur between accounts filed electronically rather than between people, creating a cash-free society. Even the cheque, which itself replaced cash in many transactions, is on the way out. The transfer of documents by mail services is also on the wane as teletex services and electronic mail systems take over. Holidays may be booked and hotel accommodation and airline seats reserved directly by computer from the home.

19. Social unrest. Computerisation should lead to a more efficient society; on the other hand, it may also lead to social unrest as many people suffer from lack of financial resources due to being made redundant. In the long term this can only be remedied by an enlightened world populace realising that technology marches on, as do 'time and tide', and it is an irresistible force which must be accepted. Change must be seen as a challenge, not viewed apathetically, which must be taken up in the quest for a new and more interesting life style.

20. Benefits of using a computer in business. At one time, mainframes cost a fantastic amount of money and only the larger company could justify their use both financially and from an administrative point of view, as it was necessary to have a computer due to the increasing volume of paper work that had to be processed and the increasing cost of administrative staff. In a number of cases computers decreased costs, but in general other types of benefit were achieved. These are outlined below. Due to the high cost of mainframes it was often necessary to operate them round the clock that is, on a multi-shift basis, to achieve an acceptable pay-back period. No doubt this factor still applies in many instances. The cost of a small business computer — or personal computer (PC) as they are called — is very low, however, even for a complete business system, and its use quickly recoups its cost even when used only on an intermittent basis. The benefits obtained depend upon the type of computer and the use made of it. Depending upon individual circumstances prospective benefits may include some of those listed below:

(*a*) Improved customer relations due to fewer computational errors, more timely invoices and statements and speedier response to enquiries regarding the status of accounts and the availability of products.

(*b*) Improved cash flows due to improved sales accounting systems particularly those relating to credit control, invoicing and statement preparation.

(*c*) More effective control procedures including production control, sales control, cost control, budgetary control and credit control.

(*d*) Improved flow of information and information retrieval by means of on-line direct access enquiry systems.

(*e*) Greater control of raw material and other stocks allowing the investment in stock to be optimised and stock-out occasions to be minimised.

(*f*) Greater degree of systems integration on the basis that the output of one part of a system (sub-system) provides the input to a related sub-system, which has the effect of eliminating duplication and delay.

(*g*) Simplification of problem solving by the use of problem solving software.

(*h*) Supply of information for improving managerial decisions.

Similar benefits to those outlined above may also be achieved by using a microcomputer in the business environment.

Progress test 1

1. Specify the nature of data processing. **(1)**
2. What is meant by data? **(4–10)**
3. List the primary operations relevant to processing business data. **(11)**
4. Specify the elements comprising a data processing system. **(12)**
5. Indicate your views on the need for computer literacy in modern society. **(14, 15)**
6. Write an essay about the problems caused by increasing computerisation, suggesting how they might be solved. **(16–19)**
7. What benefits would you expect a business to achieve from using a computer? **(20)**

2
Profile of computers

Nature of computer systems

1. Primary factors. A computer system consists of a number of different devices, which are collectively referred to as 'hardware'. The hardware consists of input, processing, storage and output devices (*see* Fig 2.1.). Computers used for business applications are digital computers, 'digital' referring to the way in which data is processed — in discrete digits, called bits. (The term 'bits' is a contraction of *bi*nary digi*t*.) The only two values a computer understands are '0' and '1', which are represented by electrical flows. When these flows are not present this represents 0, when present a 1, characters are therefore represented in combinations of 0s and 1s. Such combinations form the basis of the ASCII code — this is an abbreviation for American Standard Code for Information Interchange, adopted as standard by the American National Standards Institute in 1963. It is widely used on small business computers (microcomputers) and provides the means for transferring data between devices such as from a processor to a printer or terminal to/from a processor. The ASCII code is a seven-bit code in which, for example, the number 65 is represented as 1000001. The position of each 1 indicates its binary value (*see* also 4:**12**). Any book dealing with binary arithmetic will discuss this topic in more detail. An alternative code is EBCDIC, an acronym for Extended Binary Coded Decimal Interchange Code. This code is used on IBM mainframe computers, and uses eight binary positions (bits) for each character forming the basis of the eight-bit byte, an alternative term for character. The letter 'A' would be represented by the combination of bits: 11000001. The first four positions are zone bits, the last four numeric bits. A seven-bit code can provide for 128 different characters whereas an eight-bit code can generate 256.

The heart of a computer system is the central processing unit (CPU) (*see* Chapter 4), which accepts data for processing from an input device such as a terminal or computer keyboard or disc drive. The data is stored in the internal memory of the processor and is subjected to logical and computational operations by means of instructions contained in an internally stored program. Such operations are carried out by the arithmetic/logic unit (ALU, or simply AU). The results of processing are transferred to an output device — which may be a printer for producing hard copy documents and reports or a storage device such as a floppy or hard disc drive for the storage of updated records. Most computer systems also output results either in textual or graphical form on a monitor screen known as a video or visual display unit (VDU) (*see* Fig. 2.2).

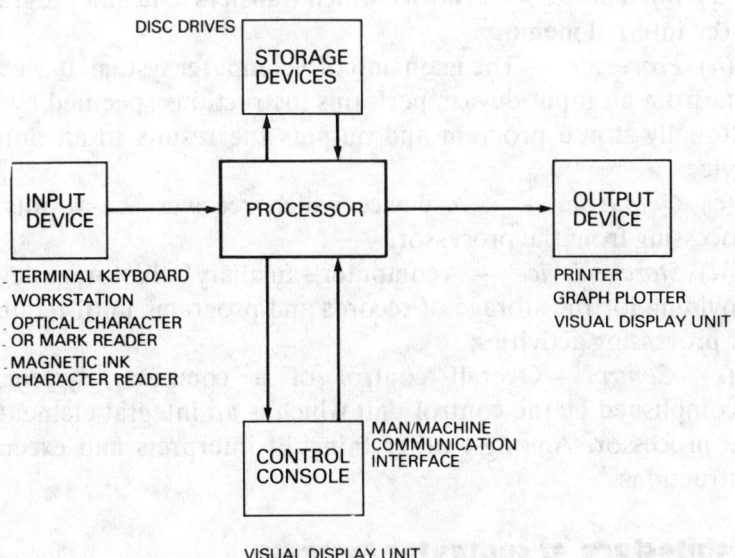

Figure 2.1 *Elements of a computer system.*

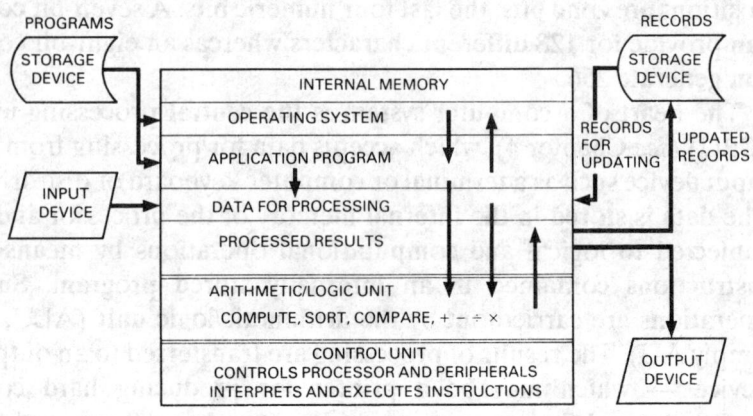

Figure 2.2   *Mode of operation of a computer.*

2. Summary of the elemental structure of a computer system.

(*a*) *Input device* — A device which transfers data and programs to the internal memory.

(*b*) *Processor* — The main unit of a computer system. It accepts data from an input device, performs instructions specified by the internally stored program and outputs the results to an output device.

(*c*) *Output device* — A device which receives the results of processing from the processor.

(*d*) *Storage device* — A computer's auxiliary bulk storage device providing for the storage of records and programs until required for processing activities.

(*e*) *Control* — Overall control of a computer system is accomplished by the control unit which is an integral element of the processor. Amongst other things it interprets and executes instructions.

Architecture of computer systems

3. Architecture defined. The term 'architecture' is used to describe the way computer systems are constructed and organised so that the processor functions efficiently and controls the flow of data between the various circuits and devices which combine to provide an integrated computer system. Computer architecture also specifies the interactions between the electronic circuitry (the hardware) and programs (the software), so as to achieve a particular level of performance.

4. Modular construction. All computer manufacturers do not design computers incorporating identical architectural features. They do, however, design them on a modular basis, i.e. a building-block basis. This technique allows the current computer configuration to be upgraded either by implementing a more powerful processor with increased processing speed and a larger internal memory capacity, or by implementing faster printer or larger-capacity and faster disc drives. The capacity of internal memory can also be increased by add-on memory modules.

Interfacing computer systems

5. General features of interfacing. In general terms, 'interfacing' describes the connecting together of various entities which interact with one another. It relates to the connection of memory chips to the main circuit board of a CPU to increase memory capacity; interconnecting two or more machines, such as input and output devices, to a central processor to form a complete computer system; connecting workstations to form a local area network for intercommunication purposes; the interconnection between computer hardware and software (the primary interconnecting elements of any computing system); and the means by which users gain access to a computer, by applying relevant dialogue and other techniques such as form displays on a monitor or selecting activities from a menu.

6. Interfacing devices to a computer. The most usual type of interfacing in a computing system is the connection of peripheral devices by cables and ports to the processor. Examples are disc expansion ports for connecting an additional disc drive or parallel and serial ports for connecting output devices. The number and type of ports a computer has determine the devices which can be interfaced. Problems arise when attempting to connect devices to a processor made to different standards and which function under the control of different software. This makes it essential to be aware of industry standards (*see* below).

Special devices such as disc controllers need to be interfaced as they handle reading and writing operations — reading data from discs to the processor and writing data to discs from the processor. Printer controllers translate signals from the processor and transfer them to the printer's electronic buffer, which is a type of memory for assembling lines of characters to be printed out.

Standards are set by various bodies, e.g. the CCITT (the Consultative Committee for International Telegraph and Telephone), which acts as a clearing house for standards of international communications over telegraphy and telephone lines, the ISO (International Standards Organisation) and the IEEE (Institution of Electrical and Electronic Engineers). Together they produce standards covering matter such as codes, coupling devices and use of public switched data networks.

7. **RS–232C interface.** A cable is plugged into a processor's input/output port by an adaptor conforming to the RS–232C standard. The other end of the cable is connected to a device, a printer for instance. by another adaptor. This provides for serial transmission of data from the processor to the printer. Serial transmission implies that each bit of a character code is transmitted one after the other. A serial printer collects the bits forming a character code in a buffer, which is a magnetic memory, until a complete ASCII character is formed which then triggers the printing of the character. A modem requires to be interfaced to the computer for transmitting signals to terminals or other computers. A graph plotter may also be connected to the processor by means of the serial channel.

8. **Centronics parallel interface.** A parallel channel allows a parallel printer to be connected to the processor by means of a ribbon cable connected to the processor by a multi-pin adaptor. The processor transmits character codes eight bits at a time. The adaptor contains a number of connecting pins which transmit various types of signal, some for character codes and others for control purposes. When

the keys on a keyboard are depressed, characters coded in ASCII are transmitted to the processor, which stores the characters in its internal memory in the code of the particular machine — which may be BCD (binary coded decimal), pure binary, octal or hexadecimal. After data has been processed the internally stored, coded results are converted into human-sensible characters either for display on a monitor or transmission to a serial or parallel printer or a graph plotter.

9. Interconnecting hardware and software. The primary software of a computing system is the operating system which provides an environment in which the user's application program can operate. The operator communicates with the operating system by inputting relevant commands via the computer keyboard. An operating system performs many important activities automatically, including data handling and file organisation. Before processing can commence the operating system must be loaded ('booted') into the internal memory (RAM) from disc backing storage. Commands are then instantly available to deal with the various aspects of processing as they arise. Many microcomputers function under the control of a disc operating system (known as DOS).

User interface

10. Menus and form displays. The nature of the man/machine interface can vary — one way is to display a menu on the monitor, which enables the user to select an option according to the nature of the processing activity or application required. This tells the computer system what it must do, and the system then deals with the selected option and gives the user appropriate prompts. Menus may list different applications, such as sales ledger, purchase ledger or stock control routines, from which the user is guided to sub-menus according to the option selected. When using a menu-driven application, options can be selected in various ways depending upon the computer in use:

(*a*) Locate the cursor adjacent to the required option and depress the ENTER OR RETURN key on the keyboard.

(*b*) Key in the number or initial letter specifying the required option.

(*c*) Use a mouse to point to the desired option on a pull-down menu.

(*d*) A touch screen facility enables the user to point with a finger to the desired option on a pull-down menu.

11. Horizontal bar menu. A horizontal bar menu is often the main menu of an application. It displays options at the top of the screen, as shown in the following example of a Macintosh nominal ledger menu bar (*see* Fig. 19.1):

File Edit Data entry Reports End-day End-period Options

12. Pull-down and pop-up menus. A 'pop up' menu is a general term that describes both pull-down and any other vertical menus which are connected to a horizontal bar menu. In the Macintosh example above, selecting the 'Reports' option (by locating the cursor on the main menu bar) will cause a pull-down menu to appear containing a list of options from which a particular report may be obtained:

(*a*) Trading statement
(*b*) Balance sheet
(*c*) Stock management report
(*d*) Profit analysis report
(*e*) Departmental summary.

13. Form display. Another interfacing method, which simplifies processing tasks for the non-expert user, is to display a form layout on the video screen, which is filled in by the user entering data into the appropriate boxes (fields) by a keyboard, just as though completing a normal form by hand (*see* Fig. 19.6).

14. Dialogue. A dialogue provides a man/machine interface enabling a user to process data interactively by responding to prompts generated by the software. The user response may consist of commands which are abbreviated to speed up their entry to the computer. When using spreadsheet software, for instance, a series of options may be shown on the bottom line of the screen. Each option is an abbreviated command such as S for 'save the current spread-sheet to disc', or Z for 'ZAP to remove the spreadsheet from the screen and from the workspace', i.e. the internal memory storing the spreadsheet.

15. Other interfacing methods.

(*a*) A *keypad* provides the interface between a user and a public on-line information system such as Prestel.

(*b*) The use of a *natural language* provides the man/machine interface enabling the computer to recognise commands input by the user. Commands are entered as normal sentences, which avoids the user having to acquire programming knowledge to access the computer system. *Fourth generation languages* are designed to provide the user with the means of gaining access to a database by way of a query language affording facilities for creating, retrieving, updating, appending, deleting or amending data. A fourth generation language translates the user's requests into procedural steps to produce the desired output. *See* 18:**28** for further details.

(*c*) *Interfacing without a formal query language* — all that is necessary to enter a query is to press an ENTER QUERY function key and type in the selection criteria, such as all customers with account balances over £4,000 (>4000).

16. GEM interface. Gem is a software package providing a user interface which, by avoiding the complexities of DOS commands, makes the computer as simple as possible to use. Instead of typing DOS commands, a mouse can be used to select icons (*see* Fig. 2.3) on the screen. When GEM is loaded a desktop with two rectangular windows appears on the screen. The upper window indicates by means of icons the folders, programs and documents contained on the disc in the A: drive, the lower contains two or three icons representing the floppy and hard disc drives (*see* Fig. 2.4). *See also*

14: 25 for further details of icons. For systems with two floppy disc drives there will be a separate icon for each. Any one of the disc drives can be opened by pointing to its icon with the pointer, which is positioned by means of the mouse. A button on the mouse is then double-clicked to select the particular icon.

A new window then opens showing the files and directories on the selected disc. A directory is shown as a folder which can be opened into a window showing the names of the programs it contains. A program can be selected with a double click. If a copy of a file is required, instead of using the DOS COPY command the pointer is moved to the required file and the button on the mouse is depressed but not released. The icon is then dragged to the relevant disc icon and when the button is released a copy of the file is made. Alternatively, instead of transferring a file to another disc drive it may be transferred to another directory. At the top of the desktop screen there is a menu bar containing a number of headings: File, Options, Arrange and Desktop. Locating the pointer on one of the headings causes a menu to drop down. The mouse can then move the pointer down the menu to select a specific option. By this means it is possible to open and close files, create new files, output data to a printer, and sort data by name, type, size or date, etc. The Desktop menu provides access to three utilities: clock, calendar and calculator.

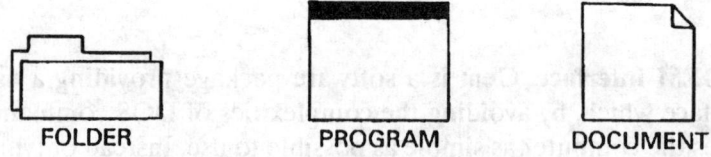

FOLDER   PROGRAM   DOCUMENT

Figure 2.3 *Icons.*

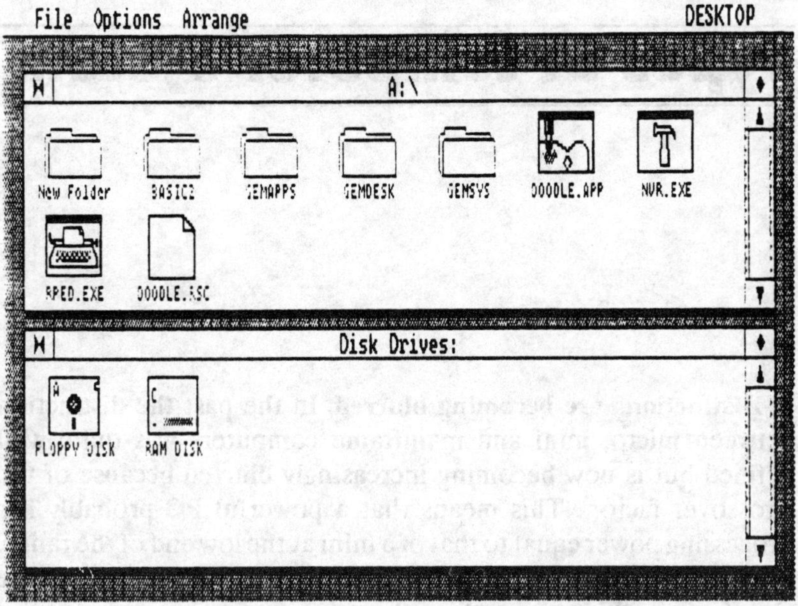

File Options Arrange   DESKTOP

Figure 2.4 *GEM screen display.*

Progress test 2

1. A computer consists of a number of different devices. State the nature of the devices. **(1)**

2. Define what is meant by digital. **(1)**

3. What is the meaning ASCII? **(1)**

4. The heart of a computer system is the central processing unit. Discuss. **(1)**

5. Define what is meant by computer architecture. **(3, 4)**

6. What is meant by interfacing? **(5–16)**.

7. What is the purpose of a GEM interface? **(16)**

3
Types of computer system

1. Distinctions are becoming blurred. In the past the distinction between micro, mini and mainframe computers was quite well defined but is now becoming increasingly blurred because of the 'crossover factor'. This means that a powerful PC probably has processing power equal to that of a mini at the low end of the range. Similarly, powerful minis have a capability equal to lower-range mainframes. However, this chapter provides a number of distinguishing features and characteristics of the various class of computer. In fact, small computers are being produced equal in size to a PC but with the power of mainframes.

Mainframes

2. High volume requirements. A mainframe is the most powerful type of computer system used for business and accounting applications. Larger businesses usually require this type to deal with large volumes of data efficiently. Such systems are usually installed at the head office of widely spread organisations such as supermarket chains, banks, insurance companies or building societies, or in town halls for municipal accounting and administrative applications. Mainframes require to be operated by expert DP professionals because of the complex use of commands to the operating system. etc.

3. Stand-alone or networking. Mainframes can be used as stand-alone computer systems or to support a large network of terminals, facilitated by their telecommunications capabilities. Input is usually by multiple keyboards manned by users operating in a multi-tasking environment. Many of the terminal keyboards are remote to the central installation, being linked to it by communication lines. A powerful operating system provides for multi-tasking (multiprogramming) as it facilitates the interfacing of many visual display units (terminals) including industrial, retail and financial terminals. Printer output is by means of various models, including laser printers; graph plotters provide graphical output. Modems are required for communication-orientated configurations for linking terminals to the computer via a multiplexor (*see* Fig. 3.1). *See* also data communications — Chapter 11.

4. Backing storage. Backing storage consists of banks of disc drives each with a capacity in the region of 1,000 Mbytes or, in some instances, one GB, known as a Gigabyte (1,000 million bytes). The discs may be fixed or exchangeable but fixed discs are necessary for on-line operations. Mainframes support a large database for applications such as car registrations, share dealings, personnel information, order processing, airline reservations, holiday bookings, banking operations, etc. They also facilitate report generation and on-line program development.

5. Architecture. The various manufacturers of mainframes, such as ICL, IBM and NCR, build them on the basis of different architectures, but usually on a modular basis incorporating independent sub-systems. The structure of a mainframe is very complex with specialised microprocessors supporting the main 32-bit processor. A memory interface provides the logical connection between memory chips and the address translation chip. Mainframes are constructed on very large scale integration (VLSI) technology, which enables computers to be smaller, less expensive and more reliable because their lower power consumption makes them less liable to blow integrated circuits (ICs) (*see* 4:1).

6. Internal memory. Internal memory capacity is in the region of 20 million bytes (20 Megabytes) of RAM. Its addressing capabilities are very high and it functions on the basis of internal and external 'virtual memory' — a storage management technique which enables

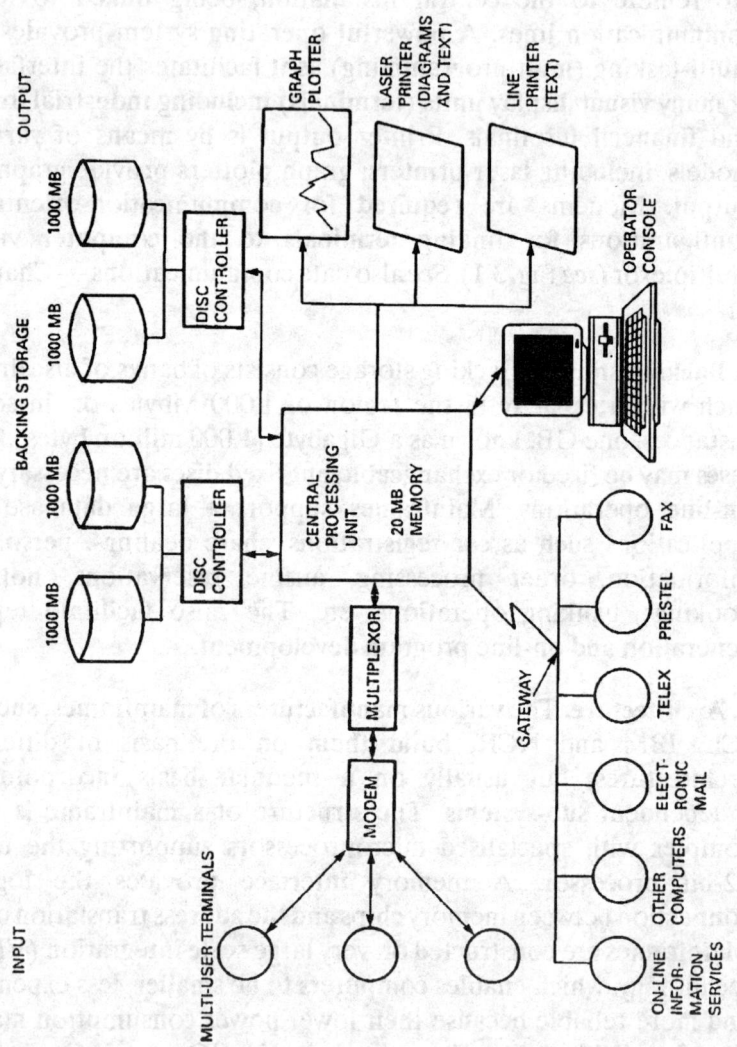

Figure 3.1 *Mainframe computer configuration.*

the limited internal storage capacity to be enhanced by disc backing storage which stores software which is segmented into pages. Only those pages required for immediate processing are called into internal memory. The pages previously stored in memory are overwritten by the latest segments (pages) of software required for processing. The internal high speed storage is classed as 'real storage' while the external disc backing storage device is called 'virtual storage'. (*See* Figs. 3.1 and 3.2 for a mainframe configuration and computer.)

Minicomputers

7. Multi-purpose computer. Minis are produced by a number of manufacturers including DEC (Digital Equipment Corporation), Hewlett Packard, IBM, ICL and GEC. They tend to be used by medium sized organisations which do not require the power of a mainframe. Applications processed on a mini include accounting routines, databases and other management information systems. They are also used in factories for the numerical control of machine tools and to monitor various types of processes. A great deal of expertise is required to operate a mini, and specialist training is needed because of its complexity compared to the operation of a PC. Minis are often used in various dispersed operating units for distributed processing as opposed to centralised processing. Each mini deals with local processing, covering such applications as accounting, payroll, stock control and order processing, etc. Minis may, however, be connected to other minis in a network for data interchange or for gaining access to information in a corporate database. On the other hand, a mini may function as a stand-alone system with its own database.

8. Configuration. Transaction data is usually input by keyboard and output by a printer. The processor is based on 32-bit technology with a memory capacity in the region of 6–16 Mbytes. The processor has a built-in Winchester hard disc drive with a capacity of between 80 and 320 Mbytes, which may be supplemented by an integral tape spooler for backing up files (taking copies). In addition, backing storage may be further complemented by exchangeable and floppy disc drives (*see* Figs. 3.3 and 3.4).

Figure 3.2 *IBM 3090 Model mainframe computer (courtesy IBM United Kingdom Limited).*

Microcomputers (PCs)

9. Versatility. Manufacturers of microcomputers for business use include IBM (the IBM PC), Apple (Apple Macintosh), Amstrad and Compaq, all of whom market a range of models. Micros are normally stand-alone machines operated by end users for their own particular processing needs such as payroll, stock control and general accounting routines. They are also widely used by accountants for problem solving using spreadsheets. They can also be used in the following ways:

(*a*) linked into a network consisting of mainframes, minis and other micros for the purpose of interchanging data between operating units and accessing a corporate database;

(*b*) connected to facsimile systems which transmit and receive images, drawings and diagrams; and telex systems which transmit and receive textual messages;

(*c*) share the resources of high speed printers and high capacity disc storage.

Micros are smaller than minis and much simpler to operate — the non-professional can become quite proficient in their use in a short space of time. Micros have brought offices and accounting practice into the twentieth century while also providing a greater degree of job enrichment to the user.

10. Internal memory. The internal memory capacity of a micro is typically 640 kbytes (640,000 bytes) but this can be increased to one Megabyte (one million bytes) or even to 8 Mbytes as some computers allow a memory upgrade to this level on the main circuit board (the 'motherboard'). Magnetic discs can be simulated on electronic circuits (chips), which allows programs to be permanently stored in a computer. This provides the means for increasing the internal memory capacity, which avoids the need to transfer programs to the internal memory from disc storage where they are normally stored until required thereby saving time.

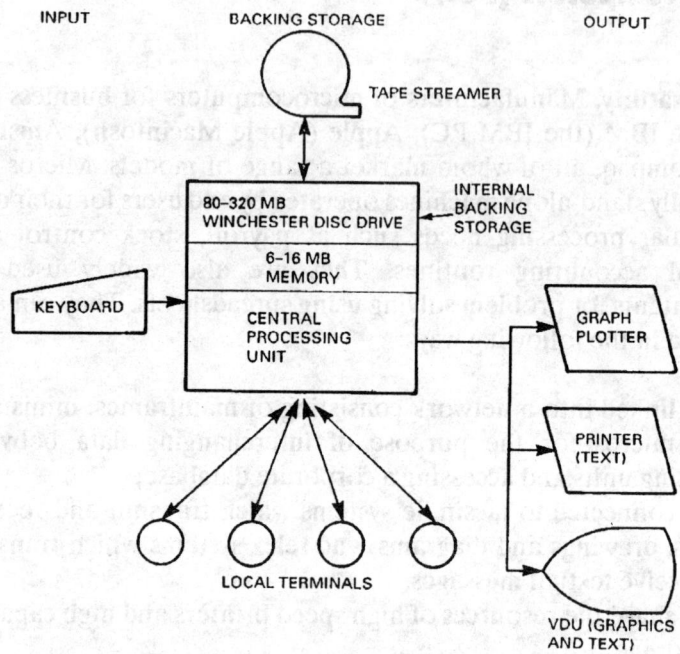

Figure 3.3 *Minicomputer configuration.*

11. Backing storage. Floppy discs are normally used for backing storage and may be either 3.5 or 5 inches in diameter. A 3.5-inch disc may have a capacity of 720 kbytes but the new IBM PS/2 computer incorporates a double-sided 3.5-inch disc with a capacity of 2 Mbytes. PCs also have integral Winchester hard discs with a capacity of 20–40 MBytes, built into the system. Also available are:

(*a*) what is known as a 'fast card' — a 20-Mbyte hard-disc expansion board designed to fit into a single IBM PC or compatible expansion slot;

(*b*) back-up storage cartridges about the size of a matchbox, which can be plugged into many business computers and will store up to 40 Mbytes of data.

12. Operational factors. Transaction data consisting of alphabetic or numeric characters is input by keyboard for processing to produce invoices and payrolls, for instance. Data may also be input for developing spreadsheet models of business situations such as break-even analysis or for producing documents in word processing applications.

Figure 3.4   *IBM minicomputer AS/400 (courtesy IBM United Kingdom Limited).*

Output can be produced in a number of ways: graphs and diagrams can be prepared using a graph plotter: text and graphs can be displayed on the monitor screen; or if required hard copies of reports or documents can be produced on a printer.

Multi-tasking, which enables a user to switch from one task to another, is becoming more widely applied. The task being performed may be the preparation of text by word processing software, the user may then switch to another task for the construction of a spreadsheet or to an accounting routine. Multi-tasking is facilitated by the use of software known as 'windows' (*see* 14:24) The use of integrated software allows the transfer of data from spreadsheets or accounting records to text files for inclusion in a report.

Small lap-top portable micros are available for use by executives while travelling on business. They have communication facilities which enable data to be transmitted to the organisation's mainframe computer from, say, a hotel room provided that the computer can be connected to the public telephone network. (*See* Figs. 3.5 and 3.6.)

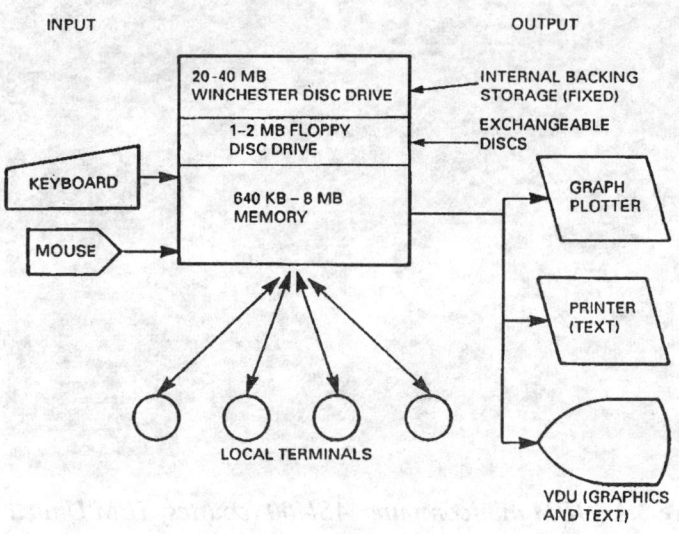

Figure 3.5 *Microcomputer configuration.*

Conclusion

13. Summary. We have considered the major differences between mainframes, minis and micros. It can be seen from the text and diagrams that the different types of computer do not consist of just one machine but a combination of related devices. These include the processor and its supporting (or surrounding) devices, also called 'peripherals'.

Minis and micros do not need those specially controlled environmental conditions, in terms of voltage, temperature, dust and humidity, which are essential for the effective operation of mainframe computers. This consideration is, however, less critical with modern mainframes as they are structured with smaller

electronic components which do not generate so much heat, and
the fixed disc drives are sealed units — which prevent dust settling
on the disc surfaces.

Figure 3.6   *IBM PC with tape streamer (courtesy M4 Data Limited).*

Progress test 3

1. In what circumstances is a mainframe computer most
suitable? **(2)**
2. How may a mainframe computer be used to advantage?   **(3)**
3. What type of backing storage is used by a mainframe?   **(4)**
4. What architecture is a mainframe based upon?   **(5)**
5. What is the typical memory capacity of a mainframe?   **(6)**
6. Outline the characteristics of a minicomputer.   **(7)**
7. What is the typical capacity of backing storage and internal
memory of a mini?   **(8)**
8. List the characteristics of a small business computer.   **(9–12)**

9. What is the capacity and type of backing storage used on a PC? **(10, 11)**

10. For what type of processing is a PC used?   **(12)**

4
The processor

General considerations

1. Processor architecture. Modern powerful processors are often constructed on the basis of multi-microprocessor architecture whereby each microprocessor has a dedicated task to perform, thus reducing overall processing time. This is achieved by the concurrent processing, or overlapping, of several different tasks such as input, processing and output. The IBM AS/400 family of computers, for example, has many specialised microprocessors dedicated to tasks such as controlling the flow of data to and from the main memory and backing storage devices, workstations and communications lines. This leaves the main processor free for primary computing tasks, which increases processing productivity (*see* 2: 3).

2. Eight-, 16- and 32-bit processors. Processors function at different speeds: 16 or 20 MHz for instance, while others run at a clock speed of 25MHz. In March 1989 Intel introduced a 33-MHz version of the million-transistor chip, a 40-MHz version is also planned (*see* 15). Earlier PCs consisted of an 8-bit processor chip which transferred information between the internal memory, various registers and the ALU eight bits at a time. Later models had 16-bit processor chips allowing transfers of numeric data consisting of 16 digits rather than 8, and capable of 16-bit addresses rather than 8, allowing the capacity of internal memory to be increased. Many computers are now based on 32-bit technology capable of processing, numeric data 32 bits in length. Intel has developed a 64-bit processor chip, the i860, which places the power of a Cray-1 (a super-computer) on a desktop. *See* **12**.

3. Structure of a processor. The processor consists of a system board — which is a circuit board on which are mounted micro-processor chip(s), memory chips and other components linked together by conductive lines or channels in the form of control, address and data buses — and adaptor boards, which are electronic circuits providing specialised functions such as graphics or which connect a system board to input or output devices. The system board also contains electronic devices such as a clock to control the speed of operation (*see* **14**), accumulators to store numeric data during the course of processing, and various registers including those for sequence control, address and instruction. The manner in which these various parts of the processor interact will be discussed later.

It is interesting to note that the main system board was once previously a printed circuit board with the various channels etched upon its surface and components mounted by means of location pins (referred to as 'pin-in-hole' technology). It is more usual now to apply 'surface mount' technology by which circuits are bonded to the surface of the system board(s), eliminating the need to drill holes in them. Components are located on the board accurately by automated equipment.

4. Main elements of a processor. Although the physical construction of different processors varies they typically consist of three main sections: the arithmetic/logic unit, control unit and the internal memory.

The arithmetic/logic unit

5. Arithmetic and logic functions. This unit performs arithmetic operations and logical functions. It consists of an adder/subtractor, one or more working registers to store the data being processed and accumulators for storing the results of calculations. Although a computer performs all types of arithmetic operations it is important to appreciate that subtraction is carried out by adding the 'complement' of the number to be subtracted to the other number used in the calculation. Multiplication is accomplished by 'shifts' to the left and addition; division by 'shifts' to the right and subtraction.

6. Logic functions. Logic functions are concerned with logic operators including AND, NAND (Not AND), NOT or INVERTER, OR (inclusive OR), X-OR (exclusive OR) and NOR. The logic is based on Boolean algebra and the use of truth tables. Logical operations are performed by logic circuits or logic gates. Further details are discussed later in the chapter.

Control unit

7. System co-ordinator. This part of the processor co-ordinates all parts of the computer system controlling the transfer of data to and from various devices. It can, for instance, send a command to a disc drive to read from a file or to transfer data from the internal memory to a printer. It performs its activities automatically according to the program requirements for a given application. The program may contain instructions, requiring data relating to despatches to customers to be read into the processor from a transaction file stored on disc or input by a keyboard; compute the data to produce invoice values in respect of sales to customers; print invoices and update the customer's account stored on disc, etc. In effect the control unit acts as a traffic controller, switching control to various channels to allow the movement of data from one part of the system to another.

8. Demonstrating the functions of a control unit. Before proceeding with the sequence of tasks performed by the control unit during processing it is necessary to be conversant with three terms:

    (*a*) operator — the action to be performed on operands;
    (*b*) operand — a data item to be operated upon;
    (*c*) accumulator — a register for storing the results of arithmetic calculations.

The operators, which are representative of an assembly code, a low level language and may be interpreted as follows:

(a) LDX   =   Load accumulator;
(b) ADD   =   Add;
(c) SUB   =   Subtract;
(d) STO   =   Store;
(e) MUL   =   Multiply;
(f) PRT   =   Print.

An instruction in assembly language for a single-address computer consists of the operator, a nominated accumulator and the operand. The example that follows will provide an understanding of the instruction and execution cycle of the control unit. It relates to a payroll application which includes the computation of gross wages by multiplying the hours worked by each employee by the relevant hourly rate. Each employee's gross wages are to be printed out to provide a list of earnings, and then accumulated to obtain a total of the gross wages of all employees. Two machine cycles will be illustrated in Figs. 4.1 and 4.2. The following data may be assumed:

(a) *Employee number 1*
  (i)   Hours worked = 50
  (ii)   Hourly rate = £2
(b) *Employee number 2*
  (i)   Hours worked = 45
  (ii)   Hourly rate = £1.50.

The program instructions for this application are shown in Table 4A. The operands used are symbolic names, which are allocated actual addresses by the assembler software. The operands used in the program instructions are:

(a) HOURS   — the hours worked by each employee;
(b) HRATE   — the hourly rate;
(c) GWAGE   — gross wage, i.e. the product of HOURS AND HRATE;
(d) CWAGE   — accumulated gross wages.

Table 4A Program instructions

Instruction address	Operator	Accumulator	Operand	Operand address
100	LDX	1	HOURS	200
101	MUL	1	HRATE	201
102	STO	1	GWAGE	202
103	ADD	2	GWAGE	202
104	STO	2	CWAGE	203
105	PRT		GWAGE	202

The memory addresses of the operands are shown in Table 4A for reference purposes to allow easier interpretation of the meaning of the program instructions.

The instructions may be interpreted as follows:

100—Load to accumulator 1 the content of address 200, which stores the hours worked by each employee . This location is cleared before entering the hours worked by the next employee.

101—Multiply the content of accumulator 1 by the content of address 201, which stores the hourly rate of pay for each employee.

102—Store the content of accumulator 1 in address 202. This address will contain the gross wages.

103—Add to accumulator 2 the content of address 202, which contains the gross wages of the last employee.

104—Store the content of accumulator 2 in address 203, which contains the cumulative gross wages.

105—Print the content of address 202, which contains the gross wages of each employee after each fetch–execution cycle.

Note: Instruction addresses are normally incremented in tens e.g. 10, 20, 30, but have been numbered as above for simplicity.

The fetch–execution cycle is summarised below (*see* **9**) for convenience before interpreting the action of the program.

9. The fetch–execute cycle.

(a) *Fetch* —	Examine sequence control register for the memory address of the next instruction to be executed.
—	Transfer operator to function register for translation.
—	Transfer operand to address register.
—	Increment the sequence control register.
(b) *Translate* —	Interpret instruction.
(c) *Execute* —	Carry out instruction.
(d) *Repeat* —	Perform loop until program completed.

10. Example: Fetch–execute cycle — running a payroll program.
Prior to the first machine cycle (*see* Fig. 4.1) the sequence control register is initialised with the address of the first instruction to be executed: 100. The first 'fetch' cycle examines this memory address, which specifies an 'operator', LDX 1, which is transferred to the 'function register' to translate the operation to be performed. The operand in address 200 (hours) is transferred to the address register to connect the required circuits to enable the data to be transferred to the accumulator. The sequence control register is incremented to 101. The execution cycle issues a command to the control bus (*see* 13) to transmit the contents of address 200, containing the value 50 (hours worked), to the accumulator via a data bus (*see* Fig. 4.1). The second machine cycle (*see* Fig. 4.2) is similarly dealt with. The sequence control register is examined and it contains 101, the address of the next instruction to be executed. This address is examined and it specifies an operator, MUL 1, which is transferred to the function register to translate the operation to be performed. The operand HRATE in address 201 is transferred to the address register and the sequence control register is incremented to the value 102, the address of the next instruction. The execution cycle then issues a command to the control bus to transmit the content of address 201 (£2 — the hourly rate) to the arithmetic unit to obtain the product of hours worked and hourly rate (*see* Fig. 4.2). The cycles are repeated for each employee until the program is completed.

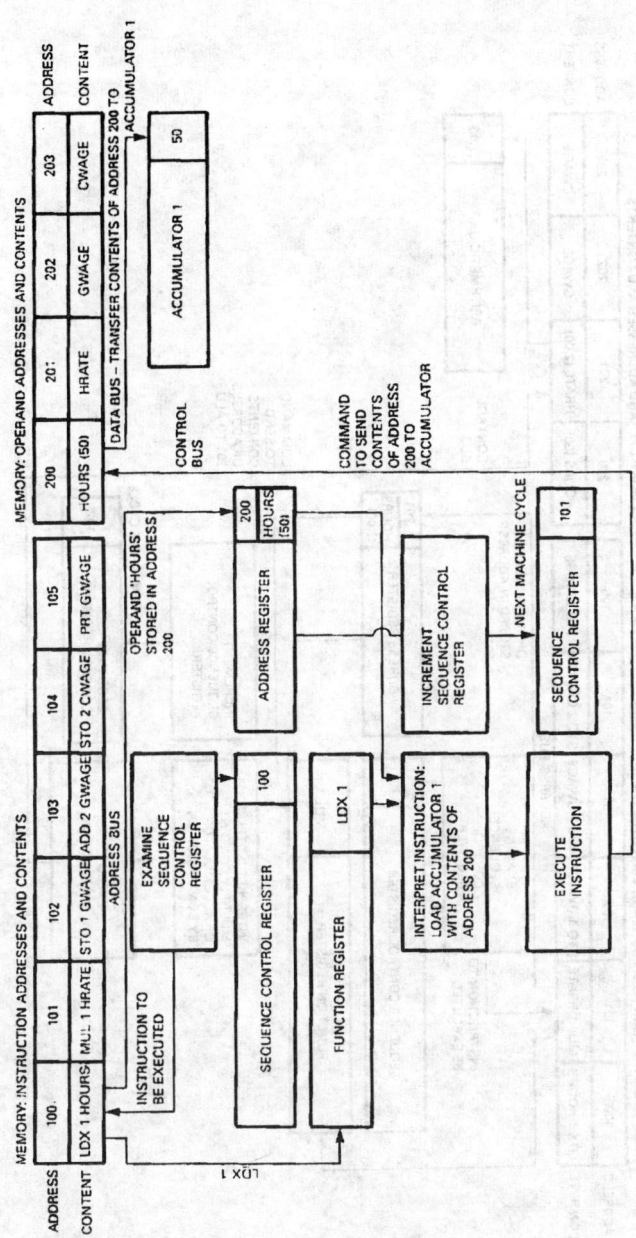

Figure 4.1   *Processor instruction and execution cycle:*
first machine cycle.

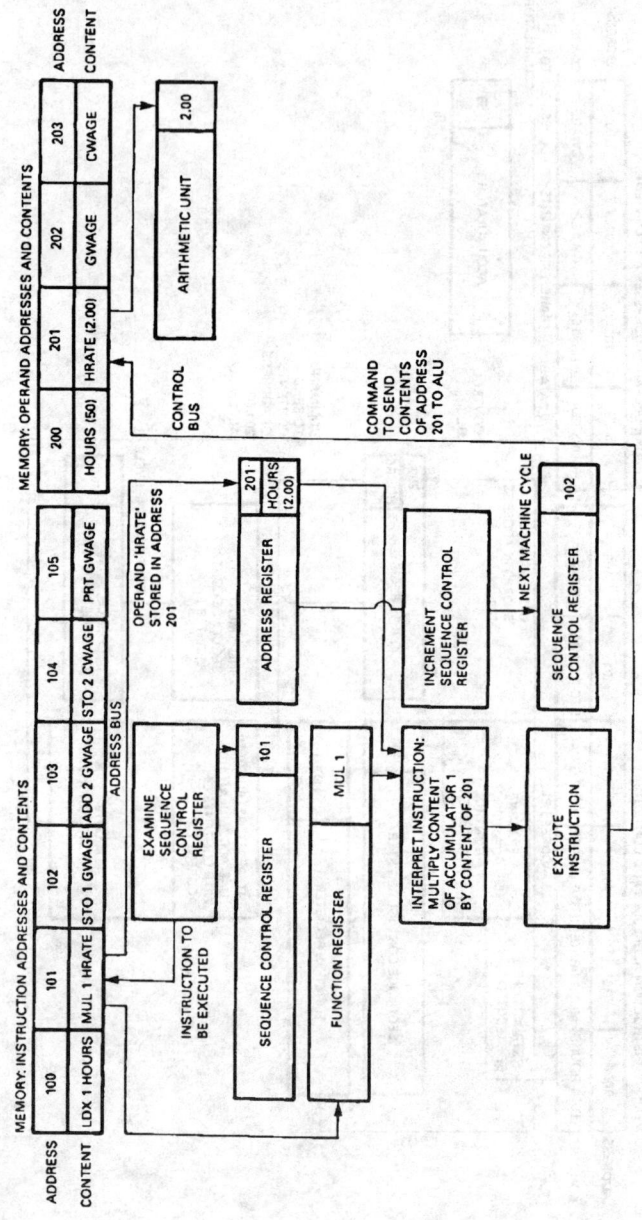

Figure 4.2 *Processor instruction and execution cycle: second machine cycle.*

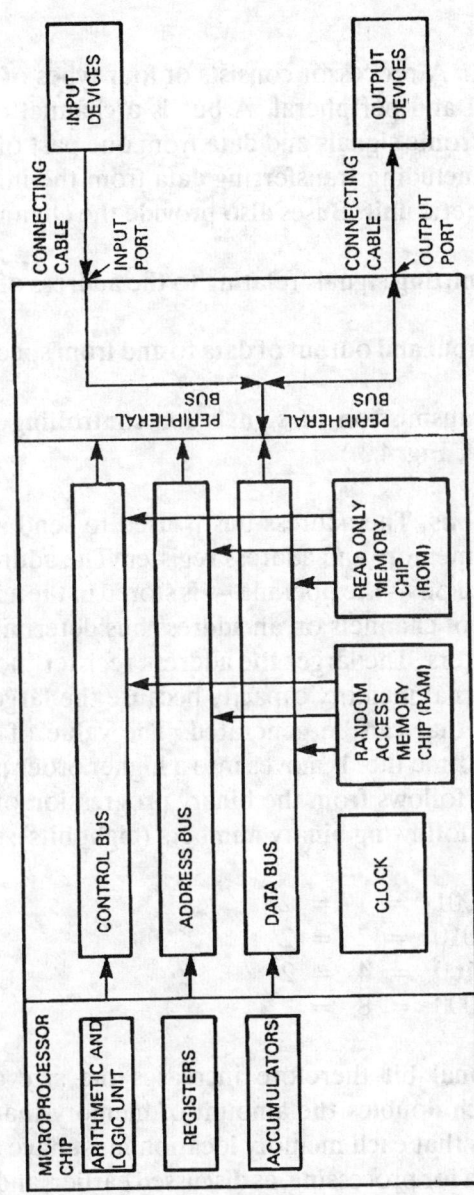

Figure 4.3 *Simplified processor configuration illustrating control, address and data bus.*

Buses

11. Channels. A processor consists of four types of 'bus': address, data, control and peripheral. A bus is a channel or pathway for routing electronic signals and data from one part of the processor to another, including transferring data from the internal memory to the arithmetic unit. Buses also provide the channels for:

(*a*) transmitting signals relating to the address of the data to be operated on;

(*b*) the input and output of data to and from specific peripheral devices;

(*c*) the transmission of signals for controlling all processing activities. (*See* Fig. 4.3.)

12. Address bus. The address bus is used to send address details between the memory and address register. The address of the data to be operated on — the operand — is stored in the address register. The number of channels on an address bus determines the size of address registers. The larger the address register the greater is the possible internal memory capacity because the larger the number of addresses that can be generated. The value of a binary digit doubles each time the '1' moves into a higher order position, i.e. to the left. This follows from the binary progression of $2n$. Take, for example, the following binary numbers (eight bits):

(*a*) 00000001 $= 1 = 2^0$
(*b*) 00000010 $= 2 = 2^1$
(*c*) 00000100 $= 4 = 2^2$
(*d*) 00001000 $= 8 = 2^3$

Each additional bit therefore increases the size of an address register, which doubles the amount of memory that can be used. The reason is that each memory location must have an address for 'fetching' data for processing, as discussed earlier, and therefore the greater the addressing capability of a processor the greater its prospective memory capacity. Typically, 8-bit processors have 16 channel address buses providing 64K bytes internal memory capacity — actually 65,536 bytes, i.e. 2^{16}. An address bus of 20 channels provides one million bytes, i.e. 1 Mbyte internal memory capacity — actually 1,048,576 bytes, i.e 2^{20}. Some models have three data paths, which greatly increases the volume of data that can be handled.

13. Data bus, control bus and peripheral channel. When data is to be transferred from a memory address to an accumulator or other memory location, a command on the control bus transmits the data to its destination on a data channel. The destination may be another memory location, an accumulator or an output port. Eventually data can be output from the output port to a peripheral device by a peripheral channel (*see* Fig. 4.3).

Processor clock

14. Electronic timing pulses. The processor's clock is an electronic circuit, often a quartz crystal, that generates electronic pulses at fixed time intervals to control the timing of all operations in the processor.

15. Clock speed. The speed at which pulses are generated is a function of clock speed which is measured in MHz (Mega — one million — Hertz, which is a measure of speed in terms of cycles per second). Cycles per second is a measure of frequency, therefore the clock speed is measured in terms of the oscillating frequency of the quartz crystal in cycles or pulses per second. The higher the Hz rating the more powerful the processor, as it performs tasks at a higher speed than lower rated processors.

Microprocessor

A microprocessor contains the circuitry for performing arithmetic and logic operations, usually contained on a single silicon chip. It also interprets and executes instructions (*see* Fig. 4.4).

16. Silicon chip. A small piece of silicon containing a completely unpackaged semiconductor device, i.e. a transistor, diode or integrated circuit (IC). Due to technological developments it is now possible to have many thousands of transistors and diodes on a single chip of silicon with dimensions of not more than five mm square. This is largely due to the development of photolithographic techniques capable of forming transistors and their interconnecting circuits on a very small scale generating VLSI (very large scale integration). A silicon chip is produced by creating microscopic layers of metal and component material on a silicon wafer using successive photolithographic masks to obtain the required electronic components and the relevant microcircuits. A chip is encapsulated in a ceramic cover which has a number of connector pins for mounting on a printed circuit board (*see* Fig. 4.4).

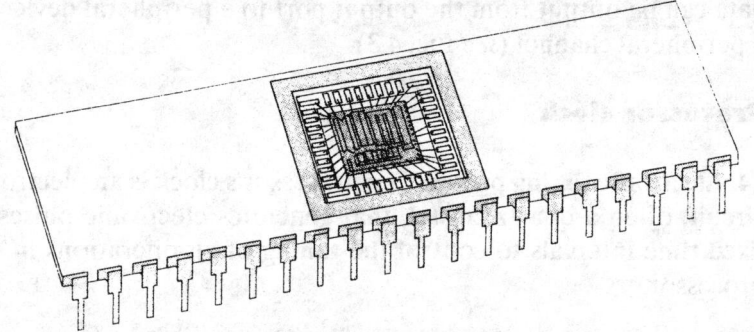

Figure 4.4 *Microprocessor chip.*

17. Wafer. Chips are produced from a wafer, which is a circular slice of semiconductor material cut from a single crystal of silicon. The slice is exposed to steam to form an oxide film on its surface. It is then treated by a photoengraving/diffusion/oxidisation process to form the circuits of the processor. The slice is then cut into many individual chips (*see* Fig. 4.5).

Computer logic

18. Logic operations and automatic decision making. Logic operations, as distinct from arithmetic operations, are concerned with comparing, selecting, matching, sorting and merging data. When comparing data factors, the logical ability of the arithmetic/logic unit differentiates between positive and negative differences between the data factors and, in accordance with the results of the comparison, the alternative sequence of instructions to be executed is determined automatically. This is known as a 'conditional' transfer, and it provides the means for processing data on the 'exception' basis — that is, data requiring special processing according to the circumstances disclosed by the data. Conditional transfers of this type are appropriate when it is necessary to compare the credit limit of each customer with their account balance for the purpose of indicating, by means of a special print-out, those customers whose balances exceed the credit limit for credit control. This is referred to as 'exception reporting'. In a stock control application the program may provide for the comparison of stock balances with reorder levels to indicate those items which require replenishment. This may be done either by printing out a reorder list or a purchase order directly. This may be referred to as 'automatic decision-making'. Similarly, within a budgetary control application actual costs may be compared with budgeted costs and variance reports printed out, again on the basis of exception reporting. It is this important attribute of computers that makes them so useful as a tool of management.

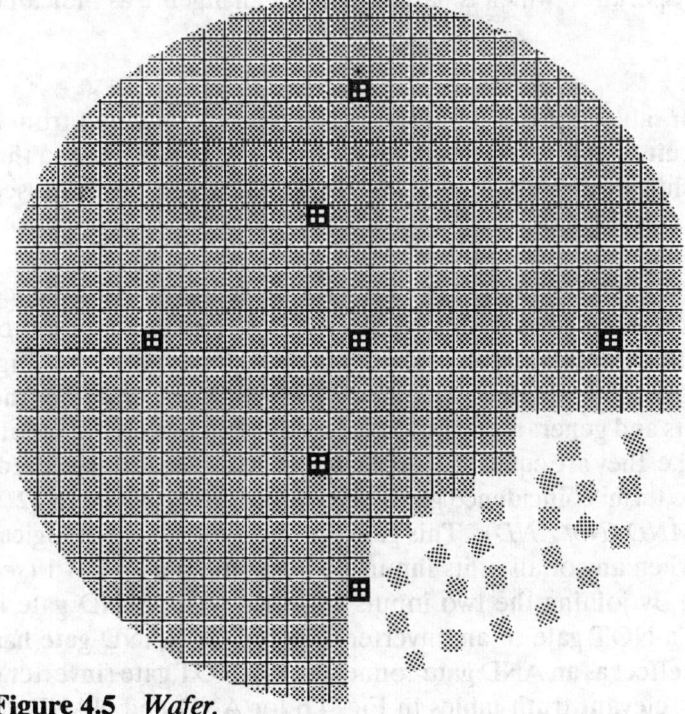

Figure 4.5 *Wafer.*

19. Boolean algebra. The name is derived from the mathematician, George Boole. The relevance of Boolean algebra to the logic of computers is based on two possible 'truth values' of a statement, i.e. true and false. These values are represented by the binary values 1 and 0 respectively, thus enabling Boolean principles to be applied to the logical circuitry of a computer. As a computer operates on the basis of electrical states, on or off, representing binary digits 1 and 0, circuits can be designed to facilitate Boolean operations by means of logic circuits (or gates).

20. Logic gate/logic circuit. These are synonymous terms for describing the logic circuits which have several inputs and one or two outputs depending upon the nature of the logic gate. Gates provide the foundations of all logic circuits which are etched on the surface of a silicon chip. Logic gates include: AND, NAND (Not AND), NOT, Inclusive OR, Exclusive Or and NOR. These are illustrated in Fig. 4.6. Each logic gate has a truth table outlining its mode of operation which is based on Boolean algebra as indicated above.

21. Truth table. A truth table shows the outputs obtained from a logic circuit or gate as a consequence of specific inputs. Due to this relationship both truth tables and logic gates will be discussed together (*see* Fig 4.6).

(*a*) *AND.* AND gates are sometimes referred to as 'coincidence gates' for reasons to be indicated. An AND gate gives an output of logical value 1 only when all of its inputs are logical value 1 (*see* Fig. 4.6). This may be explained as follows. The AND gate examines the two inputs and generates an output of true only when all the inputs are true, i.e. they are equal to 1. A particular action is then triggered, hence the term 'coincidence gates'. Examples are provided in **22.**

(*b*) *NAND (Not AND).* This gate produces an output of logical value 1 when any or all of its inputs do *not* contain a logical 1 (*see* Fig. 4.6). By joining the two inputs together on a NAND gate it becomes a NOT gate or an 'inverter' (*see* (*c*)). A NAND gate has the same effect as an AND gate connected to a NOT gate (inverter). Refer to relevant truth tables in Fig. 4.6 for AND and NAND. It will be seen that the outputs are the complete opposite of each other.

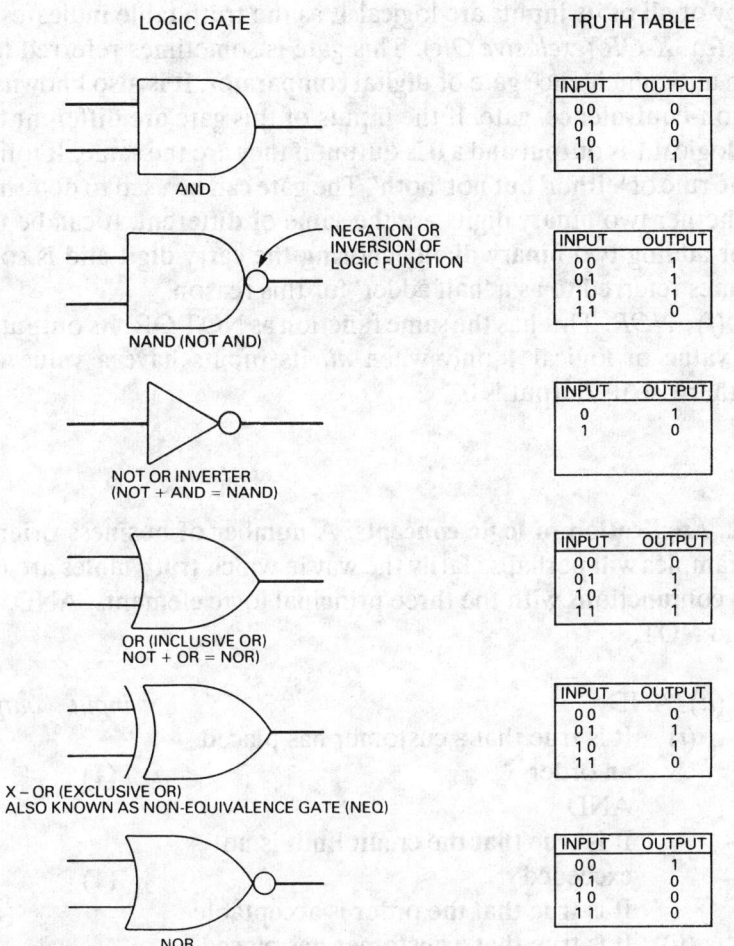

Figure 4.6   *Logic gates and truth tables.*

(*c*) *NOT or INVERTER.* The logical value of the output of this gate is always the opposite to that of the input, as shown on the truth table in Fig. 4.6. When combined with an AND gate it inverts the output to that of a NAND gate. When combined with an OR gate it inverts the output to that of a NOR gate.

(*d*) *OR (inclusive OR).* The output of this gate is a logical 1 when *any* or all of its inputs are logical 1, as the truth table indicates.

(*e*) *X-OR (exclusive OR).* This gate is sometimes referred to as an anticoincidence gate or digital comparator. It is also known as a 'non-equivalence' gate. If the inputs of this gate are different then a logical 1 is output and a 0 is output if they are the same. It follows the rule of 'either' but not 'both'. The gate can be used to determine whether two binary digits are the same or different. It can be used for adding two binary digits ignoring the carry digit and is sometimes referred to as a 'half adder' for this reason.

(*f*) *NOR.* This has the same function as NOT OR. Its output has a value of logical 1 only when *all* its inputs have a value of 0 otherwise its output is 0.

22. Application of logic concepts. A number of business-oriented examples will perhaps clarify the way in which truth tables are used in conjunctions with the three principal logic elements, AND, OR and NOT.

		input	*output*
(*a*) AND			
(*i*) It is true that a customer has placed an order		(1)	
AND			
It is true that the credit limit is not exceeded		(1)	
It is true that the order is acceptable			(1)
(*ii*) It is true that a customer has placed an order		(1)	
AND			
It is not true that the credit limit is not exceeded		(0)	
It is not true that the order is accepted			(0)
(*b*) OR			
(*i*) It is true that the level of stock has reached the reorder level (equal to)		(1)	

	OR		*input*	*output*
	It is true that the level of stock is below the reorder level (less than)		**(1)**	
	It is true that stock should be reordered			**(1)**
(*ii*)	It is true that the value of the order is less than £50		**(1)**	
	OR			
	It is not true that the delivery distance is greater than 20 miles		**(0)**	
	It is true that delivery is to be charged			**(1)**
(*iii*)	It is true that the value of the order is greater than £50		**(1)**	
	OR			
	It is not true that the delivery distance is less than 20 miles		**(0)**	
	It is true that delivery is not to be charged			**(1)**
(*iv*)	It is not true that the value of the order is less than £50		**(0)**	
	OR			
	It is not true that the delivery distance is greater than 20 miles		**(0)**	
	It is not true that delivery is to be charged			**(0)**
(*c*) NOT				
(*i*)	It is true we have excess stock		**(1)**	
	It is not true that a purchase order is required			**(0)**
(*ii*)	It is not true that we have excess stock		**(0)**	
	It is true that a purchase order is required			**(1)**

Internal storage

23. Working storage. The internal memory of a computer is an integral element of the processing unit and may be referred to as the computer's working memory. It is used for storing software in the form of operating systems, application programs and utility routines, etc. In addition, the data input for processing is stored in the memory, as are the results of processing until they are output either to backing storage or to an output device such as a printer or VDU.

Data stored in the memory, as well as instructions, can be addressed and accessed very quickly and for this reason internal memory is often referred to as 'immediate access storage' (IAS). This attribute is ideal for having all programs and master files (consisting of business records and reference files) stored internally for immediate access when required. Internal storage has to be complemented by external storage, that is, storage external to the processor, which is referred to as 'backing storage'. This is used for mass storage needs whereas internal storage is used for immediate access requirements.

Backing storage has a higher storage capacity but a slower access time than internal storage. Programs, master files and reference files are stored in backing storage until required for processing, when they are transferred to the internal memory. All programs and data must be resident in the internal memory before processing is possible (*see* Fig. 2.2).

24. Summary of types of internal memory. The most usual types of memory in current use are:

(*a*) core storage;
(*b*) semiconductor memory (MOS)
    (*i*)   RAM;
    (*ii*) ROM;
    (*iii*) PROM;
    (*iv*) EPROM;
(*c*) bubble memory
(*d*) holographic (optical) memory;
(*e*) cache memory.

25. Units of storage. The units of storage in a computer system are usually expressed in bytes and/or words, which indicates the number of binary digits (bits) in a unit of storage. At one time computers had units of storage expressed in terms of characters consisting of six bits but these have tended to be replaced by the byte which consists of eight bits. Mainframes tend to have 32-bit words equivalent to four bytes. The modern small computer tends to have a unit of storage in the form of a 16-bit word.

26. Capacity of storage. Until recently medium scale mainframe computers had internal storage capacities, typically in the region of 32 to 48 kbytes, but even the small mini or micro now has a capacity which greatly exceeds this. Typical storage capacities may be summarised as follows

(*a*) micros 640 kbytes to 8 Mbytes;
(*b*) minis in the region of 6–16 Mbytes;
(*c*) modern mainframes 20 Mbytes.

The abbreviation 'K' is used to denote 1,000 units of storage but it is actually 1,024 units of storage, i.e. 2^{10} which is an expansion of base 2, the base of the binary number system 'K' should not be confused with 10^3 which is an expansion of base 10, the base of the decimal number system.

27. Semiconductor memory. This type of memory has tended to supersede core storage in most computers, i.e. micros, minis and mainframes. The reason for this is attributable to four factors: it is smaller, has a higher capacity, is less costly and is faster with regard to access time.

Semiconductor memory is produced from silicon chips and is based on *m*etal *o*xide *s*emiconductor (MOS) technology. It is also referred to as '*m*etal *o*xide *s*emiconductor *f*ield *e*ffect *t*ransistor technology', i.e. MOSFET. *F*ield *e*ffect *t*ransistor technology is abbreviated to FET.

There are two types of semiconductor memory:

(*a*) random access memory (RAM);
(*b*) read-only memory (ROM)

28. Random access memory (RAM). This type of memory is used for working storage requirements when running application programs. Its capacity can usually be increased on-site on many computers (large and small) by adding RAM chips to the circuit boards. This type of memory can be directly addressed in the same way as core storage to access specific data or instructions.

RAM is either 'static' or 'dynamic'. Static RAM remains unchanged until an electrical pulse is generated to change it. Dynamic RAM is volatile as it requires continual refreshing by electrical pulses. When the processor is switched off the contents are destroyed and the memory must be reloaded with the same program to restart the job. The same considerations apply for processing a job again at a later date — it is necessary to reload the program. To overcome the consequences of a power failure some computers have a memory support system using batteries to energise the memory when necessary to avoid loss of data.

29. Read only memory (ROM). The contents of ROM are physically fixed and cannot be accessed to alter them as can be done with RAM. The reason for this is that the writing circuit is disconnected during manufacture. Small computers use this type of internal memory for storing a BASIC interpreter which converts program statements in BASIC programming language into machine code. This is done during the running of a program. The contents of ROM are not destroyed when the computer is switched off as ROM is non-volatile because its contents have been burnt in during manufacture. Microprograms for input/output operations are stored on ROM chips. ROM also stores the operating system.

30. PROM. There are variations of ROM, e.g. PROM which stands for 'programmable read-only memory'. Whereas ordinary ROM is preprogrammed at the factory, PROM can be programmed by the user. A special device is required for putting the 'bit' pattern into a PROM chip; this is called a PROM programmer.

31. EPROM. This is a further variation of ROM, which stands for 'erasable programmable read-only memory'. When data is recorded on this type of memory it is in effect the same as ordinary ROM in its behaviour but if the user requires to change the content of the chip an ultraviolet light is used to revert all the cells to '1s'. New data or programs can then be written on the chip.

32. Bubble memory. Bubbles may be described as cylindrical magnets which are formed from magnetic regions called 'domains' after the application of a critical bias value magnetic field. The bubbles are created on memory chips with capacities of typically 64 and 256 kbytes. Rockwell has a bubble memory system with a megabyte of storage and a module with a capacity of one megabit.

Developments are taking place to reduce the size of the bubble or magnetic domain to less than two microns to enable one megabyte of memory to be stored on a chip not greater than about half a cubic inch (approximately 8,000 mm^3) in overall size. Strings of bubbles allow streams of bits carried by the bubbles to become a series of electrical pulses providing output from the bubble memory. The ICL DNX–2000 digital PABX system uses bubble memory so it seems that this type of memory is likely to be widely used in future.

33. Holographic (optical) memory. This is a ROM optical memory system whereby a pattern is recorded on a photosensitive plate by mixing laser light from a reference beam and laser light scattered from the object bearing the information to be recorded. The data in the hologram is effectively 'smeared' over the whole of the plate. A degree of redundancy is built into the system so that dust and scratches on the emulsion have little effect on the recorded information.

Data in the reconstructed image is arranged as an array of dots – one dot for each 'bit'. Information may be read out by directing a laser beam on the hologram so that the reconstructed image falls on to a photodiode array on a silicon chip. At present the main limitation is that information on a holographic store is generally fixed and is presently of value for storing large amounts of fixed information such as machine instructions.

34. Cache memory. A high-speed memory capable of keeping up with the CPU. It acts as a buffer between the CPU and the slower main memory. As the CPU is not delayed by memory accesses the overall speed of processing is increased. Segments of program and data are transferred from disc backing storage into the cache buffer by the operating system. This type of memory is mainly applicable to the larger computer.

Progress test 4

1. What is meant by multi-microprocessor architecture?   **(1)**
2. Processors function at different speeds. Why is this?   **(2, 14, 15)**
3. Outline the structure of a processor.   **(3)**
4. Define the nature of the arithmetic/logic unit.   **(5, 6)**
5. The control unit may be defined as the system co-ordinator. Discuss.   **(7)**
6. What are the stages of the fetch–execute cycle?   **(9, 10)**
7. A processor consists of four types of bus. State each type and define its purpose.   **(11–13)**
8. What is a processor clock and what is its function?   **(14, 15)**
9. State the nature of a microprocessor.   **(16, 17)**
10. Define the terms Boolean algebra, logic gate and truth table.   **(19–21)**
11. Define the nature and purpose of internal storage.   **(23)**
12. What is a unit of storage?   **(25)**
13. State typical internal storage capacity for the different types of computer.   **(26)**
14. Define the following types of internal memory: RAM, ROM, PROM, EPROM, bubble, holographic memory and cache memory.   **(28–34)**

5

Organisation of a data processing and management services department

Organisation of a data processing department: by function or activity

1. Main sections and types of staff. The sectional organisation of a batch processing installation is shown in Fig. 5.1 and may be summarised as follows.

(*a*) Head of department — data processing manager:

    (*i*) responsible to: director of administration, managing director or company secretary according to specific requirements;

    (*ii*) immediate subordinates: chief systems analyst, chief programmer, operations manager and database administrator.

(*b*) Chief systems analyst responsible for activities of systems analysts.

(*c*) Chief programmer responsible for activities of programmers.

(*d*) Operations manager responsible for activities of chief computer operator and all operators, data preparation supervisor, tape and disc librarian and data control supervisor.

2. Principal duties of data processing manager. The duties of a data processing manager may be summarised in the following manner:

(*a*) interpretation and execution of data processing policy as defined by the data processing steering committee or board of directors;

(*b*) controlling immediate subordinates in the attainment of project objectives;

(*c*) participation in policy formulation;

(*d*) liaison with user departments to ensure their interests are fully provided for;

(*e*) ensuring that company policy is adhered to;

(*f*) ensuring that computer operating instructions are updated when the need arises;

(*g*) assessing the effectiveness of the file maintenance procedures;

(*h*) assessing the suitability of file security procedures;

(*i*) ensuring that program modifications are applied effectively;

(*j*) monitoring test runs;

(*k*) post-implementation evaluation;

(*l*) ensuring that staff attend suitable training courses for their development;

(*m*) assessing performance of staff for salary awards and promotion;

(*n*) co-ordinating the whole of the data processing operations and ensuring that work flows smoothly;

(*o*) resolving conflicts between subordinates;

(*p*) providing guidance on data processing problems;

(*q*) development and implementation of data processing standards.

3. Principal duties of chief systems analyst. The duties may be summarised as follows:

(*a*) liaison with user departments to ensure their requirements and problems are fully discussed before systems design and implementation;

(*b*) interpreting terms of reference before embarking upon systems investigations in order to establish the problem, areas of investigation and limits to the assignment;

(*c*) comparing the cost and performance of alternative processing methods and techniques;

(*d*) organising and co-ordinating the activities of systems analysts;

(*e*) reviewing performance of systems analysts;

(*f*) organising and reviewing systems documentation to ensure it complies with data processing standards;

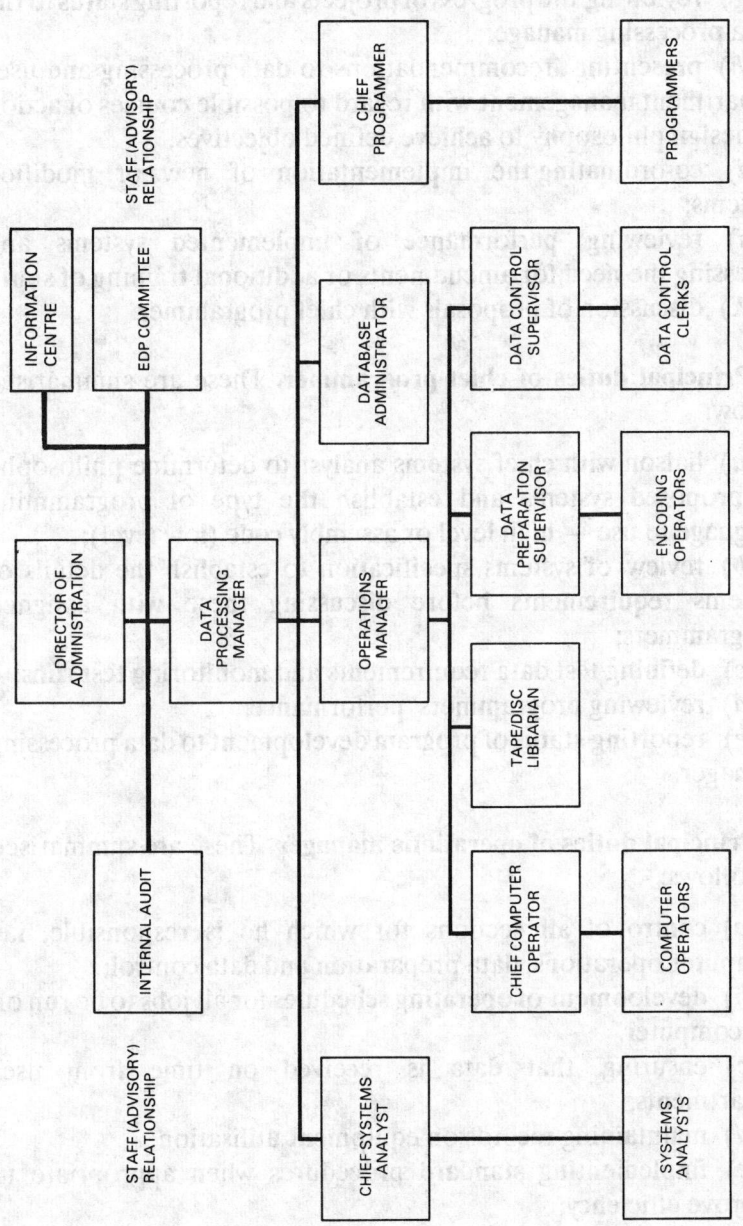

Figure 5.1   *Organisation chart: by function or activity.*

(g) reviewing the progress of projects and reporting status to the data processing manager;

(h) presenting recommendations to data processing and user department management with regard to possible courses of action or design philosophy to achieve defined objectives;

(i) co-ordinating the implementation of new or modified systems;

(j) reviewing performance of implemented systems and assessing the need for amendments or additional training of staff;

(k) discussion of proposals with chief programmer.

4. Principal duties of chief programmer. These are summarised below:

(a) liaison with chief systems analyst to determine philosophy of proposed systems and establish the type of programming language to use — high level or assembly code (low level);

(b) review of systems specification to establish the details of systems requirements before discussing these with assigned programmers;

(c) defining test data requirements and monitoring test runs;

(d) reviewing programmers' performance;

(e) reporting status of program development to data processing manager.

5. Principal duties of operations manager. These are summarised as follows:

(a) control of all sections for which he is responsible, i.e. computer operations, data preparation and data control;

(b) development of operating schedules for all jobs to be run on the computer.

(c) ensuring that data is received on time from user departments;

(d) maintaining records on equipment utilisation;

(e) implementing standard procedures when appropriate to improve efficiency;

(f) controlling stocks of data processing supplies, tapes, stationery and discs, etc;

(g) maintaining a log of computer operations;

(*h*) report to data processing manager situations such as hardware malfunctions, staffing problems and other operational matters.

6. The database administrator. As the whole concept of a database is to rationalise business systems by the integration of such systems it follows that the data needs of an organisation must be co-ordinated at a very high level. This is basically the responsibility of a database administrator who may not yet exist in many organisations. Nevertheless someone has no doubt been vested with such responsibilities, perhaps a senior member of the systems staff.

When data is common to two or more applications then programmers are not allowed the freedom they previously enjoyed to name data elements and subject them to processing independently of other application requirements. This is where the database administrator assumes command, as it were, because he must consider the data needs of the several applications under consideration for consolidation into a database.

He must first of all be conversant with business policy and strategy, particularly for the long term, as the very fabric of a business is dependent upon an efficient and effective management information system of which a database is a fundamental part — the roots of such a system in fact. He should play an active part in the planning of information systems particularly with regard to feasibility studies.

He should be an expert in all file management techniques and be able to advise management and system planners of the capabilities and shortcoming of various file management systems with regard to the application under review. It is essential that he liaise and consult with project teams with regard to the development of design specifications, program specifications, systems documentation and programs, etc. It is imperative that he monitor the implementation of a database ensuring that time and cost constraints are adhered to. It is of extreme importance that the administrator ensures that system objectives are achieved. Also of importance is that the initial preparation and maintenance of a data dictionary should be the responsibility of a database administrator, as this is essential for the success of a database system (*see* Chapter 9).

Organisation of a data processing department: by purpose

7. Structure of activities. It is sometimes found that a computer department is organised by 'purpose' (*see* Fig. 5.2) rather than by 'function' or 'activity' as shown of Fig. 5.1 In this type of structure the various activities are grouped together to achieve a defined purpose. In the case of a computer department the 'purpose' may be multifold, i.e. to develop several systems for computerisation concurrently, in which case programmers and analysts would be combined into a project team for each project undertaken reporting to team leaders.

8. Examination question. The following question relating to this topic was set in an ACCA paper.

ABC Ltd's computer department contains 35 members of staff, including the computer manager. Analysts and programmers work together in project teams under team leaders.
Required:

(*a*) Draft what in your opinion would be a typical organisation chart for this computer department. The distribution of staff should be clearly shown.
(*b*) Identify the principal responsibilities of the operations manager in a computer department.

The solution to part (*a*) is shown in Fig. 5.2 and the solution to part (*b*) is outlined above (*see* 5).

Organisation of a management services department

9. Structure. Some organisations especially the larger ones, may structure management services (*see* Fig. 5.3) as a separate department or division incorporating operations research, data processing, work study and organisation and methods. Each of these disciplines would be under the control of a specialist manager reporting to a common superior, the manager of management

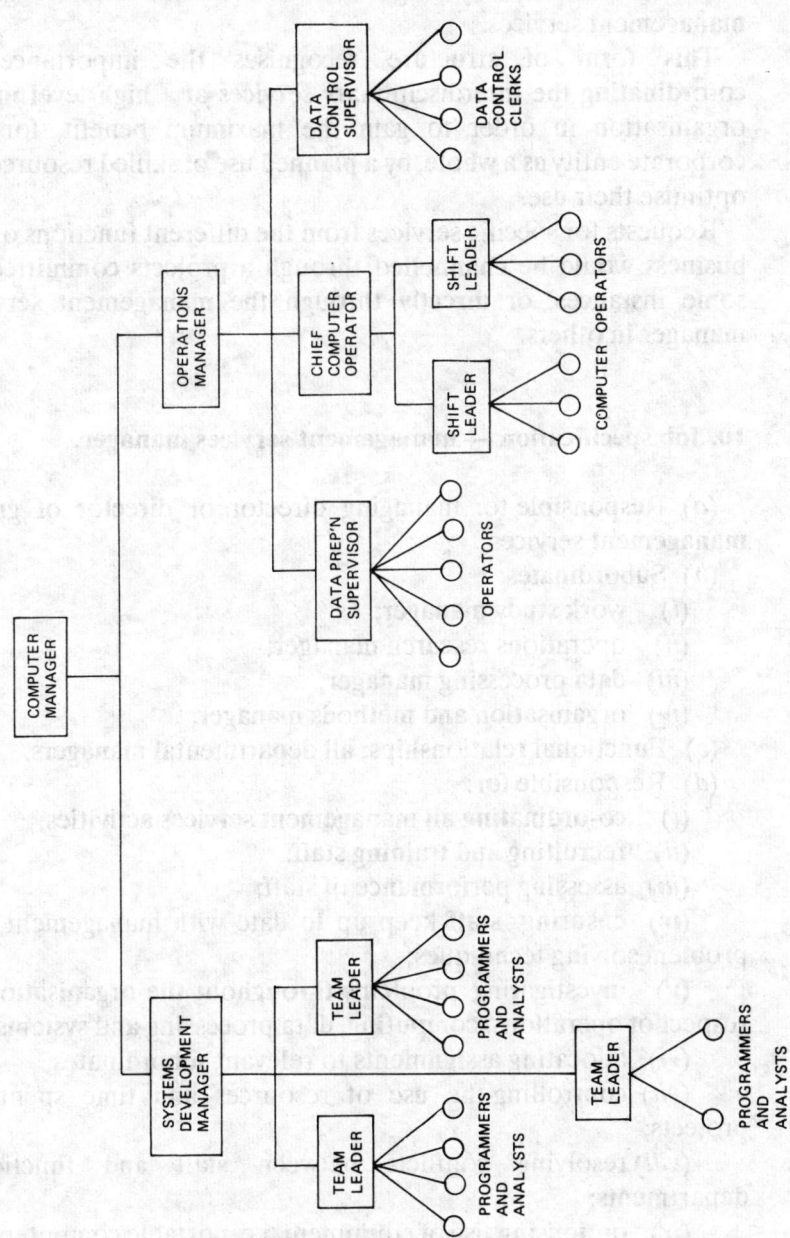

Figure 5.2   *Organisation chart: by purpose.*

services, or in a very large combine, the director of group management services.

This form of structure recognises the importance of co-ordinating the interdisciplinary services at a high level in the organisation in order to gain the maximum benefit, for the corporate entity as a whole, by a planned use of skilled resources to optimise their use.

Requests for specific services from the different functions of the business would be channelled through a projects committee, in some instances, or directly through the management services manager in others.

10. Job specification — management services manager.

(*a*) Responsible to: managing director or director of group management services.

(*b*) Subordinates:

    (*i*)   work study manager;

    (*ii*)   operations research manager;

    (*iii*) data processing manager;

    (*iv*) organisation and methods manager.

(*c*) Functional relationships: all departmental managers.

(*d*) Responsible for:

    (*i*)   co-ordinating all management services activities;

    (*ii*)   recruiting and training staff;

    (*iii*) assessing performance of staff;

    (*iv*) ensuring staff keep up to date with management and problem solving techniques;

    (*v*)   investigating problems throughout the organisation in respect of operations, computing, data processing and systems;

    (*vi*) allocating assignments to relevant subordinates;

    (*vii*) controlling the use of resources and time spent on projects;

    (*viii*) resolving conflicts between staff and functional departments;

    (*ix*) optimising use of equipment, i.e. portable computers for capturing data relating to work study and operations research projects;

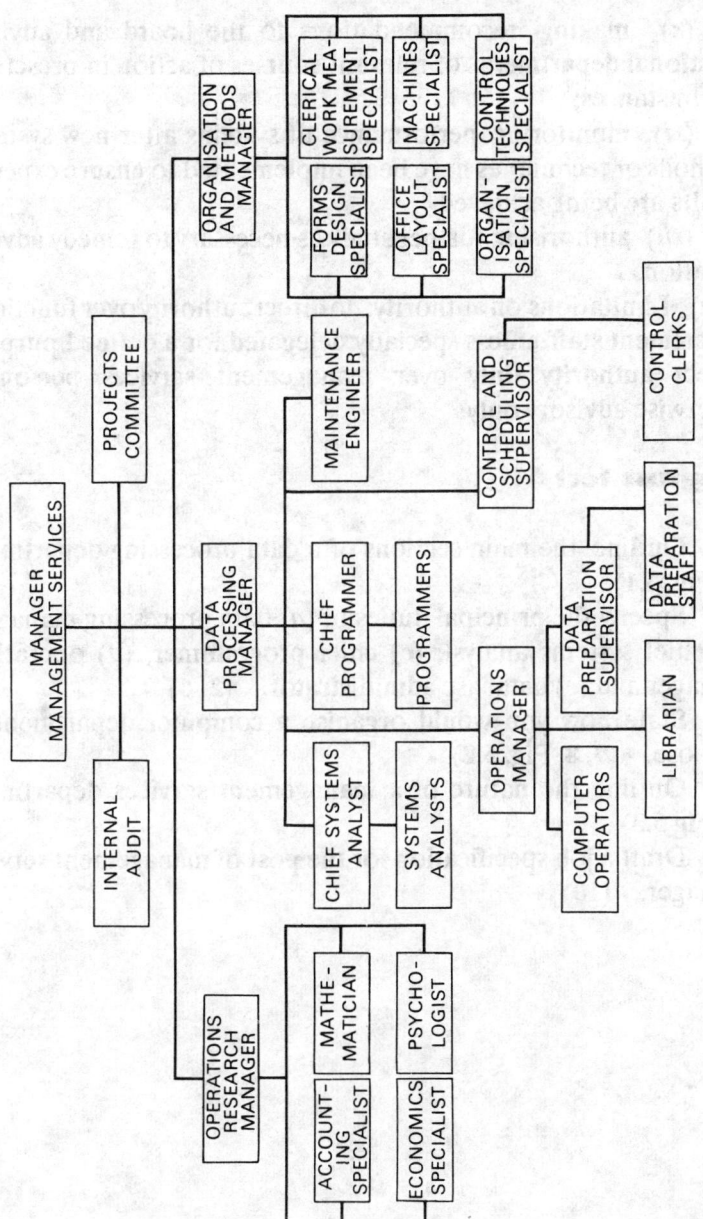

Figure 5.3 *Management services — organisation structure. Work study related to factory-based operations may also be incorporated.*

(*x*) making recommendations to the board and advising functional departments of relevant courses of action in prescribed circumstances;

(*xi*) monitoring performance of systems after new systems, methods or techniques have been implemented to ensure expected results are being achieved;

(*xii*) authorising further study as necessary to remedy adverse situations.

(*e*) Limitations on authority: no direct authority over functional department staff unless specially delegated for a defined purpose. Direct authority only over management services personnel; otherwise advisory only.

Progress test 5

1. Outline the main sections of a data processing department. (**1**, Fig. 5.1)

2. Specify the principal duties of (*a*) data processing managers; (*b*) chief systems analyst; (*c*) chief programmer; (*d*) operations manager and (*e*) database administrator.   (**2–6**)

3. State how you would organise a computer department by purpose.   (**7, 8**, Fig. 5.2)

4. Outline the nature of a management services department. (**9**, Fig 5.3)

5. Draft a job specification for the post of management services manager.   (**10**)

Part two

Computer input, output, data storage and retrieval, databases and backing storage and media

6

Computer input

Computer input media and data capture methods and techniques

1. Varying needs. There exist many different ways in which data can be collected or captured for processing by computer. The specific method or medium chosen for input depends on the type of computer configuration installed, which to some extent depends on the nature of business operations. Some businesses require real-time systems for their effective operation, in which case data is input to the computer by on-line terminal. Other businesses, with less critical information requirements, have batch processing configurations with data encoded on hard or floppy disc for input, in order to optimise the speed of inputting batches of data, for processing the payroll or for producing invoices, etc. In this instance, direct entry by means of the keyboard of a terminal device or workstation may not be suitable — being too slow for the volume of data to be processed. Large computers in the past tended to use either punched card or paper tape input but this has largely been phased out. The type of input selected also depends on the environment to which the data relates, which is why the 'shop floor' in the factory sometimes has factory terminals installed at strategic locations or portable computers, for the collection of data relating to factory orders and other requirements (*see* 23). Supermarket check-out points need some speedy method of capturing data relating to the items sold as customers come to the check-out point to pay for the goods. Bar code scanning is widely used in this situation for speeding up the flow of customers and minimising the length of queue, particularly at peak times.

2. Direct and indirect input. Input can broadly, but not precisely, be categorised into two divisions: direct and indirect. The term 'direct' should be interpreted to mean that data is in a form suitable for processing without the need for data conversion. Some systems have what may be called direct input media, such as optical marks on source documents but convert them into magnetic tape media prior to input to the computer. A typical example is the way in which meter readings are processed by electricity boards. Consumers' electricity usage is captured by having the meter read and by recording the reading in optical marks on a meter reading sheet. These sheets are read by an optical mark reader which transfers the data to a tape deck for recording the meter readings on magnetic tape. The details on the tape are then input for processing (*see* 16). In this instance, the optical method is 'indirect'. It would be 'direct' if the data was input into the computer without conversion. The same considerations apply to the use of Kimball tags as they are pre-punched ready for input to the computer when transactions occur but the data they contain is usually converted to magnetic media prior to being input for processing. Such conversions are performed electronically and automatically and do not involve time-consuming and costly punching and verifying operations, as is necessary for punched cards and paper tape. It is for this reason that punched cards and paper tape are being phased out in favour of more cost-effective and efficient media methods.

On-line systems input data direct from the keyboard for transaction data but this depends upon the nature and size of the micro, as some are equipped with devices for graphical input such as light pens, or a mouse. A 'mouse' is a small electronic device with one or two buttons on top and a ball bearing underneath which rolls on top of a desk. When the mouse is moved the cursor on the screen follows the direction of movement. This device allows the cursor to be moved to point at the required 'icon'. A click of a button selects this icon. This is a feature of electronic desktop display systems (*see* 2:16).

Table 6A summarises the various methods of input to a computer.

Table 6A Summary of input devices

Medium	Device	Type of business
Kimball tags	Tag reader	Retail clothing trade
Floppy disc	Disc unit	General for data interchange
Magnetic ink characters	Magnetic ink character reader/ sorter (Magnetic ink character recognition: MICR)	Banks
Optical characters	Optical character reader (Optical character recognition: OCR)	Gas boards, Electricity boards and local authorities
Bar code	Laser scanner	Supermarkets
Audio	Audio input	General applications
Keyboard plastic badge	Factory terminal	Factory work-in-progress control

Kimball tags

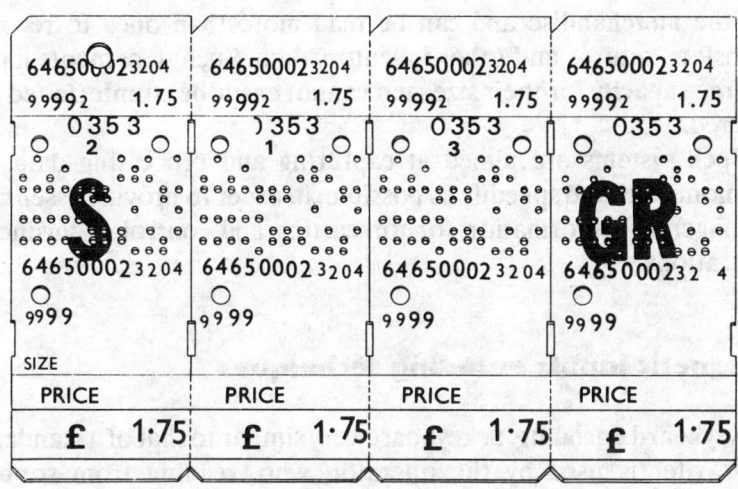

Figure 6.1 *Kimball tags (courtesy Litton Business Systems Limited).*

3. Retailing. Kimball tags are a special type of price tag used in retailing which contain printed and punched or magnetically encoded information (*see* Fig. 6.1).

Tags are used to improve the control of merchandising by means of automated tag systems which provide automatic facilities for printing and punching information into tags. The tags are then attached to the appropriate merchandise ready for sale. When the merchandise is sold, the tags are removed and the information they contain is converted to magnetic media or processing by electronic computer.

4. Data transmission. The information is then transmitted from remote locations by telephone line to a data centre where it is converted into a magnetic medium for computer input. This method eliminates mailing delays and provides management reports much more quickly.

Machines are available which encode both printed and magnetic language on tags and labels. The magnetic language is easily and accurately read by means of a hand-held magnetic scanning device such as the Datapen reader. By means of the reader information can be automatically captured at the point of the transaction from the magnetically-encoded documents. The encoded documents stay on the merchandise and can be read more than once to record transfers, returns and other inventory data. Such documents have a large capacity for their size, and cannot easily be counterfeited or altered.

Such systems are aimed at capturing and processing data as economically and speedily as possible, in order to provide essential management information for forecasting and control of business operations.

Magnetic input: encoding techniques

5. Keyboard encoding. A keyboard very similar to that of a standard typewriter is used by the operator, who, reading from source documents depresses appropriate keys on the keyboard, causing the character to be recorded on seven- or nine-track magnetic tape. For verification, the encoder compares the recorded data when it is keyed in a second time. This system is now being replaced by key-to-disc systems.

A variation of this method has the following features:

(*a*) As the operator keys data from source documents, *it is displayed on a monitor screen*, enabling a visual check to be made. In this case, data preparation also includes verification.

(*b*) To enable keyboard errors to be reduced, *magnetic tape cassettes* can be supplied which have a special format for display on the screen as a visual replica of the source document. The operator then keys in the information as if completing a form on a typewriter. As the data being keyed is displayed in the appropriate data boxes it enables the operator visually to check and correct the data as appropriate before depressing the 'send' key, which causes the data to be recorded on to magnetic media.

(*c*) *Pooling is possible,* whereby a maximum of 12 operators can key into up to four tape drives.

6. Key-to-disc. Key-to-disc systems include a number of key stations (in the region of 12 to 32) which enables that number of operators at one time to read data from source documents and encode the data on to magnetic disc. This type of system is more than a data preparation system because in addition to encoding and verifying data, it also provides for the validation of data fields, the generation or validation of check digits and the creation of batch totals, all under the control of a read-only program in the memory of the miniprocessor. Some systems are communications-orientated and transmit batches of data to a mainframe computer which may be located at a great distance away, such as another town.

After data has been encoded on disc, verified and validated, etc., records are ready for processing by a mainframe computer. The mainframe is then able to process the data which is free of errors and fully validated without having to carry out validation checks, which saves valuable processing time.

Key stations may be located up to 300 metres from the processor, which enables them to be strategically sited near to data origination points in factory departments, stores or warehouses, etc.

The essential elements of a key-to-disc system include the key stations, miniprocessor, disc drive, tape deck and a supervisor's console for monitoring the status of the system.

When an operator keys in data, by means of a keyboard similar to that of a typewriter, it is automatically checked and invalid data generates a signal from the processor to the key station which causes the keyboard to lock, together with an audible or displayed warning. Error correction is facilitated by a VDU or panel display, which indicates the erroneous data by means of a cursor on the VDU or a light on the panel display.

Data is keyed into an entry buffer and when this is full the data is transferred to a defined area of the disc. When a key station is set to verify the appropriate record is retrieved from the disc and inserted into the key station's entry buffer so that it can be compared with the same record when keyed in for verification. Differences are displayed on the VDU for correction, either to the original record or the keyed in character by the verifier operator. Records are then moved to an output buffer on disc before being transferred to magnetic tape.

As with all magnetic file media, which can be accidentally erased or overwritten, security measures are necessary and in this instance data is retained on the disc until it has been processed successfully by the mainframe computer. Data is then erased from the disc to provide storage areas for the new batches of data (*see* 6:2).

7. Key-to-diskette. A data station is used for recording data on diskettes. As data is entered it is stored in a buffer on the data station and displayed on a screen for the purpose of correcting errors before being recorded on diskette. When data is received it can be recorded to diskette and stored until a further batch of similar data is received. Data is entered by means of a keyboard similar to an electric typewriter. The data station can be set to verify mode so that a second operator can re-enter the data from source documents to detect any errors before the data is input for processing. Input to a computer is accomplished by means of an integrated floppy disc unit built into a processor's cabinet or by a freestanding floppy disc unit depending upon the type of computer and the manufacturer.

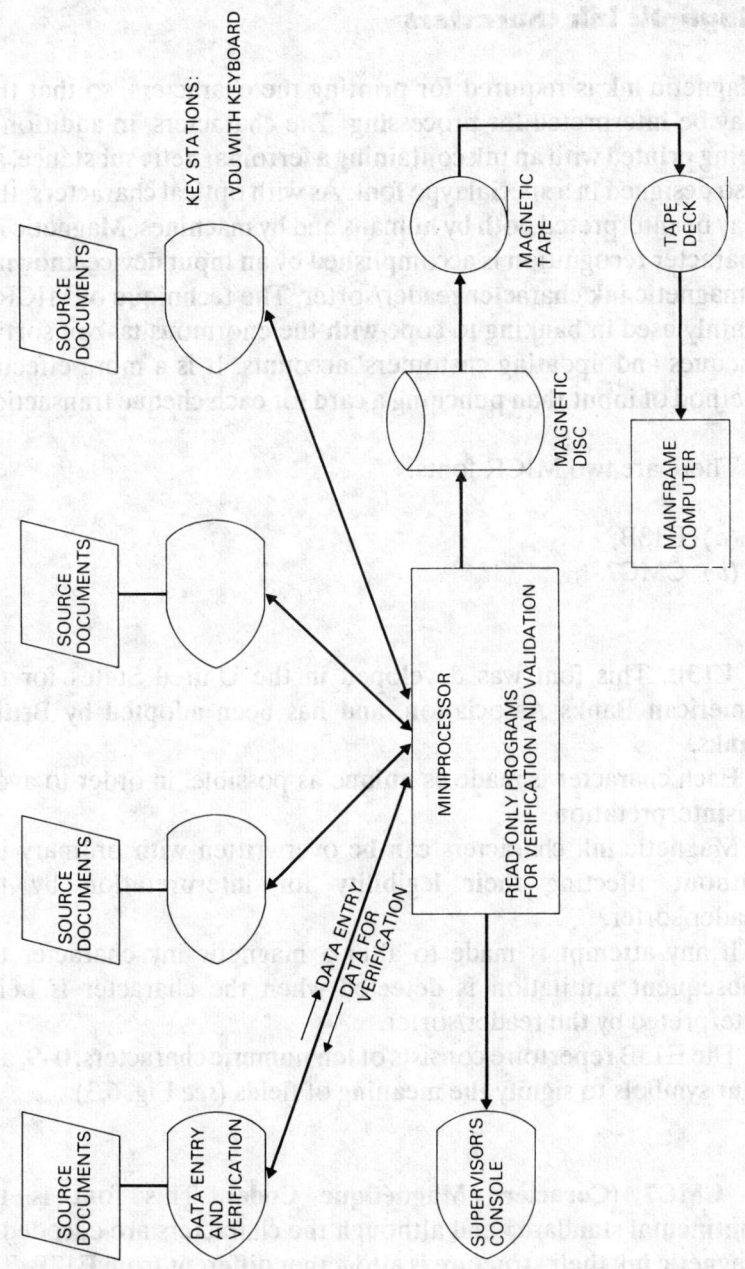

Figure 6.2 *Key-to-disc.*

Magnetic ink characters

Magnetic ink is required for printing the characters, so that they may be interpreted for processing. The characters, in addition to being printed with an ink containing a ferromagnetic substance, are also designed in a special type font. As with optical characters, they may be interpreted both by humans and by machines. Magnetic ink character recognition is accomplished by an input device known as a magnetic ink character reader/sorter. The technique of MICR is mainly used in banking to cope with the enormous task of sorting cheques and updating customers' accounts. It is a more effective method of input than punching a card for each cheque transaction.

There are two MICR fonts:

(*a*) E13B;
(*b*) CMC7.

8. E13B. This font was developed in the United States for the American Banks Association, and has been adopted by British banks.

Each character is made as unique as possible, in order to avoid misinterpretation.

Magnetic ink characters can be overwritten with ordinary ink without affecting their legibility for interpretation by the reader/sorter.

If any attempt is made to alter a magnetic ink character the subsequent mutilation is detected when the character is being interpreted by the reader/sorter.

The E13B repertoire consists of ten numeric characters, 0–9, and four symbols to signify the meaning of fields (*see* Fig. 6.3).

9. CMC7 (Caractère Magnétique Code). This font is the continental standard, and although the characters are encoded in magnetic ink their structure is altogether different from E13B. The characters are formed from a 'gapped font' code, consisting of seven vertical bars.

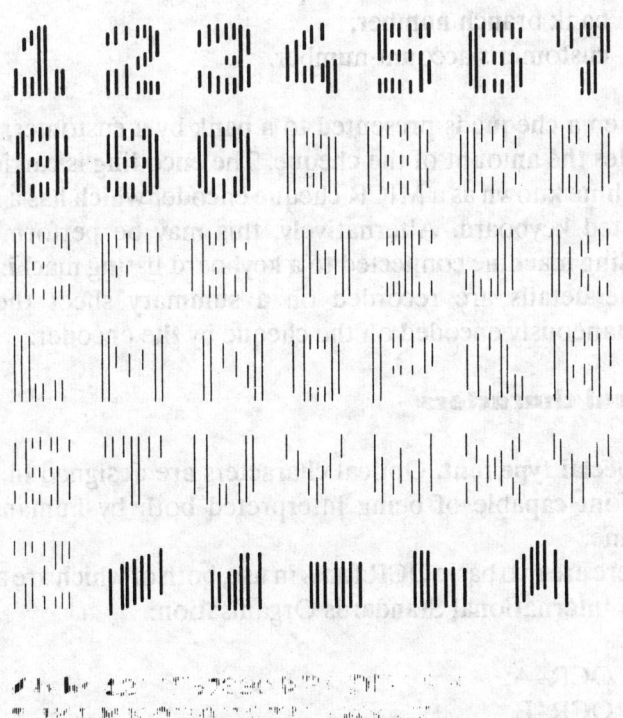

Figure 6.3 *MICR characters, E13B font (courtesy International Computers Limited).*

Figure 6.4 *MICR characters, CMC7 font (courtesy International Computers Limited).*

Each character is identified by the format of the bars, which create a six-bit code. Each bar is separated by a gap; a wide gap equals 1 and a narrow gap equals 0. The magnetic ink character reader recognises each character by the variable distance between the vertical bars.

The CMC7 repertoire consists of ten numeric characters, 0–9, 26 alphabetic characters and five special symbols (*see* Fig. 6.4).

10. Magnetic ink character encoding. Magnetic ink characters may be encoded on cheques when they are printed. The data pre-encoded would include:

- (*a*) serial number of the cheque;
- (*b*) bank branch number;
- (*c*) customer's account number.

When a cheque is presented to a bank by a customer, the bank encodes the amount of the cheque. The encoding is carried out by a machine known as a MICR cheque encoder which has a manually operated keyboard. Alternatively, this may be performed by an encoding machine connected to a keyboard listing machine. When cheque details are recorded on a summary sheet the data is simultaneously encoded on the cheque by the encoder.

Optical characters

11. Special type font. Optical characters are designed in a special type font capable of being interpreted both by humans and by machine.

There are two basic OCR fonts in use, both of which are approved by the International Standards Organisation:

- (*a*) OCR–A;
- (*b*) OCR–B.

Special ink is not required for printing OCR characters.

Optical characters are sensed by an input device, an optical character reader, which transfers data to the processor.

12. OCR–A. This font was developed, and is widely used, in the United States. It comprises 66 different characters — alphabetical characters, numbers and symbols — and four standard character sizes (*see* Fig. 6.5).

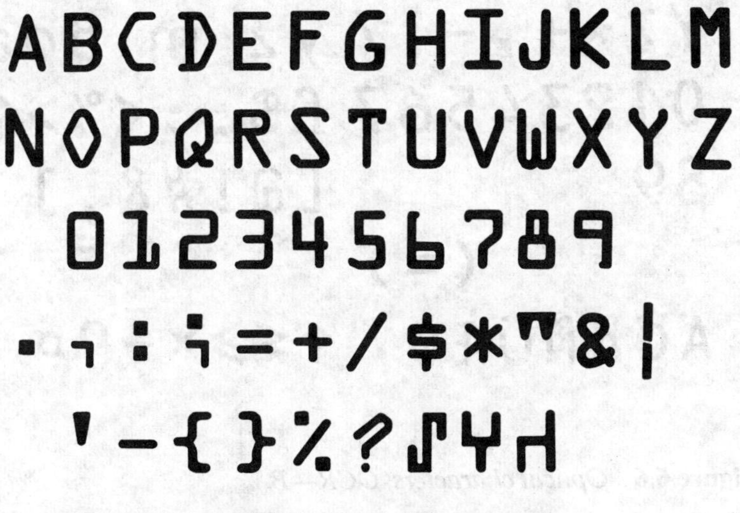

ABCDEFGHIJKLM
NOPQRSTUVWXYZ
0123456789
■ ┐ : ╕ = + / $ * ″ & |
' – { } % ? ♪ Ч Н
Ü Ñ Ä Ø Ö Æ £ ¥

Figure 6.5 *Optical characters, OCR—A.*

13. OCR–B. This font is the result of the work carried out by the European Computer Manufacturers' Association (ECMA), and is widely used in Europe. It comprises 113 different characters and four standard character sizes (*see* Fig. 6.6).

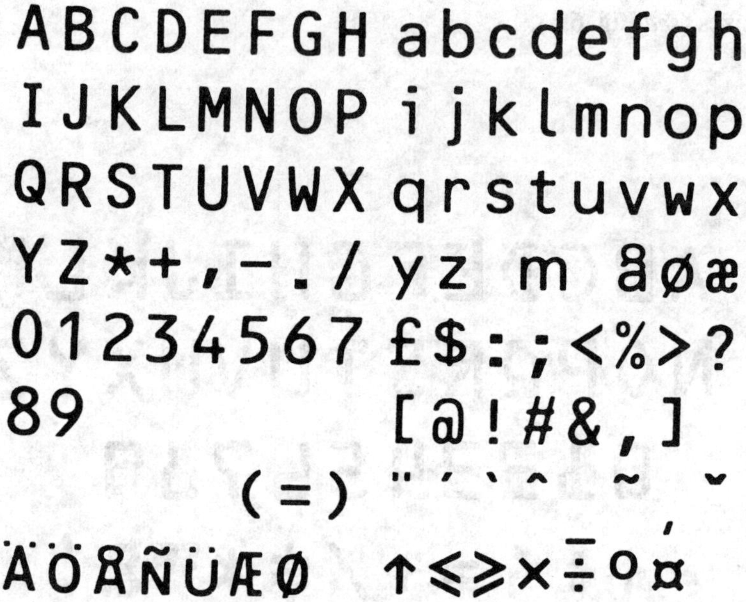

ABCDEFGH abcdefgh
IJKLMNOP i jklmnop
QRSTUVWX qrstuvwx
YZ*+,-./ yz m åøæ
01234567 £$:;<%>?
89 [a!#&,]
(=) "´`^~�‿
ÄÖÅÑÜÆØ ↑≤≥x÷°¤

Figure 6.6 *Optical characters, OCR—B.*

14. OCR character encoding. Printing characters on documents for optical reading is not so complex as printing magnetic ink characters, mainly because the font is not so intricate and the use of the special ink is unnecessasry. It is still necessary, however, to print the characters with a high degree of precision.

Encoding of characters may be performed in the following ways:

(a) *hand printing,* in accordance with specified rules for the formation of characters;

(b) *by typewriter* equipped with OCR font characters;

(c) *automatically,* by a line printer fitted with a print barrel embossed with OCR font characters;

(d) by cash registers *equipped with OCR font characters.*

Optical marks

15. Nature of optical marks. This method of collecting data utilises pre-printed source documents such as employee clock cards, confectionery order sheets and meter reading sheets as used by gas and electricity boards. It is a very speedy method of collecting data but care must be taken to ensure that marks are recorded, usually by hand, in the correct column otherwise invalid data will be processed causing error correction problems at a later date.

The documents are designed with predesignated column values and a mark is recorded in the appropriate column to indicate the number of hours worked on a specific job by an employee, etc. or to record the units consumed as indicated on a gas or electricity meter (*see* Fig. 6.7).

16. Example of OMR combined with OCR, demonstrating the use of turnaround documents. The Midlands Electricity Board produces meter reading sheets by computer, which contain details printed in optical characters. The sheets are used by meter readers who record readings (electricity consumed by customers) by marks in pre-designated meter reading columns. The details are then transferred to magnetic tape by optical mark and optical character reading.

The magnetic tape file is then used to produce consumer bills with stubs. These are sent to the consumer who detaches the stub and returns it with the remittance. The stub is then read by an optical character reader and transferred to magnetic tape to provide a file of cash receipts. The cash receipts are then recorded against the consumer record to provide an updated file of consumer details on magnetic tape. Both the meter sheet and the bill stub are turnaround documents as they are initially produced by the computer as an output and subsequently become the basis of input to the computer for further processing. The computer has actually produced its own input data at an earlier output stage (see Fig. 6.8).

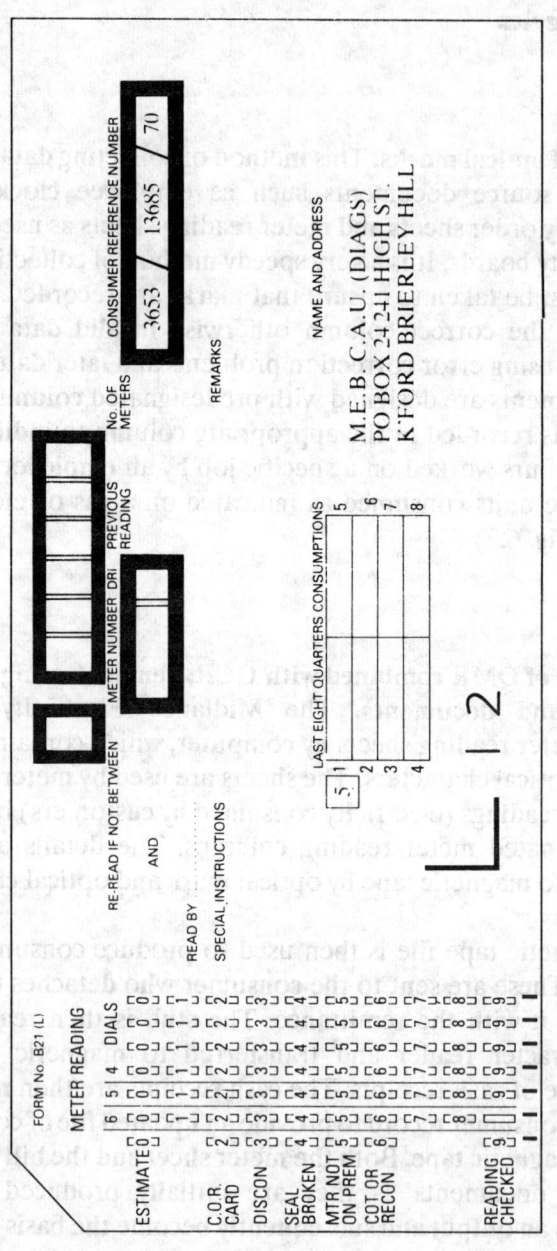

Figure 6.7 *Meter reading sheet: OMR and OCR: offpeak supply (courtesy Midlands Electricity Board).*

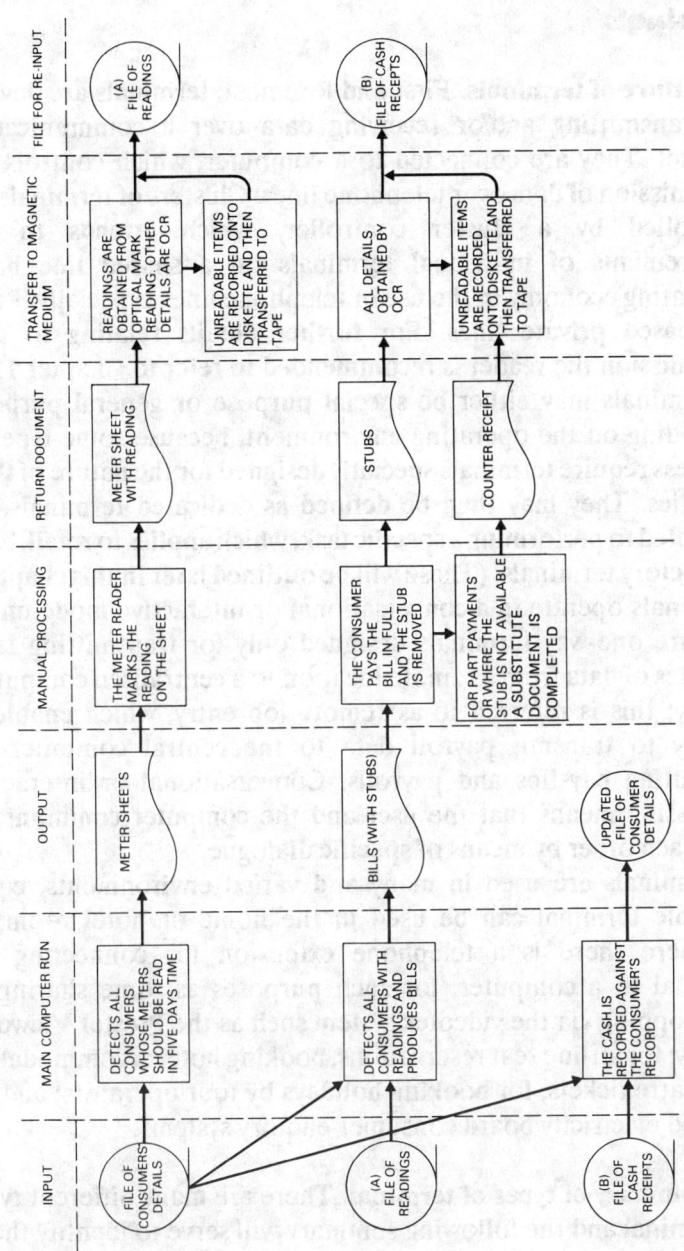

The flow chart contains the following labelled bands from top to bottom:

FILE FOR RE-INPUT
- (A) FILE OF READINGS
- (B) FILE OF CASH RECEIPTS

TRANSFER TO MAGNETIC MEDIUM
- READINGS ARE OBTAINED FROM OPTICAL MARK READING, OTHER DETAILS ARE OBTAINED BY OCR
- UNREADABLE ITEMS ARE RECORDED ONTO DISKETTE AND THEN TRANSFERRED TO TAPE
- ALL DETAILS OBTAINED BY OCR
- UNREADABLE ITEMS ARE RECORDED ONTO DISKETTE AND THEN TRANSFERRED TO TAPE

RETURN DOCUMENT
- METER SHEET WITH READING
- STUBS
- COUNTER RECEIPT

MANUAL PROCESSING
- THE METER READER MARKS THE READING ON THE SHEET
- THE CONSUMER PAYS THE BILL IN FULL AND THE STUB IS REMOVED
- FOR PART PAYMENTS OR WHERE THE STUB IS NOT AVAILABLE A SUBSTITUTE DOCUMENT IS COMPLETED

OUTPUT
- METER SHEETS
- BILLS (WITH STUBS)
- UPDATED FILE OF CONSUMER DETAILS

MAIN COMPUTER RUN
- DETECTS ALL CONSUMERS WHOSE METERS SHOULD BE READ IN FIVE DAYS TIME
- DETECTS ALL CONSUMERS WITH READINGS AND PRODUCES BILLS
- THE CASH IS RECORDED AGAINST THE CONSUMER'S RECORD

INPUT
- FILE OF CONSUMERS DETAILS
- (A) FILE OF READINGS
- (B) FILE OF CASH RECEIPTS

Figure 6.8 *Procedure chart: use of turnaround documents in quarterly billing (courtesy Midlands Electricity Board).*

Terminals

17. Nature of terminals. First and foremost, terminals are devices for transmitting and/or receiving data over a communication channel. They are connected to a computer, which controls the transmission of data over telephone lines. Clusters of terminals are controlled by a cluster controller, which attends to the requirements of individual terminals on a shared line basis, facilitating economy in the use of telephone lines especially if they are leased private lines. For further details relating to data transmission the reader is recommended to refer to Chapter 11.

Terminals may either be special purpose or general purpose, depending on the operating environment, because some types of business require terminals specially designed for the nature of their activities. They may then be defined as dedicated terminals, i.e. dedicated to performing a specific task, which applies to retail, bank and factory terminals. (These will be outlined later in this chapter.) Terminals operate in a conversational or interactive mode unless they are one-way terminals designed only for transmitting large volumes of data from a remote location to a centralised computing facility; this is referred to as remote job entry, which enables a factory to transmit payroll data to the central computer for computing payslips and payrolls. Conversational or interactive processing means that the user and the computer communicate with each other by means of specific dialogue.

Terminals are used in many and varied environments, e.g. a portable terminal can be used in the home or hotel room, or anywhere there is a telephone extension for connecting the terminal to a computer, for such purposes as: time sharing or teleshopping via the videotex system such as the Prestel Viewdata facility; for airline seat reservations, booking hotel accommodation or theatre tickets; for booking holidays by tour operators; and for gas and electricity board consumer enquiry systems.

18. Summary of types of terminal. There are many different types of terminal and the following summary will serve to identify them:

(a) teletype;
(b) visual display unit (VDU);

(c) intelligent terminal;
(d) factory terminal;
(e) bank cashpoint terminal;
(f) retail terminal;
(g) bulk transmission/remote batch terminal;
(h) handprint data entry terminal;
(i) workstations;
(j) branch terminal.

19. Purpose of terminals. It has already been stated that the primary purpose of a terminal is to transmit and/or receive data, but a brief summary, prior to further study of the different forms this may take should be beneficial.

(a) Transmission of data from one location to another or between computers in a local area network environment for text, data or electronic mail processing purposes.
(b) Access to a computer for time sharing facilities either for program development, problem solving or file processing.
(c) Random enquiry facilities for credit status enquiries, product availability, account status or hotel or airline seat availability.
(d) Real-time control of manufacturing processes and airline seat reservations.
(e) Point of sale data capture in supermarkets.
(f) Access to cash outside banking hours by means of cashpoint terminals.
(g) Processing business operations such as:
   (i) on-line order entry;
   (ii) on-line stock control;
   (iii) on-line payroll processing.
(h) Collection of data relating to works orders.
(i) Transmission of handwritten data and signatures by handprint data entry terminal.
(j) Console unit for controlling computer operations.

20. Teletype. This type of terminal is actually a teleprinter or telex machine as used in the telex system of British Telecom. It is now used for other data communication purposes due to the growth in data communications between computers. It is probably the best known keyboard/printer terminal which transmits data via a telephone line by depressing keys on the keyboard. In a telex system data is transmitted along a telegraph line. Each telex machine is connected through the telex network to other telex machines. However, we are interested in the use of the teletype as a terminal device for transmitting and receiving data in time sharing systems and as a control console for man/machine communications in the older mainframe installations.

A modem or acoustic coupler is required for connecting the terminal to the telephone line, as it is necessary to convert the digital signals transmitted by the terminal into analogue signals required by the voice grade telephone lines. When the signals are received at the computer end of the line they are converted back into digital signals from analogue signals prior to processing. This may change in the future with the advent of the digital PABX telephone system, which facilitates the digital transmission of both data and voice communications. Provision is made for prepunching paper tape for subsequent transmission of data at a faster speed than is possible by keyboard entry of data for direct transmission. Data can also be received on paper tape as well as being printed on the printing unit.

21. Visual display unit (VDU). The VDU, which is often referred to as a video unit or monitor, is a general purpose terminal which can be used for a wide range of business applications including those itemised in **19** (*a*),(*b*),(*c*)(*d*),(*g*). It is more modern than the teletype and much quieter in operation, which is why the VDU is tending to replace it in most environments. In appearance a VDU is like a television set with a keyboard or even like a microcomputer. In fact a micro can function as an intelligent VDU. The screen is a cathode ray tube (CRT) which displays images such as graphs, diagrams and text. This is in contrast with the teletype which prints text and graphs on paper by means of the printing unit. If a copy is required of the screen image this can be accomplished by copying the screen display to a printer connected to the processor. A light pen may be used in conjunction with the VDU for graphical applications (*see* Fig. 6.9).

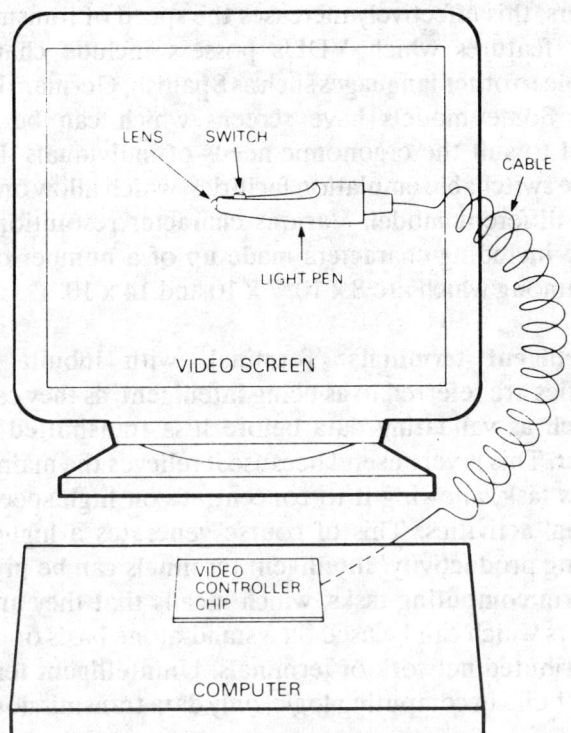

Figure 6.9 *Video screen and light pen.*

Data is displayed on the screen from incoming signals or direct from the keyboard as everything that is keyed in is displayed. The screen can be cleared by a function key without destroying the contents of the memory. Data can be corrected (edited) on the screen before transmitting it to another terminal or computer. Windows or split screens are available for displaying several different elements simultaneously; different document images for instance.

A cursor, a moving bright spot on the surface of the screen, indicates the next position for entering characters. Sometimes, a winking cursor is used as a prompt for drawing attention to a specific section of the screen. Data is usually buffered, allowing it to be transmitted in blocks of characters instead of individual characters; this effectively increases the speed of transmission.

Other features which VDUs possess include character sets switchable to other languages such as Spanish, German, French and English. Some models have screens which can be tilted and swivelled to suit the ergonomic needs of individuals. In addition they have switchable emulation facilities, which allow one model to act as a different model. Various character resolutions are also available including characters made up of a number of bits in a matrix, among which are 8 x 10, 7 x 10 and 14 x 10.

22. Intelligent terminals. Terminals with inbuilt processing capabilities are referred to as being intelligent, as they can perform tasks such as validating data before it is transmitted to a main computer. This is very useful because it relieves the main computer from this task, allowing it to concentrate on high speed 'number crunching' activities. This of course generates a higher level of processing productivity. Intelligent terminals can be programmed to perform computing tasks, which means that they are in effect computers which can be used on a stand-alone basis or can be part of a distributed network of terminals. Unintelligent terminals do not have built-in computing logic, only data transmission facilities.

Data collection systems

A data collection system is used for recording and transmitting data from remote locations either to a central point or directly to a computer. In general, data collection systems are applied where it is necessary speedily to collect data from dispersed locations within an organisation with a minimum of recording and in a form suitable for processing to obtain the desired information for the control of operations.

Applications include recording sales transactions at the point of sale and recording production data in respect of factory departments.

23. Factory terminal. The details which follow apply to the ICL Model 9603 factory terminal. It is a microprocessor-based terminal which allows data to be input via a keyboard, 10-column badge and

80-column punched card. It has a large, clear display for input instructions, error messages and replies to enquiries.

The prime types of data recorded include the completion of specific tasks, the movement of materials and components and attendance of personnel. Authorised personnel can retrieve up-to-date file information via the display. Typical enquiries include job status, next job details, component location or stock availability.

Variable information is entered via a 12-key numeric keyboard or a 42-key alphanumeric keyboard. The keyboards are pressure sensitive. To simplify data entry, fixed information such as personnel or part numbers can be read in via a plastic badge.

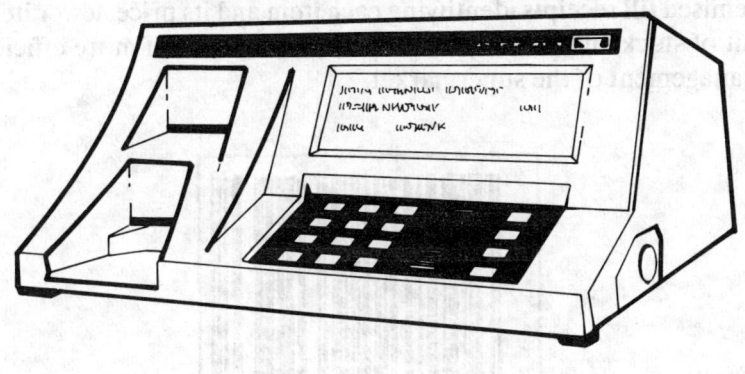

Figure 6.10 *ICL 9603 factory terminal (courtesy International Computers Limited).*

The terminal has a card reader to accept standard or plastic 80-column punched cards. The terminal can hold up to ten basic transaction programs which, together with guidance instructions, can be easily specified and amended by the user's own staff.

Initial program loading is directly from the 9600 System Controller, or via the card reader. A user identity check can be included in any program. The terminals can be located up to 7.6 wire km (4.7 miles) from the processor but this can be extended by a modem booster. The transmission speed is up to 4,800 baud (bits per second) (*see* Fig. 6.10).

24. Article numbering and check-out scanning. Article numbering and check-out scanning is one of the most dynamic developments in retailing since self-service was introduced. It is being adopted by many supermarkets. Article numbering takes the form of an EAN (European Article Number) bar code (*see* Fig. 6.11), which is a series of bars and spaces of varying width to a predetermined structure and standard. A bar code is the machine-sensible version of a product's article number which is unique to each size, colour and pack of every item. Check-out scanning involves the scanning of the bar code on items sold by a low-intensity laser scanner and other electronic scanning devices such as light pens or slot scanners. The advantage to shoppers is more efficient check-out service, itemised till receipts identifying each item and its price, fewer items out of stock and possibly lower prices as a result of more efficient management of the supermarket.

Figure 6.11 *Example of a bar code (courtesy Cadbury Limited).*

25. Auto teller terminals. These terminals are for automating payments to bank customers and data collection. Many bank branches have facilities for providing customers with a cash withdrawal service outside normal banking hours. The availability of the service is determined by each bank. Each customer is provided with a plastic card which is placed in a special cash dispensing and recording machine (the auto teller terminal) installed through the wall of the bank. The customer keys in the personal number previously provided on the numeric keyboard of the terminal and enters the amount of money required on the same keyboard. The data is entered by the depression of a data entry key.

The cash required is dispensed automatically (auto teller). The customer then removes the cash and the card from the terminal.

The transactions are recorded on the customer's statement, indicating which facility was used. A weekly withdrawal limit is given to each customer. The personal number ensures security because this is used in conjunction with the card. In the eventuality of the card being lost no one can use it without the personal number.

26. Remote batch terminals (distributed processing). Some remote batch terminals are designed as data communication systems for direct communication with a computer or as part of a comphrehensive communications network forming a distributed processing system. Such terminals, at various remote locations, communicate with one another for the purpose of transmitting source data and printing documents from the transmitted data. They may also print documents from data prepared locally.

Figure 6.12 *Handprint data entry terminal (courtesy Quest Micropad Limited).*

27. Handprint data entry terminal. One such system is marketed by Quest CIL and is called Micropad Handprint data entry terminal (*see* Fig. 6.12). It is a local or remote terminal which enables handprinted data to be captured at the time of writing and the data is validated simultaneously. The device converts the handprinted alphanumeric characters into ASCII code and transmits this code to any host computer via a standard interface.

It comprises a pressure-sensitive writing surface, an inbuilt microprocessor and an integral 40-character line display. Data and signatures are written using an ordinary ballpoint pen or pencil on documents designed by users to suit their specific applications. This method of data capture may be used for entering customer order details, retail point of sale recording, payroll and file amendments, etc.

Available options allow the data to be transmitted immediately it is written or stored within Micropad and transmitted as a block of up to 512 characters, or validated locally within Micropad. Additional features include the ability to output alphabetic characters as upper or lower case and ASCII special and control characters. The Q-Sign option allows Micropad to function as a dynamic signature verification terminal by comparing the user's signature as it is written with the reference signature. This provides immediate authorisation for transactions.

Data is validated character by character and field by field before being transmitted. Standard validation checks include:

(a) alpha/numeric/special characters;
(b) left/right/full field justification;
(c) mandatory/optional field;
(d) logical data checks;
(e) maximum data field length: 32 characters;
(f) maximum number of fields per document: 50.

Special European character sets are available including Swedish/Finnish, Danish/Norwegian, and Spanish/Portuguese.

Workstations

28. General characteristics. Workstations provide the means of improving office productivity by using technologically based tools for creating records, amending records, processing and communicating information, inter-company transactions, electronic mail, electronic filing and word processing, etc.

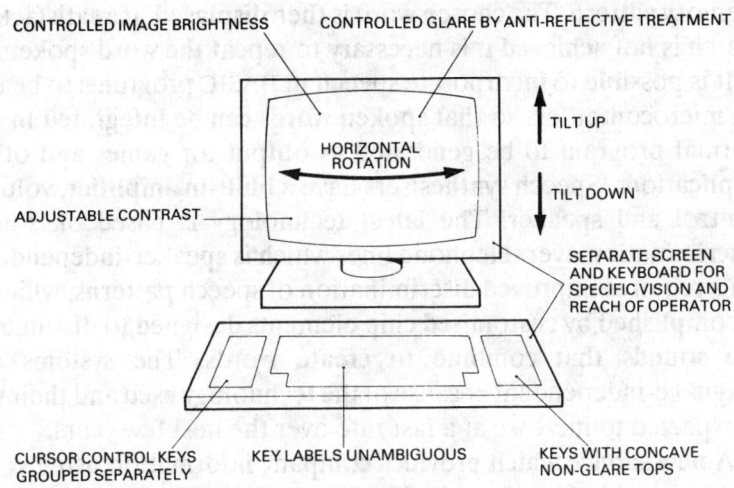

Figure 6.13   *Features of a workstation.*

The workstation consists of a visual display unit (VDU), a keyboard, a microprocessor for text and image processing and an internal memory. Workstations usually share printing and central storage resources when part of a network. They may also have voice handling capabilities which enable voice messages to be stored and electronically mailed to other users on the network, and may also be connected to mainframe computers for gaining access to a corporate database and to act as a data collection terminal (*see* Fig. 6.13).

Speech synthesis and analogue input

29. Speech synthesis. The recognition of speech is achieved using allophones, the basic speech sounds, by storing a digitised pattern in the form of a reference matrix. This is a pattern of signals unique for each vocabulary word; any English word can be constructed and spoken by this means. Words are recognised by a matching technique and the speech patterns of several speakers can be stored simultaneously. Having obtained a matrix pattern of the words the computer performs a search routine for the nearest match. When this is located it compares the bit count relationship with the memory pattern. The chosen word is then displayed. If a satisfactory match is not achieved it is necessary to repeat the word spoken.

It is possible to incorporate speech in BASIC programs to be run on microcomputers so that spoken words can be integrated in the normal program to be generated as output for games and other applications. Speech synthesisers have a built-in amplifier, volume control and speaker. The latest technology is based on sound discrimination over telephone lines which is speaker-independent. This requires improved discrimination of speech patterns, which is accomplished by customised chip elements designed to distinguish the sounds that combine to create words. The systems are language-independent because of the technology used and their use is expected to increase at a fast rate over the next few years.

A new service which provides company information using voice technology has been launched by Dun and Bradstreet. The service, called DunsVoice, operates through a standard multi-frequency pushbutton telephone and is probably the first credit-control computer to speak with a friendly human voice. To make a credit enquiry the caller simply dials up the Dun and Bradstreet database, which currently holds records on more than a million businesses in the UK alone.

30. Analogue (digital) input. This type of input is applicable to process and machine control, data logging, patient monitoring systems and laboratory projects, etc. A sensor collects details relating to the status of the system being controlled in the form of analogue signals which are converted to digital signals by a digitiser. Analogue data is represented in a continuous form as contrasted with digital data, which is in discrete form, i.e. finite values. Analogue data is represented by physical variables such as voltage, resistance, temperature, pressure and rate of flow. As variations take place they are input to the digitiser which is continuously scanned by the computer.

31. Light pen. A light pen is an electronic device in the form of a photo-diode on the end of a cable which is used in combination with a visual display unit or video screen. It is used to display, modify or detect images on the screen often in CAD (computer aided design) applications. This is achieved by passing the light pen across the surface of the screen to trace the outline of the image to be displayed. The computer can detect the position of the pen on the screen by counting the number of vertical and horizontal synchronisation pulses (*see* Fig. 6.9).

32. Graphics tablet. Sometimes referred to as a digitising tablet, this is constructed from a sensitive semiconducting material which can trace the movement of a stylus forming graphical shapes. The shapes are converted into digital signals which are input directly into the computer. A mouse may be used as an alternative to a graphics stylus for achieving the same purpose.

Progress test 6

1. Write short notes relating to computer input and data capture. (1, 2)
2. Specify the nature of Kimball tags. (3)
3. Specify methods of preparing magnetic media for computer input. (5–7)
4. Describe, with the aid of a block diagram, a computer controlled keying system (key-to-disc or key-to-tape). (6, Fig. 6.2)
5. Write brief notes on the following techniques. Describe a situation in which EACH technique would be used: (*a*) optical character recognition (OCR); (*b*) magnetic ink character recognition (MICR); (*c*) optical mark readers (OMR). (8–16)
6. List the types of terminal which may be used for computer input. (17, 18)
7. What purpose do terminals serve? (19)
8. VDUs and keyboard printer units are widely used as terminals to multi-access systems. Give for each device ONE example where it is preferable to the use of the other. Give reasons for your choice. (20, 21)
9. What are intelligent terminals? (22)
10. Write short notes on each of the following data collection systems: (*a*) factory terminal; (*b*) article numbering and check-out

scanning; (c) auto teller terminals; (d) remote batch terminals. (23–26)

11. Workstations provide the means for improving office productivity. Discuss. (28)

12. Computer input may be achieved by speech synthesis and analogue signals. Indicate the nature and use of these methods. (29, 30)

13. Define the nature of a light pen and graphics tablet. (31, 32)

7

Computer output

Output devices

1. General considerations. Output from a computer can be achieved in many different ways by various media and output devices, the primary ones being printers and VDUs. Various types of printer are used according to the size of the business, the type of computer installation and the volume of information required to be printed. Other forms of output are used for specialised applications such as image recording on microfilm or microfiche, known as 'computer output on microfilm' (COM). It is important to appreciate that magnetic media, such as discs, have multi-purpose characteristics: they can be used to store transaction files for input, to store programs and records for future use and to output results for later conversion to printed output. VDUs also serve more than one purpose: they display input data, the results of processing and system messages from the operating system and, when running interactively, prompts from application programs.

Table 7A summarises the various output devices.

Printers

2. Character printers. Serial printers print a character at a time in the same way as a typewriter except that they have facilities for bi-directional printing, i.e. from left to right and right to left. Dot matrix and daisy wheel printers are widely used on small business computers.

Table 7A Summary of output devices

Method	Medium	Output device
Printed	Hard copy	Printer: Character printers Matrix Daisy wheel Thermal Ink jet Line printers Barrel Chain Page printer Laser printer
Image recording	Microfilm or microfiche	COM recorder
Visual	Screen display	Visual display unit (VDU) — Work station or terminal
Graphical	Charts and graphs *or* diagrams	Graph plotter Printer/plotter
Magnetic (used also as input and storage media because of its multi-use features)	Magnetic tape Floppy disc Exchangeable disc storage (EDS) Winchester disc High capacity fixed discs Data module	Tape streamer Floppy disc drive EDS disc drive Sealed disc drive Fixed disc drives Integrated disc drive

3. Dot matrix printer. Each character on a dot matrix printer is constructed from a matrix of wires contained in the print head. Various combinations of wires form separate characters which are printed when the wires strike a carbon ribbon against the paper, just as on a typewriter. This type of printer does not store the pre-formed characters you find on typewriter keys or daisy wheel printers. Other features allow the selection of different print modes including condensed, enlarged, elite-sized characters, underlining and emphasised mode, etc.

The dot matrix printer has a printing speed in the region of

120–150 cps (characters per second), for NLQ and 250–400 cps for Draft attributable largely to the bi-directional printing facility. Printing takes place from the printer's buffer which is a magnetic storage device. It avoids holding up the processor which can carry on with other tasks while printing takes place. The quality of print is suitable for internal use but, with many models, is inadequate for business correspondence. Models are now available which produce near letter-quality print, generally referred to as NLQ. The speed of the printer is greatly reduced when NLQ is selected because this requires two or more passes to enable characters to be printed with greater definition. Some models also have multi-colour ribbons for colour printing.

4. Daisy wheel printers. Daisy wheel printers have a set of characters embossed on the tips of individual stalks radiating from the central hub of a wheel resembling the petals of a daisy. The wheel typically has between 96 and 130 petals. Printing is restricted to the characters embossed on the daisy wheel, but the wheel can be changed. The wheel rotates until the correct character is positioned in front of a hammer, which strikes the tip of the stalk on which the character is embossed against a ribbon to produce an image of the character.

Unlike dot matrix, a daisy wheel cannot print graphical images and it is also slower, mainly because the daisy wheel is momentarily stationary to position each character. A typical speed is 40–50 cps, and the printer can take continuous stationery or separate sheets fed by a sheet feeder. The print quality, however, is superior to that of the dot matrix printer, being equivalent to that of an electronic typewriter.

5. Line printers: barrel and chain. Line printers are impact printers which print a complete line of characters after a complete revolution of the print barrel (a barrel printer) or the chain (a chain printer). Line printers operate at various speeds depending on the model, its age and technology. Typical speeds are 200, 300, 600, 720, 1500 and 3,000 lines per minute, this last being attained by the printer having an integrated microprocessor controller and lightweight durable alloy hammers. Line printers are used for high volume printing requirements in mainframe and minicomputer installations, and cost much more than the smaller character printers.

6. Barrel printer. The barrel-type printer has character sets embossed around a print barrel. When a line is to be printed the barrel rotates so that all the As are printed followed by the Bs, in respect of the same print position.

7. Chain printer. A chain printer has characters embossed on a chain which rotates so that every character passes the print position. A hammer prints the required character. Some printers of this type have multiple sets of characters (especially numeric) in the chain in order to achieve higher speeds.

8. Laser printer. These are referred to as page printers — due to their phenomenal speed of operation, in the region of 325 lps (lines per second), they appear to print a page at a time. The quality of a daisy wheel is combined with the flexibility of a dot matrix. A laser beam fires the image to be printed on to a drum, which becomes electronically charged with the image. A toner is then applied, as in photocopying, which is attracted to the laser-treated parts of the drum only, which passes the image through a heat fixing plate and transfers it on to paper. The drum is then wiped clean before it commences the next image cycle. Laser printers provide very high quality reproduction including graphics. Preprinted stationery can be dispensed with when using a laser printer in conjunction with desktop publishing software because business documents, including invoices, statements of account, etc., can be printed complete with headings. Plug-in cartridges can be obtained for different fonts. With some models, different fonts can be downloaded by software from GEM applications (*see* 2:16), for instance. Laser printers have fallen dramatically in price since their inception. Early models cost in the region of £20,000 to £100,000, but they are now available from around £1,500.

9. Thermal printers. This type of printer uses thermal electrosensitive paper which has a thin coating of aluminium over a black- or blue-inked surface. By passing an electrical current through a needle on to the paper a spark is formed which removes a small area of aluminium which exposes the black or blue undersurface. This type of printer is both quiet in operation and inexpensive.

10. Ink jet printers. Ink jet printers are non-impact printers capable of graphical output. One type can print in colour, by means of a selection of ink wells connected to the printing head. This has a fine nozzle through which the ink is ejected.

11. Features to consider when selecting a printer. Printers are available with a wide range of features which must be taken into account when assessing the one most suitable for business needs. Whichever printer is selected it must be compatible with the computer system. Features to consider are:

(a) speed — characters per second, lines per minute;
(b) column width, e.g. 80 or 136 characters, which is relevant to the type of stationery to be used — such as payroll documents;
(c) tractor or friction feed for form-feeding considerations;
(d) colour printing;
(e) parallel or serial interface;
(f) graphics capabilities;
(g) bi-directional printing;
(h) condensed and double-width printing;
(i) alternative character sets;
(j) plain or thermal paper;
(k) cut sheets or continuous stationery;
(l) single or multi-part sets;
(m) varying character pitches;
(n) price;
(o) reliability;
(p) cost of maintenance.

Magnetically encoded

12. Magnetically encoded output. Output in this form is usually for the purpose of storing records and the media used for this purpose include floppy discs, exchangeable and fixed discs and magnetic tape.

Visual display unit and graph plotter

13. Visual display unit (VDU). A VDU is a dual purpose device which has already been discussed in detail (*see* 6: 21). It can be used as an input device for data, such as in an order-entry system, by means of the keyboard as well as being an output device for displaying text and graphical characters.

14. Graph plotter. In addition to the recently developed printer/plotter extensively used on microcomputers, a dedicated graph plotter is used for the output of graphical information on large and small computers. A plotter provides a permanent hard copy of the graphical output as opposed to a VDU, which displays graphical output in a transitory manner on the video screen as it disappears when the machine is switched off. The output can be multi-coloured.

Computer output on microfilm (COM)

15. Nature of COM. Computer output on microfilm is an alternative to printed output, which is relatively slow even for the faster type of printer compared with the speed with which COM can be produced. COM not only produces output faster but also reduces stationery costs and the space needed for storing computer print-outs. It is also an information retrieval system.

COM may be defined as a method which stems the tide of the 'paperwork explosion', which has long been a feature of computerised batch processing systems. Hard copy output is not always required; consequently, if all computer output is committed to paper, a problem soon arises, not only deciding *who* should have *what* reports but *where* they will all be stored *just in case they may be needed.* Copies of computer output can be stored on microfilm or microfiche at much reduced size compared to the size of computer stationery pages. This makes storage of output less of a problem particularly when it is supported by an effective information retrieval system.

16. Hardware and software requirements. A typical COM system is minicomputer controlled and produces alphanumeric or graphical output on imaged, cut and processed dry silver microfiche, either direct by means of a COM recorder connected directly to the host processor or via COM formatted magnetic tapes for off-line mode. Disc drives are used for storage of parameters and job details. Software provides facilities for form drawing and outputting. Reduction ratios are typically 24 x, 42 x and 48 x. Images can be stored either on film or 105mm microfiche. The COM system adds an index to each image for reference and retrieval purposes. Microfiche is more popular than roll film as images are more easily assessed by simply moving the microfiche under the viewer to the desired image. This facilitates the location of component parts for a particular unit so that it can be located in the stores of a spares organisation, for instance. Related images can be stored on the same microfiche. Fiche are more easily stored than rolls of film and fiche readers are less expensive than roll film readers, are capable of a much higher quality of image reproduction and are also less complex.

17. Information retrieval. Information stored as images on film or microfiche can be accessed for retrieval purposes by a microfilm or fiche viewer. If a hard copy is required this is provided by a 'demand' printer.

Computer aided design (CAD)

18. Nature of CAD. A technique for the development of graphical designs of various types using a computer equipped with sophisticated software and a light pen in conjunction with a video screen. These resources enable the initial design to be displayed on the screen and subsequently modified if necessary. The image on the screen can be rotated to obtain a three-dimensional view in order to assess its features from various aspects. The technique allows standard shapes to be stored on disc and accessed when required for incorporation in other designs. It saves considerable time in the design activity and improves quality as designs can be speedily checked to ensure compatibility with specifications. Errors can be corrected by light pen. The technique is widely used for the design of aircraft, cars and computers as well as a wide range of other products. *See* also 6: **32** and Fig. 6.9.

Progress test 7

1. Summarise the different methods of producing computer output. (1, Table 7A)

2. List the main features of dot matrix and daisy wheel printers. When is a daisy wheel printer more suitable than a dot matrix printer? (3, 4)

3. What is meant by NLQ? (3)

4. State the characteristics of barrel and chain printers. (5–7)

5. Define the difference between a character, line and page printer. (2, 5, 8)

6. Describe the nature of thermal and ink jet printers. (9, 10)

7. List the features you would take into account when selecting a printer. (11)

8. Outline the nature of a visual display unit and a graph plotter. (13,14)

9. Explain the meaning of COM and indicate the difference between microfilm and microfiche. What are the benefits of such a system? (15–17)

10. What is computer aided design (CAD)? (18)

8
Data storage and retrieval

Folders and directories

1. Folders. A clerical system stores documents and records in folders labelled with file names for identification. Related folders are stored together in a filing cabinet. A computer file is like an individual letter or document in a folder. The 'folder' on the disc also contains a list of the items contained in it. The list is a directory, which is why folders are often called directories. But for physical storage limitations, all files *could* be stored in one folder both in a filing cabinet and on a computer disc. Even so, for convenience, files are grouped into different folders in both instances. Each disc is comparable to a drawer of a filing cabinet and putting a disc into a drive is similar to opening one drawer. The number of disc drives the computer system has may be considered as the number of drawers of a filing cabinet that can be open at the same time. When a drawer is opened in a clerical system a set of folders appears. If a folder is opened a number of documents or further folders or combinations of the two become apparent. Similarly, when a disc is placed in a disc drive the folders it contains — directories — can be displayed on the screen by a DIR command, meaning 'list the files contained in the directory'. The other folders divide the contents of the main folder into more manageable groups, applying a hierarchical structure. The standard way of grouping folders is by directories.

2. Directories. As more files are created a disc directory can become very lengthy and may fill up completely. Directories can be created by a disc operating system, MS-DOS, for example, enabling files to be structured in convenient groups. A directory may contain any number of files but it is more convenient to separate files into sub-directories. Directories can therefore be structured on a hierarchical basis, providing a pathway to a specific file.

Fig. 8.2 illustrates a hierarchical file structure showing that the root directory 'software' consists of three sub-directories: database, spreadsheet and word processing — shown as database, spreadsh and word. Each of these sub-directories is further analysed into database files, spreadsheet models and text files.

A 'pathname' is a series of directory names followed by the required file name, each separated by a backward slash. The following examples specify the pathnames required to find a particular file or sub-directory. In practice the sub-directories would be allocated short names for convenience of specifying pathnames. The directory being worked with at any time is known as the current directory. Each of the examples assumes that the root directory is the current directory. The symbols mark each step in the path down the hierarchy to the required file.

Examples of pathnames
It has already been stated above in 2 that the root directory 'software' consists of three sub-directories which are listed below:

(a) Software\database
(b) Software\spreadsh
(c) Software\word

Each of the sub-directories may be provided with a further sub-directory with the name 'reports', 'files', or 'documents'. Each of the pathnames would then become:

(a) Software\DATABASE\REPORTS
(b) Software\SPREADSH\FILES
(c) Software\WORD\DOCUMENTS

If the database file consisted of three types of report which are given the filename of Report 1, Report 2 and Report 3, the pathnames required to access any of the reports would be: first, change the current directory to Software by the command: CD\SOFTWARE. It is then necessary to change the current directory to Reports, which is accomplished by the command CD\DATABASE\REPORTS. It is now possible to access the required report by typing the filename at the A prompt, i.e. A> REPORT 1.

Access paths for other requirements such as spreadsheet files and word processing documents are generated in the same manner. The 'reverse solidi' (backward slash) should be used to separate each step in the access path.

3. Commands for handling directories.

(*a*) A new directory is created by typing: MKDIR\ followed by the directory name. This command may be abbreviated to MD ('make directory').

The software directory was set up as follows:

MKDIR   Software   (*see* Fig. 8.1)
MKDIR   Software\ database   (sub-directory – *see* Fig. 8.2)
MKDIR   Software\ spreadsh   (sub-directory
                                    – *see* Figs. 8.2 and 8.3)
MKDIR   Software\ word   (sub-directory – *see* Fig. 8.2)

(*b*) A directory may be changed by typing: CHDIR\ followed by the directory name. (This command may be abbreviated to CD.) A file may then be specified by entering only the filename instead of the whole path.

(*c*) The contents of a directory may be displayed by typing: DIR\ followed by the directory name. If software is the current directory and it is required to see the contents of directory 'database', this may be achieved by typing: DIR Database.

(*d*) An empty directory may be removed by typing: RMDIR\ followed by the directory name. This command may be abbreviated to RD.

(*e*) To remove a directory containing files it is first necessary to delete the files then apply the RMDIR command by typing the following:

(*i*) CHDIR followed by the directory name (changes directory to the one named).

(*ii*) DEL *.* (wild card characters, as they are called, which delete all files from the directory).

(*iii*) CHDIR\(change to the directory containing the sub-directory to be removed).

(*iv*) RMDIR followed by the directory name (removes named directory).

In all MS-DOS directories apart from the root directory the first two lines indicate:

    <DIR>
    <DIR>

The . is the directory itself. The two dots (. .) are an abbreviation for the parent directory, i.e. the next directory up the hierarchy.

The print-out of the software directory indicates the details outlined above and also shows that the spreadsheet (spreadsh) contains three files: cashflow, cal, profloss, cal and cost cal. (*see* Fig. 8.3).

A directory may be printed out by the command: DIR\directory name>PRN. To print-out the software directory, the command would be DIR\Software>PRN, and for the sub-directory 'spreadsh': DIR\Software\Spreadsh>PRN.

Storage and retrieval — use of pointers

4. Optimisation of storage and retrieval. To achieve effective storage and retrieval of data the two factors can be dealt with as separate activities. Data can be saved initially on the disc or tape files to achieve high-speed input of data to storage. The file can then be organised to facilitate the data retrieval method to be employed during processing activities.

```
Volume in drive A is Apricot
Directory of A:\

CALC            <DIR>           15/03/12    3:27p
ROBIN     BAK     1536          17/03/12    1:34a
SALES           <DIR>           15/03/12    6:24p
BOOKS           <DIR>           15/03/12    9:35p
SOFTWARE        <DIR>           16/03/12   10:50p
PROFLOSS CAL     2944           11/02/88    6:16p
COST     CAL     1024           1/01/80     1:28a
ROBIN            1536           1/01/80    12:33a
PROCESSO         3456           1/01/80    12:04a
PROC3            7680           1/01/80    12:10a
PROC4            3712           1/01/80    12:30a
FILES 2          1920           1/01/80     1:15a
DIRECT           3840           1/01/80     1:34a
DIRECT2          3840           1/01/80     1:35a
          14 File(s)       658432 bytes free
```

Figure 8.1   *Root directory including the software directory.*

```
Volume in drive A is Apricot
Directory of A:\software

.               <DIR>           16/03/12   10:50p
..              <DIR>           16/03/12   10:50p
DATA BASE       <DIR>           16/03/12   10:51p
SPREADSH        <DIR>           16/03/12   10:51p
WORD            <DIR>           16/03/12   10:51p
          5 File(s)       658432 bytes free
```

Figure 8.2   *Software directory including sub-directories.*

```
Volume in drive A is Apricot
Directory of A:\software\spreadsh

.               <DIR>           16/03/12   10:51p
..              <DIR>           16/03/12   10:51p
CASHFLOW  CAL    3584           1/01/80    12:30a
PROFLOSS  CAL    1024           1/01/80     1:28a
COST      CAL    1024           1/01/80     1:28a
          5 File(s)       658432 bytes free
```

Figure 8.3   *Spreadsheet directory including spreadsheet files.*

5. Pointers. The linking up of data elements is achieved by 'pointers', which identify other related data elements. As an example, a set of related data elements for a personnel record is constituted as follows:

(a)	*Surname*	Smith
(b)	*Christian name*	James
(c)	*Relative pointer*	120
(d)	*Absolute pointer*	20812C
(e)	*Marital status*	Married
(f)	*Status*	Accounts clerk
(g)	*Department*	Accounting

The relative pointer, 120, specifies that Smith's record is the 120th record on the payroll file. Provided a start address, i.e. the beginning of the file, and length of each record are known, the 'absolute' address of a record can be computed by the file management system in the operating system.

'Absolute' pointers provide the fastest access to records, In this instance, the absolute pointer 20812C specifies the 'physical' address of associated data such as details relating to the career and training of James Smith. The address enables a record stored on a disc file to be accessed. Problems arise when data has to be relocated, because it necessitates amendment of the pointers. Records are accessed more slowly using 'relative' pointers but they have the advantage of enabling records to be physically relocated on a disc file without needing to modify the pointers. As long as the operating system knows where the file commences, the data can be accessed and retrieved. 'Symbolic' pointers, such as a name, although providing a logical link between data items, also provide the slowest means of access compared with the other methods, as the symbolic pointer has to be converted into an actual address for retrieval purposes. If Smith's record contained an extra field such as INTERESTS, this could be used as a symbolic link to access details of his interests.

Fields

6. Key fields. A key field, also referred to as a 'record key', is used to identify a specific record unambiguously. Transaction data contains a key field which is matched with its record on the relevant master file for updating. Records on a reference file are also accessed by a key field. Key fields may consist of an insurance policy number, employee number, catalogue number or product number, etc. Some key fields are made up of a 'faceted' code whereby each position in the code number has a specific meaning such as type of material, size, specification, stores location.

7. Types of key field. Key fields may be either 'unique' or 'generic'. Unique keys are used to refer to a single group of data fields comprising a complete record. If unique keys are used, which they usually are, duplicate key fields cannot appear in the file as it will be impossible to specify a particular record uniquely. Generic keys identify several groups of data which have something in common. In respect of Smith's record, previously introduced, his surname can be used as a key to access all other records of people with the same name. Any field can be used as a generic key field.

8. Fixed-length fields and records. Records consisting of a fixed number of fields, of fixed length and always in the same sequence within a record, are known as 'flat' records and they allow easier maintenance than non-flat records. Fixed-length implies that the number of character positions allocated to each field is constant for each specific record although particular fields will not all be of the same length. Some fields will not always require the full number of character positions as descriptive data varies in length. It becomes necessary to insert 'space' characters to the right in such cases so that each field has the fixed number of characters stipulated by the program.

9. Variable-length records: variable number of fields. When the number of fields in records varies they become variable-length records and are referred to as 'non-flat' records. This would occur if some records contained a fixed-length field additional to the normal number of fields in a record of a specific type. Records containing an additional field could have them stored in an overflow record associated by a pointer holding the relative address of the associated data. On the other hand, if the main record provides for the additional field which some records require then the file could have relative pointers addressing it. This avoids the complexity of processing variable-length records.

10. Variable-length records: variable-length fields. Variable length records contain fields in which the number of characters varies according to the number of characters required, which is attributable to the varying length of descriptions, prices, quantities, values and other similar data elements. This method of data storage recognises that all similar records do not always need the same number of character positions for the same field. Records which vary in length optimise storage capacity whatever the magnetic storage media used, as unnecessary character positions are not provided for. They do, however, require more complex programming. It is necessary to test for the end of one field and the beginning of the next since they do not occur in fixed positions as they do with fixed-length fields. This is achieved by an 'end of field marker', a 'bit' pattern which informs the software of the demarcation point between fields. A different bit pattern located at the end of the last field in a record informs the software that the end of a record has been reached.

11. Variable-length records: variable number of variable-length fields. Some systems require a variable number of variable-length fields. In such cases an index which identifies and separates the fields is located at the beginning of the record. The index identifies the type of field, its start position and length.

File organisation and retrieval of records

12. Methods of file organisation. The available methods include:

   (a) serial;
   (b) sequential;
   (c) indexed sequential;
   (d) direct;
   (e) inverted;
   (f) database:

(*i*)   hierarchical;
(*ii*) relationship
(*iii*) network.

13. Serial files. The records on the file are not in any specific order and this method of file organisation is therefore inefficient. If a file was recorded on magnetic tape it would be necessary to wind the tape backwards and forward to locate a specific record as they are accessed in the sequence in which they are physically stored on the file media, i.e. serially. A full index would be necessary to access a specific record on disc. It is necessary to sort a serial transaction file into the sequential order of the master file before updating so that the file can be processed with a single pass (*see* Fig. 8.4).

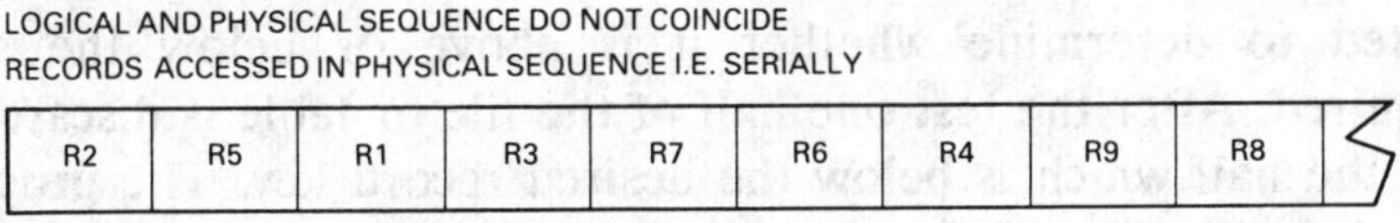

LOGICAL AND PHYSICAL SEQUENCE DO NOT COINCIDE
RECORDS ACCESSED IN PHYSICAL SEQUENCE I.E. SERIALLY

R2	R5	R1	R3	R7	R6	R4	R9	R8

Figure 8.4   *Serial organisation.*

14. Sequential files. With this method of file organisation, records are normally organised in ascending order of key field. When new records are added the sequence is maintained in respect of magnetic tape files by the insertion of records in the correct sequence on a new reel of tape. It is necessary to generate a completely new tape when applying file amendments, including adjustments, deletions and additions because it is not possible physically to insert or delete them on the same tape.

On a disc file when records cannot be stored in the correct location on a track due to an overflow condition, the logical sequence of records, not the physical one, can be maintained by using pointers and an overflow area. When the software reaches a pointer it retrieves the overflow record before dealing with the next in sequence. Serial and sequential access mean the same thing in respect of files on magnetic tape when in sequence but this may not be the case with disc files as the records accessed serially may not be in a defined key sequence due to being displaced in an overflow area of the disc (*see* Fig. 8.5).

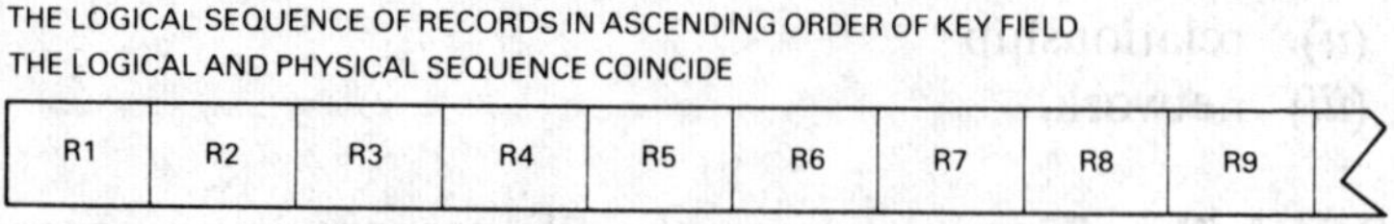

THE LOGICAL SEQUENCE OF RECORDS IN ASCENDING ORDER OF KEY FIELD
THE LOGICAL AND PHYSICAL SEQUENCE COINCIDE

R1	R2	R3	R4	R5	R6	R7	R8	R9

Figure 8.5 *Sequential organisation.*

It is possible to locate a record on a serially organised disc file without having to read each preceding record. This is achieved by the technique of 'binary chop', also referred to as 'binary search' and 'dichotomising search'. It is a speedy method of accessing specific records on a file or in a table. The method requires the various items on the file or in the table to be in a specific sequence; normally ascending order of key field.

The middle number or record key on a file or in a table is tested to determine whether it is above or below the one required. After the test one half of the file or table is discarded, i.e. the half which is below the desired record key. The process continues by examining the middle record or number of the remaining half of the file or table until the one required is located.

As an example of the functioning of 'binary chop', how many comparisons are necessary to discover the number or record key 20 in the following array of record keys?

$$1 \quad 4 \quad 6 \quad 14 \quad 15 \quad 17 \quad 19 \quad 20 \quad 22$$

The data contains nine record keys, the middle one being 15. The lower half of the record keys is below that required, i.e. 20, therefore it is discarded. This leaves record keys 17, 19, 20 and 22, the middle of which comes between 19 and 20 and therefore the left-hand side of the set is discarded. The next test refers to record keys 20 and 22. As the first number is equal to that required no further examination is necessary. Three tests were needed to find the required record key. Without the binary search technique the file would have been accessed serially, necessitating eight tests before record key 20 was reached on the file.

15. Indexed sequential. This method of file organisation is widely applied to the storage of records on magnetic disc. It allows a sequential file to be processed serially as the records are stored in ascending order of 'key' field. By means of a cylinder and track index, however, it is possible to gain direct access to records for amendment, enquiry or updating. It provides for on-line order processing and on-line building society activities, stock control, on-line banking, holiday and theatre booking systems as well as airline seat reservation systems. Records can be deleted by physical erasing and amendments or updating of records by overwriting. When file activity is low this method is more suitable than sequential as it is necessary to access only those records affected by transactions. On occasions the recording tracks on a disc become overloaded and records are stored temporarily in an overflow area until the file is reorganised. To facilitate access to overflow records a cylinder/track index records the highest record key stored in the overflow area corresponding to each track indexed. The presence of the overflow address also indicates whether new records should be stored in the data area or the overflow area. It is important to maintain the sequence of records in the file and this is achieved by 'chaining', using link fields. By this technique a record which has been displaced into the overflow area has its new location recorded within the record which logically preceded it. The displaced record also has the location of the next record in logical sequence. This enables the sequential order of records to be traced.

A cylinder (*see* Fig. 8.6) is a hypothetical but highly practical notion comprising a set of data provided by each recording surface of the disc pack. It consists of similar concentric tracks on all of the surfaces. Each track forms a ring or segment, in which records are stored in ascending order of key field, and to which are added the corresponding segments, i.e. the tracks of the other surfaces. The circular segments form a cylinder of records all of which can be accessed for a single positioning of the read/write heads. The cylinder is referred to as the 'seek' area. This is an efficient way of accessing records as the delay encountered by continuously repositioning the heads is eliminated. It is necessary to reposition the heads only for each new cylinder of records, and for a disc pack consisting of ten recording surfaces the cylinder contains ten tracks of records. Each surface has its own read/write

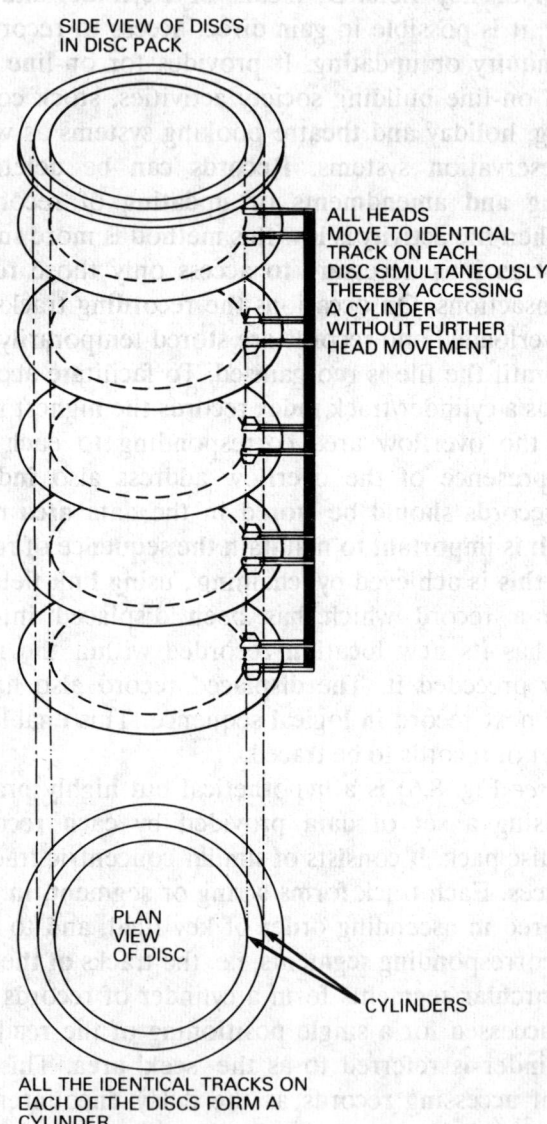

SIDE VIEW OF DISCS
IN DISC PACK

ALL HEADS
MOVE TO IDENTICAL
TRACK ON EACH
DISC SIMULTANEOUSLY,
THEREBY ACCESSING
A CYLINDER
WITHOUT FURTHER
HEAD MOVEMENT

PLAN
VIEW
OF DISC

CYLINDERS

ALL THE IDENTICAL TRACKS ON
EACH OF THE DISCS FORM A
CYLINDER

Figure 8.6 *Cylinder.*

head, which makes the cylinder concept a practical proposition. If each disc surface contains 100 tracks the disc pack has 100 cylinders.

16. Random file organisation (directly organised). Individual records are not stored in any particular sequence of key fields, i.e. they are stored randomly. It is not possible to apply a general rule for retrieving records from this type of file and it is necessary to develop an index which indicates the location of each record or, alternatively, the application of an address generation system.

	BEFORE INVERSION		AFTER INVERSION				
*PRODUCT	ATTRIBUTE 1 MAKE OF COMPUTER	ATTRIBUTE 2 TYPE OF PROCESSOR	ATTRIBUTE 1 MAKE OF COMPUTER	PRODUCT			
1	A	Z8	A	1	2		
2	A	Z12	B	3	4	5	
3	B	Z8	C	6	7	8	
4	B	Z9	D	9	10	11	12
5	B	Z12	ATTRIBUTE 2 TYPE OF PROCESSOR	PRODUCT			
6	C	Z8					
7	C	Z9	Z8	1	3	6	9
8	C	Z14	Z9	4	7		
9	D	Z8	Z12	2	5	10	
10	D	Z12	Z14	8			
11	D	Z16	Z15	11			
12	D	Z18	Z18	12			

*ADDRESS OR KEYFIELD OF RECORD   INVERTED KEYFIELD

Figure 8.7 *Inverted file.*

17. Inverted files. This type of organisation is useful when no single key can retrieve a record because a combination of keys is necessary. The record has to be searched using some combination of keys known as 'attributes'. Items possessing a specific feature are grouped together to form an inverted file. This reduces the time to retrieve records as it eliminates the need for serial searching. The keys and data are organised so that the keys (attributes) can be accessed one by one and only the relevant keys referenced. The organisation of an inverted file may be based on the structure outlined in Fig. 8.7.

Direct access methods

18. Full index. An index record contains the disc sector reference for every record in the file. The file is sorted initially into key sequence and the index is constructed as the records are transferred to disc. The index is sequential but the records may be stored randomly.

19. Partial indexing. Two or more levels of index are stored on disc. One level consists of a rough index containing the key of the last record in a specific range together with the bucket location of the fine index related to that range. The rough index contains a cylinder number while the fine index refers to a specific sector on a specified surface in that cylinder. The records need to be stored in ascending key sequence in each bucket. Comparison of the key of the required record against the rough index specifies the cylinder in which it is located. The cylinder contains the relevant fine index as its first record. Examination of the fine index indicates the surface within the cylinder. The rough index is usually transferred into internal storage during the time the file is in use.

Note: A bucket is a defined number of characters for data transfers from/to disc to/from the processor. Some computers have discs with a bucket size of 512 characters which can be handled in ones or multiples to store records in bucket sizes of 512-, 1,024-, 2,048-, or 4,096-character capacity.

20. Self-indexing. This type of organisation requires records to be stored in addresses that are related to their keys. File organisation is on the basis of:

(a) address = key;
(b) address = key + constant;

(*c*) address = (key + constant)/blocking factor.

There are many variations of this type of equation because of differing disc starting addresses, different blocking factors and the structure of keys.

If storage locations are available from location 400, each location holding one record, then the address of the record would be obtained in the following manner:

Record keys
120	Address = 120 + 399 =	519
141–180	Address = 141 + 399 =	540–579
190–300	Address = 190 + 399 =	589–699

Note: 399 is the 400th location as storage addresses commence at 0, therefore, 0–399 = 400. Some key sequences have too many gaps to be organised in this way as it is inefficient in the use of storage but when it is possible to link the address and key of a record directly, self-indexing files are feasible.

21. Algorithmic address generation. The basis of this method is a mathematical formula which is applied to the key of the required record which generates the bucket reference containing the record. The bucket is then searched to access the specific record. It is possible for the formula to generate the same address for different keys, which will create an overflow situation necessitating several accesses to locate the desired record. Space is wasted too when records are deleted from a disc file as they will not be reassigned because of the nature of the algorithm. The formal manner of establishing a suitable algorithm is to examine the code number sequence in use or to be implemented. Code numbers should be numeric only. It is then necessary to establish a formula which will generate an even distribution of bucket addresses. Constants can be added to the formula to close large gaps in the sequence to avoid wasting storage space. It is essential to determine that the bucket address is acceptable to the type of disc drive in use.

Algorithms are computed in a number of ways:

(*a*) Random allocation of records is achieved by squaring the key, or part of it, and using some digits from the square, perhaps the centre digits, as an address. This technique can allocate more than one record to the same address and none to other addresses. The first record is stored in an address called a *home* record. If addresses can hold only a single record the subsequent records allocated to this address will have to be stored in overflow areas. These records are known as *synonyms*.

Example (*i*): Compute the address of the following keys by squaring the central two digits.

Keys	1111	1112	1113
Digits	11	11	11
Square	121	121	121

As can be seen all records are allocated to the same address and are therefore synonyms.

Example (*ii*): Compute the address of the same keys by squaring the last two digits.

Digits	11	12	13
Square	121	144	169

As can be seen gaps occur in the addresses of consecutive records.

(*b*) Divide the key by a prime number and use the remainder as an address. This method will generally provide a good distribution of records. Runs of keys produce remainders that do not generate synonyms as they each differ by 1. Constants can be added if necessary.

Example (*i*): Compute the address of the following record keys by dividing the keys by the prime number 13 and use the remainder as an address.

Keys:	1111	1112	1113
Remainder	6	7	8

As can be seen a good spread of records is achieved.

Example (*ii*): Using the same record keys compute the address using prime number 11 and use the remainder as an address.

Remainder   0   1   2

This also generates a good distribution of records.

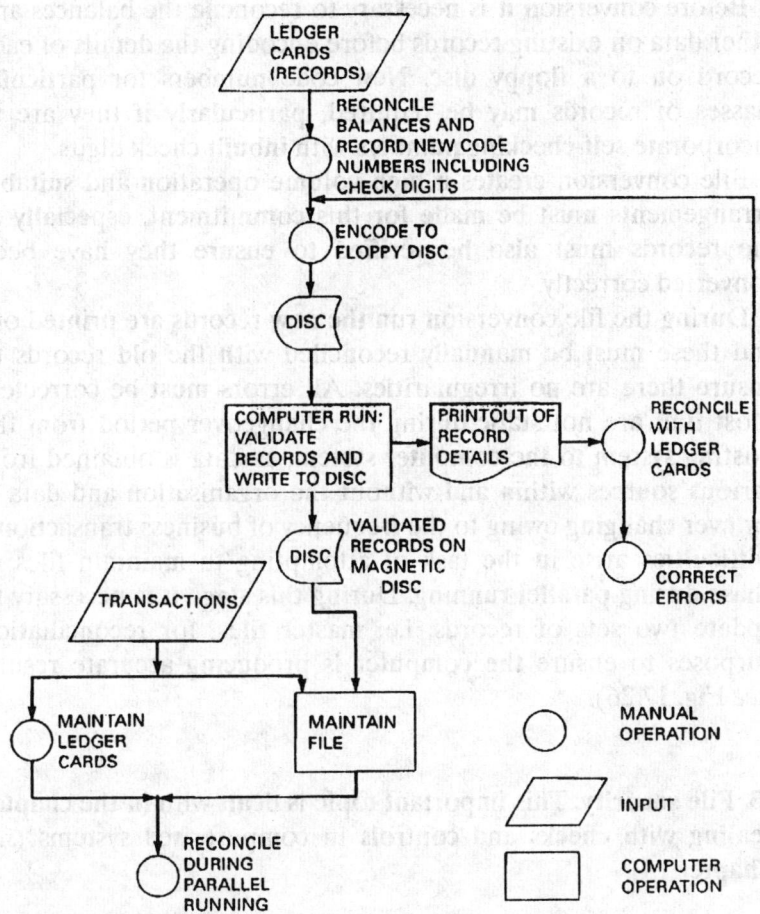

Figure 8.8   *File conversion and creation.*

File activities

22. File conversion and creation. When applications are to be transferred to a computer the master files must be converted from their present form, perhaps ledger cards, to a computer compatible form, i.e. magnetic media. In effect this means the conversion of records from a visible form, on ledger cards, to an invisible form as magnetic spots on magnetic disc (*see* Fig. 8.8).

Before conversion it is necessary to reconcile the balances and other data on existing records before encoding the details of each record on to a floppy disc. New code numbers for particular classes of records may be required, particularly if they are to incorporate self-checking numbers with inbuilt check digits.

File conversion creates a high volume operation and suitable arrangements must be made for this commitment, especially as the records must also be verified to ensure they have been converted correctly.

During the file conversion run the new records are printed out and these must be manually reconciled with the old records to ensure there are no irregularities. All errors must be corrected. Most files are not static during the changeover period from the existing system to the computer system, as data is obtained from various sources within and without the organisation and data is for ever changing owing to the frequency of business transactions. Difficulties arise in the task of attempting to maintain files in phase during parallel running. During this stage it is necessary to update two sets of records, i.e. master files, for reconciliation purposes to ensure the computer is producing accurate results (*see* Fig. 17.26).

23. File security. This important topic is dealt with in the chapter dealing with checks and controls in computerised systems (*see* Chapter 13).

24. File updating. An important feature of data processing is file updating and in this respect it is important to appreciate that all data and the records, to which the data relates, must be stored in the internal memory of the processor before any data processing operation or file updating is possible. Records are transferred by means of the appropriate backing storage device, which is normally a disc drive but may be a tape deck in some instances (*see* Figs. 8.9 and 8.10).

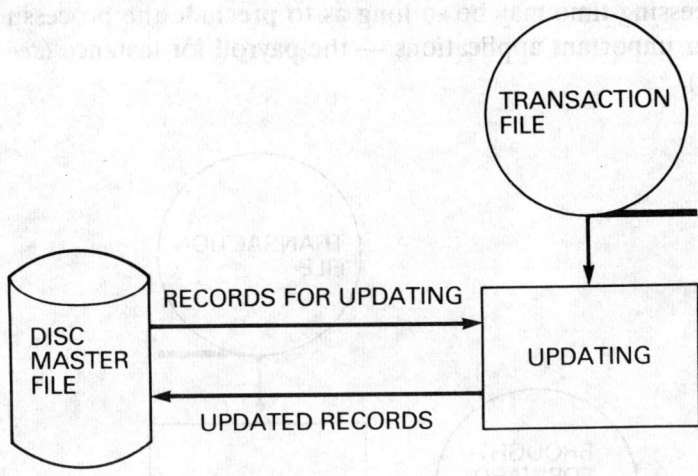

Figure 8.9   *Disc updating.*

Before processing commences the appropriate files are obtained from the tape and disc library by the computer operator particularly if they are exchangeable rather than fixed discs. After updating they are returned to the library for storage until they are required for the next updating run. In the meantime the files are stored off-line and are not accessible by the computer until the next run and this creates problems with regard to facilitating random enquiries from user departments unless the files are permanently on-line.

File updating is performed systematically at predefined periods of time depending upon circumstances. Considerations which would affect the frequency include:

(*a*) the volume of transactions;

(*b*) the need to avoid a build-up of data;

(*c*) the need to maintain a smooth work throughput;

(*d*) the demand for up-to-the-minute information for business control.

The preparation of invoices and updating the sales ledger master file may necessitate a daily run because of the relatively high volume of transactions involved. If performed weekly the processing time may be so long as to preclude the processing of other important applications — the payroll for instance (*see* Fig. 8.11).

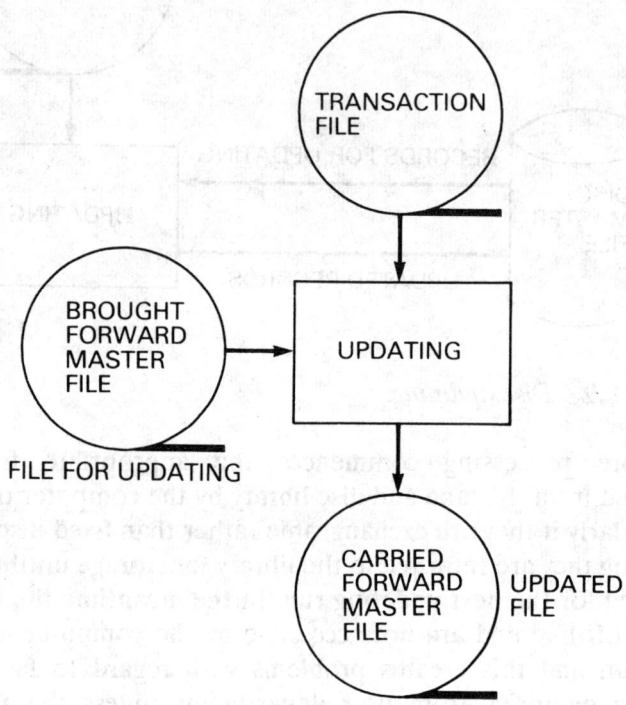

Figure 8.10 *Magnetic tape updating.*

Some applications have natural updating and processing frequencies: factory payroll has a natural weekly updating frequency; on the other hand a monthly staff payroll will naturally be updated monthly.

The frequency of updating often depends on the information needs of management for business control. One instance of this is when the status of stocks is a key factor in running a business effectively, which necessitates daily updating because management require a daily schedule in order to be aware of

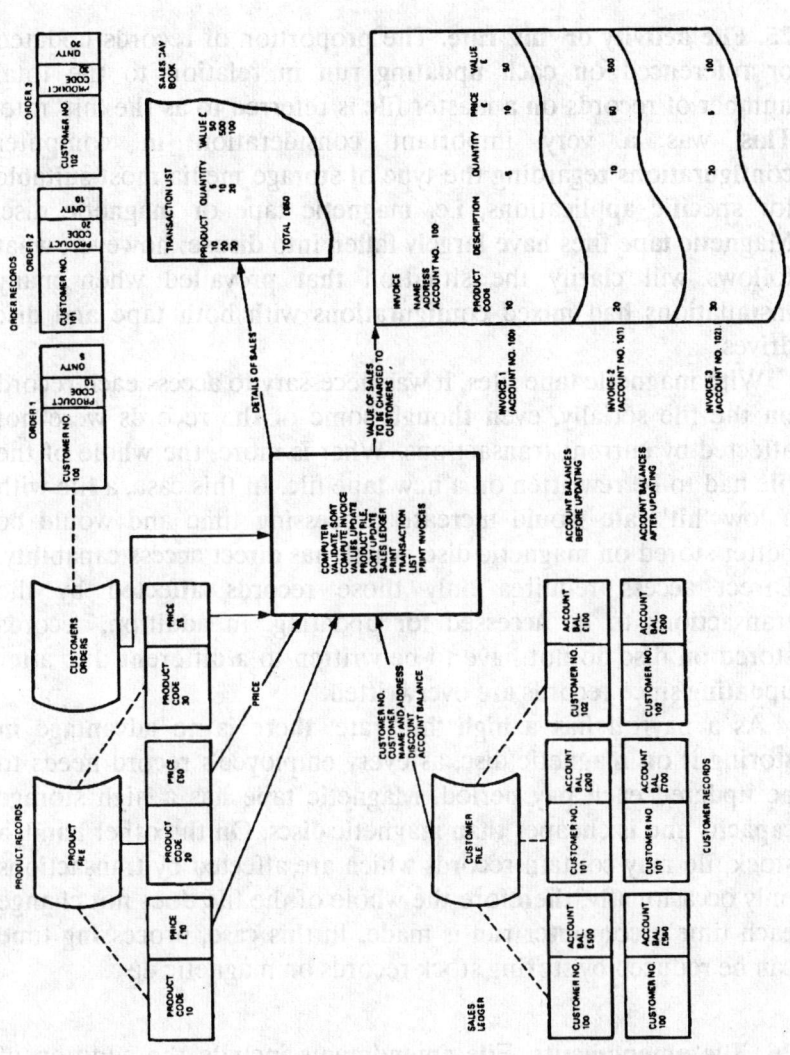

Figure 8.11   *Invoice preparation and sales ledger updating routine.*

shortages and excess stocks. Appropriate action is then taken in respect of purchase orders for raw materials and production orders in relation to sales orders.

25. File activity or 'hit' rate. The proportion of records updated or referenced on each updating run in relation to the total number of records on a master file is referred to as the 'hit' rate. This was a very important consideration in computer configurations regarding the type of storage media most suitable for specific applications, i.e. magnetic tape or magnetic disc. Magnetic tape files have largely fallen into disuse; however, what follows will clarify the situation that prevailed when many installations had mixed configurations with both tape and disc drives.

With magnetic tape files, it was necessary to access each record on the file serially, even though some of the records were not affected by current transactions. What is more, the whole of the file had to be rewritten on a new tape file. In this case, a file with a low 'hit' rate would increase processing time and would be better stored on magnetic disc, which has direct access capability. Direct access requires only those records affected by the transactions to be accessed for updating. In addition, records stored on disc do not have to be written to a different disc after updating since records are overwritten.

As a payroll has a high 'hit' rate, there is no advantage in storing it on magnetic disc, as every employee's record needs to be updated each pay period. Magnetic tape has a high storage capacity and is cheaper than magnetic discs. On the other hand, a stock file may contain records which are affected by transactions only occasionally, therefore the whole of the file does not change each time a computer run is made. In this case, processing time can be reduced by storing stock records on magnetic disc.

26. File amendments. File amendments include the addition of new records or the deletion of obsolete records from a master file, for example the addition of new starters and the deletion of terminations from the payroll or employee master file. Reference files may require amendment occasionally in respect of changes

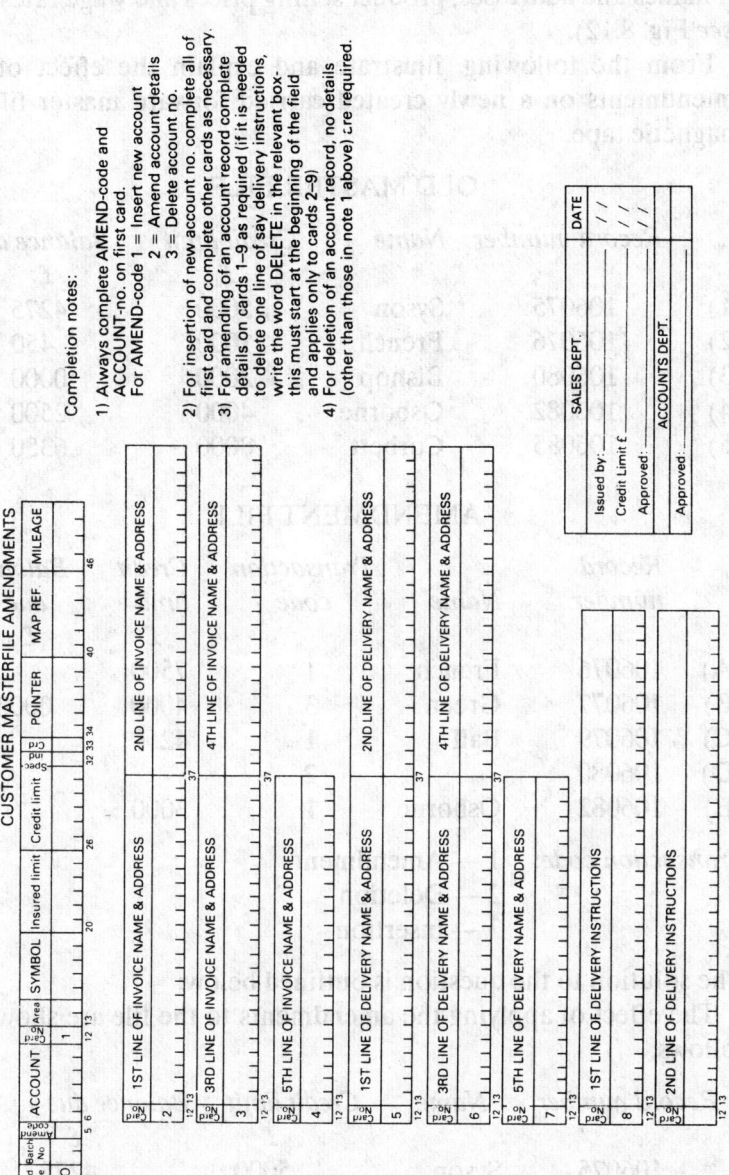

Completion notes:

1) Always complete AMEND-code and ACCOUNT-no. on first card.
   For AMEND-code 1 = Insert new account
   2 = Amend account details
   3 = Delete account no.

2) For insertion of new account no. complete all of first card and complete other cards as necessary.

3) For amending of an account record complete details on cards 1–9 as required (if it is needed to delete one line of say delivery instructions, write the word DELETE in the relevant box-this must start at the beginning of the field and applies only to cards 2–9)

4) For deletion of an account record, no details (other than those in note 1 above) are required.

Figure 8.12   *Customer masterfile amendment form.*

of names and addresses, product selling prices and wage rates, etc. (*see* Fig. 8.12).

From the following, illustrate and explain the effect of file amendments on a newly created carried forward master file on magnetic tape.

OLD MASTER FILE

	Record number	Name	Credit limit £	Balance due £
(1)	106075	Syson	5000	4275
(2)	106076	French	1000	450
(3)	106080	Bishop	2000	0000
(4)	106082	Osborne	4000	2500
(5)	106085	Corbett	8000	6350

AMENDMENT FILE

	Record number	Name	Transaction code	Credit limit £	Balance due £
(A)	106076	French	1	7500	
(B)	106077	Green	3	4000	0000
(C)	106079	Ball	1	4250	
(D)	106080		2		
(E)	106082	Osborne	1	3000	

Transaction code: 1 — Amendment
2 — Deletion
3 — Insertion

The solution to the question is outlined below:

The effect of applying the amendments to the file are shown as follows:

Record number	Name	Credit limit £	Balance due £
106075	Syson	5000	4275
106076	French	7500	450
106077	Green	4000	0000
106082	Osborne	3000	2500
106085	Corbett	8000	6350

The following details provide an explanation of the amendments.

106075	Remains unchanged and is copied to the carried forward file
106076	Amendment to credit limit on carried forward file
106077	A new record to be added to the file
106079	Indicated as an amendment but does not exist on the file. The record is signalled as an error and excluded from the master file
106080	Deletion from the file
106082	Amendment to credit limit on carried forward file
106085	Remains unchanged and copied to carried forward file.

Activities concerned with file amendments on magnetic tape include the reading in of a record to the processor's memory from the master file together with an amendment from the amendment file. The 'key' fields are compared to establish if there is a match. Appropriate action is then taken either to write the record unchanged on the new file if it is not affected by an amendment, or, if it is affected by an amendment, to adjust it in the memory before it is written to the new file. If the amendment is a deletion, then the record is omitted from the new file but if it is a new record then it is added to the new file. All this must be effected before the master file is updated by transaction data. It is essential that records are amended before being used in processing.

Relationship between master files, transaction files and reference files

27. Definition of a master file. A master file is a group of related records, e.g. stock file, customer file, employee file, supplier file. This type of file is periodically updated with current transaction data, in order to show the current status of each record in the file. Other types of master file contain reference information such as product prices, names and addresses and wage rates, etc. Such files may be used for general reference, or can form an integral part of data processing activities. Each record in a file is allocated an identification number or reference key and filed in ascending number order to facilitate ease of access or reference.

There are also several types of master file, and the type used is also dependent upon the processing method employed.

(a) Loose leaf ledger or binder.
(b) Container of ledger cards.
(c) Reel of magnetic tape or exchangeable disc packs.
(d) Floppy or fixed discs.
(e) Cassette tape.

28. Transaction file. A collection of data relating to business transactions is referred to as a transaction or changes file. This contains details relating to stock movements — stock transaction file; wages — payroll file; items required by customers — orders file; and so on. Such details are input for processing, including computing the value of stock movements, gross wages and the value of goods sold to customers. These values are then used as part of the information printed out on documents and schedules as well as being recorded on the relevant records in the appropriate master file to which they relate.

Transaction data may be collected for a period of time and processed in batches or may be processed as it arises on an interactive transaction processing basis. A file may not always be in evidence in such cases but if batches of transactions are dealt with as they arise then this process forms a transaction file dealt with on a transaction basis, i.e. on an individual rather than a batch basis.

29. Reference file. This is a file which contains reference information, i.e. information which is referred to during data processing operations, whether for random enquiries or for details required during batch processing. Such files contain details pertaining to product prices to be used for invoice computations, names and addresses of customers and suppliers to be used for the production of mail shots and for addressing documents such as invoices, statements and purchase orders, etc. Wage rates may also be recorded in this way.

If names and addresses are required predominantly for general mailing needs then the file may be structured separately, otherwise it may be integrated with the relevant master file, such as the customer or supplier file. If wage rates are reasonably stable they may be incorporated in the payroll master file in respect of those employees paid on the basis of attended hours. The rates may otherwise be input as current wages data and omitted from the file completely.

Virtual storage

30. Concept of virtual storage. Some computers incorporate a storage management technique known as 'virtual storage'. The technique increases the apparent capacity of internal storage by an amount many times its actual capacity. Concurrent processing of several programs, that would otherwise exceed the main internal storage capacity, is made possible.

31. Mode of operation. Virtual storage uses magnetic discs to store programs required for processing. This is instead of loading them to internal storage (main storage), which is the normal method employed.

In order that the main storage available is used in the most efficient manner, the technique splits the program into small segments called 'pages'. Only those pages required for processing are called into main storage at one time. The remainder of the program stays in virtual storage.

The addresses within a page refer to virtual storage locations and when transferred to main storage the addresses must refer to main storage locations before processing can be executed. It is necessary, therefore, to effect address translation, which is achieved by a hardware-assisted table look-up.

Other storage aspects

32. Volume. This term is often used to mean a unit of magnetic storage such as a set of exchangeable discs, i.e. a disc pack, or a reel of magnetic tape. Discs, hard and floppy, can be divided into multiple volumes each having a discrete entity, e.g. the sectors on a disc surface which effectively divide the surface of the disc into blocks. It is then necessary to specify the disc volume which stores the program required. This applies to Winchester discs in particular.

33. Formatting/soft and hard sectoring. A computer, by means of a DOS (disc operating system), keeps track of the location of records on a disc and can access any record by moving the head to the relevant track and then waiting for the sector (block) containing the required record to come into position. Two methods are used to indicate the location on a track where each sector starts:

(a) soft sectoring whereby special signals are recorded on the disc surface and detected by the software; and

(b) hard sectoring, whereby holes are punched through the disc around the central hole, one per sector.

These are referred to as formatted discs.

34. Archiving. The process of removing infrequently used files from the filestore. A filestore consists of files organised in a library under the control of an operating system. Archived files are omitted from the directory of current files and are normally stored on magnetic tape, reducing the number of discs required to be on-line. This effectively reduces operating costs and increases the efficiency of computer operations. Tape files can be converted to disc files when operational necessity requires it.

35. Logical and physical records. The records on a file are normally grouped by type, whereby all similar records are stored on the same medium. The individual records relating to a specific entity, e.g. account of customer X, the earning and tax records of employee Y or the stock record of item Z, are logical records. The file medium on which they are stored, i.e. the reel of tape or the specific disc pack, is the physical storage medium, therefore many logical records will be stored on a physical file (*see* Fig. 8.13).

The individual records are referenced, updated, amended and information is extracted from them according to the needs of the business. For effective file handling and processing a computer handles physical records, i.e. groups or blocks of logical records. A block may be 512 bytes (characters) in length and the number of records in the block is determined by the systems designer on the basis of the number of characters in each record and the size of the block.

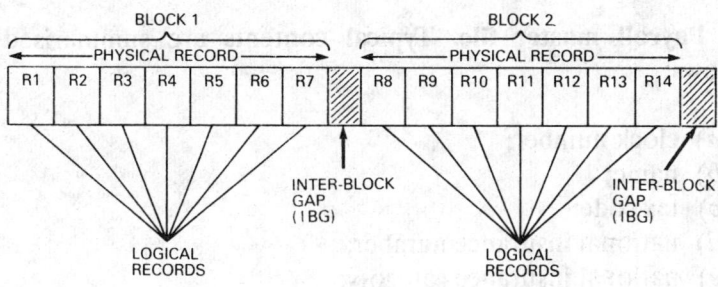

Figure 8.13 *Blocked records illustrating the relationship of physical and logical records.*

This achieves efficiency in the transfer of data from the physical file to the processor as it is impractical to stop/start a tape deck after transferring single records as there would be more stop/start time than data transfer time. A disc drive does not stop when transferring records but functions on the basis of the 'block' as blocks of records are transferred from the disc drive to the processor, not single records. The block containing a specific record for processing needs is searched after being transferred to internal memory to locate the record required (*see* Fig. 8.14).

An 'inter-block gap' is used to allow the tape to slow down and stop after a block of data has been read or written, and to allow the tape to re-start and accelerate to the appropriate reading or writing speed for the next block of data to be input or output.

If data blocks are short, the deceleration and acceleration of the tape between blocks can exceed the time actually taken in transferring data to and from the computer. To eliminate this unproductive time, the block size should be increased as much as the available internal storage locations will allow.

Logical records and files

What follows outlines the contents of master files of various applications.

36. Payroll master file. Typical contents are summarised as follows:

(a) clock number;
(b) name;
(c) tax code;
(d) national insurance number;
(e) national insurance category;
(f) taxable gross to date;
(g) tax to date;
(h) taxable gross previous employment;
(i) tax previous employment;
(j) holiday credit to date;
(k) sickness holiday credit weeks to date:
(l) employee's National Insurance to date;
(m) total National Insurance contributions to date;
(n) fixed deductions

   (i) charities;
   (ii) overalls;
   (iii) savings;
   (iv) loans;

(o) weekly salary amount (as appropriate);
(p) hourly rate (as appropriate);
(q) holiday credit flat rate;
(r) employee bank details.

37. Customer file. Typical contents of this file include:

(a) account number;
(b) name and address;
(c) credit limit;

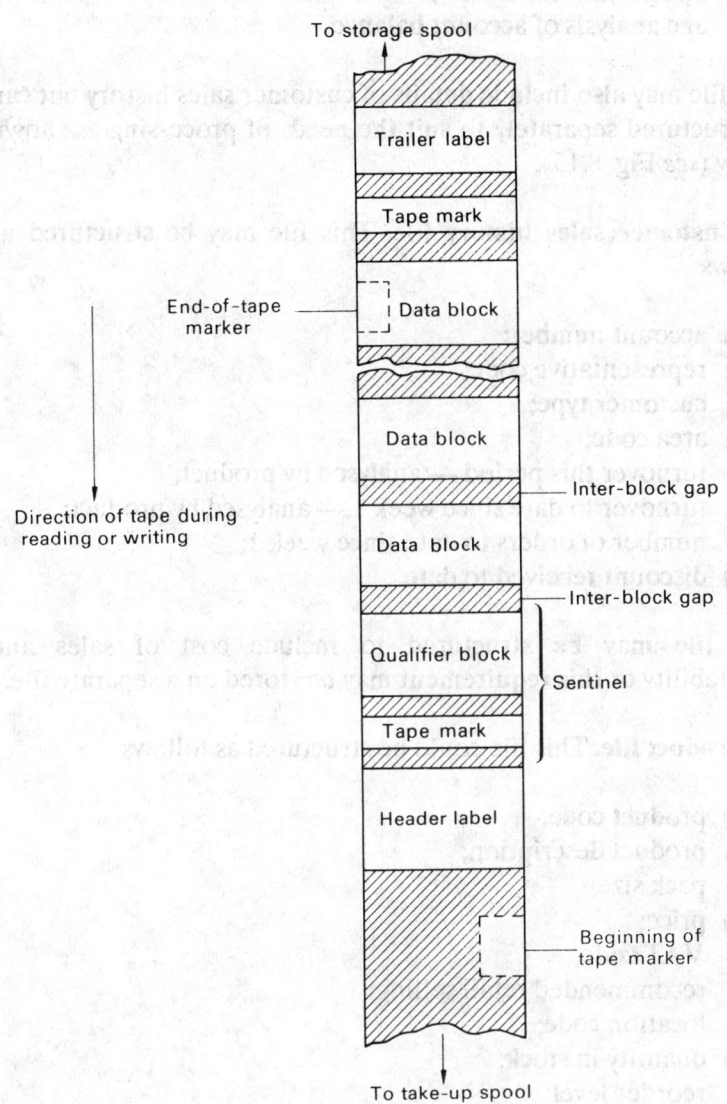

Figure 8.14 *Layout of a data file on magnetic tape (courtesy International Computers Limited).*

(d) account balance;
(e) category/discount rate;
(f) age analysis of account balance.

This file may also include details of customer sales history but can be structured separately to suit the needs of processing as shown below (*see* Fig. 8.15).

38. Customer sales history file. This file may be structured as follows:

(a) account number;
(b) representative code;
(c) customer type;
(d) area code;
(e) turnover this period — analysed by product;
(f) turnover to date since week 1 — analysed by product;
(g) number of orders to date since week 1;
(h) discount received to date.

This file may be structured to include cost of sales and profitability or this requirement may be stored on a separate file.

39. Product file. This file could be structured as follows:

(a) product code;
(b) product description;
(c) pack size;
(d) price;
(e) VAT code;
(f) recommended retail selling;
(g) location code;
(h) quantity in stock;
(i) reorder level;
(j) reorder quantity;
(k) ordered but outstanding.

40. Stock file: raw material or components. This file (*see* Fig. 8.16) may be structured in the following way:

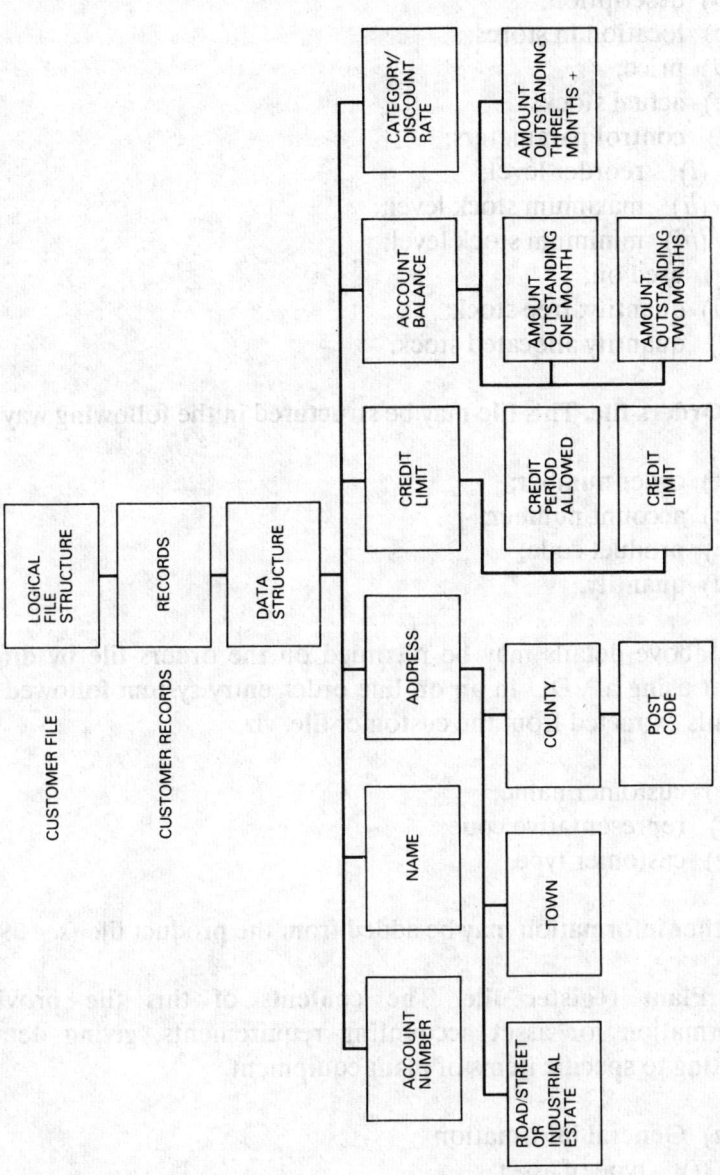

Figure 8.15 *Structured file: customer records.*

(a) stock number;
(b) description;
(c) location in stores;
(d) price;
(e) actual stock;
(f) control parameters:
   (i)   reorder level;
   (ii)   maximum stock level;
   (iii)   minimum stock level;
(g) used on;
(h) quantity: free stock;
(i) quantity allocated stock.

41. Orders file. This file may be structured in the following way:

(a) order number;
(b) account number;
(c) product code;
(d) quantity.

The above details may be recorded on the orders file by direct input using a VDU in an on-line order entry system followed by details extracted from the customer file, viz.:

(e) customer name;
(f) representative code;
(g) customer type.

Further information may be added from the product file (*see* **39**).

42. Plant register file. The contents of this file provide information for asset accounting requirements, giving details relating to specific items of plant equipment.

(a) General information
   (i)   type of asset;
   (ii)   plant code;
   (iii)   supplier;
   (iv)   manufacturer;

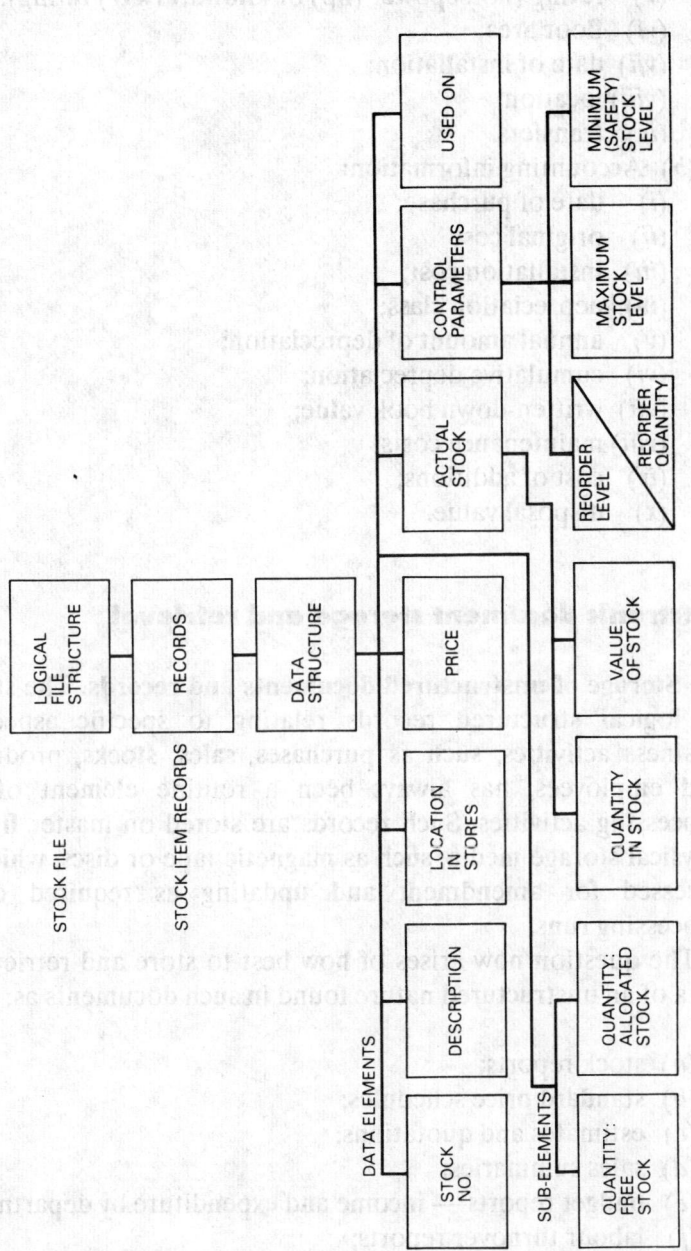

Figure 8.16 *Structured file: stock records.*

    (*v*)   rating (horsepower (hp) or kilowatt (kW) rating);
    (*vi*) floor area;
    (*vii*) date of installation;
    (*viii*) location;
    (*ix*) transfers.
  (*b*) Accounting information:
    (*i*)   date of purchase;
    (*ii*) original cost
    (*iii*) installation cost;
    (*iv*) depreciation class;
    (*v*)   annual amount of depreciation;
    (*vi*) cumulative depreciation;
    (*vii*) written-down book value;
    (*viii*) maintenance costs;
    (*ix*) cost of additions;
    (*x*)   disposal value.

Electronic document storage and retrieval

43. Storage of unstructured documents and records. The storage of logical structured records relating to specific aspects of business activities, such as purchases, sales, stocks, production and employees, has always been a routine element of data processing activities. Such records are stored on master files on physical storage media, such as magnetic tape or discs, which are accessed for amendment and updating as required during processing runs.

    The question now arises of how best to store and retrieve the data of an unstructured nature found in such documents as:

  (*a*) stock reports;
  (*b*) standard price schedules;
  (*c*) estimates and quotations;
  (*d*) sales summaries;
  (*e*) budget reports — income and expenditure by department;
  (*f*) labour turnover reports;
  (*g*) candidate assessment forms;
  (*h*) minutes of meetings.

The types of document outlined above normally reside in office filing cabinets in the relevant secretary's office but this area of business activity has been overtaken by the new electronic technology as electronic filing and retrieval systems using floppy disc based microcomputers are now becoming very common.

44. Electronic filing and retrieval systems. These systems are often referred to by various descriptive titles. However, it is unclear whether the nature of the systems under consideration differs or if it is a matter of a shovel being called a spade. The terms which may be encountered include

> (*a*) electronic document storage and retrieval systems;
> (*b*) text filing and retrieval systems;
> (*c*) file management systems;
> (*d*) electronic retrieval of free text documents.

45. Electronic retrieval of free text documents. Systems which store documents electronically and which enable complete documents or sections of documents to be retrieved are predominant as floppy disc based microcomputers are being used instead of normal office filing cabinets. This is a good thing because even in the most efficient filing system documents tend to go astray and it is often difficult to trace them as they can be classified under various titles. Such electronically stored documents can be retrieved by specifying words or phrases that occur within the text. The words can be located anywhere within the text, eliminating the need for key fields. Such systems require the ability to capture and retain documents electronically and retrieve them from a partial description of their contents.

Retrieval technique in general utilises 'user friendly' language but more complex queries can be effected by using Boolean operators 'AND', 'OR', and 'NOT'. These can be applied when combining two factors, i.e. search terms which may be phrased as 'find all documents which include both the words male AND single' or, 'find all documents relating to personnel who have "O" level passes in Mathematics AND "A" level passes in English', or, 'find those records of employees who are male AND staff NOT in the pension scheme'.

Synonyms can be applied in a query to expand a search term when different words can have the same meaning or can be spelled differently. If the search term is 'computer' it may have the synonym 'electronic computer' or 'digital computer'. When applying the synonym facility the system automatically interprets the query as 'computer' OR 'electronic computer' OR 'digital computer'.

Truncation is applied for a root search whereby all subjects with a similar root are signalled by the system, very often by the asterisk sign, e.g. finance*, which could generate the following subjects — financial, financing, etc.

Masking may be applied when the user is not sure how a name should be spelled for searching purposes. This allows the middle characters of a word to be masked out, e.g. the name of a company Hindacem may be masked as Hind*cem if one is not certain whether it is Hindicem or Hinducem.

Note: The subject of databases is dealt with in Chapter 9.

Progress test 8

1. Contrast the storing of data in a clerical and computer system. (1)
2. State the nature and purpose of a directory. (2, 3, Figs. 8.1–8.3).
3. In the context of data storage what are the nature and purpose of pointers? (5)
4. Define the terms 'relative pointer' and 'absolute pointer'. (5)
5. Define the term 'key field'. (6)
6. Define the meaning of 'unique' and 'generic' in the context of key fields. (7)
7. Records and fields can be fixed or variable/length. Discuss the significance of this statement. (8–11)
8. Specify the essential differences between serial and sequential files. (13, 14)
9. Define the term 'indexed sequential' in the context of organising records on magnetic disc and state the significance of the 'cylinder'. (15)

10. How can records be retrieved on a randomly organised file? **(16)**

11. Define the nature and purpose of an 'inverted file'. **(17)**

12. Define the following terms: (a) full indexing; (b) partial indexing; (c) self-indexing. **(18–20)**

13. The basis of the algorithmic method of address generation is a mathematical formula. Specify two typical formulae which may be adopted for this purpose. **(21)**

14. When applications are transferred to a computer the files must be converted to a computer-compatible form. Outline the procedure for file conversion. **(22, Fig. 8.8)**

15. An important data processing activity is file updating. State the nature of this activity distinguishing between the method of updating disc and magnetic tape files. **(24, Figs. 8.9 and 8.10)**

16. Before deciding to store records on magnetic disc or tape it is necessary to consider file activity, or the 'hit' rate as it is known. Define the meaning of this term and why it is important. **(25)**

17. File amendments are an essential requirement of a data processing system. Specify the nature of file amendments. **(26)**

18. What is a master file? **(27)**

19. Distinguish between a master file, transaction file and reference file. **(27–29)**

20. What is 'virtual' storage ? **(30, 31)**

21. What is meant by the terms: (a) volume; (b) formatting/soft and hard sectoring; (c) archiving? **(32–34)**

22. Specify the difference between logical and physical records. **(35)**

23. List the contents of the following typical master files: (a) payroll file; (b) customer file; (c) customer history file; (d) product file; (e) stock file; (f) orders file; (g) plant register. **(36–42)**

24. Outline the nature of electronic document storage and retrieval systems. **(43–45)**

9
Databases

Concepts

1. File of structured data. A database is a file of structured data in the form of records which are accessible to authorised managers and other personnel for administrative purposes and for use in making decisions and controlling business operations (*see* Fig. 9.1). Databases may relate to specific functional requirements such as accounting or may provide for interfunctional information needs. A *query language* facilitates enquiries using English-style words to define commands, and is discussed in 18:28–31, and 5 and 6 below.

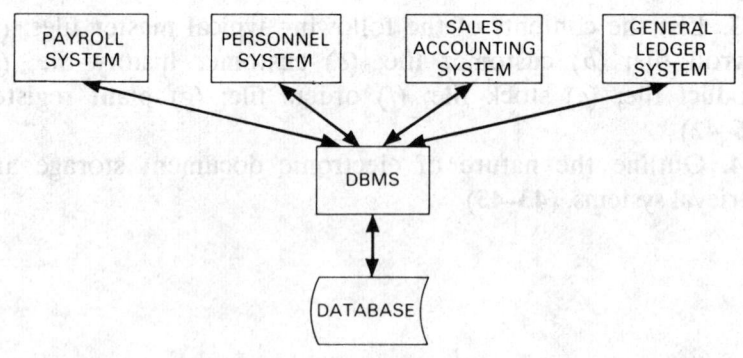

Figure 9.1 *Database file structure.*

2. Functional files eliminated. A database eliminates traditional files, which often store the same data in several functional files. This situation duplicates data unnecessarily, creating what is referred to as 'redundancy'. One functional file, for instance, stores employee records for use in payroll processing. Each record contains details of individual employees including name, address, employee number, wage rate, department, tax code and NI number etc. Another file used for personnel administration also contains details relating to employees including many already existing on the payroll file. If common data on the several files is not updated concurrently they would be incompatible and likely to create confusion by providing conflicting facts from the different files. This could arise when employees are given a wage award or are transferred to other departments and the changes are not recorded on all relevant files. Data need be input to the database only once since all relevant records are updated, thus providing a greater degree of confidence in the data retrieved by users because of its enhanced integrity or reliability (*see* Figs. 9.1 and 9.2).

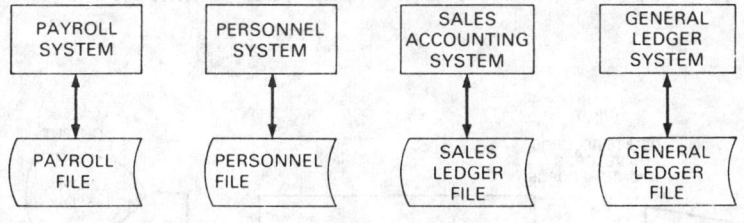

Figure 9.2 *Structure of conventional functional files.*

3. Database management systems. A database management system (DBMS) is a set of programs which deal with database management activities, including updating, deleting, adding and amending records. This is accomplished by selecting the required option from a menu displayed on the video screen or by keying in the relevant command from the keyboard. Fig. 9.3 illustrates the screen display showing the control centre of dBASE IV for creating a new file. The DBMS also allows the user to validate,

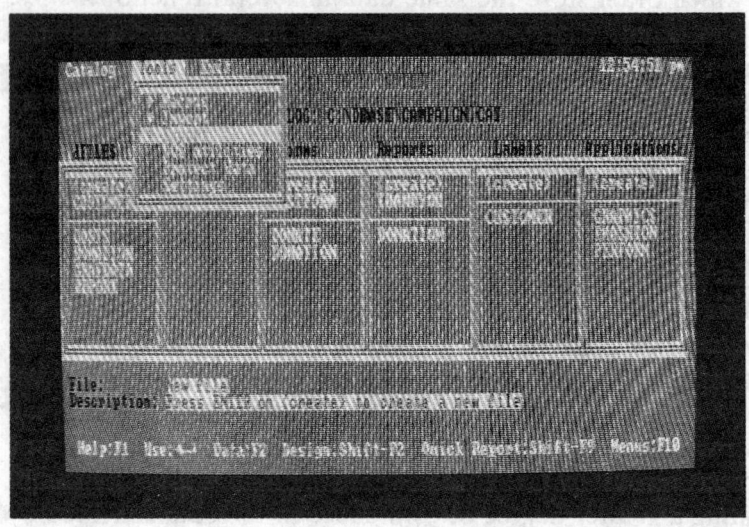

Figure 9.3 *DBase IV screen display showing control centre and drop-down menu (courtesy Ashton-Tate (UK) Limited).*

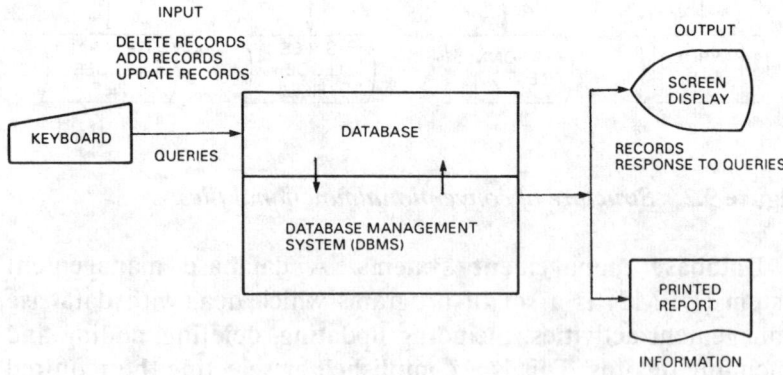

Figure 9.4 *Outline of database functions.*

sort, search and print records from the database as well as providing facilities for performing calculations and maintaining a dictionary. Some systems provide for printing standard letters and reports and merging text with data such as names and addresses. Records can be displayed on the screen and browsed through, making amendments as necessary. Files are reorganised automatically to allow for overflow conditions on disc tracks. Fields may be removed from records and files may be merged or separated according to needs. Fig. 9.4 shows the various functions diagrammatically.

4. Access and security issues. File security is provided for as database systems automatically save files at the end of processing and also make back-up copies of disc files. Elaborate security and privacy checks may require to be incorporated in a database to prevent unauthorised access to the system. Some personnel may be barred from the system as a whole or be given restricted access to specific parts of the database. Some databases require entry of a user name before allowing access and also a password for sensitive or restricted information. Each information owner needs to specify those user names allowed access to that owner's data. A list is also required of other information owners who can view but not alter records in the database. Non-sensitive information may be made available to any user by adding this fact to the user name access list. The DBMS checks a user name with the parts of the database the user requires to access and only if the user name is on the list will access be allowed. Names and/or passwords are not displayed on the video screen when keyed in, so preventing unauthorised users obtaining possession of them.

5. Database query systems. A natural English language database query and retrieval system is used for query and *ad hoc* reporting. It provides easy and instant access to information by retrieving the data, computing and presenting the information in a sophisticated columnar display on the video screen. This type of system requires English conversion of the data dictionary describing the database into a lexicon which lists alphabetically all the words and phrases used. The lexicon is used for reference purpose during the processing of natural language queries. This type of query language responds to questions phrased, for example, in the following way: 'How many cars of each model did we sell last week compared to target?'

The system will retrieve from the database the target and actual sales for each model and display them on the screen together with the actual and planned sales and percentage deviation from the planned sales for each model.

6. Fourth generation languages. Fourth generation languages (*see* 18:28–31) are designed to assist the manipulation of a database by way of a query language providing facilities for creating, retrieving, updating, appending, deleting or amending data. The query language is an element of the DBMS. When designed to access a database from a terminal keyboard it is classified as an *interactive query language*. Fig. 9.5 illustrates a screen display showing the structure of a query in the condition box. In this instance, items costing more than £2,000 require to be retrieved from the database.

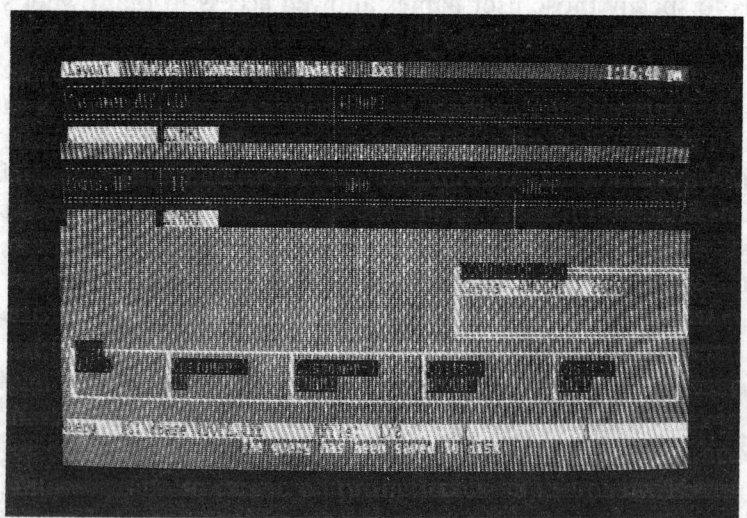

Figure 9.5 *DBase IV screen showing queries (courtesy Ashton-Tate (UK) Limited).*

The primary purpose of query languages is to provide non-computer specialists in the various business functions (the 'end users') with the means to do their own information processing without having to become programming experts. A fourth generation language translates the user's requests into procedural steps to produce the desired output. In this way user views of an application are separated from the mechanics of the system — the end result is important to the user, not how it is accomplished. Fourth generation languages enable personnel changing from clerical to computerised database applications to understand the new working procedures more easily. For example, a database may contain a plant register of machines located in the factory, which includes fields (items of information) for machine type, cost, location, depreciation and book value. If the cost of a particular class of machine is required the query language allows the question to be asked in the following way.

LIST COST, MACHINE, FOR MACHINE = 'PROFILER'

This is interpreted by the database management system as: List the cost of the machine type 'Profiler'. The response provides the record number containing the specific machine and its cost as follows: 00005 8500 PROFILER. This means that the cost of the machine 'Profiler' is £8,500. (*See* also **12.**)

7. Searching. A database has searching facilities ranging from limited searches on keywords to full text searching. This facility provides the means of extracting from a large volume of data useful facts which could not possibly be found by physical search methods in sufficient time to make a decision. Database commands are becoming increasingly powerful and the application of natural language database query systems is increasing, so greatly assisting users to find the information they are seeking.

8. Database applications. Internal private databases may be used for many and varied applications, such as the storage of asset records, which allows acquisitions and disposals to be added to and deleted from the database very easily. The database also facilitates the modification of records when plant and machinery is moved to new locations. Asset schedules may also be printed out for accounting and administrative needs. For instance, it is possible to print a report of assets nearing the end of their useful life as a basis for plant replacement.

Personnel records may be similarly stored and processed, which greatly assists their administration as it is an easy matter to add new employees and delete terminations from the database. A personnel database also allows transfers between departments to be speedily recorded and information to be retrieved in respect of employees with specific attributes, such as number of years' service, which will be required for the grant of long-service awards. Order processing systems are simplified as a database can store customer, order and product records which may be cross-referenced for processing purposes. The records in the database may be network, hierarchical or relationally structured, as shown in Figs. 9.6, 9.8 and 9.11.

9. Data dictionaries. A data dictionary contains details of the data in a database including definitions of each record type, the programs which use the data and its purpose. It may also cover the relationship of data elements, including functional dependencies as well as their format and size, i.e. the minimum, maximum and average number of characters. The dictionary assists in the design of a database and in reducing the level of redundancy to a necessary minimum; it also avoids duplication of data elements and makes for easier identification of 'synonyms' (data groups having more than one name) and 'homonyms' (one name for several data groups). Details of data structures may also be incorporated in the dictionary outlining the way in which data is grouped.

Database structures

10. Network structure. This type of database has a complex structure, resembling the logical data relationships existing in the real world of business. It is structured around the concept of a set which is a relationship between two record types, e.g. a customer's order and an order item (*see* Fig. 9.6). An 'owner' of a set, e.g. a customer's order, can have a number of 'members, i.e. order items. A record type may be a member of several sets, an owner of several sets or a member of one set and owner of another.

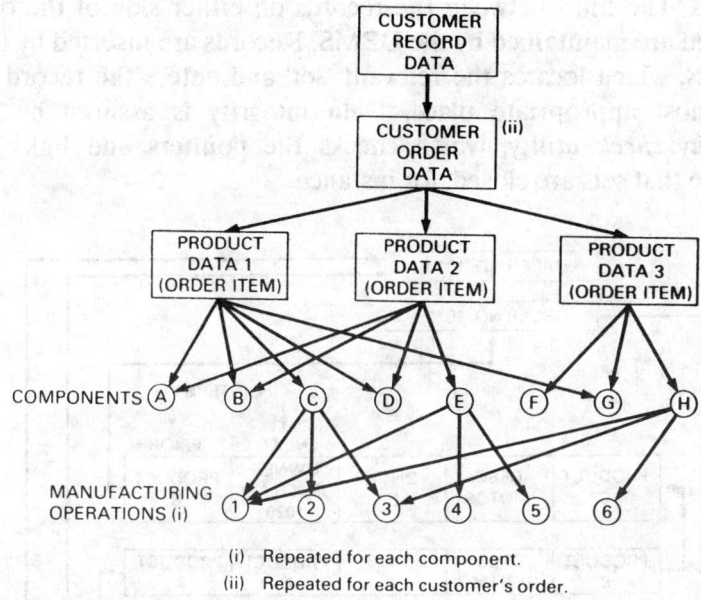

(i)   Repeated for each component.
(ii) Repeated for each customer's order.

Figure 9.6   *Network structure.*

Sets can be incorporated without members or without owners, for example when new product details are introduced before orders are placed or new employee details are recorded in the database prior to the first pay day. They are known as 'memberless' sets.

The network defines the route through the database but the user must know what linkages have been established in the database in order to be aware of the basis for data retrieval. Links between records are established through the user of pointers; a customer record can point to several order records which relate to it. Pointers inform the DBMS where the logical record is located. The next record is indicated by a 'next' pointer. Within any occurrence in a set the route to be traversed is to read the 'owner' and then access the 'members' sequentially, eventually returning to the 'owner'. It is not possible to proceed directly from the 'owner' to any specific 'member' but only via all the 'members' consecutively until the required one is reached (*see* Fig. 9.7). This is accomplished by 'next' and 'prior' pointers. Deletions are achieved by destroying the pointers which access a record. The links between the records on either side of the one deleted are maintained by the DBMS. Records are inserted by the DBMS, which locates the relevant 'set' and enters the record in the most appropriate place. Data integrity is assured by an *integrity check* utility, which checks the pointers and links to ensure that sets are closed, for instance.

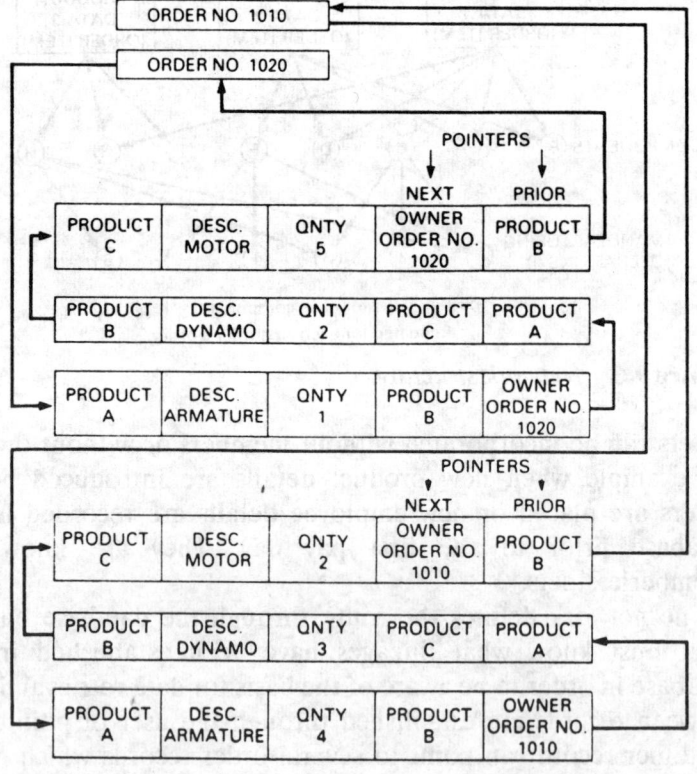

Figure 9.7 *Route through network illustrating next and prior pointers.*

11. Hierarchical structure. A hierarchical structure takes the form of an inverted tree structure consisting of the main trunk from which stem main branches and which in turn have smaller branches (sub-branches) emanating from them. The structure of the hierarchy determines the record types needed and the amount of redundancy required. In the case of customers' orders, each customer may have several orders consisting of the same product details (the product details would need to be repeated in the database for each order) (*see* Fig. 9.8). In addition, the structure outlined in Fig. 9.8 would be required for each customer. The hierarchy defines the route through the database. Access starts at the top and proceeds downwards through the hierarchical structure. Each element may be related to any number of elements at any level below it but only one element above it. One of the problems of this type of structure is that cross-linkages are not catered for. In respect of a sales office, for instance, it would need to know the items ordered by each customer as shown in Figs. 9.9 and 9.10. The production control function, on the other hand, needs to know the total quantity of each product ordered from all customers because any order from any customer can consist of any one of the range of products. To obtain this information the whole database would need to be searched. The type of structure required to allow for the production of manufacturing schedules and purchasing requirements is outlined in Fig. 9.8.

12. Relational. A database may be designed on the basis of what are referred to as 'relations', which are two-dimensional tables of data consisting of columns and rows. A relation is also known as an 'entity' or 'record'. The columns, which must be uniquely identified by a field name, are generally known as data elements or attributes as well as fields. They store data containing values relating to a particular relation, which may be a customer, stock item or employee record. Relational data analysis describes a relation by listing its columns. A customer relation contains data categories (columns) called 'Customer number' and 'Customer name' etc. An employee relation contains categories called 'Employee number' and 'Employee name', and so on. Each row in a table contains one record relating to a specific occurrence of an

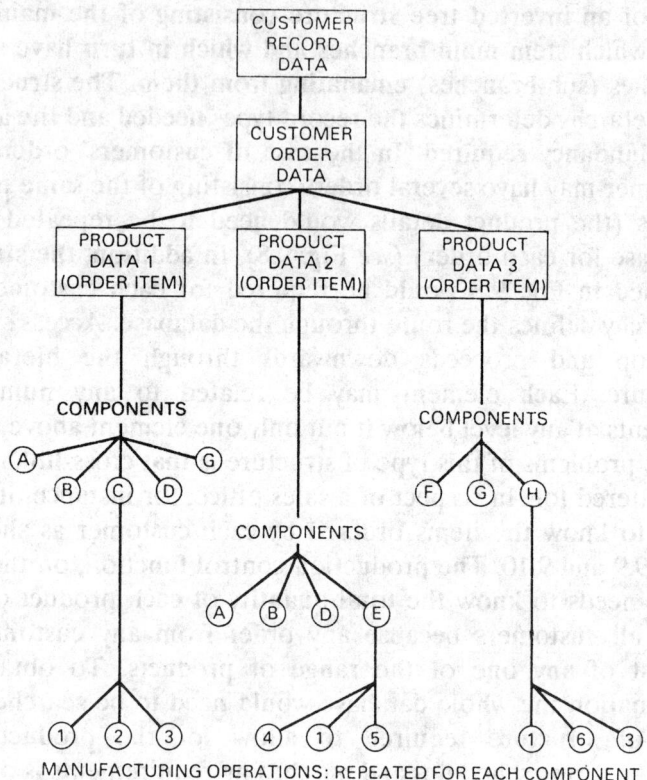

Figure 9.8 *Hierarchical structure.*

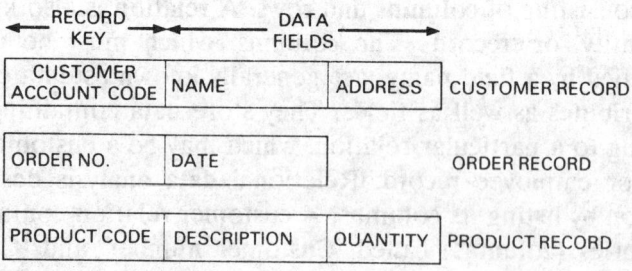

Figure 9.9 *Sales order records.*

entity, which is referred to as a 'tuple'. Thus Atkinson, James, Smith and Brown are all occurrences of the employee entity. This is analogous to records in a file where the file is comparable to a table of relations and the fields are comparable to the columns. Links between tables are maintained by repeated fields.

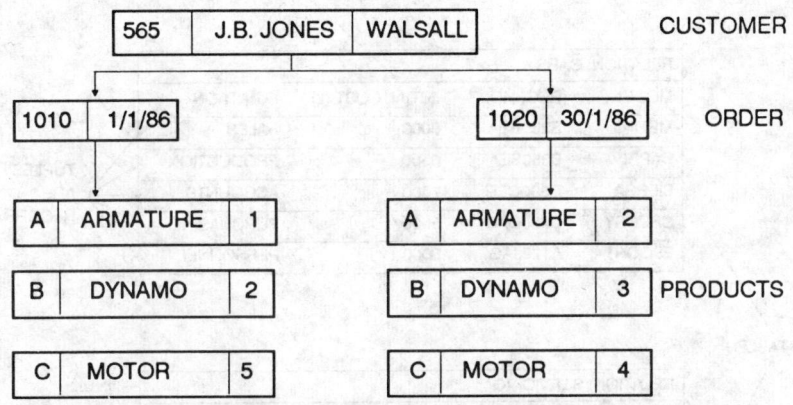

(i)   The product record is repeated for each order from the same customer.
(ii) The complete structure is repeated for each order for every customer.
(iii) The structure summarises the requirements of each order.

Figure 9.10   *Sales order hierarchical structure.*

Fig. 9.11 outlines a number of the features of a relational database discussed above. It portrays two relations, 'cars' and 'servicing'. A link may be established between the two relations by the repeating fields 'model' and 'reg(istration) number'. By means of a query language it is possible to access data from the database in respect of the various models in relation to initial cost, servicing cost, date of servicing and the function to which the car is allocated. For example, a query to retrieve information relating to which function a particular model of car is allocated may be phrased as LIST FUNCTION, FOR MODEL = 'SIERRA': the response would be ACCOUNTS SIERRA. A list of the registration numbers of each model can be obtained by phrasing a query as, for instance, LIST REGNO, MODEL. The screen would then display:

E255 REA METRO
B360 BEA CAPRI
D890 CEE SIERRA
C450 DAC CHERRY
A125 JAG ESCORT

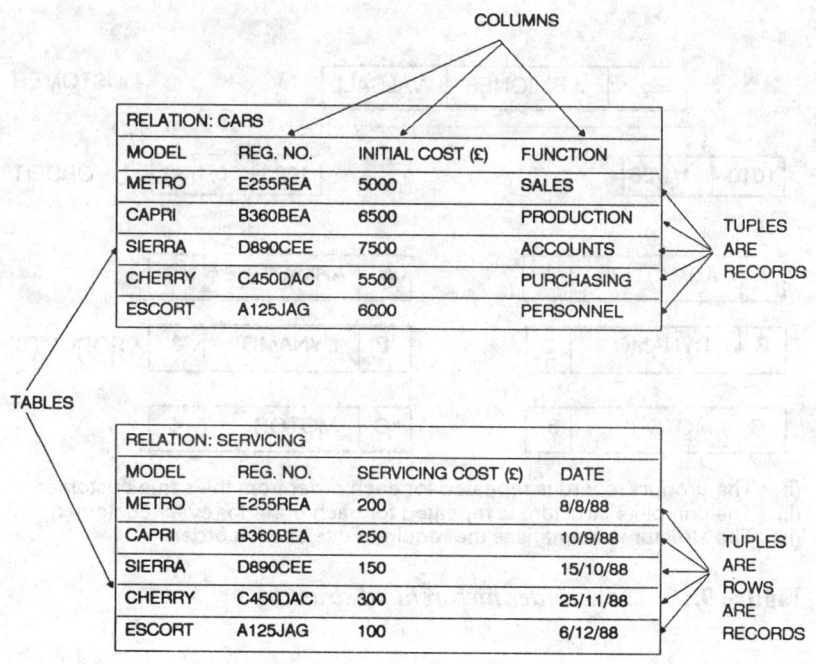

Figure 9.11 *Two-dimensional relational tables: cars and servicing.*

Some databases provide the technique of 'query by example' so that the need to learn a formal query language to retrieve data is dispensed with. To enter a query it is necessary to press an ENTER QUERY function key and type the selection criteria into the appropriate columns. For example, to obtain a list of cars which cost more than £6,000 all that is necessary is to type > 6000 in the initial cost column. The list would then be displayed as:

CAPRI B 360 BEA 6500 PRODUCTION
SIERRA D890 CEE 7500 ACCOUNTS

Multiple selection criteria can also be performed by typing the condition into each column. For example, purchasing records stored in a database may consist of columns containing supplier, part number, description and price. If a list is required of parts from a specific supplier with a price greater than a stated amount it would be necessary only to enter the supplier's name into the supplier column and the amount into the price column.

13. Data independence. Data is stored so as to achieve independence from the programs which use the data. Physical data formats may change without affecting programs as the physical format of the data is held separately (*see* 9 — data dictionaries) and not contained in the programs, as it is for conventional processing. Because of this, programmers are not concerned with the size of data items or the way in which a data item is physically stored. It is necessary only to state the records to be accessed and the DBMS presents these. If any fields are changed the only programs that will need to be amended are those that access the specific field. Under DBMS if another field is to be added to a record with data independence, only those programs which actually use the field will need to be recompiled. The operating system refers to a physical file on a specific disc but, because of the facility of data independence, this may be changed without affecting the application software using the data.

It is important to appreciate, however, that if a data structure changes this will affect the relationship between records and the way a program navigates around the database will require modification. If, for instance, the existing *order-item* record in the database contains the part number, an on-line enquiry about a specific part number will generate a list of *all* current order-items for that part. However, if the part number is removed from the *order-item* record and located in a *part* record, this new structure will require access to the *owner* of the part-order set, i.e. the part record, to obtain details of order-items (members) in the part-order set. All existing programs which access order-items via the order-item set will have to be modified so that they can obtain access to the owner of the part-order set and so identify the part being ordered. This process necessitates the insertion into the programs of additional database calls (DML statements). This example indicates the importance of effective data modelling and normalisation to reduce such complex structural changes after implementation

Summarising the advantages and disadvantages of a database

14. Advantages.

(*a*) Reduces the amount of data duplication which occurs using conventional file structures.

(*b*) Avoids duplicating input data to update multiple functionally independent files holding the same data.

(*c*) Provides fast and flexible access to information

(*d*) Improves consistency of data stored.

(*e*) Reduces processing for retrospective changes.

(*f*) Because of all the above advantages the quality of management information is improved throughout the organisation.

(*g*) Provides both data and program independence.

(*h*) Encourages integration of functional areas in an organisation.

(*i*) Offers useful query and report generation languages which help to offset the cost and time disadvantages mentioned below.

15. Disadvantages.

(*a*) Data structures in a database are complex; this means they:

(*i*)   take a long time to design and implement;

(*ii*) cost more than conventional systems;

(*iii*) require high calibre, experienced and specialised personnel.

The subject of databases is discussed further with practical examples in Volume 2.

Data modelling

Data models define the structure of files and make clearer the data needs of a business. They also help to segregate data into separate files or to integrate data structures when developing databases.

16. Normalisation. An initial requirement of data modelling is 'normalisation'. This is the process of separating items which are independent of one another into groups for recording in different files. It is necessary to ensure that each file has a 'key' which uniquely identifies the object the data describes. Relationships between fields must be established, e.g. the relationship between the key field and the other fields of an object. All details should be recorded in a data dictionary.

In some instances a record relating to an entity may have two or more distinct groups of data which should be segregated into separate stores, i.e files. As an example of this situation, details relating to an organisation's personnel may be classed as 'employee data' and may consist of the following elements:

(*a*) employee number;
(*b*) employee name;
(*c*) department number;
(*d*) monthly pay;
(*e*) tax code;
(*f*) gross pay to date;
(*g*) tax to date;
(*h*) standard deductions;
(*i*) bank sorting code;
(*j*) employee bank account number;
(*k*) bank name and address;
(*l*) marital status;
(*m*) age;
(*n*) sex;
(*o*) number of children;
(*p*) education;
(*q*) qualifications.

It can be seen that the employee data is more general than that required for payroll processing and can be grouped into two separate aspects, i.e. payroll data and personnel data (defined as the first normal form (INF)).

    (*a*) *Payroll data:*
        (*i*)   employee number;
        (*ii*)   employee name;
        (*iii*) department number;
        (*iv*) monthly pay;
        (*v*)   tax code;
        (*vi*) gross pay to date;
        (*vii*) tax to date;
        (*viii*) standard deductions;
        (*ix*) bank sorting code;
        (*x*)   employee bank account number;
        (*xi*) bank name and address.

The personnel data fields depend on the employee number key. The second group of data is:

    (*b*) *Personnel data:*
        (*i*)   employee number;
        (*ii*)   employee name;
        (*iii*) department number;
        (*iv*) marital status;
        (*v*)   age;
        (*vi*) sex;
        (*vii*) number of children;
        (*viii*) education;
        (*ix*) qualifications.

Changes to personnel data, such as that relating to marital status, number of children and qualifications, would not necessitate a change to processes which used only the payroll data. Neither would changes to payroll data, e.g. changes in monthly pay, tax code or standard deductions, necessitate a change in the processes concerned only with personnel data. The structures 'payroll data' and 'personnel data' do not contain repeating groups except for employee number, name and department, which are necessary when accessing the personnel file particularly as departmental statistics are often required.

The payroll data contains dependencies which can be segregated into two data structures because bank data and employee data can be separated as illustrated below:

(a) *Employee primary data*:
  (i)   employee number;
  (ii) employee name;
  (iii) department number;
  (iv) monthly pay;
  (v)   tax code;
  (vi) gross pay to date;
  (vii) tax to date;
  (viii) standard deductions;
  (ix) employee bank account number.
(b) *Bank data:*
  (i)   employee bank account number;
  (ii) bank sorting code;
  (iii) bank name and address.

An element of redundancy occurs since the employee account number is required in both structures for cross-referencing. This would be eliminated in a composite database structure, but for separate files benefits may be obtained because changes to bank details would not affect processes needing to access only employee primary data and vice versa. There also exist fields which can be derived from other fields because the bank name and address can be derived from the bank sorting code.

Normalisation of employee data has here generated three separate data structures. The process identified the fields which belonged to the separate groups with a minimum of redundancy, but some redundancy was necessary in the personnel data because of the need to use the key fields 'employee number', 'employee name' and 'department number' for cross-referencing and for sorting on the various keys within each file. This is defined as the third normal form (3NF).

17. Courting. This process is concerned with finding data which is held twice so that unnecessary redundancy can be eliminated. This could apply in a sales accounting system in which one data structure stores 'sales accounting data' in the sales ledger and another stores 'sales history data' in a history file. They would both contain common fields, i.e. customer code and product code. In addition, when items are despatched to customers it affects the 'value of sales' field in the customer record and the 'sales to date' field in the 'sales history' record. Both could be merged, which would avoid inputting the same unit of data twice.

When common keys occur in data structures it is probable that the same data is being considered from two points of view which, in this instance, relates to despatches or sales history. This is indicative that the structures should be reviewed to see if there is a case for merging.

All details should be recorded in the data dictionary.

Progress test 9

1. What is a database? **(1)**
2. What is a database management system (DBMS)? **(3)**
3. By what means is database security assured? **(4)**
4. It is often necessary to extract information of a specific nature from a database. How is this accomplished? **(5)**
5. What purpose does a fourth generation language serve in the manipulation of a database? **(6)**
6. For what type of applications would a database be used? **(8)**
7. What is the purpose of a data dictionary? **(9)**
8. Outline the characteristics of the following database structures: (*a*) network: (*b*) hierarchical: (*c*) relational. **(10–12)**
9. What is the significance of data independence in the context of databases? **(13)**
10. List the advantages and disadvantages of a database. **(14, 15)**
11. Define the terms 'data modelling', 'normalisation' and 'courting'. **(16, 17)**

10
Backing storage devices and media

The nature of backing storage

1. External storage. Although a computer could retain all business information in its internal memory it would be rather impractical to do so as it would require millions of bytes of storage capacity such as semiconductor memory in the form of RAMs, i.e. random access memory. It is usual to provide the computer system with off-line storage, referred to as auxiliary storage, for the storage of master files and programs relating to specific applications until they are required and transferred into the internal memory. Computers generally employ magnetic storage of one type or another but new developments are taking place such as optical discs which record data by means of a laser.

2. Types of backing storage. Magnetic tape is not so widely used for the storage of records on computer systems as in the past, being superseded largely by disc storage of one type or another. The reason for this is the speed with which records can be retrieved due to the direct access nature of disc storage. Although at a disadvantage for general data processing requirements because of its serial access nature, magnetic tape is useful for archival purposes because of its low cost and for data interchange between PCs and mainframes. Nine-track tape with packing densities of 800, 1,600 and 6,250 bpi (bits per inch of tape) has become known universally as the data interchange standard. PC manufacturers have in the past been prohibited by cost and physical size from providing 9-track sub-systems. However, recent developments by tape drive manufacturers utilising streaming tape drives have tended to reduce this problem. A 9-track tape system is capable of transferring data at a speed of 2 Mbytes per minute. Tape streamers are small tape drives used for back-up, archival storage and data interchange purposes. When files are updated on a Winchester hard disc, for instance, they are copied to a tape streamer at very high speed (*see* Fig. 3.6). This avoids having to use expensive hard discs for back-up purposes and eliminates what would otherwise be the need to handle many relatively low capacity floppy discs for the purpose. Table 10A summarises the position.

Table 10A Summary of backing storage media and devices

Storage medium	*Device*
Magnetic tape	Tape drive (tape streamer)
Hard discs	
Winchester discs	Fixed disc drive
Exchangeable discs (known as EDS— exchangeable disc storage)	Exchangeable disc drive
Soft discs	
5.25-inch (133mm) 3.5-inch (88.9mm)	Floppy drive
RAM disc	RAM card
Optical (laser) disc	Disc drive
Integrated disc	Integral disc drive pull-out unit in processor cabinet

Magnetic discs: Winchester and exchangeable

3. **Hard discs: general characteristics.** Winchester and exchangeable disc packs are 'hard discs', made from a rigid light alloy coated on both sides with a layer of magnetisable oxide. The discs rotate at very high speed on the drive and access to records

is made as the disc rotates. Data is stored on the disc surfaces along concentric tracks. These tracks are divided into sectors similar to blocks on a magnetic tape. A track index locates specific records directly without having to search the file as with magnetic tape. Data on the discs is stored in binary code and data is written to the disc from data stored in the processor's internal memory. Similarly, data is read from the disc and transferred to the processor's memory for reference or processing purposes.

Read/write heads do not come in contact with the disc surface but float above it on a cushion of air. Thus hard discs do not suffer from so much wear as floppy discs and are therefore suitable for frequent usage. A disc cartridge is another type of hard disc used on some minicomputer systems. Other systems use very large-capacity fixed discs for storing large volumes of data which is frequently referred to. Such discs are sealed within the disc drive and cannot be interchanged as with EDS. An IBM 3380 fixed disc has a transfer rate of 3 Mbytes per second and a capacity of 630 Mbytes and the 3344 model has a transfer rate of 885 Mbytes and a capacity of 280 Mbytes.

4. Winchester discs. This type of hard disc is being used to complement floppy discs or replace them in some instances on some models of microcomputer. They have a much greater storage capacity than floppies typically 5, 10, 20 and 40 Mbytes, up to 150 Mbytes. The capacity of floppies is in the region of 250 kbytes — 1 Mbyte. The Winchester is rigid and sealed in a case. It rotates at a much faster speed than a floppy, which allows data to be transferred much faster. As an example of this, floppy discs typically rotate at between 200 and 360 rpm but hard discs rotate in the region of 3,600 rpm. The Winchester's data transfer speed is, therefore, much higher — around 800 kbytes per second compared with 100 kbytes per second for floppy discs.

Portable computers such as the Panasonic PL-H7100 now have built-in hard disc drives with 10 Mbytes of storage capacity complementing floppy disc storage. The discs are 5.25 inches in diameter — the same physical size as some floppy discs.

There now exist exchangeable hard discs which are inserted in a disc drive in the same way as a floppy disc.

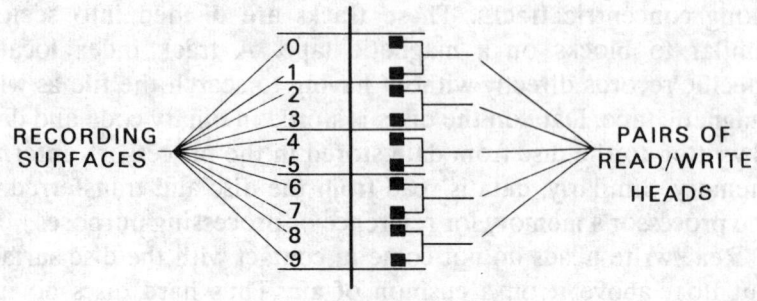

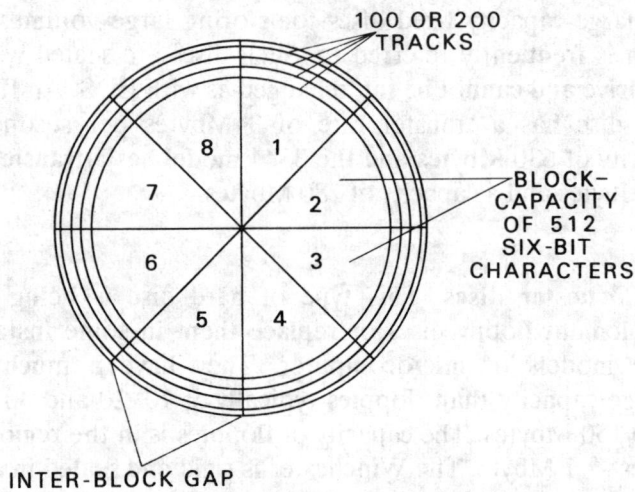

Figure 10.1 *Exchangeable discs.*

Security measures need to be taken with Winchester discs for the same reason as any other discs. Moreover, due to the high volumes of data stored on such a disc an economical medium needs to be used for back-up purposes. Copies of the files are normally stored on magnetic tape using a high-speed tape spooler (*see* Fig. 3.6).

5. Exchangeable disc storage. This type of disc is known as EDS. Such discs are widely used in batch processing environments as

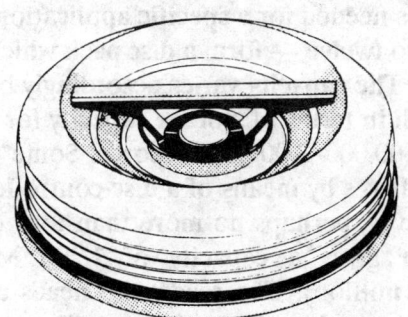

Figure 10.2 *Exchangeable disc pack.*

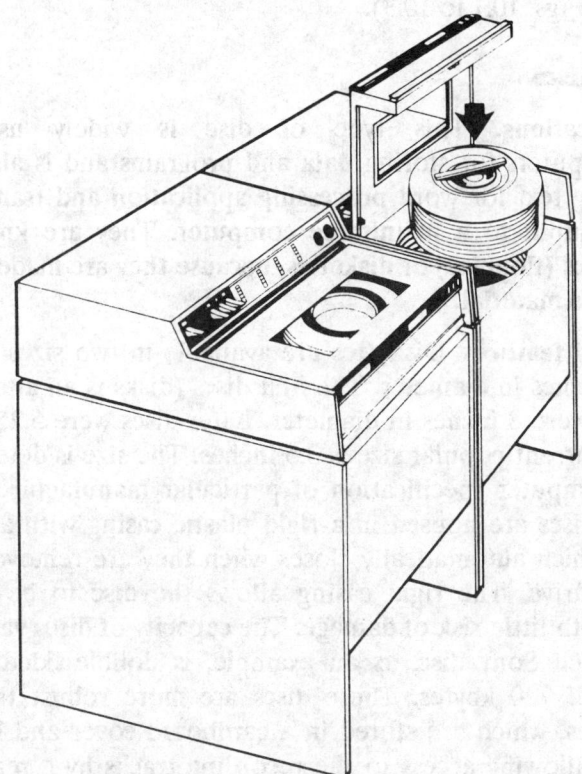

Figure 10.3 *Exchangeable disc drives.*

they are very flexible and can be exchanged in accordance with the programs and files needed for a specific application. A number of discs — from six to twelve — form a disc pack which is stored in a plastic container. The capacity varies accordingly between 60 and 300 Mbytes, which in terms of storage capacity for records of 100 characters gives 600,000–3,000,000 records. Some computers can handle four disc drives by means of a disc controller while others have banks of drives, perhaps no more than four drives for each controller, which gives a capacity of 1,200 Mbytes, or 1.2 Gigabytes (1,000 million). The read/write heads are an integral part of the disc drive and are located in pairs for each disc surface as shown in Fig. 10.1. There are disc modules, however, in which the read/write heads are part of the disc module and not the drive itself (*see* Figs. 10.1 to 10.3).

Floppy discs

6. Applications. This type of disc is widely used on microcomputers for storing data and programs and is also used for storing text for word processing application and transaction data for input to a mainframe computer. They are known as floppy discs (floppies) or diskettes, because they are made from a soft pliable material.

7. General features. Diskettes are available in two sizes — 5.25 and 3.5 inches in diameter. The first discs (disks is an alternative spelling) were 8 inches in diameter. Later discs were 5.25 inches and the current popular size is 3.5 inches. The size is determined by the computer specification of particular manufacturers. The 3.5-inch discs are housed in a rigid plastic casing with a sliding shutter which automatically closes when they are removed from the disc drive. The rigid casing allows the disc to be carried around with little risk of damage. The capacity of discs varies but the 3.5-inch Sony disc, as an example, is double-sided with a capacity of 720 kbytes. These discs are more robust than the larger ones, which are stored in a cardboard cover and have an aperture allowing access to the recording tracks by a read/write head — either for reading or writing data from or to the tracks. The surface of a disc is magnetised and data is recorded on it in ASCII code by most PCs.

A variety of discs is available, apart from differences in size. Some are single- or double-sided, single- or double-density or single-sided, quad-density. Double-density and double-sided features increase the data storage capacity.

Discs provide direct access or random access to specific records, documents, text or programs by the use of an index which indicates their location on the disc tracks without having to read through the disc tracks until the desired record or program, etc. is found, as is the case with magnetic tape files. This is accomplished by means of a disc directory (*see* **9**). (*See* Fig. 10.4.)

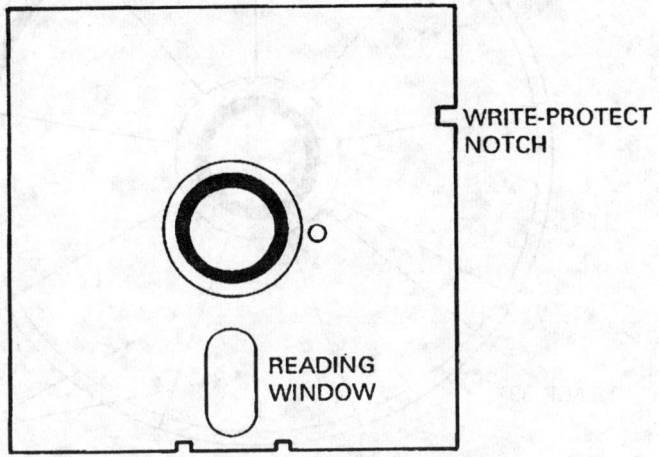

Figure. 10.4   *5.25-inch floppy disc inside its cover.*

8. Tracks, sectors and blocks. Data is recorded on the surface of a disc in a series of concentric tracks — not one continuous track as on a phonograph record — but a hypothetical track(s) consisting of a stream of binary digits (bits) representing characters. A sector is a section of a track which is used for storing text, data or programs. A sector usually consists of 256 bytes, which are transferred to and from the processor at one time. Each sector has a sector header which tells the computer that information is to follow which is stored in a sector data area. A sector gap, like an inter-block gap on magnetic tape, separates each sector. During disc operations a cyclic redundancy check, a field comprising several bytes, is read and a number of calculations are carried out. If the result differs from a pre-computed value it signifies that a read/write error has occurred. Each sector has a file control block containing details such as drive code, file name and file type which are used by the operating system and disc controller (*see* Fig. 10.5).

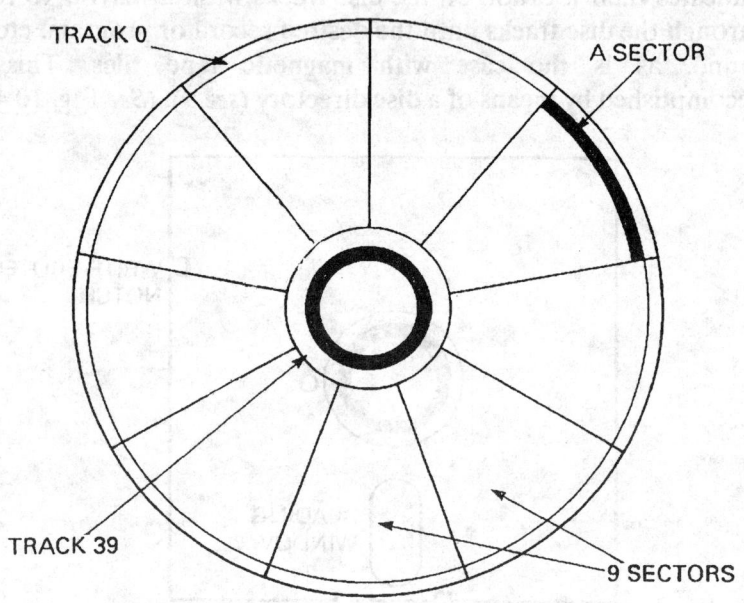

Figure 10.5 *5.25-inch floppy disc tracks and sectors.*

9. Disc operating system. Control of the location of records, files or programs stored on disc is maintained by the computer in conjunction with a disc operating system, or DOS for short. Often the first three tracks on a disc are used for storing DOS. The operating system works out where to locate files and programs and maintains a directory of the files or programs on the disc. Disc directories are usually situated on tracks in the centre of the disc. The operating system also controls the copying of files from one disc to another for file security purposes. DOS begins storing text, data or a program wherever it can find an unused sector. When a sector is filled, DOS searches for a free sector and continues recording the data or program at that location. As a file is stored on disc a track/sector list is compiled by means of a pair of bytes assigned to each file, one byte with the track reference and the other with the sector location. These bytes are called the track/sector pair. A link pair of bytes contains the location of the next portion of the track/sector list.

10. Disc security. A number of rules are worth remembering for ensuring the safety and security of discs. These are listed below.

(*a*) Maintain back-up copies of programs and important, lengthy text or data files to avoid having laboriously to re-enter them by the keyboard in the event of loss or corruption.

(*b*) Never use the original master program disc during processing as it can be very costly to replace if the disc drive or disc is damaged or corrupted. For security, construct a back-up copy and put the original in a place of safety. If the surface of the copy disc is damaged due to the disc drive malfunctioning it is then possible to replace it by making another copy from the original.

The frequency of generating back-up copies depends, to some extent, on how often files are updated. If this is a daily process, back-up copies could be made weekly — if this degree of risk is acceptable. Daily back-up, however, would offer greater security. If updating is a weekly routine the updated file should be copied immediately.

Many computers automatically generate back-up copies of files.

(*c*) The latest 3.5-inch discs are provided with a sliding tab in a groove located on the reverse side, lower left-hand corner. When the tab is moved downwards to uncover the hole in the disc casing it 'write-protects' the disc. This can be verified by looking through the disc casing — if you can see daylight it is write-protected. The computer can still read the information but accidental overwriting is prevented. It is necessary deliberately to adjust the position of the tab in the groove to enable writing to take place on the disc. This will be necessary before a file can be updated by writing new data to the disc and overwriting previously recorded data. Overwriting is destructive as it destroys the previous contents of the disc at a specific location, which is why it is essential to make back-up copies. The larger discs have a notch near the bottom left-hand corner which, when covered by sellotape, prevents accidental overwriting.

11. General rules for handling discs.

(*a*) Avoid touching the recording surface of a disc.

(*b*) Ensure the disc is placed in the disc drive the correct way round.

(*c*) Do not bend the disc.

(*d*) Do not expose disc to dust as this can corrupt data on the tracks.

(*e*) Do not remove a disc from the drive while the disc light is glowing.

(*f*) Never leave discs in the disc drive while the computer is switched on or off as the disc can be corrupted.

(*g*) Do not place disc near magnetic fields such as on the top of the computer or hi-fi unit or even near a telephone when in use.

12. Formatting discs. A new disc must be formatted by a special program before information or programs can be written to it. The program writes identifying data on to the tracks for reference by the disc operating system. Formatting is done by either of two techniques according to the particular model of computer. Some adopt 'soft sectoring', which is a sector-identification technique whereby the sectors on a disc are identified by coded signals recorded on the disc tracks. 'Hard sectoring' is a technique which identifies sectors on a disc by means of holes punched through the disc around the central hole marking the beginning of each sector.

Disc formatting is often accomplished by selecting a 'disc icon' on the screen of the monitor. The blank disc is then inserted into the disc drive.

Comparison of storage devices

13. Electro-mechanical vs. electronic storage devices. In most data processing installations data is stored on a magnetic disc utilising an electro-mechanical rotating direct access storage device which, in most cases, is a hard disc drive. The input and output performance of this type of storage is constrained by the limitations of electro-mechanical technology because the disc has to be rotated mechanically and the speed with which a mechanical device can rotate is limited. The fastest rotational speed cannot compete with electronic speed, hence semiconductor storage is tending to replace the use of discs. Data is stored on RAMs electronically and its access time is not subject to 'latency' delays due to disc rotation and 'seek' delays due to having to locate the read/write head over the required track on the disc surface. The total time to access and transfer data to or from disc consists of three factors: latency + seek + transfer time. Semiconductor memory access time is faster than disc because the total time taken to access and transfer data is little more than the data transfer time. The price/performance of semiconductor memory provides it with an economic advantage.

14. Capacity of semiconductor storage. Semiconductor storage was greatly enhanced by the development of 256-kbit chips, even more so by the availability of 16-Mbit and 256-Mbit chips.

15. Semiconductor storage sub-system. This sub-system typically consists of a controller with a standard channel interface and a semiconductor storage device which takes the place of the head–disc assembly of a conventional disc drive. The sub-system emulates standard devices and the hardware and software accept the semiconductor storage sub-system as though it were a disc drive. A semiconductor storage system can consist of between one and four storage directors connected to between one and four semiconductor storage devices each of between 16-Mbit and 256-Mbit capacity. A storage director may be connected to as many as four channels on four separate CPUs.

16. Advantages of semiconductor memory. Using semiconductor memory for on-line applications increases the rate at which transactions can be dealt with due to a reduction in the response time required to gain access to information. For batch processing applications the time to access records is also reduced, which leads to an overall reduction in total processing time.

17. Volatility. The first generation of semiconductor storage devices were volatile, causing data to be lost when the power was switched off. Volatility and loss of data through accidental loss of power are avoided with current RAM systems thanks to the availability of battery back-up facilities which function with an integral hard disc. Before power is switched off at the end of processing data is written to a Winchester disc. When power is switched off accidentally, before the end of processing, the battery back-up system powers the semiconductor memory and the Winchester discs, allowing data to be transferred to hard disc auxiliary storage. When power is restored data is read from disc and transferred back to semiconductor storage automatically. There is a penalty for this back-up, however: the time taken to unload the contents of RAM to disc and reloading from disc to RAM. It is important to be aware that data is written to disc only when the power is *off* — during the course of normal operations data is stored only in RAM thereby attaining semiconductor speed of response and transfer.

18. Semiconductor and virtual storage. Semiconductor storage can have a dramatic impact upon a virtual storage system, which is constrained by the characteristics of the actual (real) electro-mechanical disc drive. The actual device in use transfers data to the internal memory of a processor in pages (*see* 8:**30, 31**), which occupies considerable retrieval and transfer time. The response time provided by RAM storage allows the time to transfer pages to be eliminated, which improves system performance.

Optical and integrated discs

19. Optical disc. Optical data discs are rotating storage devices which use lasers to read and write data from and to disc. They are read-only devices, but erasable systems are expected to become available. Information is held on a metallic layer sandwiched in a protective transparent envelope made from glass or plastic. The information is stored on the disc by a laser beam which burns a hole in the metallic layer or raises a small blister. Information is read by a beam bounced off each hole or blister on to a light-sensitive device which interprets or reads the beam's angle of refraction. The use of this technique is also expected to expand greatly because of its vast storage capacity. To appreciate the storage capacity of optical discs a few comparisons will be made. An office filing cabinet containing in the region of 10,000 A4 documents of 2,000 characters (bytes) each, holds the equivalent of 20 million bytes. An optical disc of one Gigabyte capacity, i.e. 1 billion bytes, is capable of storing 500,000 such A4 pages. This would require: 2,000 floppy discs each of 500,000 bytes capacity; 50 20-Mbyte Winchester discs or 50 reels of magnetic tape of 20-Mbyte capacity. Moreover, Winchester discs are fixed, which can be rather expensive if vast amounts of data need to be stored and accessed as each disc requires its own drive. Optical disc devices are expensive but the costs must be related to the amount of data they are capable of storing compared with that of fixed discs for an equivalent capacity. From a security point of view data on an optical disc cannot be erased accidentally as is the case with magnetic discs (*see* Fig. 10.6).

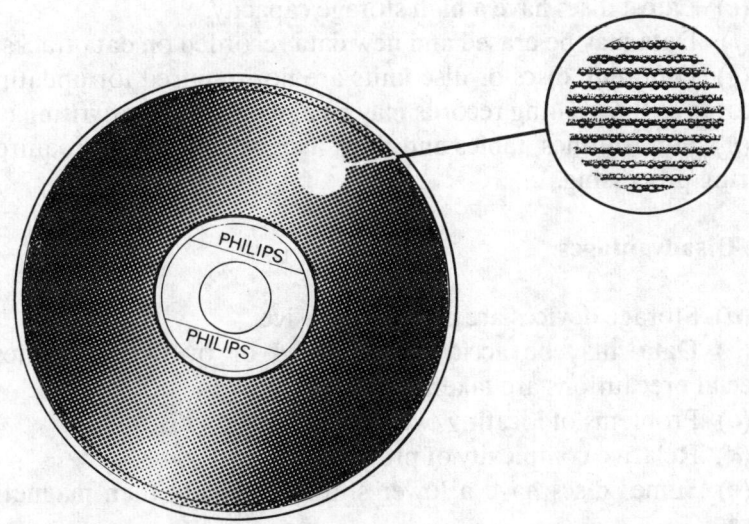

Figure 10.6   *Philips (optical) disc (courtesy Philips Organisation).*

20. Integrated discs. Some modern small computers have integrated discs stored in the same cabinet as the processor and memory. The discs are mounted in a pull-out unit and a single spindle unit holds one fixed two-surface disc and one removable two-surface disc. Each disc has a capacity of approximately 4.9 Mbytes and a transfer speed in the region of 312 kbytes per second.

Advantages and disadvantages of direct access storage

21. Advantages.

(a) Any item of data can be directly addressed depending upon the method of the file organisation used.

(b) High data transfer speed.

(c) Data can be input in random order (without the need for sorting).

(d) Discs may be used for real-time remote enquiry systems.

(e) Latest discs have a high storage capacity.

(f) Data may be erased and new data recorded on data tracks.

(g) Different discs or disc units are not required for updating records as the existing records may be amended by overwriting.

(h) Sub-routines, tables and rates may be called in as required during processing.

22. Disadvantages.

(a) Storage devices are rather expensive.

(b) Data may be accidentally erased or overwritten unless special precautions are taken.

(c) Problems of locating overflow records on discs.

(d) Relative complexity of programming.

(e) Some discs have a lower storage capacity than magnetic tape.

Progress test 10

1. Why is it necessary to have backing storage? **(1)**
2. Summarise the types of backing storage available which are used on micros, minis and mainframes. **(2, Table 10A)**
3. Define the following types of disc storage: exchangeable discs, Winchester discs and floppy discs. **(3–12)**
4. What factors would you take into account for the careful handling of discs? **(11)**
5. State the nature and purpose of disc formatting. **(12)**
6. Specify the nature of RAMdisc, optical disc and integrated disc. **(13–20)**
7. List the advantages and disadvantages of direct access storage. **(21, 22)**

11

Data communication

Basic concepts

1. Nature and benefits. Data communication is the process of transmitting (moving) data/information in coded form over some kind of electrical transmission system for the purpose of interchanging details of business transactions. Communication between business units is aided by modern systems such as local and wide area networks. Instead of despatching data internally by messenger, electronic mail facilities enable it to be interchanged efficiently and expeditiously between workstations sited in functional locations and executives' offices. This avoids the frustrations of having to make repeated internal phone calls when staff and executives are not at their desks. Messages can be left in electronic mailboxes (memory locations) on relevant workstations. With external communications, between branch works for example, it is much faster to send information by local or wide area network, fax or telex than by the normal mail services. Speed is the essence of modern business communications.

Analogue communications

2. Acoustic coupler and modem. The older telephone systems function using analogue signals to represent voice modulation patterns by means of variations in waveforms. When using telephone lines for transmitting data from a terminal to a computer, the terminal's digital signals need to be converted to analogue signals by an acoustic coupler or modem prior to transmission. A

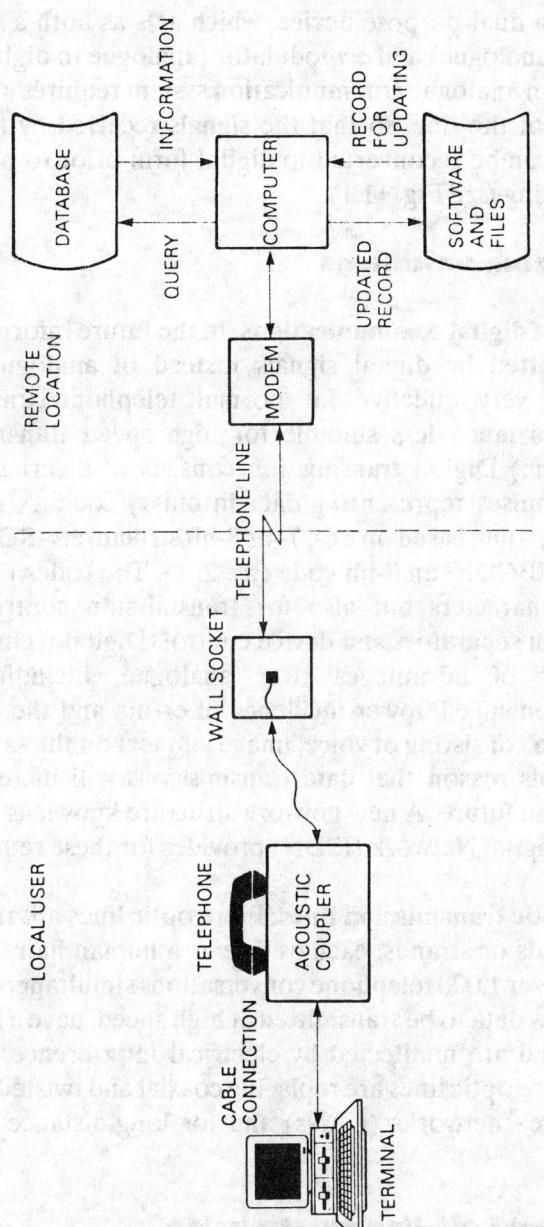

Figure 11.1   *Terminal with acoustic coupler.*

modem is a dual-purpose device, which acts as both a *mo*dulator (digital to analogue) and *dem*odulator (analogue to digital), hence its name. An analogue communication system requires a modem at both ends of the line, so that the signals received by the distant computer can be reconverted to digital form prior to being input for processing (*see* Fig. 11.1).

Digital communications

3. Nature of digital communications. In the future information will be transmitted by digital signals instead of analogue (*see* 2). (Although very effective for normal telephone transmission, analogue is much less suitable for high speed transmission of information.) Digital transmission consists of a series of on/off electrical pulses representing data in binary code. A number of codes exist, some based on a 6-, 7- or 8-bit structure: ASCII is a 7-bit code and EBCDIC an 8-bit code (*see* 2: 1). The codes provide not only for characters but also for transmission control signals, information separators and device control. Digital technology has a number of advantages over analogue, including higher transmission speed, lower incidence of errors and the facility for mixing data consisting of voice, image and text on the same circuit. It is for this reason that data transmissions will increasingly be digital in the future. A new network structure known as Integrated Services Digital Network (ISDN) provides for these requirements.

4. Fibre optic transmission lines. Fibre optic lines are transparent glass threads or strands, each as fine as a human hair, capable of handling over 1,000 telephone conversations simultaneously. Fibre optics allow data to be transmitted at high speed, have a high signal capacity and are unaffected by electrical interference. For these reasons fibre optic lines are replacing coaxial and twisted pair cable in local area networks (LANs) and for long-distance telephone networks.

On-line and off-line transmission

5. On-line data transmission. On-line data transmission indicates that the communication lines are connected directly to the

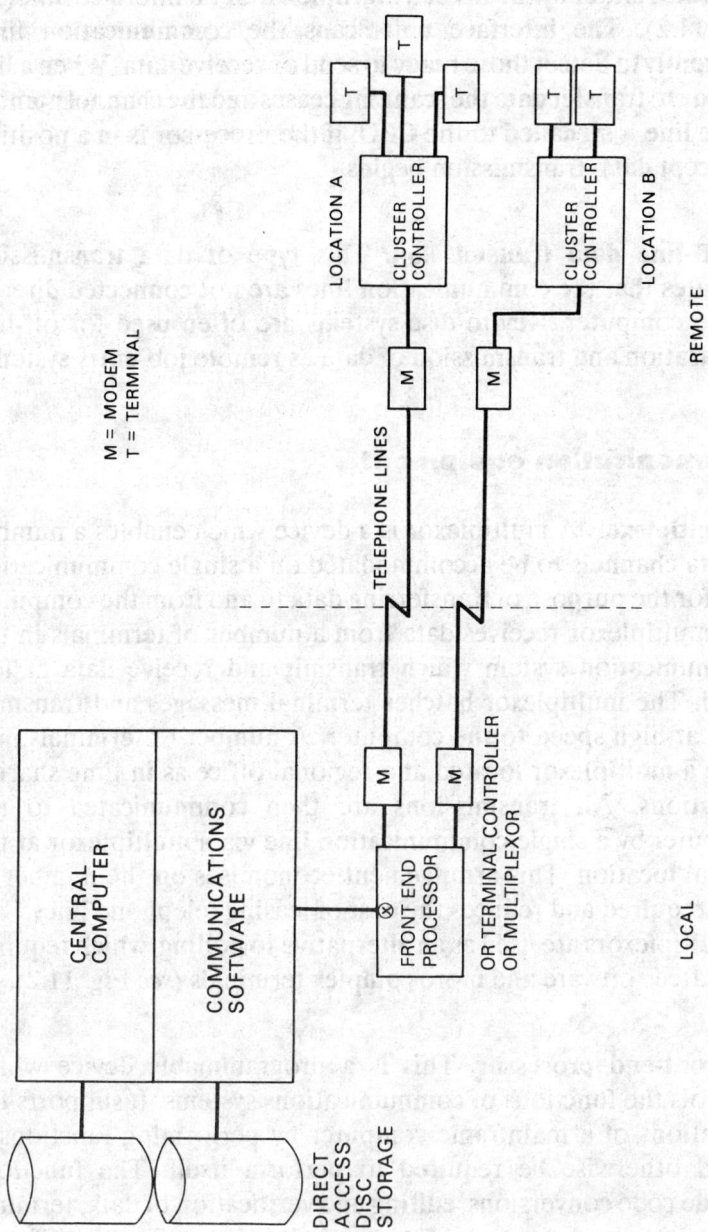

Figure 11.2 *On-line data transmission — clusters of terminals.*

computer either by means of a multiplexor or an interface unit (*see* Fig. 11.2). The interface unit scans the communication lines frequently to detect those ready to send or receive data. When a line is ready to transfer data the scanning ceases and the channel number of the line is signalled to the CPU; if the processor is in a position to accept data, transmission begins.

6. Off-line data transmission. This type of data transmission indicates that the communication lines are not connected directly to the computer. Key-to-disc systems are often used for off-line preparation and transmission of data as remote job-entry systems.

Communication equipment

7. Multiplexor. A multiplexor is a device which enables a number of data channels to be accommodated on a single communication line, for the purpose of transferring data to and from the computer.

A multiplexor receives data from a number of terminals in the communication system which transmit and receive data at low speed. The multiplexor batches terminal messages and transmits them at high speed to the computer. A number of terminals may share a multiplexor located at a regional office as in time sharing operations. All transmissions are then communicated to the computer by a single communication line via a multiplexor at the central location. This arrangement economises on the number of lines required and reduces the cost of leasing telephone lines.

Multiplexors are used as an alternative to polling, which requires dedicated software and more complex terminals (*see* Fig. 11.2).

8. Front-end processor. This is a programmable device which controls the functions of communications systems. It supports the operations of a mainframe computer by performing functions it would otherwise be required to perform itself. The functions include code conversions, editing and verification of data, terminal recognition and control of transmission lines. The mainframe computer is then able to devote its time to data processing rather than data transmission (*see* Fig. 11.2).

Accuracy and speed factors

9. Error checking. In most data transmission systems redundancy checking is used to detect errors, which are then corrected by retransmission of the blocks containing errors. Redundancy checking detects errors by computing additional bits from the data, which are added to blocks of data. The receiving terminal then performs checks by comparing bit patterns in the data blocks, which identifies bits which have been lost or corrupted during transmission. Blocks containing errors are then automatically retransmitted. Parity checking can also be applied whereby an additional bit is added to the frame of bits forming a character before transmission. Parity checking can be either even or odd parity. This requires the count of 1 bits to be either even or odd according to the mode of parity selected. Errors may also be detected by retransmitting signals received back to the transmitting terminal on a separate channel. The signals are then compared with the original transmission, differences indicating the presence of transmission errors.

10. Speed of data transmission. Although the speed of data transmission is usually expressed in terms of bits/s, i.e. bits per second, a term used to define the speed of transmission in terms of the number of pulses which can be transmitted in a second is the baud. If data is transmitted serially one bit at a time then 100 baud is equivalent to 100 bits per second. If, however, the data consists of two-bit groups then 100 baud is equivalent to a baud rate of 200 bits per second. Typical baud rates are 110, 300, 600, 1,200, 2,400 and 4,800.

Telecom Datel services

11. Definition of Datel. Telecom considers data transmission facilities of such importance to commercial, business and industrial undertakings as to merit the provision of a separate group of communications services known as 'Datel services'. Datel is a word derived from (Da)ta (tel)ecommunications and the services available are described below (*see* **12–15**). It is important to appreciate that permission must be obtained from Telecom to connect any communications equipment to Telecom services.

Datel services are summarised in Table 11A.

Table 11A Datel services at a glance

Service	Signal path	Transmission speed — bits per second	Operating mode	Remarks
Datel 200	Public telephone network	300	Asynchronous	300 bit/s may not always be attainable with older equipment
	Private circuit	300	Asynchronous	
Datel 600	Public telephone network	600	Asynchronous	Speeds of up to 1,200 bit/s are also possible
	Private circuit	1,200	Asynchronous	4-wire private circuits are required for duplex working
Datel 1200 Duplex	Public telephone network	1,200	Synchronous or asynchronous	
Datel 2412	Public telephone network	2,400	Synchronous	Over some connections it may be necessary to switch to 1,200 bit/s
	Private circuit	2,400	Synchronous	A 4-wire private circuit is required
Datel 4800	Public telephone network	4,800/2,400	Synchronous	Over some connections it may be necessary to switch to 2,400 bit/s
	Private circuit	4,800/2,400	Synchronous	A 4-wire private circuit is required
Datel 4832	Private circuit	4,800/3,200	Synchronous	A 4-wire private circuit is required
	Public telephone network (standby)	4,800/3,200	Synchronous	PSTN only operation is not available
Datel 9600	Private circuit	9,600/7,200/ 4,800	Synchronous	A 4-wire private circuit is required
	Public telephone network	9,600/7,200/ 4,800	Synchronous	
Datel 48K	Wideband circuit	40.8k/48k/ 50k	Synchronous	

(Courtesy British Telecom)

12. International Datel services. International Datel 200, 600 and 2400 services provide for the transmission of data over the PSTN to most of Europe, the USA and many other countries. The transmission of data internationally can be arranged over privately leased circuits, whether or not the International Datel service is available to the country concerned.

13. Datel Network Control Systems (DNCS). DNCS are available for use with most Datel services. Specially equipped racks, housed in an attractive cabinet, provide the termination points for the circuits and hold the modems, control units and other necessary equipment. The system is modular; as the user's needs increase, more 'building bricks' are added to it. Where a customer uses more than one Datel service, DNCS may contain a mixture of these different services.

14. Multipoint circuits for data transmission. In addition to point-to-point circuits, data may also be transmitted over a multipoint circuit. This allows from two to twelve terminals to be connected to a central station and allows the transmission of data from the central station to any terminal and from terminals to the central station. Direct communication between terminals is not possible.

15. KiloStream and MegaStream. These are digital private circuit services which transmit text, data, facsimile or speech. They can also be used for slow-scan visual services including closed circuit television, confravision and videostream — a videoconferencing service. KiloStream is available in various speeds including 2,400, 4,800 and 9,600 bits per second. KiloStream Plus combines the high data rates of MegaStream with the wide availability of KiloStream. The service offers a 2-Mbits/s path provided up to 31 channels are sited on the customer's premises, and individual circuits link a number of locations. For users requiring a large number of KiloStream circuits over various routes KiloStream Plus is ideal. MegaStream is the highest capacity digital private circuit service available from BT. It is available nationally and can be used to link high-speed terminals, private branch exchanges, local and metropolitan area networks, visual services and mainframes; voice and data can be mixed. MegaStream is ideal for corporate networks.

Other Telecom services

16. System X. This is British Telecom's name for its computer controlled telephone exchanges linked by digital transmission and signalling systems. Older exchange equipment is scheduled to be progressively replaced by the new technology system over a number of years. With this system caller voice patterns are represented by on-off digital pulses. The system greatly improves the quality of transmission and calls are connected more quickly. The equipment is also cheaper to buy, install and maintain than older systems and takes up much less space.

Digital exchange systems, like System X, rely on the latest microchip technology. This means that exchanges no longer have moving parts prone to crossed lines, wrong numbers, and line noise as was the case with the older electro-mechanical exchanges and the more modern cross-bar and electronic read relay exchanges.

System X also facilitates integrated links between local and trunk exchanges, referred to as Integrated Digital Access (IDA). In addition to voice services IDA offers both circuit and packet switched data facilities which can be used for a wide variety of purposes, e.g. facsimile, electronic mail and slow-scan TV.

17. Packet switching. Packet switching is a technique whereby the terminal or computer in a data transmission system collects data into a block which is allocated an address. The block is sent to the local packet switching exchange, which transmits it to its destination exchange. The communication lines between exchanges are engaged only when a packet is being transmitted. During lapses in transmission, lines are available to other users. If data is transmitted by the normal telephone network a charge is incurred for the length of time the line is used, even for the time when no data is being transmitted. Packet switching is designed to eliminate this. In the UK this applies where telephone calls or data transmissions on public switched telephone lines are charged on a time used basis.

Digital PABX telephone exchange

18. General outline of PABX. Digital PABX telephone exchanges are an essential communication catalyst for the electronic office of the present and future. Digital voice and data communication systems provide the foundations for extending office automation.

The digital exchange translates voice analogue signals into digital signals, which are the common language of computers and electronic equipment such as workstations, word processors and terminals in general. This technology will widen the horizons for developing automated offices as it makes it possible to access all electronic devices comprising the electronic office. This includes access to local area networks, mainframe computers, terminals, word processors, electronic mail stations, telexes, microcomputers and electronic printing equipment. The devices are connected to the wiring of the digital switchboard at no additional cost. PABX systems can also act as message switching centres for terminals and other devices. They also control the routeing of data or text from workstations.

19. ICL DNX–2000 digital PABX distributed network exchange. The DNX–2000 is a *d*istributed *n*etwork *e*xchange which provides the means for integrating office communications as it can talk to and work with computers, word processors, telexes, electronic printing equipment and traditional telephones.

The system has bubble memory (which eliminates tape and disc) as the primary non-volatile storage medium. The exchange can be interlinked or used with other switching systems to provide integrated communications. It can handle 150 to 10,000 lines.

Features include discriminatory barring, automatic route selection, extension metering, automatic number identification and traffic analysis.

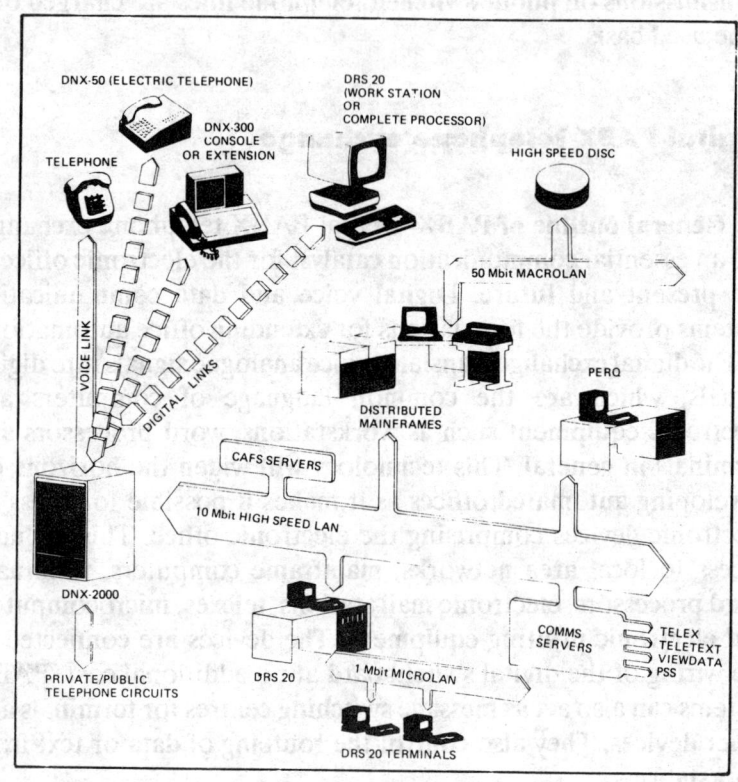

Figure 11.3 *ICL DNX–2000 digital PABX distributed network exchange (courtesy International Computers Limited).*

The DNX–2000 supports standard dial and MF telephones together with two special terminals — the DNX–50 and DNX–300. The DNX–50 is an electronic telephone providing display capability, flexible key assignment, hands free operation and an optional data port into the DNX–2000. Features include abbreviated dialling, dial by name, date and time display, numeric keypad for normal telephone operation and alphabetic keys for message generation. The DNX–300 dataphone can function as a console, maintenance position or a secretarial/executive extension. It has DNX–50 features plus electronic mail, diary, directory, full message switching capability and system statistics recovery. Other features include VDU, standard keyboard layout, fixed designation keys including dial keypad and fixed feature keys. It is built on distributed microprocessor architecture (*see* Fig. 11.3).

Satellite transmission

20. Nature and objective. The primary object of satellite communications is to provide an efficient worldwide communication system affording simultaneous transmission/receiving of all forms of communications including telephone, radio, television, data and facsimile. Some businesses have already installed rooftop dishes for satellite communications, replacing surface lines for high speed transmission of large volumes of data between dispersed locations.

21. Advantages. Satellite communications provide distinct advantages over ground-based radio transmission, which suffers from a number of problems: interference between different transmissions, for example, and atmospheric disturbances, which distort signals. The altitude of the satellite is such that radio waves are not materially affected by the topography of the terrain. Satellites are equipped with an antenna which receives radio beams from an earth station transmitter which are then retransmitted to another earth station. The satellite's orbit is determined so that signals can be received at specific locations. A worldwide system of satellites exists which enables signals to be transmitted round the world by bouncing them from one satellite to an earth station and then retransmitting them to another satellite. The whole of the earth's surface is covered by this arrangement. Compared to cable communications, satellites tend to be more flexible and less expensive to use. The power of satellite transmissions is to be increased so that the size of earth station aerials can be decreased. This will allow the use of aerials in the home to receive satellite television transmissions in competition with cable television and other television services (*see* Fig. 11.4).

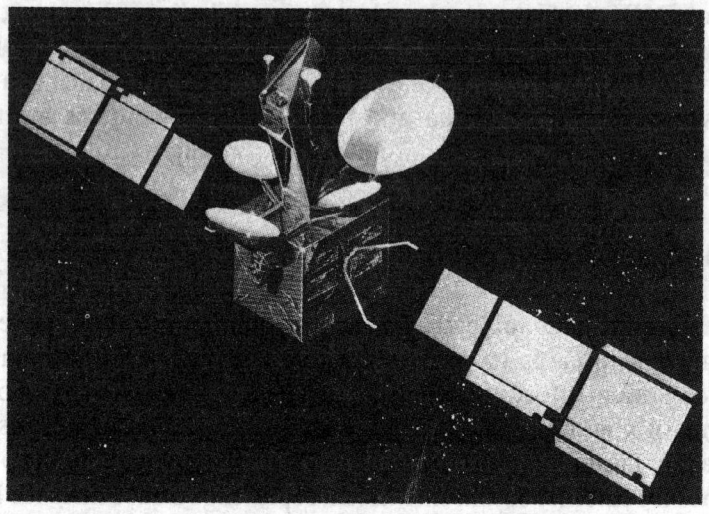

Figure 11.4 *Intelsat V (courtesy Picture Unit, British Telecom).*

Services other than British Telecom

22. Mercury Communications. This is Britain's national and international communications organisation in competition with British Telecom. Mercury's national telecommunications network links together the principal business centres in England. International communications for voice, data and TV are provided by two satellite communication centres.

Progress test 11

1. Define the nature of data communication. (1)
2. What benefits are obtained from data communications? (1)
3. What purpose do acoustic couplers and modems serve? (2)
4. Describe the nature of digital communications. (3)
5. What benefits are derived from fibre optics? (4)
6. Distinguish between on-line and off-line data transmission. (5, 6)
7. State the purpose of a multiplexor and a front-end processor. (7, 8)

8. What is the purpose of redundancy checking in data transmission systems?   (9)

9. How is the speed of data transmission defined?   (10)

10. List a number of Datel services.   (11, Table 11A)

11. Describe the nature of Datel Network Control Systems. (13)

12. State the nature of KiloStream and MegaStream services. (15)

13. Describe the nature of packet switching.   (17)

14. State the nature and relevance to office automation of digital PABX.   (18, 19)

15. What is the objective of satellite communications?   (20, 21)

12
Networks

Types of network: local area networks

1. Nature and purpose. A local area network, often referred to as a LAN, is in its simplest form a 'cluster' of interconnected microcomputers forming a network. A LAN is designed to serve a local establishment such as a factory and its administrative offices, providing a speedy and effective means of communication between the various sections and improving day-to-day efficiency. Networks may consist of interconnected workstations, intelligent terminals, microcomputers, word processors and electronic mail facilities. LANs provide for the sharing of expensive hardware resources such as a high-speed printer and high-capacity hard disc storing programs, data files or a database which can be accessed by any authorised user of the network. Networks have different topologies, protocols, methods of data transmission and the type of cable used — which may be twisted-pair, coaxial or fibre optic cable. (*See* Figs. 12.1, 12.2 and 12.7.)

(*a*) *Twisted-pair wires.* A transmission medium used in telephony which consists of a single wire with an earth return. The cable pairs are twisted to reduce the effect of 'crosstalk' with other pairs of wires. They are used for links between individual telephone terminals and local exchanges. They have limited use for broadband multiplexed channels because crosstalk can be excessive.

(*b*) *Coaxial cable.* A communication link consisting of an inner central conductor, insulated from an outer conductor which functions as a shield to reduce electrical interference and crosstalk.

Several tubes, as they are called, can be combined into a single bundle to form a cable. There is a very low loss of energy when high frequencies are transmitted.

(c) *Optical fibre cable.* Optical fibre cable carries light pulses, not electric current, hence there are no electromagnetic fields to interfere with transmissions. The fibres are of very small diameter and they can be bundled to create cables in which each fibre may provide a broadband channel.

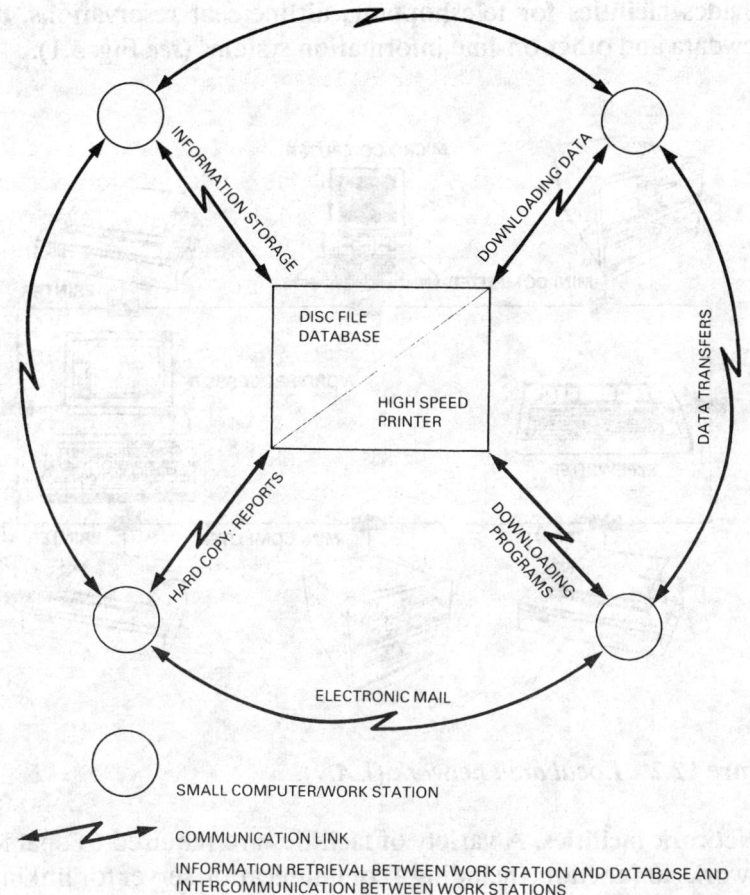

Figure 12.1 *Outline structure of a local area network.*

There exist over 50 different proprietary networks including Acorn's Econet; Ethernet of Rank Xerox; Corvus Omninet and IBM's PC-Net.

Two-way communication is possible between the various computers in the network for transferring data or messages electronically, i.e. electronic mail. The speed of transmission varies between one and twelve million bits per second. Ethernet transmits data at ten million bits per second, much faster than the speed of telephone lines. Modems can link LANs to British Telecom's telephone system and to gateways to other networks, which provides facilities for teleshopping, airline seat reservations, to Viewdata and other on-line information systems (*see* Fig. 3.1).

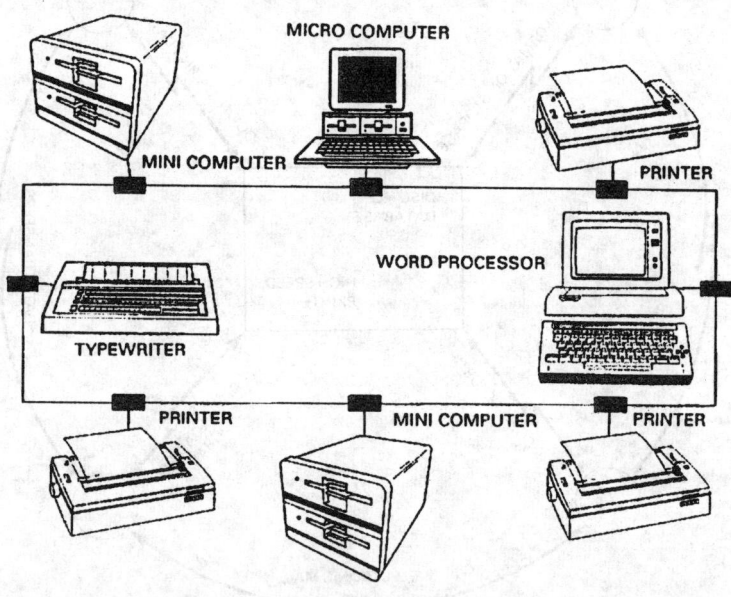

Figure 12.2 *Local area network (LAN).*

2. Network facilities. A variety of facilities are required to enable networks to function, including a communication server for linking network users to a variety of communication devices by telephone line connections; a print server providing each network user with high-speed printing facilities, and a file server which facilitates the storage of documents which can be retrieved and updated as necessary (*see* Fig. 12.3).

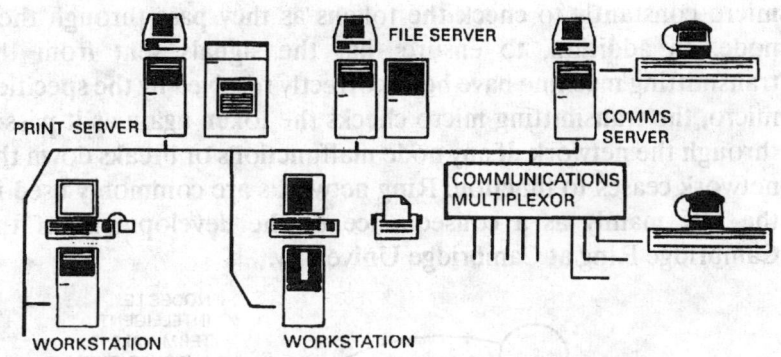

Figure 12.3 *Part of a network illustrating print, file and comms servers.*

3. Broadband and baseband networks. LANs can be either broadband or baseband. Broadband networks have a number of channels multiplexed together, one of which serves as a high-speed data channel the other being available for other purposes such as video. Broadband has a bandwidth greater than a voice-grade line, which makes it faster but more expensive than baseband. A baseband channel provides for data transmission in only one direction at a time. It uses lower-cost cable than broadband because of the lower bandwidth required for a single channel.

Network topology — ring, star and bus networks

There are three primary types of topology: RING, STAR and BUS networks.

4. Ring network. This type of network is formed by a continuous ring of nodes, i.e. devices, each linked to the next. The devices may be a workstation, terminal or microcomputer, each having a unique address for identification purposes. Messages are passed from one node to the next until the one to which the message is addressed is reached. Tokens, which may be defined as labelled packets or units of data, constantly revolve around the loop or ring, which is why they are referred to a 'token' passing rings. The tokens have data written to and read from them continuously. As the tokens could be carrying data from any micro to any other it is necessary for each micro constantly to check the tokens as they pass through their node. In addition, to ensure that the signals sent from the transmitting machine have been correctly received by the specified micro, the transmitting micro checks the token again as it passes through the network. If any node malfunctions or breaks down the network ceases to function. Ring networks are commonly used in the UK mainly as a consequence of the development of the Cambridge Ring at Cambridge University.

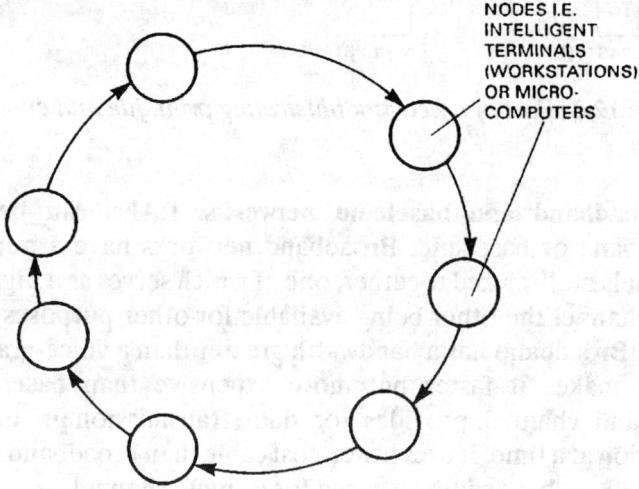

NODES I.E. INTELLIGENT TERMINALS (WORKSTATIONS) OR MICRO-COMPUTERS

Figure 12.4 *Ring network.*

A ring network developed by IBM is known as the Token Ring Local Area Network. The token ring works by sending free tokens around the ring. A user wishing to transmit data round the network has to wait until a free token arrives before being able to do so. IBM, who developed this type of network in its laboratories in Zurich, considers it to be the future foundation of office automation. The system is flexible as it is possible to increase the speed of transmission and incorporate additional users or new equipment at any location on the network pathway. This type of network can support up to 260 terminals. Signal boosters are necessary for dispersed networks requiring a number of kilometres of cable.

Speeds of 16 Mbits/s (16 million bits per second) are possible, which is a vast increase over the current 4 million. Moreover, tests are under way on prototype systems using fibre optic cables (replacing twisted-pair copper cables) which it is expected will attain speeds of 100 Mbits/s. IBM provides software for connecting a token ring network to PC-Net, a lower performance network. It is also possible to connect mainframe computers on a token ring LAN either directly using a specially programmed PC or a Series 1 minicomputer. Links are also facilitated via other gateways. Because data is in labelled packets the network can carry traffic using IBM's Systems Network Architecture protocols and the internationally accepted Open Systems Interconnection (OSI) protocols (*see* Fig. 12.4).

5. Star network. Star networks have a central network controller or file server, usually a microcomputer controlling a disc drive, to which all nodes are connected. The network transmits data to specific nodes in accordance with the destination address. This type of network is used in time sharing systems whereby the central controller is a host computer to which all terminals are connected via modems (or acoustic couplers), multiplexors and telephone lines. If the central controller, whether a file server or central time sharing computer, breaks down the network ceases to function (*see* Fig. 12.5).

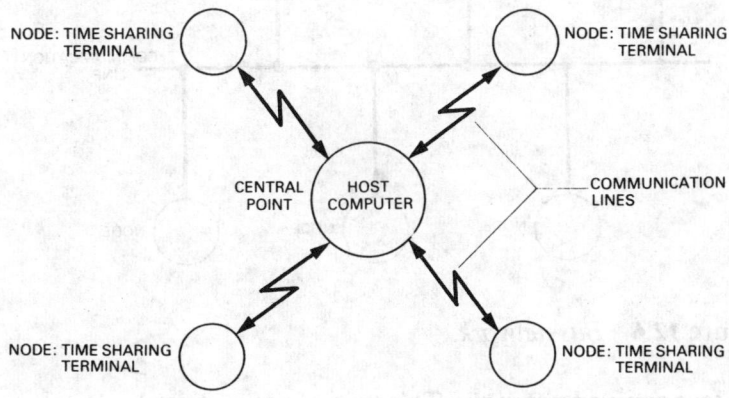

Figure 12.5   *Star network.*

6. Bus network. A bus may be defined as a communication line or channel to which is connected the various workstations, word processors or microcomputers by means of cable taps. Any device can easily to removed or added to the network as required. Each device or node has a specific address and messages are routed to all nodes until the one to which the communication is addressed is reached. If one or several devices fail, the network continues to function.

An example of a bus network is Ethernet, which uses a system known as CSMA/CD, an abbreviation for carrier sense multiple access with collision detect. With this system, terminals listen to the carrier wave to detect if any other terminals are transmitting data. All terminals on the network can do this at any time because of the multiple access nature of the system. If two terminals listen simultaneously and both detect that no transmissions are occurring then both transmit data concurrently. Consequently both transmission signals collide. Both terminals detect this situation by the collision detect facilities and both wait a random period of time before retransmitting the data (*see* Fig. 12.6).

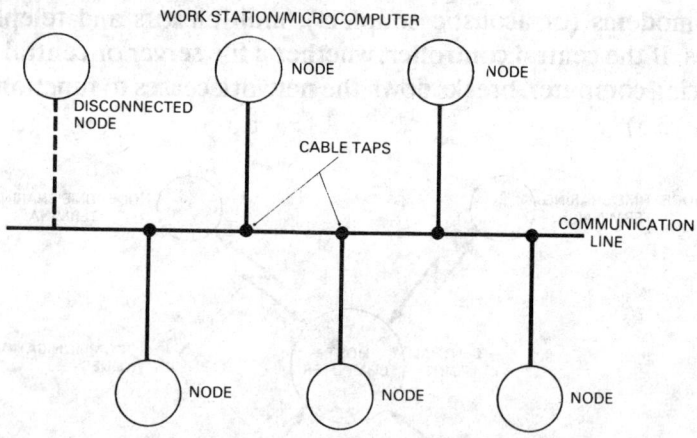

Figure 12.6 *Bus network.*

7. Close coupled networks. This type of network is also known as a multi-processor system. Each terminal has its own processor for local processing needs. Communication takes place on a bus (electronic board) which has a file-serving processor alongside the application processors each of which is able to share any other's memory. The communication distances are very short which enables transmission speeds to be achieved in the region of one million characters per second, which is much faster than local area networks using coaxial or twisted-pair cables. The central processor does not poll each user's processor for detecting data to be transmitted but is 'demand' activated or 'interrupt driven'. The protocol to handle data transmissions is less complex than that required for LANs and the complex protocols to deal with data collision and for ensuring the integrity of data are dispensed with.

Value-added network (VAN) and store and forward systems

8. Value-added network (VAN). This type of communication network provides additional services to the communication channels by third-party vendors under a government licence. The additional services include automatic error detection and correction as well as 'store and forward' message services, electronic mail and protocol conversions to access different computers and networks. The vendors can provide point-to-point or switched services on British Telecom and Mercury circuits provided they 'add value' to those circuits.

9. Store and forward. The term relates to the temporary storage of a message in a computer system for subsequent transmission to its destination at a later time. Store and forward techniques allow for routing over networks which are not always accessible. This requires one or more computer-controlled exchanges or nodes which are able to store messages and release them for onward transmission when a transmission path is available. Messages for different time zones can be 'stored and forwarded' to the destination during normal daytime by this means.

Wide area networks

10. Versatility of wide area networks. Whereas a local area network serves the requirements of an organisation for interdepartmental

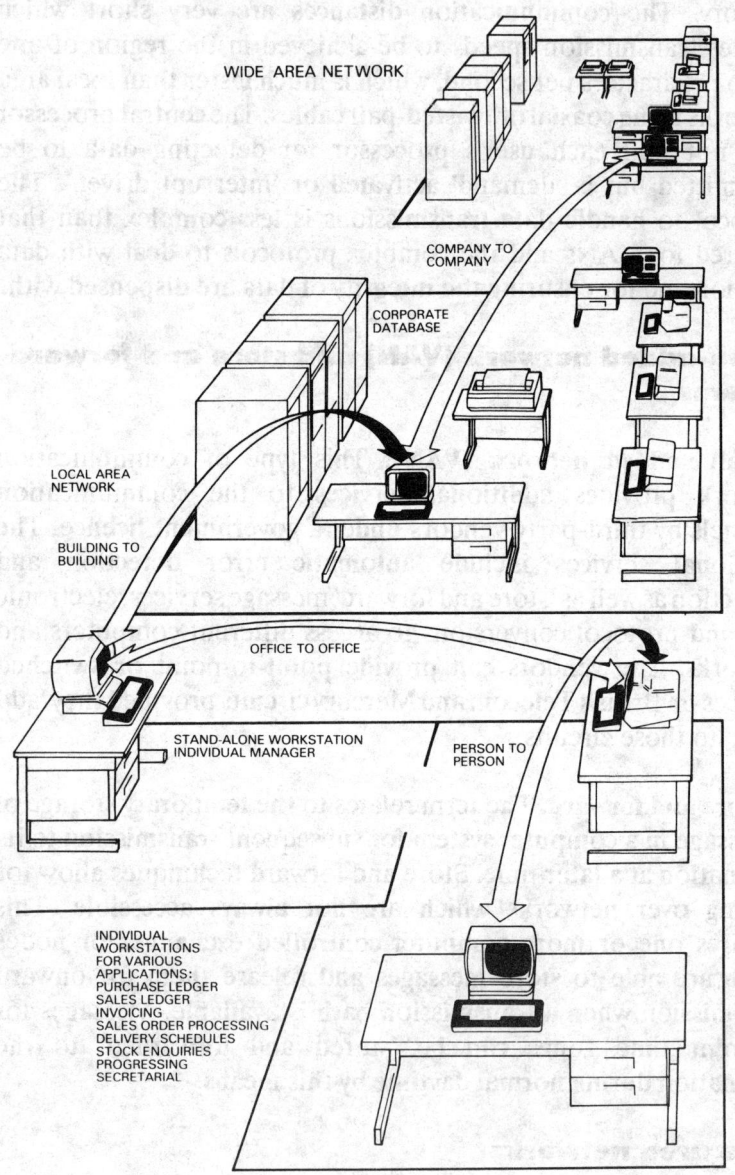

WIDE AREA NETWORK

COMPANY TO
COMPANY

CORPORATE
DATABASE

LOCAL AREA
NETWORK

BUILDING TO
BUILDING

OFFICE TO OFFICE

STAND-ALONE WORKSTATION
INDIVIDUAL MANAGER

PERSON TO
PERSON

INDIVIDUAL
WORKSTATIONS
FOR VARIOUS
APPLICATIONS:
PURCHASE LEDGER
SALES LEDGER
INVOICING
SALES ORDER PROCESSING
DELIVERY SCHEDULES
STOCK ENQUIRIES
PROGRESSING
SECRETARIAL

Figure 12.7 *Networks.*

communications, a wide area network serves a wide geographic area and may in fact embrace a whole country or even the world. A wide area network usually takes the form of a packet switching network. However, a system known as Integrated Services Digital Network (ISDN), a single network able to carry and switch a wide variety of telecommunications services, is expected to evolve from an integrated digital network (IDN), which is a telephone network in which digital transmission systems are fully integrated with digital switching systems. Such systems are likely to incorporate most of the Telecom services embracing speech and data transmission including electronic mail, facsimile document transmission (FAX), videotex such as Prestel, interactive videotex (on-line shopping), electronic funds transfer, inter-computer data transmission by packet switching and so on (see Fig. 12.7).

Progress test 12

1. State the nature and purpose of local area networks. **(1)**
2. What network facilities are required to enable networks to function? **(2)**
3. Distinguish between broadband and baseband networks. **(3)**
4. Define and distinguish between ring, star and bus networks. **(4–6)**
5. Describe the characteristics of close-coupled, value-added and store and forward networks. **(7–9)**
6. How does a wide area network differ from a local area network? **(10)**

Part three

Checks, controls, security and processing techniques

13

Checks, controls and privacy in computerised systems

Spectrum of control

1. Security measures. The extent to which security measures are applied depends on a number of factors, among which are:

(a) confidentiality of the data;
(b) the extent to which it may be subjected to unauthorised access;
(c) the possibility of system failure;
(d) the possibility of corrupting files;
(e) the possibility of a disc file being stolen;
(f) the nature of the system.

The term 'security' means ensuring that data is inaccessible to unauthorised personnel as opposed to ensuring the correctness of the data which is a matter of data validation. It also incorporates all file security measures relating to the 'dumping' of data from a master disc file to a magnetic tape file or another disc to safeguard against accidental erasure or corruption of the data or even theft of the master disc file. The security copy enables a file to be reconstructed by copying the data from the security disc or tape to the master disc (*see* **14–16**).

2. Security in on-line processing systems. Included in this category are such applications as: order processing, invoicing and sales ledger; purchase ledger, stock control and payroll, etc. To prevent unauthorised access to confidential files a password is provided to bona fide users of the applications. The password when input to the system is compared with that stored in the operational software. Access is barred if the password is incorrect. When entered, the password is not printed or displayed on the video screen for security reasons. Such applications usually have built-in enquiry programs to facilitate speedy information retrieval in response to queries. The data on the file is protected from being altered as amendments are not possible while the enquiry program is in use.

Passwords do not provide a foolproof method of obtaining the ultimate degree of security because operators are careless and leave them taped to their terminals, visible to all. It is also possible to obtain a password by trial and error as many operators use their initials, names of pop stars and other obvious words. Accordingly, the use of passwords should be allocated and controlled by a responsible official; they should also be changed frequently.

3. Databases. Some database systems are accessible by different application programs and are designed to prevent data being erased or altered accidentally by such programs. Alterations are only possible by the database software, i.e. the database management system (DBMS).

The ICL Viewdata system, for instance, has a number of built-in security measures. A user must enter a user name before access to information is possible. When information is confidential or of a restricted nature a password may be required. Access to some parts of the database can also be restricted to specified terminals. Each information owner must explicitly list those user names allowed to access his data. The list may include other information owners who can look at, but not amend, their part of the database.

Individual pages can also be restricted by giving them a list of user names. When a Bulletin user dials up the system and enters his user name the system checks this name against the parts of the database the user wishes to access. If the user name is on either the list of the information owner or the page list, access will be allowed.

4. Real-time systems. Real-time systems are designed to deal with dynamic situations in order to control a critical operation such as an airline seat reservation system which must be continually updated as events occur. Such systems accept random input at random time intervals and the status of files changes accordingly making it necessary to implement security measures. These take the form of dumping all relevant restart and audit information periodically, say every two to three minutes, to tape or disc. The dumped data can then be used to restart the system in the event of a malfunction.

Such operations are also provided with a second processor which is automatically switched into the real-time system in the event of the first machine ceasing to function for any reason.

5. Analysis of areas of control. If one views a large data processing department as a small business, which in effect it is, this will provide some indication of the range of checks and controls which need to be applied. A data processing department is a sub-system of a larger system which must be co-ordinated within the framework of corporate strategy and company policy. It can be seen then that even more checks and controls must be applied as the activities of a data processing department have a bearing on the efficiency and effectiveness of all, or nearly all, functions of a business.

The areas of control may be analysed very broadly within the following categories; they are purely arbitrary as they may be defined in different ways and referred to by different terms. If it is considered that a data processing department plays a major part in the operations of a business, the relevant checks and controls must be applied to maximise its performance however they may be defined. The categories are:

(a) organisational;
(b) administrative;
(c) environmental;
(d) technological;
(e) sociological;
(f) procedural and operational;
(g) development.

Types of control

6. Organisational controls. These may be summarised as follows.

(*a*) The data processing department in the larger organisation should function through a policy-formulating steering committee in order to ensure that only those projects are undertaken which will provide maximum benefit to the business as a corporate entity rather than merely maximising or optimising the performance of individual functions. This does not preclude the data processing manager gaining direct access to his immediate superior, the managing director for instance, as this is often essential during the course of day-to-day operations to resolve immediate problems.

(*b*) In addition to the remarks made in (*a*) above, the data processing manager should report to a higher authority than the functional level, as he himself is a functional manager. It is necessary for him to report to, and receive instructions from, a superior such as the managing director, so that overriding authority may be implemented in conflicting circumstances.

(*c*) The various activities of a data processing department should be organised to allow for the implementation of 'internal check' procedures to prevent collusion to perpetrate fraudulent conversion of data and master files regarding the transfer of funds to fictitious accounts, for instance. This course of action necessitates a separation of duties, as in the accounting function, but in this case instead of separating the cash handling from the cash recording it is necessary to separate systems development from systems operation. It also necessitates the independence of a data control section even though it is normally structured within the operations section under the control of the operations manager. The preparation of input should be shielded from the influence of operations staff as data must maintain the utmost integrity. There must also be independence of the computer file library, as in a large data processing complex chaos can occur if stringent controls are not applied to the movement of master files and program files. Strict control procedures are required to ensure 'purge' dates are adhered to, to avoid premature overwriting or prolonged storage.

7. Administrative controls.

(*a*) Access to data relating to business transactions should be restricted to functional and data preparation staff in the data processing department.

(*b*) Access to the computer room, if a centralised department, must be restricted to authorised personnel only.

(*c*) Master files and programs must be released from the library only on the presentation of an authorisation slip and they must not be allowed to leave the data processing department unless by special authority for processing at a bureau in the event of a systems breakdown.

(*d*) Internal check procedures must be implemented as indicated above (*see* **6**(*c*)).

(*e*) Adequate security measures must be incorporated to prevent fraudulent entry of data to perpetrate fraud by the use of passwords and Datakeys (*see* **2**, **3** and **35**).

(*f*) Projects must be controlled to ensure they are implemented to time schedules as far as is possible (*see* **38** and **39**).

(*g*) Projects must be formally approved by management prior to systems development, perhaps as a result of the deliberations of a steering committee.

(*h*) Budgeted levels of expenditure should be adhered to and controlled by means of a formal budgetary control system.

(*i*) Control of performance standards.

8. Environmental controls. Some computer installations require critically controlled conditions of temperature, power and humidity as well as the level of dust in the atmosphere. These factors must be continuously monitored to ensure trouble free operations. For example, dust in the atmosphere can corrupt magnetic files if it settles on the recording surfaces, and excessive heat can cause malfunctions in the hardware. This is not so critical as with the early mainframes but nevertheless must be controlled. Dust extracting mats and double doors as well as monitoring equipment achieve these requirements.

9. Technological controls. The controls to be applied in this area are mainly to ensure that the most suitable equipment is being used for all data processing activities. If an installation is still operating with punched card or paper tape input then it is certain that it is technologically obsolete and perhaps not so efficient as it could be using other methods of input, such as that achieved by the use of a keyboard or magnetic media such as magnetic discs (hard discs or floppies according to circumstances). Direct input methods requiring the use of workstations in the form of VDUs for order-entry systems may need to be installed to replace the older batch processing technique. Distributed processing using networks of minis or micros may be more suitable than the current centralised system using a second generation mainframe.

10. Sociological controls. With the continuing and expanding use of automation in the administrative environment it must not be overlooked that this, in effect, is a 'dehumanising' of tasks traditionally performed by people. We all know the consequence of this — redundancy. When developing computerised systems it is imperative that the 'human' aspect of operations is dealt with in the most humane way possible. People are not machines and need more than a little 'maintenance' to keep them motivated to their tasks. These tasks need restructuring in many instances as their former work is 'relegated' or 'farmed out' to a computer. This has the effect of 'deskilling' their work which can have a demoralising effect and needs careful control to avoid having staff with 'moronic' tendencies (*see* Chapter 1).

Procedural and operational controls

11. Summary of controls. The controls in this area embrace:

    (*a*) input controls;
    (*b*) hardware controls;
    (*c*) file security;
    (*d*) batch controls;
    (*e*) auditing and audit trails;
    (*f*) confidentiality of information;
    (*g*) software (program) checks;
       (*i*)   validation checks;
      (*ii*)   check digit verification.

12. Input controls. In batch processing applications in particular, source data is recorded on source documents by clerical staff and errors are often made. Such errors cannot be allowed to enter the computer system so it is necessary to correct obvious errors before releasing the documents to the batch control section of the data processing department (*see* **19**).

Checking would be concerned with detecting missing data fields or transposed digits. Assuming that data is to be recorded (encoded) on magnetic tape or disc to produce a transaction file, this will be done by an operator using a magnetic tape encoding machine or key-to-disc by means of a keying station. It will be necessary to verify the data in both instances and validate the data in the case of the key-to-disc system. In both instances it is advisable to utilise a different operator to avoid similar errors being made at both times, i.e. the initial recording and the verifying stages.

13. Hardware controls. Initially it is of paramount importance to ensure that all hardware is maintained regularly, perhaps by a maintenance contract, to ensure a minimum of down-time. It is necessary to 'check-out' the computer circuitry to ensure that all characters consist of the correct number of binary digits (bits) and this is accomplished during processing operations by parity checking. Check bits are automatically recorded on tape and disc during initial encoding and it is essential to detect data corrupted due to a parity failure otherwise the computer system will produce a high degree of error.

File security

14. Purpose of file security. The purpose of a file security system is to provide a basis for reconstituting master files containing important business information, as it is possible to overwrite or erase a file in error.

It is essential that file security precautions be incorporated in those electronic computer data processing systems which store master files on a magnetic medium, to safeguard against the consequences of loss of data, errors or corrupted data.

Without such precautions, it would be necessary to reprocess data, in the event of loss or corruption, from the last run when the file was known to be correct.

The reprocessing of data for a number of previous runs is very disruptive to the work scheduled for the computer, and consequently has an adverse effect on the productivity of the data

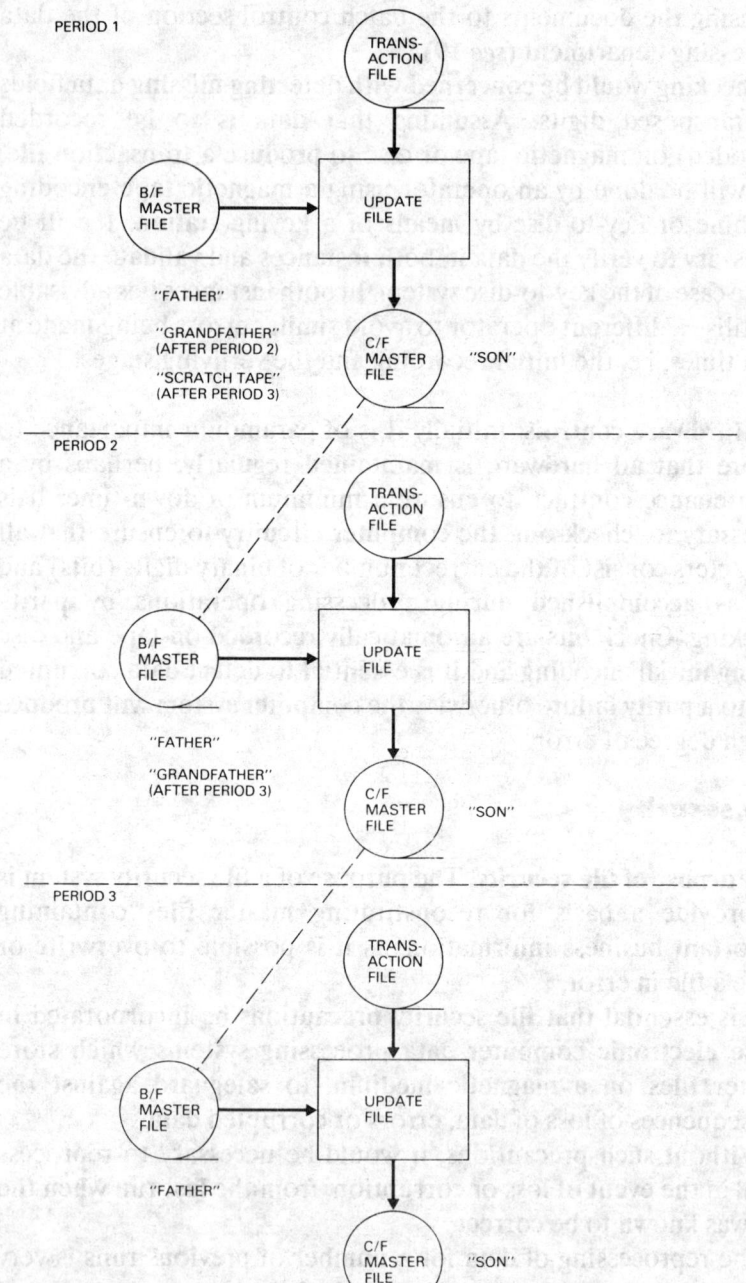

Figure 13.1 *Generation technique of file security.*

processing department. It is therefore imperative that the reprocessing of data is kept to a minimum.

15. The generation technique of file security. In respect of master files recorded on magnetic tape, the technique of file security applied is known as the 'generation' technique because files relating to two previous periods are retained transiently in addition to the current updated file and the current transaction file. The two previous period files plus the current file comprise three generations, which are referred to as Grandfather – Father – Son. The technique operates as follows.

(*a*) The first master file produced is referred to as the 'Son tape'.

(*b*) The 'Son tape' produced during the following updating run replaces the first 'Son tape', which becomes the 'Father tape'.

(*c*) The next updating run produces a new 'Son tape', the first 'Son tape' (at present the 'Father tape') becomes the 'Grandfather tape'. The previous 'Son tape' now becomes the new 'Father tape'.

(*d*) On the next updating run, the original 'Son tape' (now the 'Grandfather tape') is overwritten, and can in fact be used for producing the new 'Son tape' (*see* Fig. 13.1).

16. The dumping (copying) technique of file security. With regard to master files recorded on magnetic discs, the existing records are overwritten during updating, and consequently the previous records are destroyed.

File security in respect of disc files is often achieved by the technique of 'dumping', which involves copying the updated records from one disc to another disc or to magnetic tape. In the event of loss of data on one disc, the situation is resolved by using the records for further processing from the spare disc or the magnetic tape reel on which the records were 'dumped'.

The records are retained in this manner until the next dump is carried out and proved to be free of errors and corrupted data.

It is also possible to apply the 'generation' technique to disc files, by the retention of three generations of records either on one disc or on separate discs.

17. File safety and ensuring the confidentiality of information. The records retained for regeneration purposes are filed for safety away from the computer centre, in case of damage by fire, etc. Thus even if the files retained in the computer centre are damaged or destroyed the records will still be available in the remote filing location.

Other physical precautions which may be used to protect files from loss or damage include the following.

(a) Use of a write-permit ring to prevent overwriting of information on magnetic tape. When the ring is removed from the tape reel the file can only be read. When the ring is placed into position it depresses a plunger on the tape deck allowing the tape to be overwritten.

(b) Prevention of unauthorised access to computer room.

(c) Implementation of suitable security measures to prevent sabotage if this is a possibility. This may require security guards patrolling regularly and perhaps the installation of alarms connected to the local police station to signal a break-in.

(d) File labels encoded on the header label of magnetic files to indicate the date when the information may be overwritten. The 'purge' date validation programs are used for this.

The confidentiality of information is largely achieved by means of software and includes the following aspects.

(a) Particularly in time sharing systems it is normal practice for each authorised user to be provided with a password which is entered on the keyboard of the terminal and transmitted to the computer. The password is not printed or displayed on the terminal, however, so that it cannot be observed by anyone in the vicinity. The password allows access to specific files related to the user of the system.

(b) Information on a file may be stored in a 'scrambled' format which can be decoded only by providing the system with the decoding key to unscramble the information.

(c) Specific terminals may be prohibited from receiving transmitted information by lock-out procedures. In this way only designated terminals will actually receive file information.

Data Protection Act 1984

18. Data Protection Act 1984. With the wide use being made of electronic mail and databases the question of data privacy and integrity comes to the fore. This development has been recognised by the Data Protection Act 1984 which was approved by Parliament on 12 July 1984. The Act provides that all persons in control of personal data automatically processed on computers and all providers of bureau computer services to persons in control of such data should register with the Data Protection Registrar and comply with the data protection principles.

The data protection principles apply where data users hold personal data, and include the following.

(*a*) The information to be contained in personal data shall be obtained and processed fairly and lawfully.

(*b*) Personal data shall be held only for one or more specified and lawful purposes.

(*c*) Personal data held for any purpose or purposes shall not be used or disclosed in any manner incompatible with that purpose or those purposes.

(*d*) Personal data held for any purpose or purposes shall be adequate, relevant and not excessive in relation to that purpose or those purposes.

(*e*) Personal data shall be accurate and, where necessary, kept up to date.

(*f*) Personal data held for any purpose or purposes shall not be kept for longer than is necessary for that purpose or purposes.

(*g*) An individual shall be entitled at reasonable intervals and without undue delay or expense to be informed by any data user whether he holds personal data of which that individual is the subject; and to access any such data held by a data user and where appropriate, to have such data corrected or erased.

Where data users hold personal data or where relevant services are provided by persons carrying on computer bureaux, appropriate security measures shall be taken against unauthorised access to, or alteration, disclosure or destruction of, personal data and against accidental loss or destruction of personal data.

It is interesting to note that many installations are inadvertently in breach of the Data Protection Act. This is because the screens of PCs, terminals and workstations are in view of office staff in the immediate vicinity, allowing personal or confidential information displayed on the screen to be read by unauthorised personnel.

Batch control

19. General considerations of batch control. It is one thing to process data, quite another to know that all the necessary data required for processing has been received, processed, errors signalled and corrections made. In order to control the flow of data in and out of the data processing system, it is normal practice to incorporate a data control section in the data processing organisation.

The data control section receives all incoming data for processing from internal operating departments or outlying branches. The data may already be batched when received in readiness for data preparation operations, unless the data is already in a form suitable for direct input to the computer. Each batch of data has a batch control slip attached, on which is recorded batch number, department or branch number, document count (number of documents in the batch) and other control totals if relevant such as hash or meaningful totals.

Each batch is recorded in a register in the control section for maintaining a record of the data when the batch was received. The batches may be vetted for correctness and completeness of data in general terms and then sent to the data preparation section for encoding on magnetic media. Data is, of course, verified, to ensure the accuracy of data preparation operations before being sent for processing. After processing, the batches of documents and the printed output from the computer are sent to the data control section, where they are entered in the register as a record that all batches have been processed or otherwise. It is then necessary to check for errors discovered during processing, as outlined below.

20. Errors correction routine. When the printed documents from the computer are received by the control section, they are checked for errors, signalled by an error diagnostic code or alternatively a separate error list is printed.

One of the first tasks undertaken by the control section is to compare the control totals with those generated by the computer, as it is possible that documents may have been overlooked during data preparation and not presented for processing and it is therefore essential that the fugitive documents are identified, traced and presented for processing.

After errors have been identified, it is necessary to extract the appropriate input document from the batch for correction. Corrected errors are then re-assembled in a batch with a batch control slip attached for re-processing. The new batch number is recorded on the print-out for cross-reference and control. The control of corrections is carried out in a similar manner to the control of original data.

Auditing computerised business systems

21. The approach. The work of both internal and external auditors is affected by the introduction of an electronic computer. While they need not be computer experts, they should be familiar with the mode of computer input, processing and output in order that they may conduct test checks with understanding. Auditors should also be familiar with computer programming so that they may recommend adequate controls to be built into the programs when they are being prepared. It is difficult and costly to amend programs once they have been completed, especially as they take a great deal of time to prepare initially.

An earlier approach was known as the 'Black Box' technique; the auditor extracted a sample of records and had them calculated manually. The results were then compared with the output from the computer and if there were no differences it was assumed that everything was satisfactory. In this respect, the 'Black Box' was the computer and in order to audit records it was not necessary for the auditor to know anything about how the computer processed the data or about the programming techniques.

The auditor may, however, assume wider duties in the present electronic data processing era. He must as before observe the principles of *internal check*, the separation of functions to prevent collusion and fraudulent intent. This includes the separation of data origination, control of input by means of 'batch totals', data preparation and processing, systems and programming.

Auditors should be consulted in an advisory capacity by system designers to establish the checks and controls which should be incorporated in the various applications under consideration. Systems should be designed so that they are self-checking and self-correcting whenever possible. Auditors need to ensure that incorrect, i.e. invalid, data is rejected by the system before being subjected to processing operations. This is accomplished by inbuilt data validation checks such as range and limit checks; checks to ensure data is complete, of the correct type and for the correct period, etc.

22. System documentation. Systems documentation produced by the systems designer should pass through the audit department as a matter of routine so that auditors have the opportunity to assess the effectiveness of their recommendations and see that important checks and controls are incorporated and not overlooked. The documentation normally includes: the detailed description of the system (the system definition); decision tables which outline the conditions to be tested for and action to be taken; the flowcharts of the system structure and program flowcharts outlining the processing stages; a print-out of the program coding, error-handling routines and test data to be used, etc.

The staffing of the system should also incorporate the principles of *internal check* whereby duties are separated so that collusion would be necessary to implement fraudulent practices such as collaboration between computer programmers and operators; data recording personnel and data conversion operators, etc.

23. Design philosophy. Auditors should determine the suitability of the design philosophy behind the processing tasks to be undertaken. This requires an assessment of the relative merits and demerits of batch processing versus on-line processing; centralised versus distributed processing and whether a database would best suit the needs of prospective systems integration projects rather than separate functional files.

24. System testing. It is essential for auditors to satisfy themselves that systems are suitable for their purpose and that they are achieving the objectives laid down in the systems specification. This is largely determined by running programs with test data representative of that to be actually processed. The results obtained are compared with pre-calculated values. Any differences are noted and form the basis for program modifications or even major restructuring of the system.

Trials should be incorporated to assess the accuracy with which transaction data is recorded on source documents prior to data conversion for input to the computer. Errors should be analysed to establish their nature and their cause. The effectiveness of the built-in validation checks is tested in this way.

25. Live operation. During the live operation of a project the role of an auditor is to ensure that the inputs are reconciled for both document number counts and values with predetermined control totals. This is for the purpose of assessing whether all the transactions are accounted for.

26. Audit trail. An audit trail is provided by means of a print-out listing all the transactions processed during the run or period. In a sales ledger application this would include a list of all invoices, credit notes, remittances and journal adjustments. Details of VAT charges would also be listed. Some accounting packages facilitate the work of an auditor by printing out a system checklist indicating balances on the sales ledger and the corresponding balance in the debtor control account in the nominal ledger. The print-out may also specify the number of the last invoice, credit note and similar details relating to the payroll and purchase ledger. Copies of source documents can also be stored for future reference.

27. Audit packages. Audit packages allow selected records to be printed from master files so that they can be subjected to further scrutiny to determine if all transaction details affecting the record are shown. By this means it is also possible to examine control parameters to ensure they accord with current needs. This applies to stock control levels in a stock control system and credit limits in a sales ledger system.

28. Data validation/error reports. Error reports containing details of invalid transactions are generated by data validation routines built into programs at strategic points. Many validation routines are included in the initial program to avoid processing errors in subsequent processing stages. Details of transactions may also be tested by applying spot checks taking random samples.

29. General aspects of system auditing. The optimum time for auditors to review the checks and controls incorporated in a computer/clerical system for the first time is immediately after the system specification has been completed. It is then possible to remedy any shortcomings or omissions before the system is implemented.

Other factors to consider are: preventing unauthorised access to the computer room and to information stored in files; assessing the adequacy of program amendment procedures and back-up arrangements in case of system failure; effectiveness of interfaces to other installations or in local area network activities; checking that computations have been correctly calculated on the basis of defined formulae; adequacy of audit trails and so on.

Software (program) checks — validation

30. Data validation. The objective of a data validation system is to detect errors at the earliest possible stage, before costly activities are performed on invalid data. It is therefore essential to ensure that source data is correctly recorded initially before data preparation takes place. Similarly, it is important to check the accuracy of data preparation operations before data is processed, and this is achieved by verification procedures.

When data is input for processing, it is subjected to a vetting procedure by means of an edit program which allows valid data to be written to the medium to be used in subsequent processing — magnetic tape or disc (*see* Fig. 13.2).

Invalid data either may be written to another magnetic tape, or may be printed out on the line-printer as a special report, or errors may be indicated on the main report. The choice of method depends upon individual circumstances, and the manner in which the system is designed.

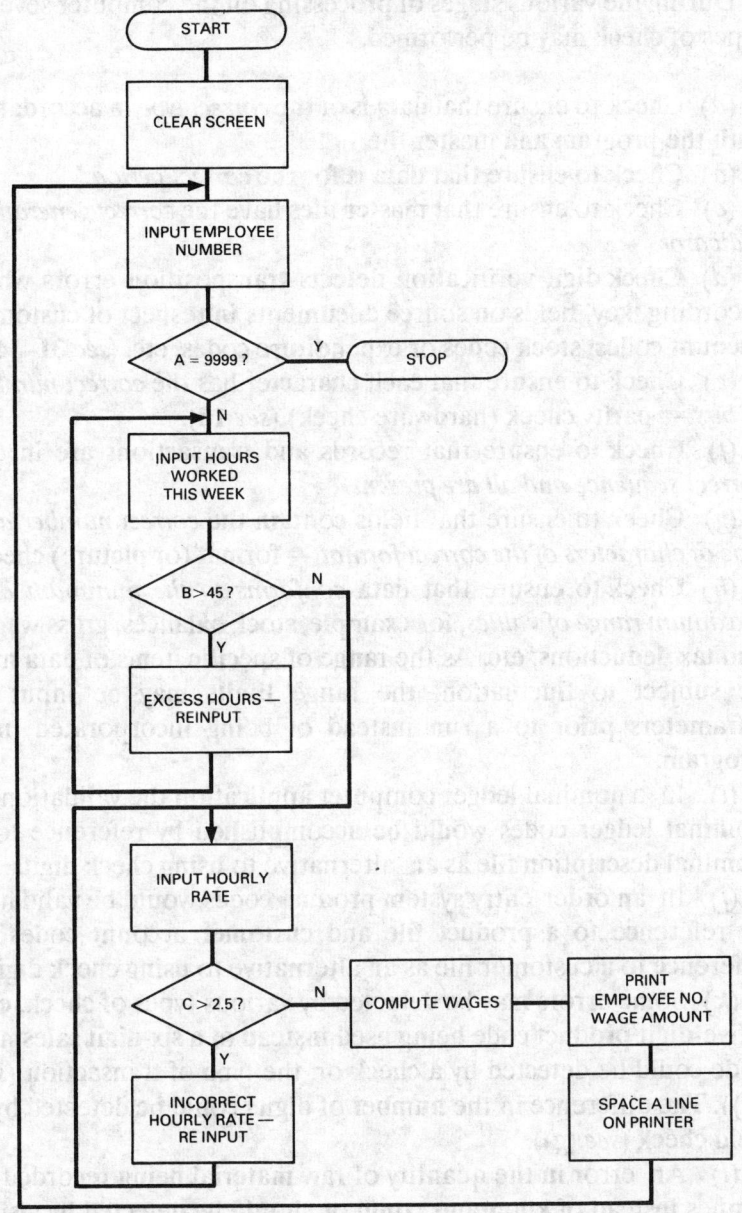

Figure 13.2 *Flowchart interactive processing: payroll application — validation checks.*

During the various stages of processing on the computer several types of check may be performed.

(*a*)   Check to ensure that data is of the *correct type* in accordance with the program and master file.

(*b*)   Check to ensure that data is for the *correct period.*

(*c*)   Check to ensure that master files have the *correct generation indicator.*

(*d*)   Check digit verification detects transposition errors when recording 'key' fields on source documents in respect of customer account codes, stock codes or expenditure codes, etc. (*see* 31–34).

(*e*)   Check to ensure that each character has the *correct number of bits* — parity check (hardware check) (*see* 13).

(*f*)   Check to ensure that records and transactions are in the *correct sequence and all are present.*

(*g*)   Check to ensure that fields contain the *correct number and type of characters of the correct format* — format (or picture) check.

(*h*)   Check to ensure that data *conforms to the minimum and maximum range of values,* for example, stock balances, gross wages and tax deductions, etc. As the range of specific items of data may be subject to fluctuation, the range limits may be input as parameters prior to a run instead of being incorporated in a program.

(*i*)   In a nominal ledger computer application the validation of nominal ledger codes would be accomplished by reference to a nominal description file as an alternative to using check digits.

(*j*)   In an order-entry system product codes would be validated by reference to a product file and customer account codes by reference to a customer file as an alternative to using check digits.

(*k*)   Some errors may be detected by various types of check, e.g. a five-digit product code being used instead of a six-digit salesman code could be detected by a check on the type of transaction (*see* (*a*)). The difference in the number of digits could be detected by a field check (*see* (*g*)).

(*l*)   An error in the quantity of raw material being recorded in tonnes instead of kilograms could or should be detected by visual inspection rather than a computer validation program. The unit of weight is normally pre-recorded on transaction data and weight designations are predefined in the program.

(*m*) Compatibility checks are used to ensure that two or more data items are compatible with other data items. For instance, discounts to customers may be calculated on the basis of order quantity but a discount may apply only if a customer's account balance is below a stated amount.

(*n*) Probability checks are used to avoid unnecessary rejection of data as data can on occasions exceed normal values in a range of purely random causes. If this arises with an acceptable frequency (probability) at a defined level of confidence (normally 95 per cent), then the data need not be rejected. This would tend to reduce the level of rejections and the time expended on investigating causes of divergences.

(*o*) Check to ensure 'hash' and other control totals agree with those generated by the computer.

Check digit verification

31. Transposed digits. It is important to appreciate that the accuracy of output from data processing can be only as accurate as the input from which it is produced. Errors often occur in the initial recording and transcription of numerical data, such as stock numbers and account codes, frequently through transposition.

Check digit verification is a technique designed to test the accuracy (validity) of such numerical data before acceptance for processing. The data vet program performs check digit verification as part of the editing routine. Data is rejected as invalid when the check digit is any number other than the correct one. The data must then be re-encoded and represented for processing.

32. Check digit and modulus. A check digit is a number which is added to a series of numbers (in the form of a code number for stock or customer identification) for the purpose of producing a 'self-checking' number. Each check digit is derived mathematically, and bears a unique mathematical relationship to the number to which it is attached. The check digit is normally added in the low-order position.

Before indicating the way in which a check digit is calculated, it is necessary to understand what is meant by a 'modulus'. A modulus is the figure used to divide the number for which a check digit is required. Moduli in common use are 7, 10, 11 and 13.

33. Check digit calculation.

(a) Assume modulus 11 is selected for the purpose of calculating a check digit.

(b) Assume the number for which a check digit is required is 2323.

(c) Divide 2323 by 11 and note the remainder. Remainder is 2.

(d) Obtain the complement of the remainder and use as the check digit: $11 - 2 = 9$ (Complement = check digit).

(e) The number including its check digit now becomes 23239.

34. Calculation of a check digit using weights. A weight is the value allocated to each digit of a number according to a specified pattern, to prevent acceptance of interchanged digits. A more refined method of obtaining a check digit is achieved by the use of weights.

(a) Assume the same number and modulus as in the above example, i.e. 2323 and 11 respectively.

(b) The selected series of weights are 5, 4, 3, 2.

(c) Multiply each digit of the number by its corresponding weight as follows:

		Weight	Product
Units digit	3	2	6
Tens digit	2	3	6
Hundreds digit	3	4	12
Thousands digit	2	5	10
		Sum of products	34

(d) Divide sum of products by modulus 11 and note the remainder. Remainder is 1.

(e) Obtain the complement of the remainder and use this as the check digit: $11 - 1 = 10$ (assigned the letter x).

(f) The number including its check digit is 2323x.

A check may be applied to confirm that 10 or x is valid as follows:

Sum of the products	34
Add calculated check	<u>10</u>
	<u><u>44</u></u>

Divide by modulus 11 and note any remainder.
As there is no remainder, the check digit is valid.

Datakey and Smartcard

35. Datakey. A Datakey is an electronic memory circuit (EAROM) embedded in plastic and moulded to the shape of a key. It is a personal, portable information device which utilises alterable semiconductor memory. It is reusable and has an unlimited read/write life span.

Another device called a Keyceptacle Peripheral Subsystem is the interface between a Datakey and a higher level host system. It acts as the electronic liaison for the Datakey. The Keyceptacle access component incorporates the contact and routing circuitry which provides the physical exchange between the Datakey and the Keytroller electronic module. The Keytroller incorporates the intelligence for interchange between the Datakey and the host system. It consists of an encapsulated microcomputer with serial input/output communications. The firmware is the heart of the Keytroller (*see* Fig. 13.3).

36. An access controller interfaced with a user's equipment enables a Datakey to serve as a restrictive data filter assimilating and distributing information on an authorised basis. The Datakey can simultaneously record these transactions, which effectively provides an additional method of monitoring a data security system.

Selective access can also be applied for personnel to gain access to buildings and data files, credit/debit systems as well as other applications. When personnel or customers are provided with a programmed Datakey, a perpetual, updatable record can be maintained for practically any information gathering purpose in a user's system.

As can be seen Datakey is a product that has an almost endless list of uses for applications including data capture, security system control, data input and data retrieval. Applications already using Datakey include shop floor data capture (where operator identity is an important factor); computer terminal security; software protection; physical access control systems; operator identity in photocopier systems; pre-payment in vending systems, as well as other applications in hotel accounting terminals and automatic test equipment.

Figure 13.3 *(a) Datakey and Keytroller; (b) Close-up of Datakey (courtesy Data Card (UK) Limited).*

In these particular applications the Datakey is used for a variety of purposes. In certain instances for a particular operation but in others carrying out a number of functions, e.g. identifying the operator to the host system, enabling specific accounts to be debited with the charge for the service, protecting the host system from unauthorised use and enabling any revised information to be written back to the Datakey.

37. Smartcard. A Smartcard may be defined as a credit card with an inbuilt microprocessor and memory. It offers more security than the normal credit card which has a magnetic strip on the reverse side. The microprocessor allows the card to be used for financial transactions and can store a bank balance. A Smartcard can also be used as a means of identification. The card is read when inserted into a reading device which transfers the details stored to a computer.

Systems development controls

Before developing computerised systems it is necessary, particularly in the larger installation, to obtain the relevant authority from the board of directors, which may be based on recommendations of the data processing steering committee. The committee provides guidance to management on the basis of the results obtained from the conduct of a feasibility study, which indicates the points for and against a specific course of action. These factors guide management in making decisions to pursue one course of action as opposed to another. Important factors which need to be subjected to some form of control or monitoring include those listed below.

38. Important factors to be controlled. The list which follows is meant to convey the important factors as a guideline for effective control of computerised projects, rather than being a complete list of all factors.

(*a*) Periodic reviews need to be undertaken to ensure that projects conform to laid down time schedules as far as is possible and that resources are not used excessively.

(*b*) It is necessary to assess the problems encountered during the course of investigations or design stages which were unforeseen during the preliminary survey.

(*c*) The highest degree of co-ordination must be sought between 'user' department staff and systems development staff to ensure a workable system is subsequently implemented.

(*d*) Design philosophy must be discussed before procuring expensive hardware and software. It is a matter of deciding the nature of processing facilities to suit the requirements of the system. Similarly, it is pointless designing a real-time system which requires expensive hardware and systems support when all that is necessary is more frequent reporting cycles. This may apply to stock management situations. Of course, it is possible to implement on-line systems using terminals for direct entry of data, such as customer order details, without going to the extreme of making it a real-time system as on-line entry can be supported by effective batch processing systems at lower cost.

(*e*) Systems documentation must be prepared and maintained during the course of developing systems, to ensure it readily portrays the status of the system at any time. This is essential for continuity of development projects, as staff may leave and be replaced by personnel unaccustomed with the stage the system had reached and with the details of the system generally. Documentation should be developed on the basis of data processing and programming standards.

(*f*) Systems must be implemented with a minimum of disruption to current operations. Parallel running must continue until the computerised system proves to be adequate for its defined purpose and is seen to be attaining projected levels of performance.

(*g*) Access to databases must be controlled by the use of passwords so that only authorised personnel can gain access to the system or to specific files.

(*h*) Effective fail-safe procedures must be implemented in the case of lengthy processing tasks or important operations such as the real-time control of a major or critical operation, e.g. airline seat reservation systems and stock management systems.

(*i*)   Accounting records must be checked after being converted to magnetic file media to ensure that they contain correct information.

39. Critical path method for project control. (*See* 17: **19–22.**)

Data processing standards and documentation

40. Purpose and objectives. The purpose and objectives of standards are for guiding staff in the general rules, conventions and code of practice relating to the development of systems. The project control system will be structured to be compatible with the various stages of development, thereby providing a standard way of controlling all projects on the basis of a standardised schedule which should enable the highest possible level of project productivity to be achieved.

41. System and program documentation. System and program documentation standards outline the way in which systems should be structured and the manner in which they should be documented. This factor relates to the method employed and the style adopted for the construction of procedure charts, system flowcharts, data flow diagrams, data structure charts, system structure charts, decision tables and run charts. Standards also embrace programming methodology in respect of the use of standard coding sheets and the application of structured or modular techniques of program design.

42. Design of system inputs, files and output. Documentation standards specify the way in which systems documentation should be constructed. They contain details and specifications relating to computer input, i.e. source documents and screen displays; the design of output from the computer either as a screen display or a printed report; and the structure of master files. The primary purpose of such standards is to adopt a uniform, effective method of documentation which enables systems to be designed in the most efficient way.

43. System continuity. The application of system and program documentation standards assists in attaining system continuity as it eliminates being dependent on system details which exist only in the mind of a system designer. It is imperative that all details of the current system and the proposed system should be committed to paper in its various forms, i.e. document layouts and specifications, as well as diagrammatically in the form of flowcharts, etc. This achieves continuity in the development of systems, which is of extreme importance as it avoids disruption to the smooth development of a project.

44. Operations standards. The implementation of operations standards requires the compilation of a standards manual. Reference to the manual on points of procedure by operations personnel will ensure the adherence to laid-down standards. The standards should typically encompass details relating to the flow of work in respect of: handling procedures; batches of source documents when received from the user departments in respect of batch control and data conversion; security measures to be applied to the files after updating; work scheduling activities; archiving procedures; purging procedures in respect of retained files for security purposes; error control routines; output distribution routines and so on.

45. Performance standards. Performance in a data processing environment is essential and performance standards are required and should be implemented for the control of output in order to ensure scheduled completion times; input schedules should be prepared for controlling input to the system to ensure it is received on time. This will prevent delays and the build-up of work affecting other jobs in the queue. The cost of operations should be controlled to ensure operations are performed economically. This may be accomplished by the implementation of cost standards or budgets. Run timings should enable the time spent on different jobs to be effectively controlled and provide the means of compiling job schedules.

46. Standards officer. The implementation of and effective adherence to standards should be under the control of a standards officer. The duties and responsibilities of such a person include advising management and staff, both in the data processing department and user departments as relevant to their activities in the data processing environment in the use of the various standards. The results attained and methodologies practised should be monitored to ensure they accord with the relevant standards. Staff suggestions for modifying established standards should be implemented if they provide the means of improving results and working practices. All modifications to existing standards and the application of new standards should be promulgated in a standards manual to ensure all details are fully up to date. The meaning and underlying philosophy of standards should be discussed with appropriate personnel.

47. Communication and co-ordination. The major benefit of standardisation relating to systems methodology and documentation is the provision of a medium for discussion. Discussions of system details are improved between designers and users, designers and programmers and designers and management. Such discussions enable misconceptions to be removed and system features to be more fully understood. When personnel from the different functions affected by systems development are able to communicate, many of the inherent problems are more easily dealt with. It is always good practice to compile a 'glossary of system terminology', which aids understanding of the language of system designers and terms used during discussions. The National Computing Centre has developed a comprehensive set of standards embracing systems documentation, programming and operating.

Progress test 13

1. The extent to which security measures are applied depends upon a number of factors. Discuss.   (1–4)

2. Indicate the main areas of control in a data processing environment.   (5)

3. Specify the nature of organisational controls relevant to the data processing function.   (6)

4. Specify the nature of administrative controls relevant to the data processing function.   (7)

5. Outline the features of environmental and technological controls which should be incorporated into the data processing activity.   (8, 9)

6. State the sociological factors which should be considered when developing computerised systems.   (10)

7. (a) Describe the sequence of checks (human, hardware and software) involved in producing an accurate transaction file on magnetic tape from source data. (b) Describe what is meant by a check digit and illustrate how a modulus 11 check digit is calculated. (12, 13, 30–34)

8. Specify the nature and purpose of input and hardware controls. (12, 13)

9. What precautions would you adopt to ensure the security and confidentiality of master files?   (14–17)

10. Outline the main provisions of the Data Protection Act. (18)

11. Describe in detail the checks and controls that can be applied to input data before it is used to update a master file. Assume a batch processing system.   (19, 20, 30–34)

12. What is an audit trail and why is it necessary?   (26, 27)

13. List the typical checks applied to input data to ensure its integrity.   (30–34)

14. Specify the nature of check digit verification   (31–34)

15. Define the nature and purpose of Datakey and Smartcard. (35–37)

16. What are the important factors to be controlled when developing computer-based systems?   (38, 39)

17. Describe briefly the role of critical path analysis in project control.   (39)

18. Outline the nature and purpose of data processing standards. (40–47)

14
Processing techniques and configuration requirements

Batch processing

1. Entry of data. Batch processing handles batches of transactions automatically through a sequence of processing runs at predefined frequencies. Processing frequency is inherent in some applications — a weekly factory payroll is naturally processed weekly. What of invoices? The frequency will depend on the volume of invoices to be produced: large volumes may need processing daily to keep down the backlog; weekly processing may well be suitable for smaller volumes.

Each batch is identified by a batch number which is recorded on a *batch control slip*. The slip also contains control information, including the number of items in the batch and any other control totals such as a hash total made up of transaction references. These controls enable missing items to be located, since the control total generated by the computer will disagree with that on the control slip. All transactions are processed together as a batch through each separate stage of processing (known as a 'run'), which are usually validate, sort, compute, update and output (*see* Figs. 14.1 and 14.2). This mode of processing distinguishes it from on-line processing (*see* **6**).

2. Processing characteristics. Batch processing is an economical method for processing large volumes of routine data relating to various business applications, including stock control, general ledger, order processing, invoicing and payroll. After data has been processed the master files relevant to the various applications are

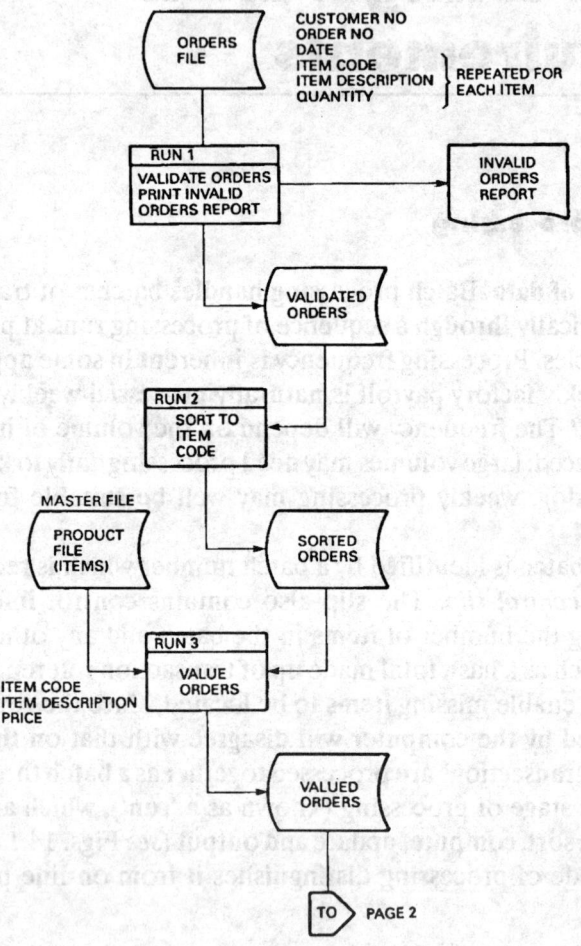

Figure 14.1 *Batch processing flowchart illustrating the preparation of invoices and updating the customer file.*

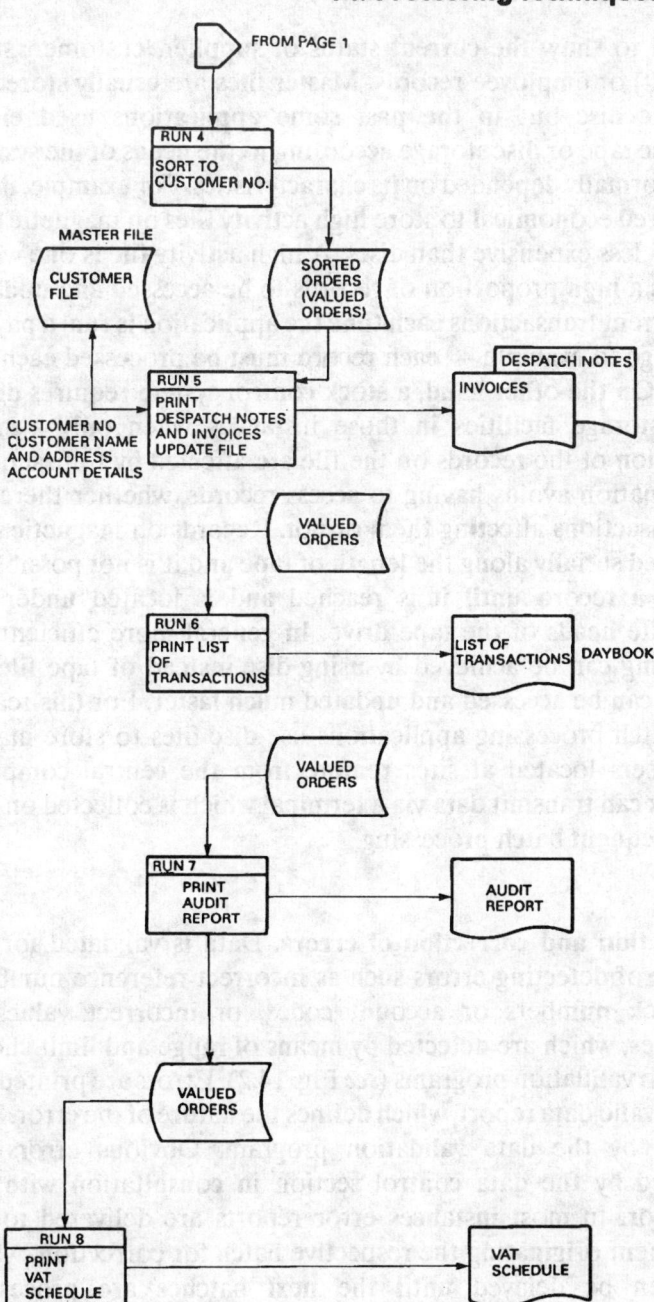

Figure 14.1 *(contd.)*

updated to show the current status of supplier, customer, stock (product) or employee records. Master files are usually stored on magnetic disc but in the past some applications used either magnetic tape or disc storage according to the needs of the system, which normally depended on its characteristics. For example, it was considered economical to store high activity files on magnetic tape as it was less expensive than discs. A high activity file is one which requires a high proportion of records to be accessed and updated with current transactions each time the application is run: a payroll file is a good example — each record must be processed each pay period. On the other hand, a stock control system requires direct access storage facilities in those instances when only a small proportion of the records on the file are affected by transactions. This situation avoids having to access records, whether there are any transactions affecting them or not. Records on magnetic tape are stored serially along the length of tape and it is not possible to process a record until it is reached and is located under the read/write heads of the tape drive. In general more efficient file processing can be achieved by using disc instead of tape files as records can be accessed and updated much faster. For this reason most batch processing applications use disc files to store master files. Users located at sites remote from the central computer complex can transmit data via a terminal which is collected on disc for subsequent batch processing.

3. Detection and correction of errors. Data is validated for the purpose of detecting errors such as incorrect reference numbers, e.g. stock numbers or account codes, or incorrect values or quantities, which are detected by means of range and limit checks built into validation programs (*see* Fig. 14.2). Errors are printed out on an invalid data report, which defines the nature of the error. This is done by the data validation program. Obvious errors are corrected by the data control section in consultation with the originator. In most instances error reports are delivered to the department originating the respective batch for correction, which will then be delayed until the next batches are processed. Amendments will then need to be made to batch control totals. Subsequently corrections must be encoded and fed into the system and processed through the system as new transaction data (*see* Fig. 14.2). An error report might appear as follows:

Invalid items report: Stock records

Stock item details
Batch number 6
Date 25/01/91

Item code	Description	Quantity	Error type
2235	NOTS	50	Incorrect description
2243	WASHERS	2000	Range error
245	FLANGES	40	Incorrect item code
	BUTTERFLY NUTS	20	Missing item code
2267	HANDLE		Missing quantity
2234	BOLTS	30	Missmatch code and desc
2285	SCREWS	BBB	Quantity not numeric

As can be seen from the report, most of the errors are self-explanatory. The first item — incorrect description — should read NUTS not NOTS. The second item indicates a range error detected by a range check: the maximum permissible quantity is perhaps 1,000. The third item has the first digit missing from the item code; the fourth has the item code omitted, the fifth a missing quantity and the sixth item is invalid because of a missmatch between item code and the description. The last item has alphabetic instead of numeric characters in the quantity field.

4. Back-up facilities. Back-up facilities (file security) for master files are normally achieved by making a copy of the file either to another disc or to a tape streamer — a device, usually used on minicomputers, which allows high speed copying of files while avoiding the use of expensive hard discs. Back-up facilities for transactions can be achieved by retaining the original file and/or making a copy of the file, which may be supported by producing printed records of the transactions.

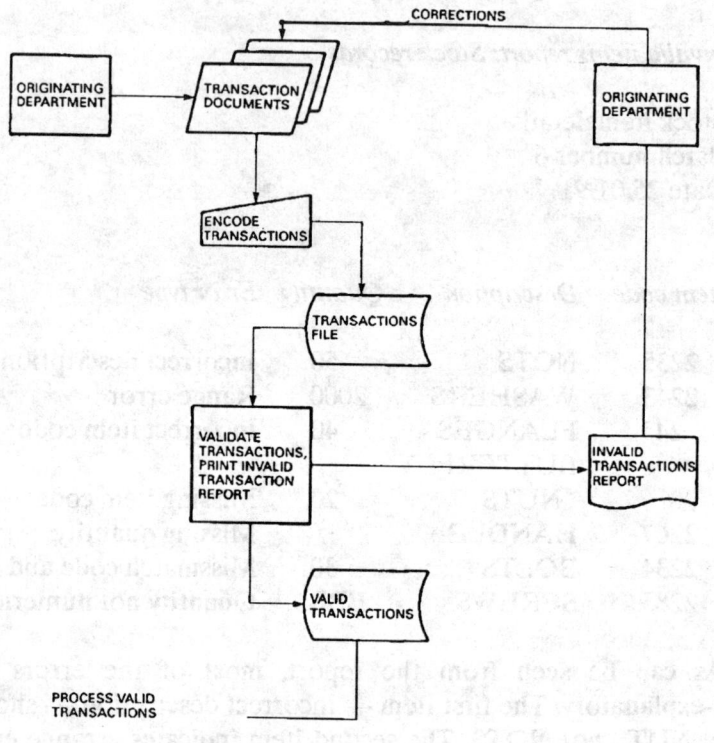

Figure 14.2 *Batch processing flowchart illustrating data validation routine.*

5. Configuration. A fairly powerful mainframe or minicomputer is required with a large internal memory capacity capable of controlling terminal operations with multi-tasking and multi-user capabilities. The specific input devices used relate to the nature of the business, as previously discussed, but for general requirements details of transactions can be collected by a key-to-disc system which produces a transaction file from which data is input for processing. In other instances data may be transmitted by terminal from remote locations and collected on a disc which stores the transactions for subsequent processing in batches. (This is known as *remote job entry* (RJE).) As this requires a communication link over telephone lines, a modem (*see* 11: 2) will be required. Discs will also be used for the storage of application software and master files. thus necessitating several disc drives and disc controllers. A minicomputer will use fixed hard discs known as Winchesters; a mainframe will use either exchangeable or fixed discs. Exchangeable discs can be removed from the disc drive and replaced with others containing the required application software or files. Fixed discs are an integral component of the disc drive and cannot be removed. Between two and four drives will be required for a small mainframe configuration, but many more for a large system serving the needs of many operating units. The most used output device is a high speed printer for hard copy, but a graph plotter may be used to present data graphically or output can be by means of microfilm or microfiche (COM). In addition, an operator console is required — normally a visual display unit (VDU).

On-line processing

6. Characteristics. An on-line system consists of terminal(s) connected to and controlled by the computer. Communication lines connect the various departments of a business directly to a computer for specific purposes dependent on the nature of the functions performed (*see* Figs. 11.2 and 14.3). It is important to appreciate that an on-line system need not be a real-time system but a real-time system must be an on-line system. This will be discussed further when dealing with real-time systems.

7. Applications. On-line systems may be used for:

(*a*) *Interactive processing* (transaction processing):
  (*i*)   on-line order processing;
  (*ii*) on-line building society transactions;
  (*iii*) on-line payroll processing;
  (*iv*) on-line point of sale (supermarket) check-out systems.
(*b*) *Real-time processing*:
  (*i*)   airline seat reservation system;
  (*ii*) on-line warehouse stock control;
  (*iii*) on-line hotel accommodation system;
  (*iv*) on-line banking.

(c) *Random enquiries*:
  (i) on-line credit enquiries;
  (ii) on-line product availability enquiries;
  (iii) on-line account enquiries;
  (iv) on-line package holiday availability enquiries.

Interactive processing

8. Processing characteristics. Interactive processing handles transactions individually in what is referred to as *conversational mode* processing, unlike batch processing which deals with them in batches. The software prompts the user, indicating the needs of the application, which may specify the data required for processing, ask if it is a debit or a credit or if there are any more transactions for the item currently being processed, to which the user responds interactively. The system may then ask if there are any more transactions and the user responds accordingly. At the end of the posting run back-up copies of master files are produced for security purposes (*see* below). Interactive processing can be done on a stand-alone basis by a single user or on a multi-user basis, which allows each user to enter and process data according to his or her specific needs (*see* **15–19**). This type of processing technique receives and processes data at random time intervals. If transactions are dealt with as events occur and the files are updated with the details immediately, it is a real-time system (*see* **11–14**). Transactions need not be processed as they occur; for example, despatches to customers can be input the following day for the production of invoices. Transactions are still dealt with on an individual basis, however, and this is the key factor distinguishing this type of processing from batch processing (*see* Fig. 14.3).

9. Back-up facilities. Prompts from the software inform the user when to load discs for obtaining a back-up copy of a master file at the end of the posting routine. As most transactions are recorded on a source document the retention of the documents provides a back-up file which may be used for reconstituting the master file in the event of its corruption or loss. For audit control and back-up requirements the transactions currently dealt with may be printed out to provide the details necessary for security purposes.

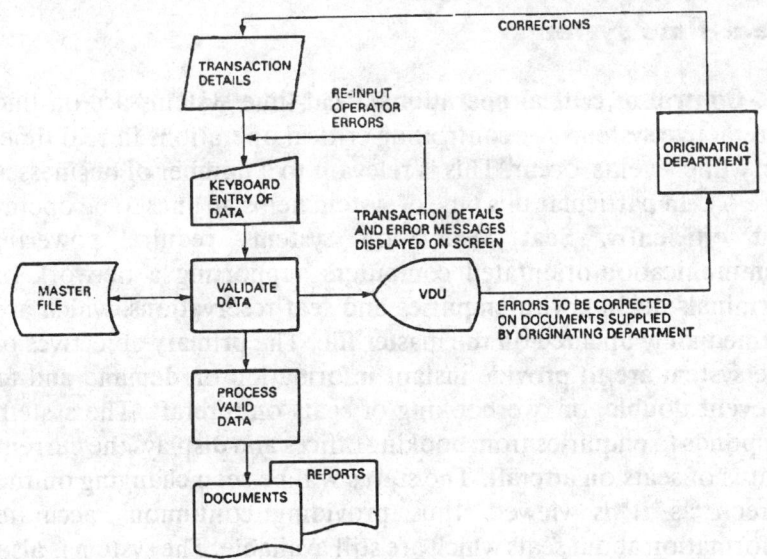

Figure 14.3 *On-line processing facilities.*

10. Configuration. Interactive processing may be carried out either on a stand-alone basis using a single PC or by a multi-user system. In both situations data will be input by keyboard. Data communication equipment will be required if the interactive system has geographically dispersed terminals. (*See* Chapter 11.) The type and size of processor required will depend on whether a stand-alone PC or multi-user system is used. In the latter instance a mainframe or mini with a large internal memory capable of handling the relevant number of terminals would be required. Backing storage for a PC may be a combination of a 3.5–inch floppy disc storing approximately 720 kbytes and a Winchester of 20–Mbyte capacity. The mainframe or mini would be supported by a number of Winchester disc units of, for example, 1 GB (gigabyte). Disc controllers would also be required. The PC will be equipped with a dot matrix or daisy wheel printer. Each location on a multi-user system may require local printers for printing documents and schedules. In addition, a high speed printer would be required at the mainframe or minicomputer installation to produce documents and reports from batch processing applications. (*See* **15–19** for further details.)

Real-time systems

11. Control of critical operations. Real-time systems are on-line interactive systems for controlling critical operations in real time, i.e. while events occur. This is relevant to a number of businesses (*see* 7). In particular this type of system helps airlines to be operated efficiently. Seat reservation systems require powerful communication-orientated computers supporting a network of terminals dealing with enquiries and seat reservations, which are immediately updated on the master file. The primary objectives of the system are to provide instant information on demand and to prevent double, or overbooking of seats on aircraft. The system responds to enquiries from booking offices and displays the current status of seats on aircraft. The status will be seen changing on the screen as it is viewed, thus providing continuous accurate information about seats which are still available. The system is also used for planning fuel and other provisioning requirements for each flight as well as normal accounting routines. This particular application requires ticket and boarding pass printers and remote communication concentrators.

12. Configuration. In some circumstances multiprocessing may be adopted, using two processors in tandem (incurring high hardware costs) to allow batch processing and real-time processing to proceed side by side. In such cases priorities must be established to enable parts of the system with a low priority to be interrupted to deal with real-time requirements. In addition, a front-end processor or multiplexor would be needed to control the communications from the various lines. Modems and terminals will be required at each location in the network. Cluster controllers may also be necessary to control groups of terminals at specific locations. (*See* Fig. 11.2.)

13. Back-up facilities. It is imperative that a critical real-time system has adequate back-up facilities. In a multiprocessing system the processor assigned to batch processing is programmed to switch immediately to the real-time operation in the event of a malfunction in the real-time processor. This is a fail-safe routine to protect the integrity of the data and to avoid the system going down, which would be chaotic in a critical, widely dispersed operation such as airline seat reservation. Restart procedures are an inherent part of the system and restart and audit data is 'dumped' (copied) to disc every two or three minutes. In the event of a malfunction the system can be restarted from the details last dumped.

14. Software. Highly sophisticated software will be required to control the real-time operation, including interrupt facilities as appropriate, with provision for controlling background tasks such as the processing of routine applications in batch mode. The software takes the form of a powerful operating system. Communications software will also be required to handle enquiries from the various terminals.

Multi-user applications

15. Characteristics. A modern method of information processing allows a number of users consisting of various people in different departments to process their own particular requirements, whether computing wages and payroll processing, preparing invoices and updating the sales ledger or updating the stock file. Such operations are known as on-line because each of the users is connected to the computer by a terminal (*on-line*) which is under the control of the processor. The nature of the processing is referred to as a 'multi-user' application. The terminals replace the key-to-disc system used for batch processing. This type of operation requires terminal controllers for controlling the operations of groups of terminals. In addition, if terminals are located remotely, modems, multiplexors and *maybe* front-end processors will be required as well as private leased communication lines.

Terminals are both input and output devices, but in addition local printers may be required at each dispersed office for printing documents and summaries. A printer would also be required at the mainframe installation as well as a console to enable the computer operator to monitor the system. Backing storage consists of banks of fixed disc drives, each allocated to the various applications, and disc controllers for controlling groups of disc drives.

A powerful processor is required to support the multi-user environment as it must be capable of polling the lines to allocate time slots to each terminal. It also requires a large memory capacity for storing the various user programs as well as the high overhead required for storing the operating system. The term 'overhead' refers to the area of the internal memory of the computer which is inaccessible to the user. It is in effect unproductive memory, in the sense that it cannot be used for storing data or records.

16. Record locking and unlocking. Multi-user systems require a hardware protection feature for preventing system crashes as a result of several users processing the same file simultaneously. Record locking and unlocking facilities are also required to prevent a record being accessed by a user at the time it is being updated by another user. The first user of a record is allocated complete control to update the record and other users are denied access until the record is updated. File locking is similar to record locking but control is applied at file level. Record locking is more desirable since file locking prevents other users accessing any records on the file during updating. Note that record and file locking techniques can be used on local area networks.

17. Multi-user in relation to distributed and centralised processing. Multi-user systems are sometimes classified as distributed processing, but effectively they provide distributed facilities by way of terminals for gaining access to a centralised processing installation. This feature may be contrasted with network systems, which do provide distributed processing, because diversified computers are connected together by means of the network and are able to intercommunicate with one another for the transfer of information. The individual computers also perform local processing requirements such as payroll, stock control and sales ledger as stand-alone systems. The individual terminals in a multi-user system cannot communicate with one another, this being unnecessary since they share common files.

18. Multi-user systems vs. networks. A disadvantage of a multi-user system is that if the connecting cable is severed the terminal becomes inoperative as it has no link with the computer. This is not the case with networks, however, for if a microcomputer becomes disconnected from the network it can continue processing — but cannot, of course, communicate with other computers on the network.

19. Multi-user operating systems. Special multi-user operating systems are required to control terminal operations as only one user can access the system in any moment of time. Delays for users while awaiting their turn to access the system for the input of data for updating files or for retrieving information are not noticeable.

Multi-tasking

20. Multi-tasking. A technique which facilitates the running of two or more tasks concurrently on microcomputers. In mainframe environments multi-tasking is referred to as 'multi-programming', but in both instances the technique allows high speed switching between different tasks while affording access to multiple sources of information as with integrated packages. This means that information can be obtained from different spreadsheets for integration with text files, functional files, graphics and databases, etc. Each task has its own window (*see* 24) on the screen, which acts as a viewing area of the computer's memory. A mouse (*see* 26) is used to select the files required from drop-down menus. Windows can be closed when switching to different tasks while the original task is being executed. Windows can be displayed on the screen at any desired location and the size of a window can be adjusted. Multi-tasking provides facilities for the transfer of information from one application to another with high speed switching between them by means of special operating systems such as Microsoft Windows, OS/2 for the IBM PCs and MultiFinder for the Apple Macintosh (*see* Fig. 14.4). The operating system needs to know details of the different programs before they can be executed; for instance, it needs to know how much RAM is required, the resources required (such as disc drives and printers) and how the program writes to the screen, etc. For this purpose each program requires what may be called a program information file which defines the various parameters. To write one's own windows-compatible applications, a programmer's toolkit is required to aid the construction of pull-down menus, dialogue boxes, mouse support and application icons.

Figure 14.4 *Screen displaying windows in a multi-tasking environment (courtesy Apple Macintosh).*

Other processing techniques

21. On-line order processing systems. On-line processing systems are quite prevalent and a number of factors need to be considered regarding the type of computer and devices required to support the system. One essential factor is to know how many terminals/workstations will be required which, to some extent, is dependent upon the location of the terminals: for example, if they are located within the same general area as the computer special communication lines will be required for linking them together. If the distance is within say, 4,000 feet, internal lines can be used but if the terminals are geographically dispersed, perhaps in branch sales offices, leased private telephone lines will be necessary in order to obtain exclusive use of them whenever they are needed. If the public telephone lines are used delays will occur due to lines being engaged when required. This tends to negate the purpose of the system, which is aimed at increasing administrative efficiency and avoiding bottlenecks in the processing of orders, eliminating shortages and reducing delivery delays. It more than one terminal is envisaged, a multi-access computer which can effectively control the number of terminals on-line is needed. The computer's memory capacity must be quite substantial to deal with multi-user operations as it needs to store sophisticated software by way of the operating system as well as the application programs. Large capacity magnetic disc storage devices may be required to take advantage of direct access capability, as an on-line order entry system must have direct access to records. For example, before an order is accepted it is necessary to access the customer's record on the customer file to check the credit status, and the product records on the product file to assess the availability of each item ordered, i.e. the stock status. The customer can then be informed of the delivery situation. Modems and multiplexors may be required for remote terminals, and perhaps cluster controllers to control groups of terminals. A line printer is necessary for printing picking lists, invoices, shortage lists, despatch documentation and various statistical reports. The speed of the printer required depends on the volume of orders to be processed daily.

22. Point-of-sale systems. The term 'point-of-sale' is used to describe the technique used for capturing transaction data as sales occur in supermarkets and department stores. Data is captured (recorded) using special laser scanners at check-out points. A scanner senses data printed in the form of a bar code on the label of the product. The bar code used in Europe is the European Article Numbering (EAN) code. The light and dark lines of the code are converted by the scanner into a number which is sent to the in-store minicomputer. The computer looks up the number in its memory to identify the product and transmits the price of the item to the check-out terminal. The price is displayed and the price and description of the commodity are printed on to the customer's receipt, together with the total amount, the value of cash received (unless a cheque or credit card is used) and the amount of change to be given. Other details are also printed including the date and check-out number, etc.

A system has been developed which uses speech synthesised microchips which generate verbalised prices for customers. The digitised sounds are stored in a semiconductor store and released on instructions from a bar code reader.

The equipment required to operate a point-of-sale system, depending upon its exact configuration, includes retail terminals at each check-out point which can function as free-standing sales registers equipped with a laser bar code scanner; keyboard and VDU which can be used as a back-up system in the event of a malfunction with the bar code scanner; an in-store minicomputer supporting the terminals at the various check-out points in the store; a printer for printing customer receipts and, if the system is linked to an electronic funds transfer system, a data communication link to the various banks' computers for credit check enquiries and the transfer of funds. The minicomputer acts as a system controller and may be linked to a control mainframe at head office.

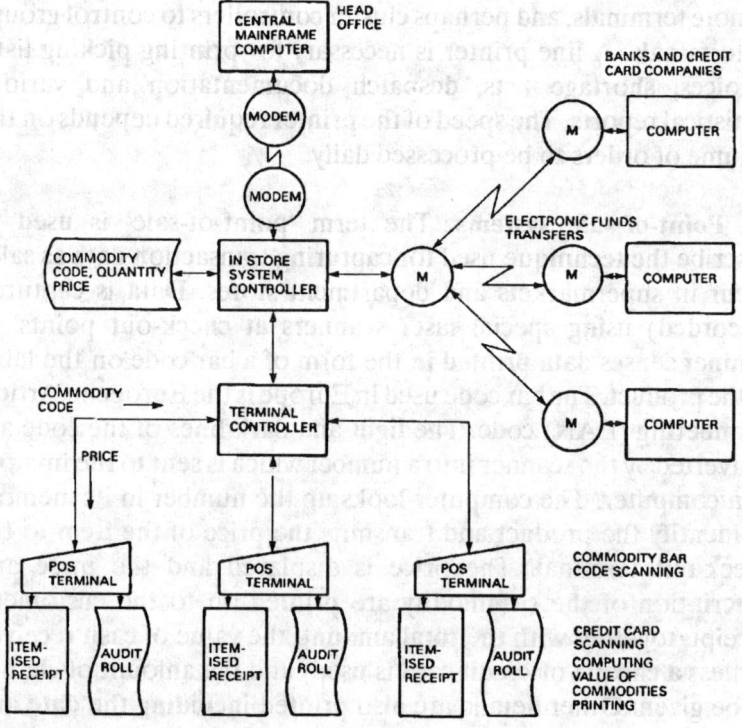

Figure 14.5 *Flowchart illustrating a retail point-of-sale configuration.*

This type of system reduces the time customers spend queueing at check-out points and provides itemised till receipts to give customers a visible check on the price of the goods.

The efficiency of stock management is increased through this system, enabling the level of stocks to be reduced, saving both funds and storage space. The overall efficiency of store administration is enhanced as management is provided with frequent up-to-date information, which has a bearing on the profitability of the business (*see* Fig. 14.5).

23. Distributed processing. Distributed processing must not be confused with decentralised processing, even though decentralisation is a feature of distributed processing. Prior to the advent of the computer, different companies in a group may well have used their own data processing installation, i.e. decentralised facility. The centralisation of data processing was the trend of the 1960s, but the tendency of the 1970s and 1980s has been a reversal of this situation, largely due to the development of workstations, mini- and microcomputers. These cost much less than mainframes, which makes it a viable proposition to install them in departments and branches on a distributed processing basis. This is the philosophy of providing computer power where it is most needed, instead of concentrating all processing in a single centralised computer system. Systems architecture is a design philosophy whereby small computers in dispersed operating units may be connected by a communications network to one another and also to a large, centrally located mainframe. The mainframe may support a large database, which would allow information of a strategic nature to be retrieved on demand for corporate planning. This would be a distributed processing network (*see* 14.6).

Simplicity of gaining access to a computer by relevant operating personnel at all levels of an organisation is not an easy matter to accomplish even within a single-unit business organisation equipped with terminals. This problem is accentuated when there are many dispersed units within the organisation, a number of which may be interdependent, e.g. marketing and manufacturing functions, as all units must be fully aware of the operational status of one another's sphere of operations.

It becomes even more of a problem when a business is a

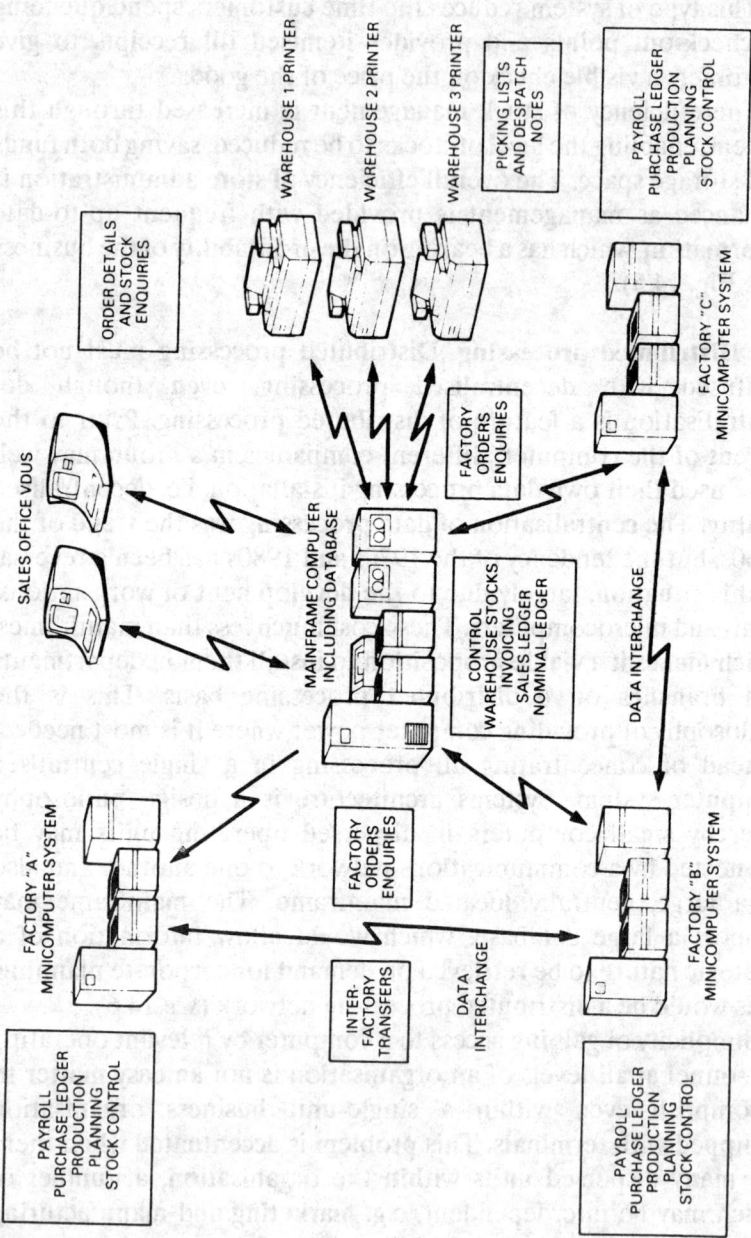

Figure 14.6 *Outline of characteristics of a distributed processing network.*

multinational organisation with widely dispersed subsidiaries. With the implementation of distributed processing systems, this is less of a problem because it is of no consequence whether the small computers are located in the same building as a mainframe computer or on the other side of the ocean. Distributed processing allows a business to select the level of processing autonomy in respect of depots, factories, warehouses or sales offices.

Distributed processing also includes the use, on a decentralised basis, of intelligent terminals, i.e. terminals with processing capabilities which may be used on a local basis for off-line operation or for on-line operations linked to a host computer. The choice of terminal may be selected according to local needs and may include badge readers and data collection terminals in factory departments, tag readers and point-of-sale terminals in retail sales outlets, visual display units (VDUs) for offices, VDUs and/or printers for warehouses, and video units in the sales department for on-line entry of order details (*see* Fig. 14.6).

Processing aids: windows, icons, mouse and pointers (WIMP)

Windows, icons, mouse and pointers are electronic techniques used to select files, applications and specific routines, avoiding unnecessary use of the keyboard to input commands.

24. Window. A window acts as a viewing area of the computer's memory. In multi-tasking operations software may be used which opens a window for a particular application. Several tasks can be viewed on the screen simultaneously, avoiding the need to exit from one program to access another. The window may be closed when switching to a different task while the original task is being executed. Less powerful spreadsheet programs do not possess this feature but do have facilities for displaying sections of a large spreadsheet, perhaps the top and bottom sections, simultaneously (*see* Fig. 2.4).

25. Icons. Icons represent a physical object or activity pictorially by means of stylised symbols. They are used in conjunction with a cursor or pointer (*see* **27**) for selecting options from drop-down menus. An icon is selected by moving the pointer to the appropriate symbol by cursor control keys or by a mouse (*see* **26**) if available. If a file icon is selected a list of files or programs on a particular disc will be displayed on a drop-down/pop-up menu. The name of the required text file or program is then selected by moving the cursor to point to the required location. Icons and pointers eliminate the need to use complex commands and so enable the non-expert to use a computer with comparative ease.

Icons also display office desk-top functions, which include 'in' and 'out' baskets, calculator, printer, file folders, diary and disc symbols, etc. Selecting a diary icon loads a diary program; when a disc icon is selected a series of other icons may be displayed from which to select the required option for file copying or formatting, etc. (*See* Figs. 2.3 and 2.4.)

26. Mouse (and pointer). A mouse is a hand-held electronic device which is used instead of a keyboard. It has one or more switches on its upper surface and ball-bearings on its lower, allowing it to be moved in any direction around the screen by traversing it in the required direction over the surface of a desk or graphics tablet. A pointer (or cursor) on the screen moves in synchronisation with the mouse. Specific options are selected by directing the pointer to the one required on a drop-down menu. The switch on the upper surface of the mouse is then depressed to make the selection. The mouse is used in this way for selecting files, programs or options for particular routines, for example 'screen painting', which selects the background and foreground when displaying graphs and charts on the screen. A mouse may also be used in conjunction with icons (*see* Fig. 14.7).

27. Pointer. A pointer is another name for a cursor, which has already been discussed in relation to keyboards, windows, mouse and icons. It is a pointer or electronic indicator —a bright bar which moves over the surface of the screen automatically when entering data and indicates the next position for entering characters. Some cursors can be moved round the screen by cursor control keys or directed by the movement of a mouse. Some pointers take the form of an arrow which traverses the screen for option selection purposes. A pointer also signals the current cell in a spreadsheet.

On occasions a 'winking' cursor is used as a prompt to draw attention to a specific section of the screen.

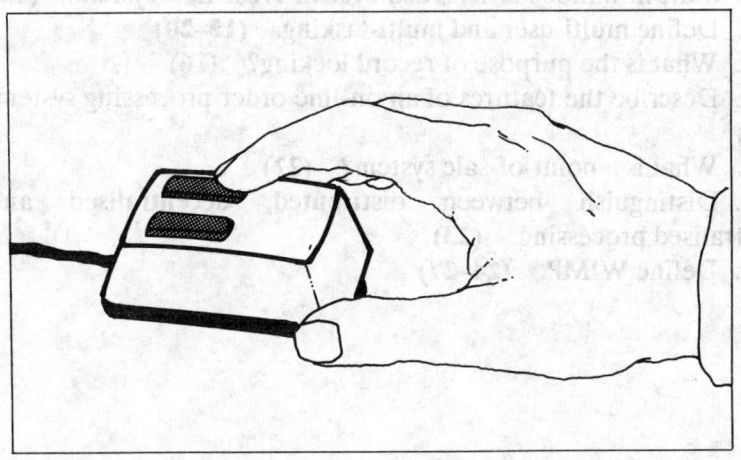

Figure 14.7 *The 'mouse' — hand-held cursor control device.*

Many business applications display a menu for selecting routines or a specific application; options can be selected in several ways, one being to locate the cursor adjacent to that required and depress the ENTER OR RETURN key on the keyboard.

Progress test 14

1. State the nature of batch processing.   **(1, 2)**
2. How are errors detected and corrected in a batch processing system?   **(3)**
3. How is file security achieved in batch processing?   **(4)**
4. Describe a typical batch processing configuration.   **(5)**
5. Describe the features of an on-line system.   **(6)**
6. What is interactive conversational mode processing?   **(8)**
7. How is file security accomplished in on-line processing systems?   **(9)**
8. Describe the nature of an on-line processing configuration.   **(10)**
9. State the important factors of a real-time system.   **(11)**

10. What type of configuration is required for a real-time system? **(12)**

11. State how file security is achieved in a real-time system. **(13)**

12. Define multi-user and multi-tasking. **(15–20)**

13. What is the purpose of record locking? **(16)**

14. Describe the features of an on-line order processing system. **(21)**

15. What is a point-of-sale system? **(22)**

16. Distinguish between distributed, decentralised and centralised processing. **(23)**

17. Define WIMP. **(24–27)**

15

Computer bureaux and computing services

Computer bureaux

1. Definition of and factors to consider in selection of a bureau. A computer service bureau is a company which operates a computer to process work for other companies, particularly those which cannot justify a computer of their own. A number of factors need to be considered when choosing a computer bureau as it is necessary to select one which is both reliable and efficient. The following factors provide a reasonable assessment of a bureau's capability relative to others:

(a) reputation;
(b) integrity;
(c) efficiency;
(d) competitiveness;
(e) number of years established;
(f) financial stability;
(g) turnround time-reliability;
(h) calibre of staff employed;
(i) market standing;
(j) approach to technological developments.

2. Types of bureaux. There are basically three types:

(a) *independent companies* specially formed to provide computing services to clients;

(*b*) *computer manufacturers* with separately structured computer bureaux;

(*c*) computer users with *spare capacity* who allow other firms to use their computer system either for standby facilities or for program testing prior to the installation of a similar computer system.

3. Services provided. In general, the range of services provided by computer bureaux is as follows.

(*a*) *Data preparation or conversion.* This service consists of the conversion of source data into a machine-sensible form for processing by computer. Conversion may be in the form of floppy disc, cassette tape, magnetic tape or optical characters. A bureau may be used for the initial conversion of master files when computerising systems.

(*b*) *Systems investigation and design.* This consists of the analysis of existing procedures and their conversion for processing by computer.

(*c*) *Program preparation and testing.* This service provides an addition to the service indicated in (*b*) above.

(*d*) *Hiring computer time.* Here the service to the client consists of processing the client's data using the programs supplied by the client. The hire-charges usually vary according to the time of day the service is provided and the length of time the bureau's facilities are used.

(*e*) *Do-it-yourself service (DIY).* The provision of computing facilities to allow the clients' computer operators to process data with their own programs. The service is usually available during off-peak periods.

(*f*) *Time sharing.* Access to the bureau's computer by means of communication links, which in effect provides each user with computing facilities as if he had an in-house computer.

4. Reasons for using a bureau. Any particular company will of course have specific reasons for using a computer bureau, but in general the following reasons are common:

(*a*) to obtain valuable initial experience of processing by computer before deciding whether or not to install an in-house computer;

(*b*) to provide standby facilities, by arrangement, in case of breakdown of the in-house computer;

(*c*) to provide facilities for coping with peak data processing loads owing to insufficient capacity of the in-house computer;

(*d*) non-availability of finance for the installation of an in-house computer;

(*e*) space restrictions for accommodating a computer installation;

(*f*) to avoid the responsibility of operating an in-house computer;

(*g*) insufficient volume of work to justify the installation of a computer;

(*h*) to obtain the benefit of computer power at reasonable cost;

(*i*) to provide more information for management control;

(*j*) to test and prove programs to be run on a similar computer, when installed, to that used by a bureau;

(*k*) to obtain the skill and experience of bureau operating staff in the processing of data;

(*l*) recognition that a bureau is likely to have powerful, up-to-date equipment, made economical by processing a wide variety of work at high volumes;

(*m*) recognition that a bureau will be using, as far as possible, the most efficient techniques and software aids;

(*n*) to process jobs that cannot be processed economically by an in-house computer.

5. Disadvantages of using a bureau. One of the main disadvantages of using a bureau is the loss of control over the time taken to process data (turn-round time) suffered by an organisation, because of the competing requirements of other clients of the bureau.

In some instances, an organisation may be better served by an in-house computer but may be reluctant to take the plunge; as a result, no experience is gained directly in operating a computer installation. This may create indirect benefits to competitors, especially in the problem solving applications for which a computer is so valuable. This means that competitors who use computers for their problem solving needs probably generate optimum solutions, whereas a business without a computer may lose this advantage.

Computing services

Many computing services organisations originally started out as computer bureaux, providing data processing facilities to small businesses which could not justify the use of a computer. This has now changed to some extent due to technological developments, which have already been discussed. Many bureaux have expanded the range of services they provide and may now be defined as computing service companies.

6. Supply and installation of computing equipment. Some organisations now supply hardware including micro-, mini- and mainframe computers either to function as 'in-house' systems or as 'front-end' processors linked to other mainframes. They may also supply networked micros, intelligent terminals, multi-user and multi-processor systems.

7. Supply of software. In addition to providing software support with computing equipment as a complete package, some companies also function as software houses developing software packages for distribution through a dealer network or developing 'custom' (bespoke) software for individual companies to their specification.

8. Facilities management. This is an arrangement whereby a company transfers all or part of its data processing facility, including hardware and staff, to a contractor, i.e. a computing services organisation, and then purchases back the processing requirements of the company. A specific level or service is guaranteed. Contracts vary according to specific needs of individual customers and may involve providing all operational and development staff to run an existing data processing installation or the transfer of the installation to the premises of the computer service company.

Facilities management can provide an efficient service at less than the equivalent 'in-house' costs. It is useful when it is necessary to limit capital expenditure for upgrading or replacing an existing system.

9. Consultancy. Some companies will require the services of a consultant before embarking on the installation of computerised systems and others will need advice on specific problems of a data processing nature. Consultancy services covering these needs are often provided by computing services organisations.

10. Turnkey services. Turnkey services may be defined as 'the supply and installation of a computer system in such a complete form that the user need only "turn a key" as it were to commence using the system'. Such a service is provided by external consultants. The user figuratively turns a key to gain access to the system for whatever purpose it is designed. This requires the initial identification of a client's needs, the selection of the most suitable hardware (computer system) and the relevant elements of software support. The service covers systems design, program coding, testing and debugging until the system is suitable for handing over to the client.

A business with very little data processing experience using sophisticated machines, or no computer specialists on the staff, would find this service of the utmost benefit as it would enable the changeover of systems to be accomplished by experts without too much involvement by management.

Progress test 15

1. Define the term computer bureau.   (1)
2. (a) Describe the range of services offered by computer bureaux. (b) List the major features which should be considered when choosing a computer bureau.   (1, 3)
3. Specify the types of computer bureau available.   (2)
4. List FOUR services offered by a typical computer bureau. (3)
5. For what reasons would you consider using a computer bureau?   (4)
6. What are the disadvantages of using a computer bureau?   (5)
7. Many bureaux have expanded the range of services they

provide and become in effect computer service organisations. What services would you expect them to provide? **(6–10)**

8. Define the following services: (*a*) facilities management; (*b*) turnkey services. **(8, 10)**

Part four

Development of
computer applications

16

Framework for the development of computer applications

Initial considerations

1. Data processing steering committee. A steering committee should be formed with responsibility for appraising the viability of computer projects, to ensure they are cost effective and would be of benefit to the business as a whole, to optimise corporate rather than functional performance. Such a committee enables the data processing needs of the business as a whole to be co-ordinated with other functional activities within the framework of corporate plans.

It is important to appreciate that a steering committee need only be formed in larger companies when considering the implementation of a mainframe computer for corporate use embracing major business systems. A committee is not usually required in small companies or in departments inside larger companies with their own computer resources.

Membership of a steering committee should consist of representatives of the various functions which will be affected by the installation of a computer into the business. The committee is likely to be chaired by the chief executive, which would enable him to have an overview of proposed computer projects and assess whether they accord with the future strategy and policy of the business. The functional interests in a typical manufacturing business would probably be represented by the production controller, stock controller, chief accountant, sales manager, chief buyer and of course the data processing manager. The data processing manager is then in a position to be aware of company policy and can interpret its requirements more objectively before executing the needs of such policy.

2. Preliminary appraisal. A mainframe computer cannot be plugged in and away she goes, as it were — its successful implementation depends upon a number of factors. Management must make a decision on the basis of a feasibility study report either to implement or not to implement a computer. Whichever decision is made can have far-reaching effects on the future efficiency of the business.

The correct decision is crucial because it is possible to make an incorrect decision in either of two instances: management may decide not to implement a computer when they should or to implement a computer when they should not. Failure to implement a computer when it is necessary will reduce administrative efficiency. On the other hand, the consequence of implementing a computer when it is not needed is chaos as systems will be disrupted, unnecessary costs will be incurred and organisational changes will be made needlessly.

3. Top management support. The time, effort and finance required for the initial implementation and development of computerised systems may deter the most enlightened managers unless the feasibility study report makes refusal difficult. This is a further pointer to the value of an accurate feasibility report. It is imperative for top management — the board of directors and functional managers — to show interest at the outset, otherwise projects will have little chance of success once a computer is installed.

Any dissension on the part of top management will filter through the organisation to the lower management levels and this in itself will detract from the successful implementation of systems. Departmental managers in charge of systems to be computerised will not, in all probability, provide the required level of support to systems staff which is so essential for the efficient operation of new systems. User departments need to participate in the design of systems with which they are concerned and for which they are responsible.

Education, training, communications and recruitment

4. Education and training programme. The reason for any lack of enthusiasm on the part of management may be ignorance of computers — or even fright — and this should be dispelled by means of a short induction course. Such a course may be conducted by internal systems staff if any are already employed in the organisation or, if they are not, selected managers and staff may attend a computer manufacturer's or college based computer appreciation course. The contents of a computer appreciation course may consist of the following:

(a) definition of a computer;
(b) the place of the computer in the organisation;
(c) duties of systems analysts and programmers;
(d) responsibilities of the data processing manager;
(e) outline of computer applications;
(f) benefits of using computers related to present systems if relevant;
(g) data preparation methods;
(h) processing techniques, batch, on-line; real-time and multi-programming, etc.;
(i) hands-on experience.

5. The need to communicate. Before a large computer is implemented within the organisation the fact that this is under consideration should be communicated to all personnel, particularly those who are likely to be the most affected once a computer becomes operational. This course of action will dispel distorted rumours circulating within the organisation which could have a damaging effect on morale.

It is also necessary to communicate company policy with regard to possible redundancies when systems are transferred to the computer. Of particular importance are the arrangements to be made for retraining staff and possible redeployment.

In most companies it will be the responsibility of the managing director to communicate these factors formally and he should also stress the importance of obtaining the fullest co-operation of staff in the difficult transition period ahead, in respect of systems development and changeover.

Feasibility study: objectives, costs and other factors

Important considerations concerned with conducting a feasibility study include the need to state the terms of reference and the boundaries of the study. It should also mention the structure of the team to conduct the study and the timescale for producing the report.

6. Objectives of study. At the outset it is important that objectives of the study be clearly defined so that the study team have a clear understanding of the requirements of the study. The objectives may be to determine if all or some of the following factors are feasible using a computer:

(*a*) reducing the number of staff in specific administrative functions because of cost;

(*b*) avoiding the need to increase clerical staff because the calibre of staff required is in short supply;

(*c*) improving the flow if information for management;

(*d*) providing problem solving facilities for management;

(*e*) improving cash flows by producing invoices and statements of account earlier;

(*f*) reducing the cost of processing each unit of data;

(*g*) streamlining accounting routines;

(*h*) providing the means for effective systems integration;

(*i*) improving the accuracy of information and data on business documents.

7. Choice of business area. In order to achieve the designated objectives it is necessary to select the areas of the business most likely to achieve them. Possible areas may be chosen on the following basis:

(*a*) those involving procedures which process a large volume of data, forms or documents;

(*b*) those involving procedures with a high proportion of repetitive operations;

(*c*) those involving procedures with a large number of clerical staff;

(*d*) those involving procedures which suffer from delays due to bottlenecks in processing perhaps due to insufficiently planned procedures, inadequate methods of processing or high-volume posting or calculating operations.

8. General considerations of a feasibility study. A number of important factors must be taken into account before any conclusions can be established and before the feasibility study report is presented to management. They include the following:

(*a*) the alternative types of computer configuration available;

(*b*) the availability of standby facilities in case of breakdown of the computer;

(*c*) business trends and their likely impact on data processing commitments;

(*d*) the extent to which the organisation would need restructuring with the advent of a computer.

(*e*) the availability of experienced computer personnel, systems analysts and programmers, etc.;

(*f*) the feasibility of using a computer bureau instead of installing an in-house computer;

(*g*) the feasibility of using several microcomputers instead of a mainframe computer;

(*h*) the incidence of redundancy in respect of clerical staff;

(*i*) the time necessary to develop computerised systems;

(*j*) the need for computer appreciation courses for management and staff.

9. Cost considerations of using a computer. Some of the elements of cost which must be considered by a management accountant include:

(*a*) the cost of purchasing or renting a computer perhaps compared with the cost of using a computer bureau;

(*b*) the cost of developing computer systems;

(*c*) the cost of computer accommodation;

(*d*) the cost of recruiting and training computer staff;

(*e*) the annual cost of operating the computer system;

(*f*) the comparative costs of alternative methods of processing;
(*g*) the cost of writing off current equipment;
(*h*) the availability of finance to purchase a computer system;
(*i*) the cost of obtaining finance to purchase a computer system;
(*j*) the cost of converting master files to magnetic media.

10. Expected benefits of using a computer. The possible benefits are numerous if computers are planned and used effectively. (*See* 1: 20.)

11. Feasibility study in a business possessing a computer. When a computer already exists in the organisation it is still necessary to conduct a feasibility study for any proposal to computerise a business system. The objectives and stages of feasibility study for a proposed system may be based on the following outline of action to be taken:

(*a*) define objectives of system to be studied;
(*b*) define objectives of the feasibility study (*see* 6);
(*c*) collect facts relating to the current system, including types and volume of input, types and volume of output, frequency of processing, time for performing each main activity, number of staff employed on the system, type of files used, number of records in files, frequency of referring to files, frequency of updating files, file activity ratio ('hit rate'), problem areas and operating costs, etc.;
(*d*) anticipated system development costs, including costs of file conversion;
(*e*) estimate run times;
(*f*) anticipate costs of computer operations;
(*g*) assess expected benefits;
(*h*) prepare feasibility study report;
(*i*) submit and discuss report with appropriate management;
(*j*) make decision to computerise and proceed with more detailed systems analysis if management consider proposals satisfactory; otherwise continue with existing system perhaps with minor modifications.

12. Recruitment of data processing staff. A computer installation will be only as efficient as the personnel who manage, develop systems and program the computer. It is essential to obtain the services of an effective data processing manager who, first and foremost, should be a good manager. He should have a wide knowledge of business systems, particularly of the business in which he is employed, and due to this essential requirement he is often appointed from within the business. Former organisation and methods specialists and line managers have been appointed to the post of data processing manager on the basis of their knowledge of key systems in the organisation.

The data processing manager should have a considerable knowledge of computers, particularly of the model in use, or about to be implemented, but he need not be an expert in programming. He is responsible for interpreting and executing the policy of the steering committee, planning, organising, co-ordinating and controlling projects to ensure they achieve objectives.

Systems analysts should be recruited from within the organisation whenever possible to take advantage of their knowledge of the business, which is of extreme importance for the development of computer systems. They must be aware of the needs of the operating functions and departments, particularly the purpose and objectives of the systems they operate. This is the reason why O & M investigators often become systems analysts when a computer is implemented into a business.

A systems analyst must have many talents and be capable of viewing the business as a total system and yet be able to analyse it into its constituent elements (sub-systems). He must be able to appreciate the interactions which occur between sub-systems and the effects computerisation is likely to have on them. He should design systems without unnecessary complexity as the simpler the design the more effective they are likely to be (*see* 17: 1–2).

Programmers are required who are capable of writing simple, efficient programs. Unnecessary complexity in programs is likely to increase computer running time and produce documents and reports which are too complex for system needs. This situation requires a higher degree of co-ordination between programmers and systems analysts to ensure that ambiguity does not enter into programming as this will result in systems failing to meet their objectives.

Traditional stages of systems development

13. System life cycle. The stages of system life cycle development methodology are summarised below. A number of the stages are dealt with in greater depth within the various topic areas, particularly those relating to feasibility study (*see* **6–11**), terms of reference, systems analysis and design. The stages are as follows.

(*a*) Define the problem.

(*b*) Management specify terms of reference.

(*c*) Conduct feasibility study:

(*i*) *Technical feasibility.* Demands on the system regarding terminal enquiries or volume of data to be processed by batch or on-line processing. Speed of system response required and the capability of hardware and software to meet these requirements.

(*ii*) *Economic feasibility.* Matters relating to cost/benefit appraisal.

(*d*) Present report to management with recommendations.

(*e*) Management decision to abort or continue with project.

(*f*) Plan the project.

(*g*) Carry out systems analysis.

(*i*) Fact finding (collect the facts including environment and functional analysis).

(*ii*) Verify the facts.

(*iii*) Record the facts.

(*iv*) Procedure analysis.

(*h*) System design.

(*i*) Design philosophy.

(1) Establish design objectives and constraints.

(2) Design alternative systems.

(*ii*) Design activities.

(1) Prepare procedure charts (for clerical activities), block diagrams and systems flowcharts.

(2) Determine actions to be taken by means of decision tables.

(3) Design input documents and output documents and reports.

(4) Design file structures and layout.

(5) Develop the structure of computer runs by means of run charts.

(6) Evaluate run times.

(7) Design screen layouts for on-line terminal operations.

(8) Develop dialogue to be used by terminal/workstation operators.

(9) Develop fail-safe and restart procedures.

(10) Develop procedures for file security.

(11) Discuss with auditors and develop checks and controls to be incorporated.

(*i*) Prepare system specification (system definition).

(*i*) Details of the system including clerical and computer procedures, block diagrams, system flowcharts, decision tables and a narrative providing a general description of the system.

(*ii*) Input, output and file specifications and layouts.

(*iii*) Schedule of equipment required by the system including new equipment needs and alternative equipment proposals.

(*iv*) Nature and use of passwords.

(*j*) Present alternative proposals to management.

(*k*) Discuss proposals with management.

(*l*) Management decision — choice of proposals, if relevant.

(*m*) Prepare program specification: statement of program requirements including initialisation, parameters, processing stages, input and output requirements, test data and testing procedure to be applied, checks and controls to be incorporated, exception routines, conditions and actions to be provided for and arrangements for test runs.

(*n*) Programming.

(*i*) Program procedure charts (flowcharts) and/or structured English (*see* 18:10–18).

(*ii*) Program coding sheets.

(*iii*) Prepare test data and testing procedures.

(*iv*) Prepare validation checks and other controls to be incorporated into the system.

(*v*) Compile source programs.

(*vi*) Debug programs.

(*o*) Convert files.

(*p*) System testing.

(*i*) Prepare precalculated results.

(*ii*) Test programs with test data by dry runs, i.e. desk checking.

(*iii*) Test run on computer: compare results with precalculated results.

(*iv*) Report to management and discuss the results obtained from system testing. Decide on future course of action.

(*v*) Make appropriate modifications to system or programs and recompile as necessary.

(*q*) Implementation.

    (*i*)   Plan system implementation.

    (*ii*) Carry out parallel running of old and new systems; implement direct changeover or pilot scheme as appropriate.

    (*iii*) Prepare manuals for supporting user departments and operation departments including data preparation and data control clerks.

(*r*) Evaluate results with expectations.

    (*i*)   Monitor system performance in co-ordination with user department.

    (*ii*) Report to management to discuss the situation and decide on appropriate action.

    (*iii*) Make relevant adjustments to the system.

(*s*) Maintain system.

    (*i*)   Develop, test and implement improvements.

    (*ii*) Modify system to accord to changing circumstances.

    (*iii*) Integrate related systems to improve processing efficiency.

It is important to appreciate that the 'system life cycle' approach to system design and development is the traditional approach but a number of structured analysis and design methodologies are currently available, one being that from Michael Jackson Systems Limited. Jackson has expanded his structured programming philosophy into the realms of structured systems design.

Structured systems development methodology

14. Logical view. Structured development methodology initially adopts a logical view of a system to assess the current data flows and activities as a basis for establishing what data flows and activities are required to accord with the current operational and environmental needs of the business. This stage assesses business requirements without considering how they will physically be accomplished. The logical needs are subsequently matched to physical machines, equipment and software during the physical design stage of system development. The structured approach incorporates data modelling by developing entity and data flow diagrams showing data relationships and dependencies. System development often applies a top-down data-driven approach, first defining top-level requirements which are progressively analysed into more detail by decomposition. Functional decomposition diagrams are used to analyse functions (activities) and provide details of the current structure of activities, which is subsequently modified to accord to current needs which is the purpose of this methodology.

The logical approach to system design allows the system developer to identify user information needs accurately. Long and complex narratives and complex flowcharts, features of the traditional systems development approach, are replaced with graphical methods and structured English (*see* 18:10). Structured systems analysis and design provides frequent walkthroughs, i.e. reviews, designed to detect errors, omissions and ambiguities in any stage of development. This prevents errors being found at the programming or live running stage which is then very expensive to correct. Data structure design creates the initial requirements for setting up a database.

15. Stages of structured systems development methodology. The stages are typically these.

(*a*) Obtain terms of reference and conduct feasibility study.
(*b*) Analyse current system in respect of:
    (*i*)   operational details;
    (*ii*) entities;
    (*iii*) data;
    (*iv*) events.
(*c*) Construct conceptual model.
(*d*) Construct entity life history diagram.
(*e*) Construct transaction history diagram.
(*f*) Construct context diagram.

(*g*) Specify data elements (attributes) relating to each input data flow.

(*h*) Specify data elements (attributes) of output data flows and the origin of each output data flow.

(*i*) Prepare data flow diagram specifying input and output data flows and an outline of processing activities.

(*j*) Transform analysis — levelling of data flows. This process refines the broad detail contained in an initial data flow diagram into detailed data flows portrayed on individual data flow diagrams which assist the development of systems.

(*k*) Data modelling using an entity diagram to depict the relationship between data items, their entry points and access paths.

(*l*) Functional decomposition of processes.

(*m*) Construct flowchart portraying logical model of the system.

(*n*) Convert procedural steps into executable code either by normal programming or by automated code generation tools.

This subject is expanded upon in Volume 2.

Prototyping

16. Model for development. A prototype is an original machine, car, aircraft or business system that serves as a model for future development. A prototype of a business system may be used to demonstrate its initial performance and the system may then be modified to enable it to achieve specified objectives. The prototype allows judgements and assessments to be formed and demonstrates to users how their information needs can be achieved by the new system. The technique may be used at various stages of the development cycle. Prototyping strategy must be determined prior to developing a system to avoid expending resources on development without achieving commensurate benefits. The development of new systems or projects in dynamic application areas of the business are likely to benefit from prototyping. A number of factors need to be considered when determining strategy, including the complexity of the system under review, the clarity of user requirements and the urgency of getting a system up and running. Prototyping is a characteristic of many fourth generation languages. It has a number of attributes, particularly that of users obtaining a high degree of satisfaction from having systems delivered much sooner than conventional methods of system development allow. It is important, however, to be aware of the objectives to be achieved and not to overlook the need for data analysis (discussed in **29**). Logical structured design methodology (LSDM) recognises three approaches to prototyping.

17. First approach. This approach uses screen development aids to build a series of menus and screens and may be used where processing is straightforward and user requirements well defined. Users process transactions as they would in a live system but this approach does not incorporate system logic or a database. Once they accept the design, users can participate in further development of the model. If the user finds the prototype unacceptable due to inconsistencies, omissions or other weaknesses, those matters are addressed. Once approved the prototype model can be developed further.

18. Second approach. This approach requires the building of a 'throw-away' version of the system for user trials. In addition to menus, screens and a database, system logic is incorporated into the prototype. This approach may be used for larger, more complex projects when user requirements are not well defined. The prototype may be refined to be compatible with user requirements. The prototyping software is unlikely to have the performance and facilities for implementation as part of the physical system. It would, however, be used to identify user requirements and to specify the most relevant dialogue design.

19. Third approach. This approach is similar to the second approach save that the software is intended to form part of the final system. The prototype may be extended into a working part of the system to be implemented. This would often become the pilot for a project with a phased implementation plan. The prototyping software must incorporate facilities to accomplish performance objectives.

Systems analysis and duties of systems analyst

20. Systems analysis defined. Systems analysis is the term used to describe the process of collecting and analysing facts in respect of existing operations, procedures and systems in order to obtain a full appreciation of the situation prevailing so that an effective computerised system may be designed and implemented if proved feasible.

The difference between an organisation and methods investigation (a review of clerical procedures and methods) and a systems analysis project is one of objective rather than of principle.

An O & M investigation sets out to improve the existing situation by the most suitable means, chosen from a number of possible alternatives. Systems analysis, however, has as its objective the design of an effective computerised procedure which will create benefits in excess of those possible by other means.

Systems analysis also embraces systems design, which is an activity concerned with the design of a computerised application based on the facts disclosed during the analysis stage. Both activities are carried out by the same person who is known as a *systems analyst*.

21. Duties of systems analyst. The duties may be summarised as follows.

(*a*) Collect, record and analyse details of existing procedures and systems.

(*b*) Develop ideas for a computerised system superior to the existing methods in use — improve system performance.

(*c*) Design system input, file and output requirements.

(*d*) Specify checks and controls to be incorporated in conjunction with audit staff.

(*e*) Define actions required to deal with various conditions arising in the system by means of decision tables.

(*f*) Specify the structure of computer runs.

(*g*) Specify the most appropriate processing technique for the prevailing circumstances.

(*h*) Estimate run timings.

(*i*) Prepare computer operating instructions.

(*j*) Define error messages to be incorporated in the system.

(*k*) Specify test data to be used for proving programs in conjunction with audit staff and programmers.

(*l*) Arrange for test runs in conjunction with programming staff.

(*m*) Document all aspects of the system in a system specification.

(*n*) Implement parallel operation of old and new systems.

(*o*) Monitor results.

(*p*) Maintain system to accord to changing circumstances.

(*q*) Communicate with user department, systems staff and programmers as appropriate.

22. Systems analysis team. Some projects require a team of analysts, the size of which depends on the complexity and type of system to be investigated. It is good policy to recruit suitable personnel from existing staff, as it is important that they should have a sound knowledge of the business, which often takes many years to obtain in sufficient depth to analyse systems effectively.

The team should also include representatives from the various departments of the organisation that will be affected by the investigation. This approach ensures that personnel with an intimate knowledge of the systems being reviewed for computerisation have the opportunity to record facts which may otherwise be overlooked and which are important for the effective design of the computer system.

After the project is concluded the personnel on secondment go back to their department (unless recruited for systems work on a full-time basis due to their experience) and take an active part in the newly installed computerised system. By this means the best results are obtained, as personnel who have been brought into the picture are more likely to co-operate and accept the changes which have been implemented.

Fact-finding techniques

23. Primary questions. Any person concerned with fact finding, whether for normal work simplification or with a view to computerising a system must apply a methodical approach to ensure important facts are not overlooked. To this end a pre-prepared checklist may be used containing the main points to which answers are essential. The checklist is based on a framework of fundamental questions:

(*a*) *What* is done?
(*b*) *Why* is it done?
(*c*) *When* is it done?
(*d*) *How* is it done?
(*e*) *Where* is it done?
(*f*) *Who* does it?

If the answer to the question, 'Why is it done?' indicates that the system provides a useful purpose, the fundamental questions outlined above may be expanded as follows:

(*a*) Purpose: *What* is done? This requires a definition of the activities performed, which may be, for instance, the calculation of wages based on the hours worked by employees as recorded on time cards.

(*b*) Means: *How* is it done? Details are required of the resources and methods used to accomplish the defined activities, including:

(*i*)   forms used;
(*ii*) machines and equipment used;
(*iii*) method/technique used, e.g. three-in-one posting method using a writing board whereby three related documents are posted simultaneously.

(*c*) Personnel: *Who* does it? Details of the personnel performing the activities are required, which may include:

(*i*)   the number of personnel engaged on the activity both full-time and part-time;
(*ii*) job titles and the skills required;
(*iii*) type of staff — male or female.

(*d*) Location: *Where* is it done? The details required in this instance relate to the place where the activity is performed:

(*i*)   which factory, branch office or site;
(*ii*) function;
(*iii*) department;
(*iv*) section.

(*e*) Time/sequence: *When* is it done? Details of the time period and the sequence in which the activity is performed are required on the basis of the following details:

(*i*)   day, week, month;
(*ii*)   sequence — before activity *x*;
(*iii*)   sequence — after activity *y*.

After completing the checklist based on the questions outlined above, it will be necessary to test the validity of the responses.

24. Interviewing. This technique collects facts by interviewing personnel connected with the system under investigation as it is considered that they possess vital information relating to the systems with which they are concerned. The interviewer should encourage the staff to give their view of how they consider the system may be improved, and accordingly should be prepared to listen rather than dominate the interview. He should possess sufficient tact, however, to steer any discussion in the desired direction.

There should be no mystery surrounding an interview and the purpose of conducting it should be stated as it must be appreciated that personnel become very apprehensive of pending changes. An interview should be concluded amicably and in such a manner that any further assistance will be forthcoming freely.

25. Questionnaire. A questionnaire may be used as an aid to interviewing as it has the advantage of containing pre-formulated questions, answers to which are essential for the development of the system under consideration. This approach avoids the possibility of overlooking important facts. Questions should be framed as simply as possible to avoid ambiguity, should be asked in a logical sequence, should not be too numerous and leading questions should not be asked. The answers obtained may be verified by interviews after the questionnaire has been completed or it may be used during the course of an interview.

26. Observation. This technique is used to obtain an overall visual impact of a systems environment. It takes into account details relating to the movement of personnel and forms, types of machines and equipment being used, the speed of operations, working conditions, idle time, number of staff, bottlenecks and delays, etc.

27. Inspection and examination. This entails the examination and inspection of documents regarding number of entries made, their general state, how they are filed and the effectiveness of the filing system. The state of machines and equipment will also be examined as will the general working conditions in the systems environment.

Collecting facts

28. Types of facts. The fact-collecting stage of an assignment is extremely important as it enables the systems staff to become familiar with the characteristics and features of the system under review. This is essential before it is possible to design a computerised version of the system. The specific facts to be collected depend upon the nature of the system and the terms of reference, but generally they will include details relating to the following matters:

(*a*) *Resources used.* Details must be collected relating to the number of personnel engaged on the various tasks, the number and type of machines in use for specific operations, the number and types of forms and stationery used and other operating supplies, the use made of computer bureaux, services provided by other departments and so on.

(*b*) *Operational data.* This data relates to the nature and volume of the various tasks and activities performed, the time taken to perform them and their volume and frequency. It also includes details of bottlenecks and delays in the system as well as other system strengths and weaknesses.

(*c*) *Operating costs.* This data relates to the costs of running the system in respect of the resources used as indicated in (*a*) above. Such costs include salaries of staff, supervisors and management; the cost of electricity for heating and the supply of power to machines; machine and building maintenance and insurance costs; operating supplies, i.e. forms and stationery; inter-department service costs and computer bureau charges; depreciation of machines and buildings, etc.

(*d*) *Organisational data.* This type of data relates to the number of personnel engaged on each activity, their job titles, superior/subordinate relationships and the span of control of the various supervisors.

(*e*) *Communication analysis.* It is often necessary to establish the lines of communication which exist within a system, i.e. the incidence of intercommunications between personnel in the same department, within a section and between other sub-systems and functions of the organisation. This is indicative of the nature of the communications which will be required by the proposed computer system. This may include the need for on-line terminals, electronic mail, access to a database, distributed processing for inter-communication between computers and random enquiry facilities, etc.

(*f*) *Company policy matters.* It is essential to be aware of the various policies which exist and the manner in which they relate to the various systems. In respect of personnel policy, for example, this would embrace matters relating to long-service increments which must be provided for in the payroll system; in respect of the sales system this would embrace matters relating to the level of discounts in relation to sales values, the credit limit and credit period allowed to specified customers and the policy in respect of delivery charges in relation to value of sales; and so on.

(*g*) *Data analysis.* Establishing the nature of the data used in the business, the users and its purpose (*see* 29).

29. Data analysis. Data needs to be analysed in great detail, particularly as information systems are primarily concerned with the right data flowing in the system at the right time to produce the required information when required. The data contained in functional files and databases must be precisely defined, accurate, complete and current. Data analysis is an activity concerned with collecting details of the data existing in the current system. It is then possible to observe which data can be eliminated and new data that needs to be incorporated in the proposed system to enable it to meet its objectives. Data analysis highlights data which does not serve a useful purpose, identifies duplicated data and establishes the data flows between related functional sub-systems, which ensures that specific data remains in existence even though it may not be used specifically by a particular system.

Data analysis may be carried out on the basis of the following checklist.

(a) *Why* is the date required?

(b) *How* is the data originated?

(c) *Where* is the data originated?

(d) *What* benefits does it provide to the efficient operation of a specific system and for the business as a whole?

(e) *What* would be the effect of eliminating the data?

(f) *What* is the structure of the data-hierarchical, network, relational, serial or sequential?

(g) *What* data relationships exist?

(h) *Which* entity or record is the data related to?

(i) *Which* system uses the data?

(j) *What* reports are produced from the data?

(k) *When* is the data used?

(l) *How* is the data used, by whom and for what purpose?

(m) *What* is the frequency of preparation and access?

(n) *What* are the volumes of data used — maximum, average and minimum?

(o) *What* is the rate of growth?

(p) *What* are the attributes:

    (i)   key fields;

    (ii)   size of fields;

    (iii) sequence of fields;

    (iv)   fields to be validated;

    (v)   type of characters in fields?

Recording facts

30. Procedure chart. A chart used for analysing the activities and their relationships within a defined procedure. It portrays the various activities in the procedure and by means of symbols indicates the type of activity performed. This type of chart is used in systems investigations to record the details of the existing procedures so that they may be subjected to further analysis. A typical procedure chart, illustrated in Fig. 16.2, is constructed by means of the symbols shown in Fig. 16.1.

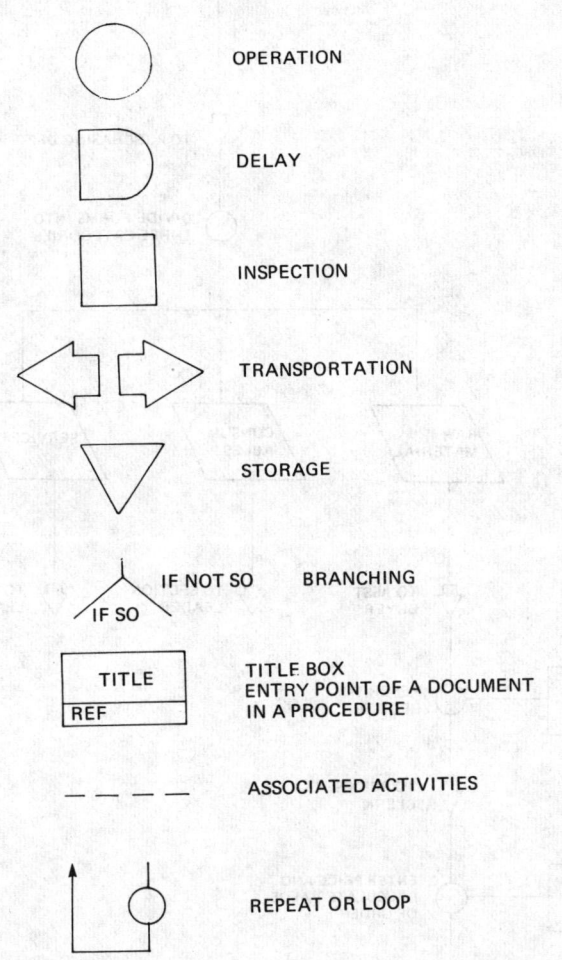

Figure 16.1   *Symbols for the construction of procedure charts.*

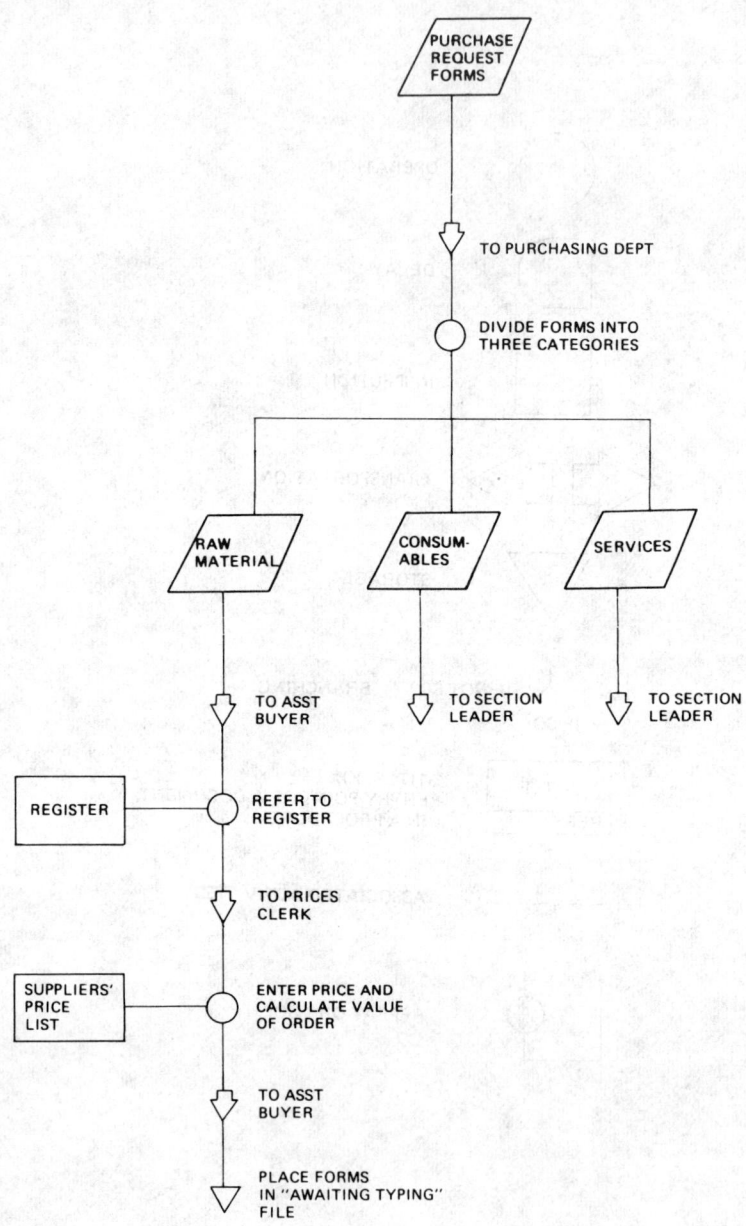

Figure 16.2 *Typical procedure chart.*

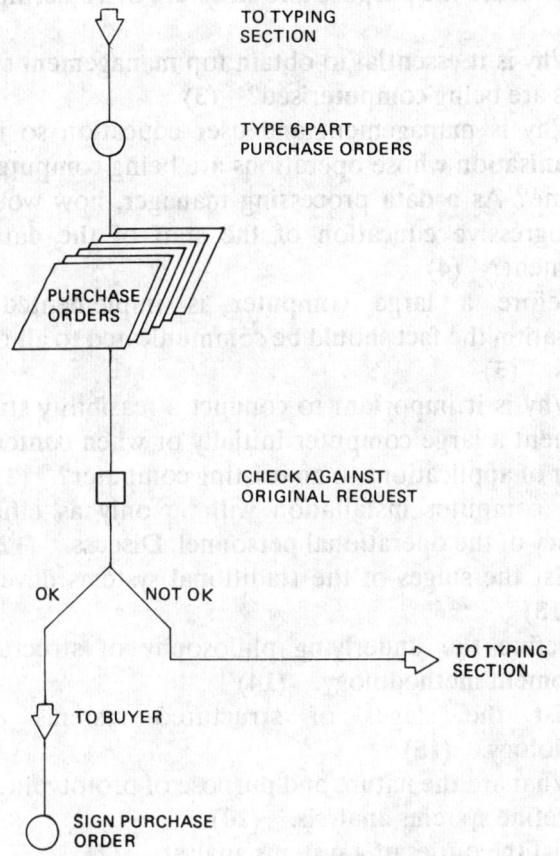

TO TYPING
SECTION

TYPE 6-PART
PURCHASE ORDERS

PURCHASE
ORDERS

CHECK AGAINST
ORIGINAL REQUEST

OK   NOT OK

TO TYPING
SECTION

TO BUYER

SIGN PURCHASE
ORDER

Figure 16.2 (*contd.*)

Other methods of recording include procedure narratives, which provide a written description of a system to support the facts recorded on a procedure chart; activity charts, which analyse the activity of personnel and machines; and a forms display chart, which displays the forms and their relationships in a procedure.

Progress test 16

1. What are the purpose and structure of a steering committee? **(1)**

2. Why is it essential to obtain top management support when systems are being computerised? **(3)**

3. Why is management and user education so important in an organisation whose operations are being computerised for the first time? As a data processing manager, how would you plan the progressive education of the staff of the data processing department? **(4)**

4. Before a large computer is implemented within an organisation the fact should be communicated to all relevant staff. Discuss. **(5)**

5. Why is it important to conduct a feasibility study either to implement a large computer initially or when contemplating the transfer of applications to an existing computer? **(2, 6–11)**

6. A computer installation will be only as efficient as the efficiency of the operational personnel. Discuss. **(12)**

7. List the stages of the traditional systems development life cycle. **(13)**

8. Define the underlying philosophy of structured systems development methodology. **(14)**

9. List the stages of structured systems development methodology. **(15)**

10. What are the nature and purpose of prototyping? **(16–19)**

11. Define systems analysis. **(20)**

12. List the duties of a systems analyst. **(21)**

13. What factors determine the need for a systems analysis team? **(22)**

14. What are the primary questions to be asked when investigating systems for development? **(23)**

15. What techniques may be employed for fact finding? **(24–27)**

16. List the types of facts which typically require to be collected. **(28, 29)**

17. How would you set about analysing data in a system? **(29)**

18. What recording techniques may be used to record systematically the facts collected? **(30)**

17

Systems design and implementation

Objectives and essentials

1. Objectives and essential considerations. The design of a
computer-based system (and any other type of system) is a creative
task which has as its objective the implementation of a system
creating benefits and improvements superior to those achieved by
other methods.

The system must therefore be designed so that basic business
documents and reports are produced as effectively as possible in
accordance with the needs of the business.

Provision should be made for automating decisions of a routine
nature whenever possible, which may be incorporated in the
program in the form of standard formulae, thereby assisting the
various levels of management by freeing them from routine
decision-making.

During the process of designing a system, it should be borne in
mind that the system(s) under review should not be considered in
isolation from other systems, as many systems are interrelated
either by the need for basic information or by the output from one
system being the input to other systems.

The processing requirements of the total system — the
organisation — should be considered, even though it may be
decided to design separate systems — 'sub-systems' — initially.
Even so, the separately designed systems should be planned in such
a way that they may be developed with a minimum of amendment
and disruption at a later date after gaining experience in the design
and processing of separate applications.

2. Essentials for effective design of systems. A well-designed system should take into account the following factors:

(*a*) production of the desired information, at the right time, in the right amount, with an acceptable level of accuracy and in the form required at an economical cost;

(*b*) incorporation of checks and controls which are capable of detecting and dealing with exceptional circumstances and errors;

(*c*) need to minimise the cost and the time spent on recording source data;

(*d*) need to minimise the cost and the time spent on data preparation;

(*e*) need to minimise the cost and the time spent on processing data;

(*f*) effective safeguards for the prevention of fraud;

(*g*) efficient security measures in order to avoid loss of data stored in master files;

(*h*) efficient design of documents and reports;

(*i*) efficient design of computer runs;

(*j*) design of suitable coding systems to aid identification, comparison, sorting, verification and the elimination of ambiguity;

(*k*) policy matters and their effect on business systems;

(*l*) legal matters and their relationship with business systems;

(*m*) adequate handling of exceptions to normal situations.

While a system can be designed to process all possible variations or exceptions on a computer, this may create a considerable degree of complexity in programming and extend processing time to an unacceptable level. Consequently it may be more efficient to design clerical systems instead of computer systems to handle them. Refer to Volume 2 for further details.

Forms design

3. Principles for the effective design of forms. This activity is concerned with designing the documents used for collecting source data relating to business transactions which is subsequently input to an information processing system. The documents or the print-outs from an information processing system also have to be designed. Forms must be effectively designed whether they are for use in clerical systems or in combined clerical/computer systems. The following guidelines will indicate the primary factors to be taken into account during the form design process.

(*a*) The paper must be of the correct type and substance for its purpose. For example, a form may contain details of the operations and departments through which an item is to proceed during the course of manufacture. The document may be placed in the work bin containing parts which are covered in oil. Non-absorbent paper will be required.

(*b*) The colour of paper for distinguishing between individual copies in multi-copy sets.

(*c*) Colour of ink used for printing.

(*d*) Type faces, i.e. type font.

(*e*) Type size.

(*f*) Punching requirements for filing.

(*g*) Sprocket holes for feeding continuous stationery on a printer.

(*h*) Cut off or rounded corners.

(*i*) Direction of grain for ease of folding.

(*j*) Blanking requirements to obliterate information on specific copies of a document, e.g. blanking of prices on a despatch note forming part of a multi-part invoicing set.

(*k*) Simplicity of design.

(*l*) Entries should flow in a logical sequence.

(*m*) Data boxes should be adequate for the size of fields to be entered.

(*n*) How to combine related forms containing similar data for various sub-system requirements thereby reducing the number of separate forms.

(*o*) Consider the type of carbon paper required for entries on to copies, i.e. interleaved re-usable carbon paper, one-time carbon paper or 'no carbon required' (NCR) paper.

(*p*) Some forms may be designed for three-in-one applications to enable common entries to be made on several documents simultaneously thereby avoiding duplication of entries.

(*q*) Some applications may require printing on a carbon insert, such as a pay advice sealed inside a pay envelope.

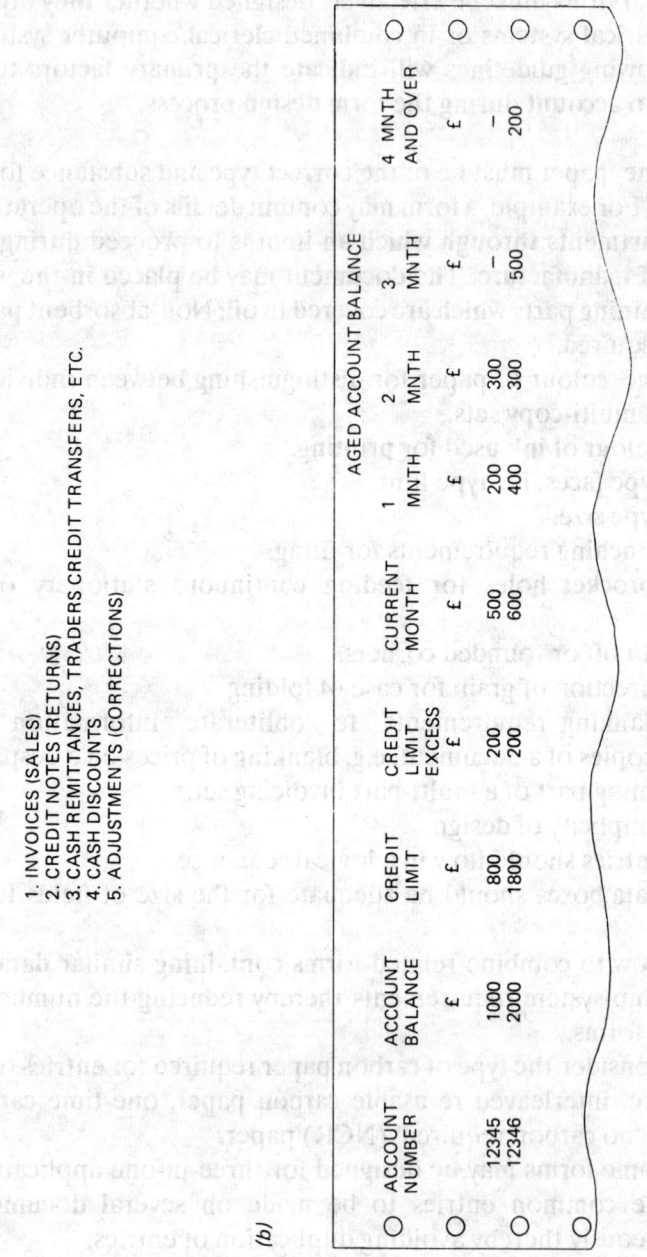

Figure 17.1 *Credit Limit Excess and Aged Balance Report.*

(*r*) Design should take into account speed and accuracy of entering data on to forms.

4. Form design question. The following question is part of a question set by the Association of Certified Accountants.

XYZ Ltd maintains its sales ledger system on a minicomputer. The sale ledger master file is held on magnetic disc. Accounts, which contain the usual standard data, are kept on a brought forward balance basis with the total balance analysed over current month, month 1, month 2, month 3 and month 4 and over. Visual display units are employed for the entry of transaction data and for the retrieval of data for answering enquiries. A variety of printed reports is produced on the line printer.

Draft, with TWO lines of sample entries, the Credit Limit Excess and Aged Balance Report which is produced monthly for the Accounts Manager. Your answer should be in the format of a typical computer-produced line-printer report.

SOLUTION

A suggested layout for the report is shown in Fig. 17.1.

System specification

5. Nature. A system specification is similar to any product specification whether for a hi-fi unit, television set, refrigerator or radio. A specification provides the interface between systems analysis and system design.

6. Contents. The specific details of a system specification depend on the nature and complexity of the system, but typically it includes a number of sections, summarised below.

    (*a*) Introduction.
    (*b*) System objectives.
    (*c*) System description.
    (*d*) Input specification.
    (*e*) Output specification.

(f) File specification.
(g) Changeover.
(h) Equipment.
(i) Test data.
(j) Program specification.

7. Introduction. This section includes details appertaining to the following.

(a) Name of the system.
(b) Glossary of terms used in the specification.
(c) Date of preparation.
(d) Statement of acceptance.
(e) Index to sections of the specification.
(f) System relationships.
(g) Details of amendments to original terms of reference.
(h) Departments involved with the system.
(i) Standards of performance.

8. System objectives. Expected benefits: tangible and intangible.

9. System description.

(a) Procedure charts and narrative relating to clerical systems.
(b) Data structure charts and data flow diagrams.
(c) System flowcharts and computer run charts.
(d) Decision tables.
(e) System structure charts.
(f) Coding system.
(g) Auditing procedures.

10. Input specification.

(a) Name of system.
(b) Name of document.
(c) Source and method of origination.
(d) Details of data elements.

(e) Frequency of preparation.

(f) Volume.

(g) Draft layout of document.

(h) Screen layouts.

11. Output specification.

(a) Name of system.

(b) Name of report.

(c) Number of print lines.

(d) Maximum size of fields.

(e) Destination of report.

(f) Draft layout of report.

(g) Screen layouts.

12. File specification.

(a) Name of system.

(b) Filename.

(c) File medium: tape reel, cassette, disc, floppy, fixed or exchangeable.

(d) File labels.

(e) Size of records.

(f) Record types.

(g) Number of reels/discs.

(h) Block size.

(i) Field names.

(j) File security, privacy and confidentiality; use of passwords.

13. System testing and changeover.

(a) Test programs with test data.

(b) Testing procedures: dry runs (desk checking).

(c) Pre-calculated results for comparison with results obtained from testing.

(d) Procedure for system modifications.

(e) Method of changeover: direct, parallel running or pilot.

(f) Changeover timing.

14. Equipment.

   (*a*) Type of computer.
   (*b*) Peripherals.
   (*c*) Run timing.
   (*d*) Computer utilisation.
   (*e*) Terminal utilisation.
   (*f*) Frequency of batch processing if relevant.

System modification requests

15. Pre-installation modifications. User department personnel participating in the development of a computer-based system may request a modification to the potential design of the system for a number of reasons. The design may, for instance, create a number of previously unforeseen problems or fail to resolve existing ones. This situation may be discovered during prototyping, i.e. when running a model of the system to assess if it will achieve stipulated objectives. Such requests can be accepted after discussions between management, operating department (user) personnel and systems staff. This will necessitate a modification to the relevant systems documentation to ensure it accords to the system eventually implemented. A record of the modification should be promulgated, i.e. committed to a formal record indicating:

   (*a*) authority for the request;
   (*b*) date of request;
   (*c*) system or sub-system in question;
   (*d*) terms of reference indicating the reason for the request;
   (*e*) agreed course of action.

It may be necessary to submit details of the modification to the audit department so that they can assess the adequacy, or otherwise, of the checks and controls incorporated, if relevant, and that it accords with accepted standards, principles and practice.

16. Post-implementation modifications. Post-implementation requests for modifications can be more serious because not only will amendments to the design of the system be required but programs or parts of programs will need recoding, recompiling and retesting. This can be very costly, time-consuming and disruptive. Inferior system design should be avoided at all costs which is why defined checkpoints should be incorporated at various stages of development. A system will need updating due to technological and economic developments and the passage of time. Such modifications must be put on record in the manner outlined above. It is also necessary to maintain control of the implementation of the modification to ensure no unnecessary delay.

Benchmark tests

17. Benchmark tests defined. Benchmark tests are used to assess the performance of different computer systems for the selection of the system which best fits the requirements of the business's data processing commitment. The tests are applied to representative data and processing functions such as reading and writing records, sorting operations and multiplication, etc. The actual times obtained can be compared with manufacturers' published performance data for evaluating the various computer systems under consideration. Tests are conducted by benchmark programs which also provide valuable information in respect of the amount of internal storage used during processing.

18. Advantages of benchmark tests. These are summarised below:

(*a*) assists in selecting the most suitable computer system for businesses' data processing requirements;

(*b*) performance data is known in advance which assists in formulating job schedules.

Project management and control

19. Analysis of project elements. A project should initially be analysed into primary activities so that the most suitable systems staff may be assigned to their investigation. Staff may be assigned to organisation or communication studies, forms, work flows, data flows, processing operations, file structures and system outputs. In other instances individual systems personnel may be assigned to investigate the whole of a system depending upon the complexity of the project and the available manpower resources.

20. Project life cycle. The next requirement of project planning is to formulate the project life cycle by defining the project start date. It is then necessary to estimate the duration time of each constituent component of the initial systems analysis stage. Time for developing a number of alternative proposals will also be required. Time estimates will also be required for writing, compiling and testing programs, systems implementation, the evaluation of results and system maintenance.

It is then possible to assess the prospective completion date of the project. The target time is always difficult to achieve because of the many uncertainties involved, such as problems which are difficult to resolve; elements of a procedure previously not considered as they were not included in the procedure manual or were not apparent but which are found to be critical to the effective operation of the system; unplanned staff absences; and so on. It is, however, important to have a time schedule and a list of essential activities to be performed so that resources may be deployed from lower priority projects when necessary in an attempt to achieve the stated completion time. Any plan is better than no plan at all.

Account must be taken of the sequence in which tasks must be performed. Some activities are dependent upon the completion of others, e.g. it is not possible to write programs until the design of the system is finalised. In other instances various tasks can be performed concurrently, e.g. one investigator can study the organisation and communication structure of a system whilst others are looking into the forms, files and data flows, etc.

21. Planning techniques. Techniques which can be applied for project planning include the use of bar charts (known as Gantt charts) on which the various activities are listed in the form of a schedule. The length of a bar signifies the amount of time allocated to an activity. A more sophisticated technique is the network analysis chart, which is useful for specifying the critical path. This consists of those activities which form the longest route through the network. If delays occur on the critical path then the project completion time will be delayed. This type of control information provides the basis for project control as it makes clear when resources need to be deployed to critical activities which are falling behind schedule. In addition, use of structured techniques should assist project planning as it introduces more identifiable checkpoints.

22. Example of project network planning. Figure 17.2 illustrates a network analysis chart and shows how some activities can be carried out concurrently while others depend on the completion of earlier activities before they can be started. The length of activity lines is not representative of actual time, which is indicated by a figure on the activity line. The chart may be analysed as follows:

Event	Activity	Activity duration time (days)
0–1	Project planning	4
	Systems analysis:	
1–2	Organisation structure	6
1–3	Communication analysis	5
1–4	Records and forms analysis	4
1–5	Data analysis	6
1–6	Work flow and processes	6
	Record the facts:	
2–7	Organisation details	3
3–7	Communication patterns	5
4–7	Records and forms details	6
5–7	Data flows and entity relationships	5
6–7	Details of work flow and processes	7
	System design:	
7–8	Input and output design	11
7–9	Design of screen layouts	9
7–10	File design	7
7–11	Data validation procedures	6

8–12	Programming	9
9–12	Dummy	–
10–12	Dummy	–
11–12	Dummy	–
12–13	Installation and testing	14

Dummy activities are those which do not incur time or use of resources. They are a means of presenting the network without dangling activities. An event is the beginning or end of an activity as indicated by a box in figure and is known as a 'node'. Nodes are often shown as circles.

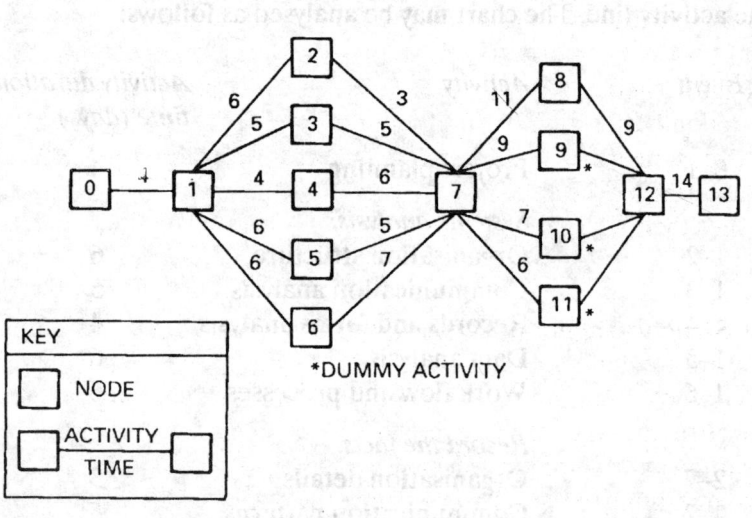

Figure 17.2 *Network analysis chart.*

It will be observed that as this is a complex project it will require segregating into a number of specific sub-projects each allocated to a project team under the control of a team leader. Each team leader reports to the project co-ordinator, who takes the steps necessary to ensure that all sub-projects maintain compatibility with overall system objectives. In this instance the project has been sub-analysed into sub-projects, which are carried out sequentially as follows:

(a) project planning;
(b) systems analysis;
(c) record the facts;
(d) systems design;
(e) programming;
(f) installation and testing.

The different activities covered by systems analysis are carried out concurrently, as shown in the list above and Fig. 17.2, as are the system design activities. This is possible because the nature of the analysis is different and the activities are carried out by different members of the project team.

The critical path lies along the activities 0–1, 1–6, 6–7, 7–8, 8–12 and 12–13. It would of course be possible to commence some system design activities before systems analysis was completed because the latter activities did not all take the same time. In practice it could prove dangerous to proceed to systems design before critically examining all the details of the current system to obtain a complete rather than a fragmented appraisal.

23. Structure of projects. A project may be structured in a number of ways depending on the scope and complexity of the system under review. A small project may be dealt with through all the constituent stages of analysis and design and perhaps programming, testing and implementation by one all-round systems and programming expert. This of course presupposes that the systems personnel possess a wide range of experience embracing the analysis of current systems and the design of inputs, records, files and outputs for proposed systems including knowledge of processing and data capture techniques, etc.

24. Pilot project. A project may consist of developing a pilot project in one section or operating unit of the business, such as a branch of a building society or a branch works. The results obtained from running the pilot system assist in evaluating its suitability for implementation in other locations in the business.

Systems installation, testing and maintenance

Once designed, the installation, testing and maintenance of the system must be implemented. This is considered below under the following topics:

(a) planning the installation;
(b) changeover: direct, parallel running, or pilot scheme;
(c) test data and dry running;
(d) monitoring and maintenance;
(e) retraining personnel.

Planning the installation

25. Determine strategy. When preparing system installation plans it is necessary to take account of the complexity of changeover as this will have a bearing on the time required. Other matters to build into time schedules will be the time needed for training staff, obtaining pre-printed stationery, system testing, resolving problems, file conversion and take-on of opening balances.

26. File conversion/and take-on of opening balances. Many computer-based systems are of an accounting nature necessitating the conversion of files to magnetic media and the transfer of opening balances to the computer files. The time it takes to accomplish this task requires careful planning and control. The longer the transfer takes the more difficult it becomes to catch up with the current status of the system. This leads to frustration as personnel attempt to run both the current and the computer system on a disjointed basis. 'Catch-up' must be given priority while maintaining the current system in an up-to-date condition.

Very often records are converted from ledger cards on which transaction details are recorded by hand or posting machine to magnetic media by suitable encoding methods. Before conversion it is essential that the balances on such records as stock record cards, suppliers' and customers' accounts and employee payroll records are reconciled to ensure only correct balances are transferred to the new system. This creates a high volume activity and suitable arrangements must be made sufficiently in advance to avoid unnecessary 'take-on' delay. (*See* Figs. 8.8 and 8.22.)

27. System changeover. The methods of system changeover are outlined below to illustrate the various characteristics which need to be taken into account during the planning stage of installation. The methods relate to the way in which a new computer system will be installed or implemented.

There are three primary methods of changeover from the current system to a new computer system.

(a) direct;
(b) parallel running;
(c) pilot scheme.

Direct changeover

28. Nature of direct changeover. By this method the new system is installed without parallel running or pilot schemes. It is suitable only for relatively simple systems, but these are very rare as even the simplest of computer systems is in fact relatively complex to get up and running. Small business computers are more straightforward than mainframe installations but even so there are many complex factors to consider. All systems have inherent problems which do not always manifest themselves until the previous system has been dispensed with.

29. When to use direct changeover. Direct changeover should be contemplated only after considering all the possible problems that can arise and their consequences. This is a high-risk method but may be adopted when the system is straightforward, when user staff are confident in running the system, and when time is short. This method may also be adopted when the current system and the new system are so dissimilar that parallel running is irrelevant. It may also be applied when the additional staff necessary for parallel operation are not available.

Parallel running

30. Nature of parallel running. This method requires the running of both the current and new system side by side on a fail-safe basis. The current system is not dispensed with until the integrity of the new system has 'been proved beyond reasonable doubt'. This is accomplished by comparing the results produced by the current system with those produced by the computer system. If they are in agreement the system integrity is assured.

As this is a fail-safe method it is costly because it is necessary to engage staff for running both systems side by side. This method also usually prolongs the testing period and delays system changeover, consequently time must be allowed for this factor. It is necessary, therefore, for a limit to be set on the number of cycles for which the two systems will run in parallel.

31. When to use parallel running. It may be said that parallel running should be adopted for all installations. Very rarely will the circumstances warrant the risky practice of direct changeover.

Pilot scheme

32. Nature of a pilot scheme. This method of system changeover also adopts a cautious approach. Resources are not committed to a company-wide implementation and the installation of a system is restricted to one location only. The results obtained from running this pilot scheme assist in determining the suitability of the system for other locations in the business. As an example, a pilot scheme may be implemented in one branch of a multi-branch business such as a bank or building society to assess its performance before it is introduced on a wider basis in all branches. This applies, for example, when putting branches on-line to a centrally located computer for dealing with daily branch transactions.

33. When to use a pilot scheme. A pilot scheme should be adopted when the system under consideration has far-reaching consequences on the efficient performance of key activities on a wide scale throughout the business. In such cases it is prudent to limit the implementation to one section of the business to be used as a proving ground. This will then avoid wide-scale disruption within the business environment.

NOTE: Whatever method of system implementation is allowed

for in time schedules under the various circumstances which may prevail, it is necessary to consider two important factors:

(1) Do not prolong changeover to live operation unnecessarily as this will incur operating costs, perhaps because of extended parallel running.

(2) Do not change over to live operation too soon as operational inefficiency may be encountered due to insufficient familiarity with the new system as a result of inadequate training.

Test data and dry running (desk checking)

34. Test data and dry running. Prior to the installation of the computerised system test data must be prepared for live testing. It is also necessary to simulate the operation of the computer application before it is installed, to detect any bugs. This is accomplished by desk checking or dry running, which involves running through the program coding as the computer would do when processing actual data. This dry running may also be performed while checking related flowcharts and decision tables.

System monitoring and maintenance

35. Follow-up (monitoring). After the system has gone live and proved to be performing satisfactory it is still necessary to monitor the system to ensure that no abnormalities occur and to remove the cause if any arise. It may be found that, although the system is achieving results as stipulated in the system specification, the system design does not provide for certain requirements. This situation will, of course, require system modification which will necessitate program recoding, recompiling and retesting. It will also require checks to ensure that system security and privacy are maintained at the stipulated level. Security checks must be made to ensure that there is no unauthorised access, for example, to confidential files such as the payroll and customer file and that access is barred to computerised automatic cheque writing facilities.

Periodic review meetings should be arranged to discuss future development of the system. Such development may take the form of system integration or links to a database.

36. System maintenance. Systems in their original form often outlive their usefulness because of the need to change business practices in accordance with changing economic circumstances and the introduction of new legislation. In addition, systems may be implemented initially on a stand-alone functional basis and management may later consider it a practical proposition to integrate related systems to avoid the input of data several times to each of several systems for different purposes. In addition, batch processing applications may be converted to on-line multi-user or multi-tasking systems. In other instances a database may need to be implemented to support the needs of a major business function or to rationalise the storage and retrieval of data for integrated systems.

Retraining personnel

37. Changing systems needs retraining of personnel. When manual systems are superseded by computerised applications there is a need to retrain existing personnel or recruit personnel from external sources for the new types of task which have been created. Before training can commence, however, it is necessary to select suitable personnel with the required aptitude and potential for specified tasks. Manual dexterity, for example, is essential for the expert manipulation of a terminal keyboard or keyboard data encoder, as this determines the speed with which data can be input for processing, the efficiency with which terminal operations are conducted, and the efficiency with which data can be encoded.

38. Training schedule. It is important to prepare a training schedule sufficiently far in advance of the date set for system changeover to ensure a smooth transition from one system to the other. It will also be necessary to arrange for personnel to be released from their current duties to attend the specified training courses or training sessions. Although this can disrupt the smooth functioning of the various departments concerned, it is a matter which must be accepted as a necessary requirement — the price to pay for future greater efficiency.

Progress test 17

1. Indicate the objectives of systems design and the essential requirements for the effective design of systems.   (1, 2)

2. Prepare a checklist for the guidance of systems analysts when designing forms for use in computer systems.   (3)

3. Specify and describe briefly the contents of a system specification.   (5–14)

4. Outline a procedure for dealing with requests for system modifications.   (15, 16)

5. Indicate the nature and purpose of benchmark tests.   (17, 18)

6. State important factors in respect of project management and control.   (19–24)

7. What factors need to be taken into account when converting files for a computerised application?   (26)

8. There are three primary methods of changing over from the current system to a new computer system. These are: (a) direct changeover; (b) parallel running; (c) pilot scheme. Discuss the characteristics of each of these methods.   (27–33)

9. Prior to live operation of a newly computerised application it is essential to test the performance of the system by means of test data. Discuss.   (34)

10. After systems have been implemented it is necessary to monitor their performance. Why is this necessary?   (35)

11. Why is system maintenance necessary?   (36)

12. When changing systems to computerised applications, retraining of personnel becomes necessary. Discuss.   (37, 38)

1. Indicate the objectives of system design and the essential fundamentals in an effective design objectives. (1-2)
2. Prepare a checklist for the adequacy of various alternatives for assigning tasks for use in computer systems. (5)
3. Specify and describe briefly the contents of program specification. (6-10)
4. Outline a procedure for dealing with requests for system modifications. (15-16)
5. Indicate the nature and purpose of benchmark tests. (17-18)
6. State important factors to keep in respect of management and control. (19-2.)
7. What factors need to be taken into account when converting files for computerised applications? (23)
8. There are three alternative ways of changing over from the current system to a new computer system. These are: (a) direct changeover; (b) parallel running; (c) pilot scheme. Discuss the characteristics of each of these methods. (27-28)
9. In testing live operation of a newly computerised application it is essential to test the performance of the system by means of test data. Discuss. (33)
10. After systems have been implemented it is necessary to monitor their performance. Why is this necessary? (35)
11. Why is system maintenance necessary? (36)
12. When changing to newly computerised applications re-training of personnel becomes necessary. Discuss. (37-38)

Part five
Programming and software

18
Computer programming and decision tables

Nature of computer programs and programming

1. Source and object programs. Programs are sets of instructions for processing data to attain the purpose and objectives of a particular application. They are written in the code of a particular programming language to produce a 'source' program, which is converted into a machine code 'object' program used for processing transaction data. The conversion is a translation operation in the same sense that an English/French dictionary translates the words of one language into those of the other. Computer programs are converted by software known as 'interpreters', 'assemblers' or 'compilers', which are discussed in Chapter 20. A computer program instructs the computer in the operations to be performed on data in the same way as a procedure manual in a clerical system tells a clerk the operations (activities) required to process a business procedure.

Users of small business computers, such as accountants, executives and office staff generally, often do not possess much programming knowledge or expertise. This does not prevent them from operating the computer since the programming for a number of business applications has already been done in the form of pre-programmed application packages supplied by distributors or software houses. Programming is largely the province of professional programmers, often employed in the systems department of a business to write and test for internal use programs for which suitable packages do not exist.

2. Predefined instructions. Each operation performed by a computer (on transaction data relating to a specific application) is in accordance with a predefined instruction.

Each instruction defines a basic operation to be performed, identifies the address of the data to be processed, the location of the data affected by the operation and the input or output device to be used. The complete set of instructions necessary to process a job is known as a 'program'.

Instructions are of five basic types:

(*a*) *Arithmetic/logic.* Add, subtract, multiply, divide, shift, round-off, collate and compare, etc.

(*b*) *Data transfer.* Read from input, read to output, read a character, read a word, read a block of data, print a line, transfer data to different locations in the memory, etc.

(*c*) *Conditional branch or jump.* The presence of specific conditions in the data being processed is established by a comparison of data factors or the testing of a counter which causes the computer to branch or jump to the next appropriate instruction.

(*d*) *Unconditional branch or jump and loop.* When it is necessary to execute an instruction which is not the next in sequence in the internal memory, this is achieved by an instruction known as an unconditional branch or jump. This provides the means of creating a loop in the program for executing a common sequence of instructions repeatedly to various units of data. A loop is terminated by a conditional branch after effecting a test.

(*e*) *Counter.* A counter is a memory location (unit of storage) used for the purpose of storing a control parameter for automatically controlling a processing sequence. A counter may be set with a specific number which is decremented by '1' after each event being controlled. The counter may then be tested to detect whether it reads '0', for instance. If a '0' is detected a conditional branch is executed to a specific set of instructions. If the counter does not read '0' a conditional branch is executed to a different set of instructions, perhaps to execute a further loop in the program.

Program development cycle

3. Important considerations. Before specifying the stages involved in the development cycle a number of important matters need to be considered, many of them emanating from the program specification provided by the system designer (*see* 17: 5–14). Before designing the program(s) it is necessary to understand fully the type of application to be programmed, be it payroll, sales invoicing and sales ledger, stock control, or whatever. The processing technique to be applied, whether batch or interactive transaction processing, etc., will be stated in the specification. The type of language to be used must be decided on — typically COBOL, C, Fortran, Pascal, etc., depending on the practice of a particular installation. The complexity of the system being developed needs to be assessed and decision tables and program flowcharts prepared accordingly, which simplifies the task of program coding. The validation checks to be incorporated in programs must be decided on to ensure the integrity of the data being processed, as must the standard sub-routines to be incorporated, i.e. program modules common to several applications, to avoid repetitive coding. The program is then coded in the chosen language and subjected to desk checking, known as a 'dry run', to detect programming errors. The 'source' code is then compiled to obtain an 'object' program in machine code which is stored on magnetic disc. Program diagnostic routines carried out during program testing indicate errors in the program. After errors have been corrected the program will need to be recompiled (or assembled) prior to further testing. The results obtained from program testing are compared with those which have been pre-computed, thus providing a means of evaluating the integrity of the program. After successful testing the program is run live and the results monitored to ensure they accord with system performance criteria and meet specification requirements. The programs are updated (referred to as maintenance) after a period of live operation, to meet changes required by the users or to eliminate inconsistencies (bugs) which do not show up at testing time.

4. Summary of stages. The stages of the program development cycle may be summarised as follows:

   (*a*) consult system specification;

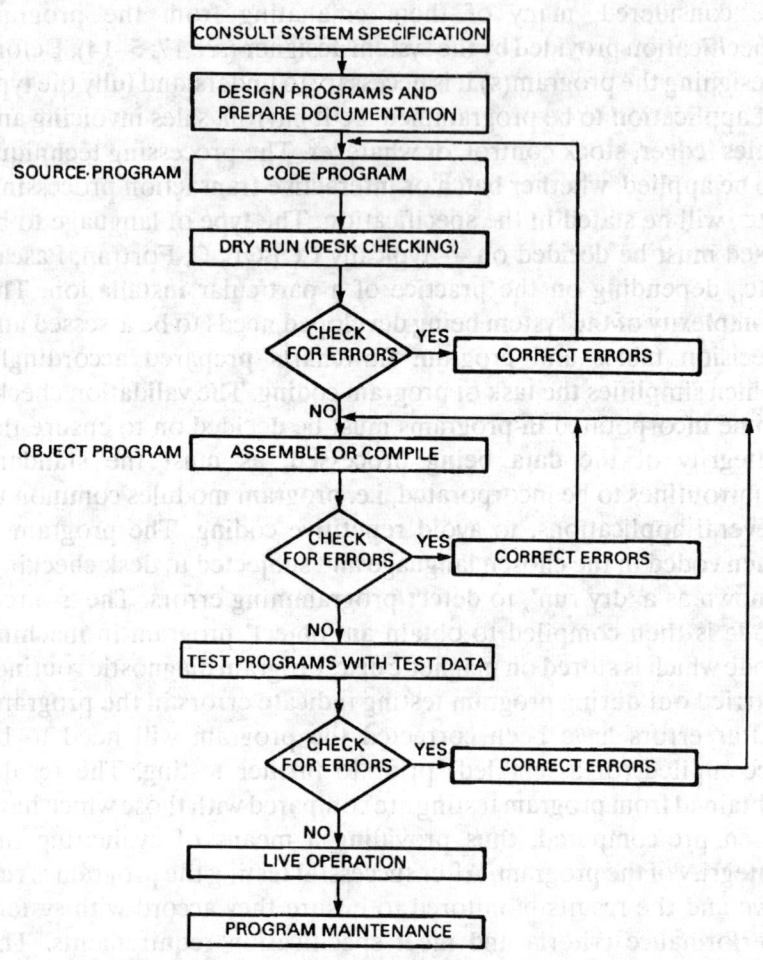

Figure 18.1 *Program development cycle.*

(b) design programs and prepare documentation, decision tables and flowcharts, etc.;

(c) code programs to provide source code on coding sheets — this is also an element of program documentation;

(d) dry run by desk checking programs for initial testing to detect programming errors;

(*e*) assemble or compile source code to obtain object programs in machine code (these are the programs used for processing);

(*f*) correct errors and recompile as necessary;

(*g*) test programs by running them on the computer and comparing results obtained with those pre-computed;

(*h*) detect and correct errors;

(*i*) recompile as necessary;

(*j*) live operation and monitoring;

(*k*) program maintenance.

See Fig. 18.1.

Program structure

The primary structure of a program may be developed on the basis described below. (*See* Fig. 18.2.)

5. Program initialise.

1. Define constants, variables, etc.
2. Open files: input and output.
3. Read first record (this is read ahead).

6. Main body of program.

Process records until end of file.

1. Input transaction data: details of business transactions.
2. Validate data: ensure data is correct before processing.

Depending upon the validity of the data, either:

3. Reject data and display error, *or*:
3. Accept and process data — perform relevant arithmetic and logical operations.
4. Update files: store revised records on disc.
5. Output results: relevant output device.
6. Read next record.

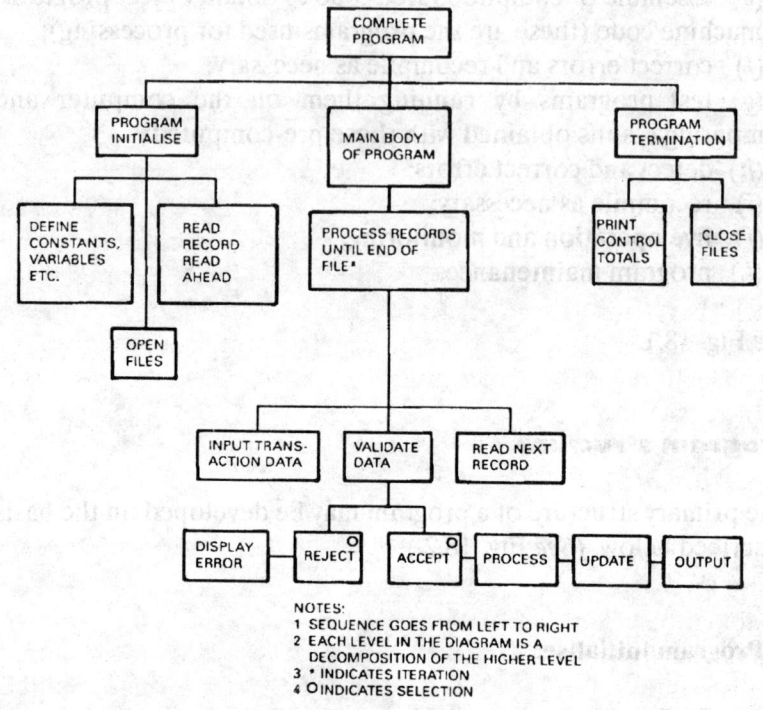

Figure 18.2   *Program structure diagram.*

7. Program termination.

1.   Print control totals: total value of transactions and number of records processed.
2.   Close files: input and output.

Structured programming

8. Independent program sections. Structured programming techniques develop a program as a series of independent sections each designed to perform only one specified task. This approach enables programming errors to be localised to one section of the overall program and also assists program maintenance by making it possible to amend one section without affecting any other. Each section must have only one entry point and one exit point and there should be no jumps to statements in other sections as this would infringe the principle of entry and exit points.

9. Problem algorithm. The objective of structured programming is to produce an algorithm of a problem which can be easily converted into a programming language. It is of course necessary to construct an algorithm only from structures which are explicitly available in the programming language to be used. Structured programming includes WHILE-WEND and REPEAT-UNTIL expressions which perform a series of statements in a loop. Program construction is based on three primary constructs: sequence (*see* 11), selection (*see* 18) and iteration (*see* 12), which are discussed below.

Structured English and constructs

10. Definition of logical processes. Structured English provides a basis for structured programming because it consists of a combination of English words and program-type constructs used to define the logical processes required by a program. Structured English is a sub-set of the English language, with a limited vocabulary consisting of:

(*a*) imperative verbs to express functions;
(*b*) data dictionary terms, including nouns for the name of data items, documents or reports;
(*c*) reserved words for logic formulation.

Its syntax is also limited and omits most punctuation and all adjectives and adverbs. Structured English enables system logic to be easily understood by user department staff, which aids productive discussions with systems analysts during system development. Other conventions which need to be considered when applying structured English include:

(*a*) When using IF or WHILE statements conditions should be inserted in parentheses.
(*b*) Subordinate sentences should be indented for purposes of clarity.

Constructs

11. **Sequence.** A sequence is the normal flow of logic in a system which indicates the sequence in which program statements are to be executed. This may be illustrated by a simple diagram, as in Fig. 18.3.

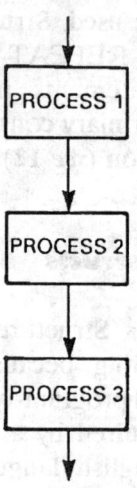

Figure 18.3 *Sequence.*

12. **Iteration.** Repetition, or iteration, utilises loop statements such as WHILE DO or WHILE WEND, REPEAT UNTIL. Iteration is concerned with repeating a group of instructions until a particular condition is detected. This creates a loop in the program to avoid having to repeat the same instructions continually. Iteration continues until a particular condition is satisfied. Fig. 18.4 portrays this construct. The WHILE-WEND expression allows a loop to be executed as long as a logical expression is true. For example: WHILE (not end of wages file) DO. This is interpreted as: It is true that the end of the wages file has not been processed in which case the loop to process wages would be continued. (This is discussed further below.)

The REPEAT-UNTIL expression is applied while a condition is untrue. Referring to Fig. 18.4, it may be interpreted as:

```
WHILE (not end of processing) DO
  IF (x < > 10) THEN
    REPEAT
      Process 1
    UNTIL (x = 10) ELSE
      Process 2
  END IF
ENDDO
```

The completion of an iteration structure should be terminated with an ENDWHILE or ENDDO or other similar convention.

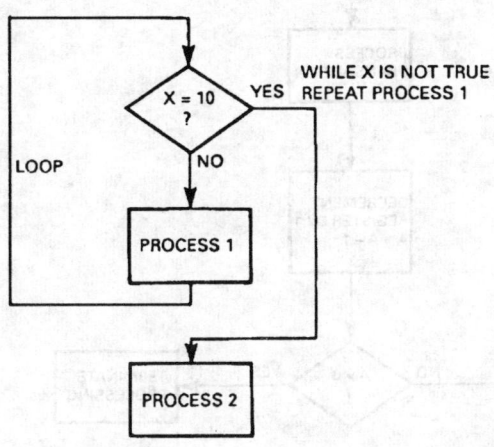

Figure 18.4   *Iteration.*

13. Incrementing and decrementing a register. An iteration can repeat an activity a specified number of times or until a file or transaction are completely processed. This can be controlled by testing the status of a register after being incremented or decremented.

14. Example 1. If 50 transactions are to be processed a register can be set to 50 (A = 50) (*see* Fig. 18.5) and decremented by 1 after each transaction has been processed. This is outlined below:

Set register A = 50
WHILE (not end of processing) DO
　　REPEAT
　　　Process transaction
　　　Decrement register by 1
　　UNTIL (register A = 0)
ENDWHILE

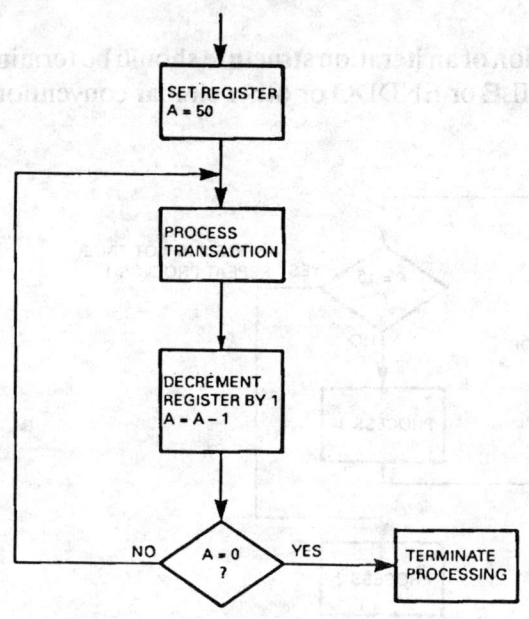

Figure 18.5 *Selection by decrementing and testing condition of register.*

15. Example 2. Alternatively, a register can be set to 0 (A = 0) *(see* Fig. 18.6) and incremented by 1 after each transaction has been processed. This may be illustrated as follows:

Set register A = 0
WHILE (not end of processing) DO
　　REPEAT
　　　Process transaction
　　　Increment register by 1
　　UNTIL (register A = 50)
ENDWHILE

The logic of this example may also be shown as follows:

```
Set register A = 0
   IF (register A < 50) THEN
      Process transaction
      Increment register by 1 ELSE
      Terminate processing
   END IF
```

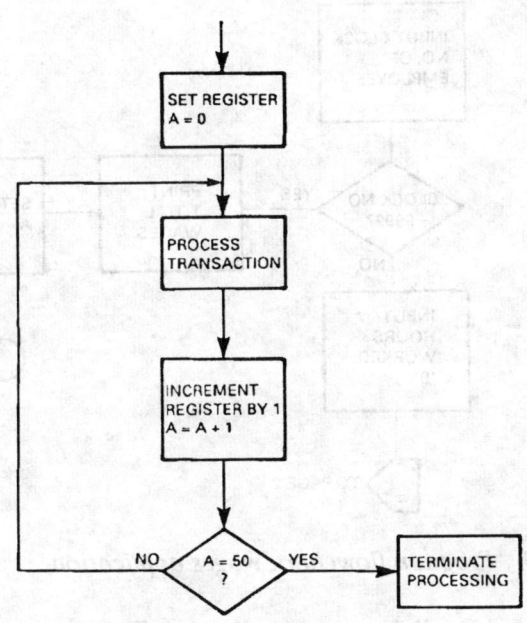

Figure 18.6 *Selection by incrementing and testing condition of register.*

16. Example 3. A wages file is processed and it is necessary to terminate the execution of the program when all transactions have been processed, i.e. when the end of the transaction file has been reached. For this purpose the condition test is: IF clock number is = 9999 THEN ... ELSE. The use of 9999 for testing for the end of the transaction file is based on the range of clock numbers in use. In this instance the range terminates below 9999, e.g. the range may be 0001 to 5999. This test signifies that when the clock number is

9999 the last transaction had been dealt with in the previous pass. This is illustrated in Fig. 18.7.

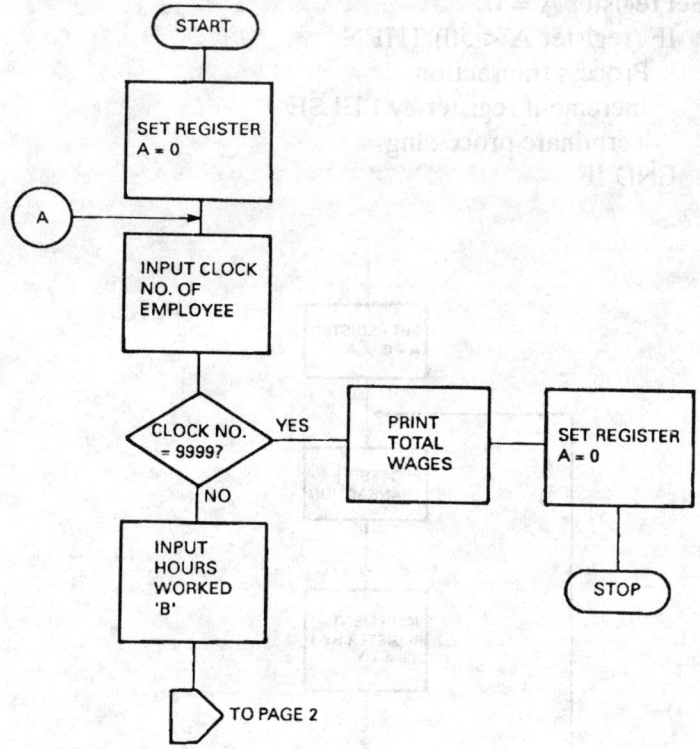

Figure 18.7 *Program flowchart: wages application.*

17. Structured English: wages application. The complete flowchart for the wages application is shown in Fig. 18.7. This is converted into structured programming format from which the program can be coded into the relevant programming language.

```
Set register A = 0
WHILE (not end of wages file) DO
     Input (clock number of employee)
         IF (clock number = 9999) THEN
             Print total wages
             Increment register ELSE
                 WHILE (not last transaction)
```

```
      REPEAT
          Input hours worked
          Input hourly rate
          Compute wages
          Sum wages
          Print clock number, hours worked, hourly rate,
          wages
      UNTIL (end of transactions)
    ENDWHILE
  ENDIF
ENDWHILE
```

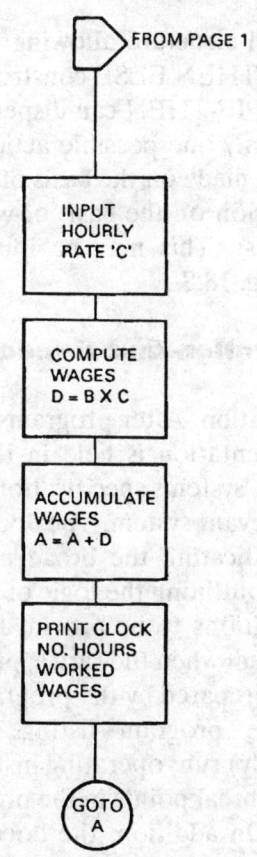

Figure. 18.7 *(cont.)*

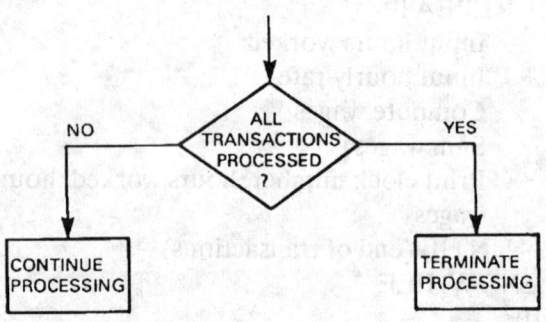

Figure 18.8 *Selection.*

18. Selection. A control structure allowing tests to be made for conditions using the IF THEN ELSE construct (*see* **16**). Selection control structures using IF-THEN can dispense with ELSE when a condition can have only one possible action to deal with it. A selection, or decision, is made on the basis of program logic which selects the next instruction on the basis of which of two or more possible conditions exist. This may be illustrated by a simple diagram, as shown in Fig. 18.8.

Program documentation and standards

19. Program documentation. After programs have been prepared all the relevant documentation is held in the systems folder or manual, referred to as a 'systems specification' because it contains all the details of the relevant system. The documentation includes low-level flowcharts indicating the broad characteristics of the system; decision tables outlining the logic of the system regarding the nature of the conditions to be provided for and the actions required to deal with them when they arise; program coding sheets of the source program prepared by the programmer together with the subsequent source program listing obtained from the compilation (or assembly) run; operating instructions for running the program, specifying breakpoints in the program and stationery changeover needs, etc. In addition, the documentation contains input, output and file formats; data structure charts; charts consisting of sections relating to input, processing and output. The input and output sections are concerned with input, output and files whereas the processing section describes the processes necessary to convert inputs to outputs; program network diagrams are also included which illustrate interactions between data and the various processing operations.

20. Programming standards. Producing programs within the framework of data processing standards will aid the continuity of program development in the event of programmers leaving the company. New programmers will be in a position to assess the documentation as far as it has been developed and continue from that point on the basis of laid down standards relating to the construction of flowcharts, decision tables and coding, etc. Accordingly, they will attain an acceptable level of productivity and expertise much sooner than otherwise would be possible.

Standards have been developed by the National Computing Centre (NCC); the British Standards Institution (BSI); IBM and other major computer manufacturers; the International Organisation for Standardisation (ISO), the American National Standards Institute, Inc. (ANSI) and the European Computer Manufacturers' Association (ECMA). The BSI represents the UK in international organisations concerned with the preparation of international standards. Standards have been established for flowchart symbols and computer languages. The standards relate to file organisation methods, checkpoint/restart routines, job control programs, routines for label writing and checking on file media. Standardisation also includes the use of standard coding sheets and modular programming.

High-level languages

21. Definition. A high-level language is any problem-orientated programmer's language which allows statements to be written in a form with which the user is conversant, such as the use of mathematical equations for a mathematician and plain English-style statements for business applications. This is as distinct from machine-orientated languages, which relate to a specific machine rather than the type of problem to be solved. Example of high-level languages are outlined below.

(*a*) *Algol.* Algol is an acronym for *algo*rithmic *l*anguage, which is a high-level problem-orientated language for mathematical and scientific applications. The language defines algorithms as a series of statements and declarations in the form of algebraic formulae and English words. Each operation is represented as a statement and each unit of data is known as a variable and is assigned a name by the programmer. An instruction or assignment statement of the form $b: = a + c + 5.0$ effectively adds 5.0 to the numbers in the locations a and c and places the answer in location b. The statement consists of the name of a variable followed by =, followed by any arithmetic expression whose answer is put into the left-hand side variable.

(*b*) BASIC. A programming language widely used for time sharing applications and for programming mini- and microcomputers. It is a high-level language relatively simple to learn by non-computer specialists. BASIC is an acronym for *B*eginners *A*ll purpose *S*ymbolic *I*nstruction *C*ode. A simple program for adding two numbers and displaying the result on the screen of a terminal (such as a VDU) or microcomputer is outlined below:

```
10 INPUT A
20 INPUT B
30 C = A + B
40 PRINT C
50 END
```

(*c*) CBASIC *Compiler.* This is the Digital Research Inc. industry standard commercial dialect of BASIC suitable for the business environment. CBASIC Compiler is a direct enhancement of CBASIC that is five to ten times faster in execution than most versions of BASIC. It is possible to write, test and combine separate modules for creating complete programs applying the modular, top-down approach. It includes facilities for graphics, expanded file processing techniques, supports multi-user operating systems and is compatible with CP/M Graphics.

(*d*) *Other versions of* BASIC. Microsoft BASIC, which is very widely used; XBASIC, which is a British engineering- and mathematics-orientated version with matrix-handling; and XTal

BASIC, another British version which has a choice of screen- or line-based editors.

(e) COBOL. This is an acronym for *common business-oriented language*. It is a high-level programming language designed to assist the task of programmers by enabling them to write programs in a more simple form than is possible with assembly code. The language is largely used for mainframe computer applications. It is problem- rather than machine-orientated as it is designed to assist the solving of business problems for such applications as stock control, payroll, sales and purchase ledger accounting.

COBOL consists of four divisions:

(i) identification;
(ii) environment;
(iii) data;
(iv) procedure.

(f) CIS COBOL. This version of the language is that of Micro Focus Ltd. The CIS stands for *compact, interactive and standard*. It is a complete system for compiling, testing, debugging and executing standard COBOL programs. It has become the most widely favoured version of the ANSI 1974 COBOL language. It can be used for running existing mainframe and minicomputer programs on a microcomputer. A micro can also be used to develop COBOL software for larger computers.

(g) *Level II* COBOL. This version of the language is also attributable to Micro Focus Ltd. It provides the full facilities of mainframe COBOL on 8-bit or 16-bit microcomputers, allowing the user to develop mainframe programs with the interactive facilities of a microcomputer. It allows portability of software between mainframe and microcomputers; employs dynamic paging to allow implementation of programs greater than 64k bytes on 8-bit microcomputers; provides for interactive screen handling.

(h) *Pascal.* This is a high-level programming language which is highly structured, enabling programs to be written more efficiently without the problem of writing long programs using monolithic structure.

It executes programs quickly, much faster than interpretative languages like BASIC, but it is more complex and time consuming to learn initially. When preparing a program Pascal words are typed in boldface such as **Procedure, begin, end, program** and write. Modules consist of separate procedures each of which is an element of the main program. The main program 'calls' the procedures in the order they are to be executed.

(*i*) *Pascal/MT +*. This is a version of Pascal by Digital Research Inc. It provides speed and accuracy for developing microcomputer programs. It is a direct-compiling dialect of the full ISO standard Pascal — greatly enhanced and extended to maximise the inherent versatility and portability of the language. Pascal/MT + native code compiler executes much faster than traditional p-code Pascal compilers. The programming system includes a compiler, a linker, run-time support library, disassembler and a symbolic program debugger. It is compatible with CP/M Graphics.

(*j*) *PL/1*. A powerful all-purpose language which rivals Fortran for scientific applications and COBOL for commercial applications. Digital Research Inc. has developed a version of the language for implementation on microcomputers. It is based on the ANSI Standard Subset G. It is easily transported from micro to mini to mainframe or from mainframe to mini to micro. The Digital Research Inc. PL/1 program development system includes an optimising native code compiler, an assembler, a linker, library manager, cross-reference generator and a comprehensive library of built-in functions. It supports CP/M Graphics.

(*k*) C. An advanced programming language built for coding power and speed of execution with a minimum of constraints. It allows skilled software developers to take full advantage of the inherent structure of the computer. C is ideal for applications which must achieve a high level of performance and for systems level programming. The Digital Research Inc. C programming development system includes a compiler, linker, run-time library containing a wide range of utilities which handles everything from transcendental functions to input-output.

(*l*) LOGO. A structured programming language which is becoming popular in the field of education as it is designed to allow very young children, in the four to five age group, to program a computer. The language was developed at the Massachusetts Institute of Technology in the late 1960s by a team led by Seymour Papert. LOGO takes the form of a 'turtle', i.e. a mechanical device or a triangle of light on the screen of a computer. Both forms provide the means for drawing lines either on a sheet of paper or on the screen.

(*m*) *Fortran.* An acronym for *For*mula *Trans*lation. It is a high-level language for scientific and mathematical use. The language was introduced by IBM in 1957 but has since developed into different forms. It has been replaced to some extent by BASIC and other high-level languages.

(*n*) *Lisp.* This language is designed to process data in the form of lists, which is indicated by the name of the language: *lis*t *p*rocessing language. It is based on Algol.

(*o*) *Coral.* A high-level programming language for real-time applications developed by the Royal Radar Establishment at Malvern, England.

(*p*) *Forth.* A high-level programming language designed for small computers, having the advantage of requiring a small amount of memory and being independent of a specific machine.

22. Portability. Digital Research Inc. develops languages that allow the user to design applications programs, which can then be applied to various processors and operating systems allowing full portability from 8-bit to 16-bit or 32-bit environments: from microcomputer to mini or mainframe. Programming productivity has been enhanced by Digital Research, which provides the most important commercial programming languages in sophisticated compiler implementations which are portable. Some aspects of these programs are outlined in the following text.

Procedural languages

23. General features. A procedural language specifies the way in which a process has to be carried out and requires statements to be executed in sequence, unless directed to branch to a sub-routine when a specific condition exists or when a new transaction requires to be repeated. The procedure is repeated by the process of looping until all transactions have been dealt with or a specific condition exists. Procedural languages include COBOL, Fortran, Pascal, C and Lisp.

24. Lisp. Lisp is one of the oldest higher-level languages, designed to process data in the form of lists (*see* **21**(*n*)). Instead of using statements and commands the language uses procedures to operate on the data. The data comprises words called 'atoms', which can be numbers or symbolic names for some object, place or event. The atoms are grouped together to form lists which are then manipulated to achieve the desired purpose. A procedure is an operation that is applied to the atoms and lists. The basic operation of Lisp is to read the procedure, evaluate and print the result. This cycle is repeated on each procedure until the required processing occurs.

Non-procedural languages

25. General features. Non-procedural languages specify what is to be achieved but not how to achieve it. They are declarative languages because instead of defining a sequence of instructions the programmer provides facts and relationships about a problem.

26. Prolog. This is a declarative, problem-orientated language used for developing knowledge-based systems. It is non-procedural because it does not define a sequence of instructions, but acts upon facts and relationships relating to a problem from which new facts are inferred and used to solve the problem. (*See* **27**(*a*)–(*b*) which contrasts procedural and non-procedural.)

27. Illustration. A simple illustration will distinguish between the two types of language:

   (*a*) *Procedural*:
     (*i*)   Key in employee number.
     (*ii*) Key in hours worked.
     (*iii*) Key in hourly rate.
     (*iv*) Compute wages earned.
     (*v*) Print employee number.
     (*vi*) Print hours worked.
     (*vii*) Print wages earned.

(b) *Non-procedural*:

(i) Compute wages earned and print hours worked and wages earned.

A non-procedural language:

(a) meets the specification of a 4GL (*see* **28**);
(b) is very brief;
(c) takes the form of a natural language;
(d) is usable by a non-specialist;
(e) is easy to understand;
(f) is user friendly.

Fourth generation languages (4GLs)

28. What it is. A 4GL is a computer-based language in which the programmer, or user, specifies *what* is to be done and not *how* to do it, written in an ultra-high-level English-like language. In *Software: Design, Implementation and Support,* by David Leigh, David Hatter and Roy Newton, a 4GL is defined as 'a member of the next generation of programming languages which will make communication with the machine easier, will allow quicker production of reliable software and will generally improve the way in which computers serve people'.

29. Requirements of a 4GL. A 4GL must be well structured, easily understood by other users, capable of easy modification and debugging and must be self-documenting. Further requirements include:

(a) it should be usable and understandable by non-computer specialists;
(b) the language must be as close to a natural language as possible;
(c) it must be able to decide on output formatting;
(d) it must be user friendly.

Fourth generation languages assist personnel when changing from clerical to computerised database applications by enabling them to understand the new working procedures more easily. They assist the manipulation of a database, providing facilities for creating, retrieving, updating, appending, deleting or amending data.

4GLs are very diverse products: approximately, one third of more than 100 available in the UK are non-procedural (*see* 25, 26 and 27(*b*)) and one third are procedural (*see* 23, 24 and 27(*a*)); the remainder have features of both. A number of the products at the bottom end of the market do not include a database but have tools to interrogate one. Many of the lower cost products are little more than program generators which have been given the up-market generic name of 4GL.

30. Procedural steps. A 4GL translates the user's requests into procedural steps to produce the desired output. In this way user views of an application are separated from the mechanics of the system, making it transparent — the end result is of importance to the user, not how it is accomplished. Fourth generation languages are also used as query languages to obtain specific information from a database. A query to retrieve information relating to a specific machine, say a capstan lathe in a factory, in respect of its initial and maintenance costs may be structured as:

List ICost, MCost, For Machine = 'Capstan'

The response to the query would be displayed on the screen as follows:

ICost 1000 MCost 200 Capstan.

When a 4GL is approaching the characteristics of a natural language, a query may be phrased as:

List the names of personnel in department X with less than ten years' service AND who are aged over 50

or, perhaps:

Find all employees in department X with less than ten years' service AND who are older than 50.

For these requirements the 4GL must be able to deal with varied syntax.

31. Fourth generation languages are applicable to:

(a) database query languages;
(b) prototyping languages;
(c) spreadsheets;
(d) screen painters;
(e) application generators;
(f) report generators;
(g) expert systems.

Aids to programming

32. General features. The traditional method of preparing programs, first by the preparation of detailed program flowcharts from which programs are written using a specific programming language, is being superseded to some extent by program development software which uses either a 4GL; menus and prompts for guiding the user through all the stages of development; or structured programming techniques using interactive graphics.

The traditional systems life cycle approach will be affected by this change of methodology as will the use of program flowcharting techniques which are likely to be replaced by structured programming techniques which develop structure diagrams automatically. See below.

33. Program generators.
System C
Program generators are software packages, like Sycero marketed by System C Limited. The package may be used to develop traditional business applications such as payroll, accounts, invoicing and stock control. It can also be applied to the development of programs for applications where ready-made programs are unavailable. This type of package can also be usefully employed by experienced programmers as the Sycero programs are structured and documented in a manner which facilitates linking with other programs. By means of prompts and menus, new records or files can be incorporated.

Building a program in seven steps

Using Sycero, as a example of a program builder or generator, the process of program building is very straightforward and can be accomplished in seven steps.

(*a*) *Plan the system.* Define the elements of the system you want to create, the types of data to be input, the screen layouts for required displays and how many files are needed. Determine how the program is to handle the information.

(*b*) *Specify the system.* With the micro running proceed to select items from the main menu. By following the prompts proceed to define the types of files required and what items of information they will contain. The menu offers the following options:

- (*i*)   system configuration;
- (*ii*) initialisation;
- (*iii*) system — file — field definition;
- (*iv*) screen definition;
- (*v*)   screen processing;
- (*vi*) report definition;
- (*vii*) report processing;
- (*viii*) program definition;
- (*ix*) generate a program;
- (*x*)   create a 'live' data file;
- (*xi*) run a generated program;
- (*xii*) utilities;
- (*xiii*) end session.

(*c*) *Draw the screens.* Having specified where and how data is to be stored it is necessary to specify how the data is to be entered and displayed on the computer screen. On each screen type are descriptions of the items to be entered and the exact position on the screen where the item is to be displayed. Graphics facilities can be used to sketch in lines and boxes giving the system a professional finish.

(*d*) *Check the data.* It is prudent to incorporate a validation/verification procedure to detect when data has been entered incorrectly. Prompts indicate what needs to be input at any point, such as stock number, and also advise on the range of figures acceptable. Error messages can be displayed.

(*e*) *Define the program.* Define the program to operate on the data. Certain standard operations will almost always need to be carried out. Each system will require a file maintenance program to enter, amend and delete information. An enquiry program allows instant on-screen access to all data in any chosen form. Posting programs handle the logic of recording all transactions against a single item and updating files.

(*f*) *Produce the print-out.* The system is now built and it is necessary to specify the printed output requirements — the report definition, i.e. the formatting. The system provides facilities for defining where on a printed page columns are to appear, how they look, what their headers are like and so on. Column totals can be generated, each page can be numbered and print-outs can be stamped with the date and time.

(*g*) *Generate.* The Sycero software requires to know the name of the program. It then translates the data defined and specified into a computer program. The code produced is very lucid and structured.

34. Michael Jackson structured programming. Software known as Program Development Facility (PDF) provides for program development using structured programming methodology. It dispenses with the traditional program methodology of preparing detailed program flowcharts followed by program coding. The PDF technique uses interactive graphics to develop structure diagrams known as 'hierarchy' charts, which replace traditional program flowcharts. The structure diagrams are stored on disc and facilities are provided to modify them as necessary. The screen may be considered to be a window through which a diagram is viewed. A simple command generates pseudo-code (JSP structure text) and source code ready for compilation or preprocessing. Refer to program flowcharts and system life cycle (16: 13).

Program dumps and restart procedures

35. Program dump. When programs are tested it is usual either to print out sections of the program from memory or to display them on a video screen for the purpose of tracing sequence errors which prevent the execution of the program. Sometimes when editing program errors on the screen of a micro they are not always effected in memory so it is advisable to print out the program or list it on the screen to verify whether the corrections have been implemented.

36. Dump and restart procedures. To avoid the consequence of hardware or software malfunctions a fail-safe procedure is adopted, particularly for lengthy or critical programs which are essential for the control of a real-time system. In such instances it is usual to implement checkpoint/restart routines. These provide for the periodic dumping of the contents of the internal memory which signifies the status of the system at that moment of time. Dumping is usually effected to disc or magnetic tape, thus enabling the system to be restarted from the point of the last dump without having recourse to the beginning of the program (which would be impossible to do in any event when controlling dynamic systems). It would, however, be possible to recommence from the beginning jobs running in batch mode, but this would hardly be a practical proposition.

Compile time and execution time errors

37. Compile time errors. When a source program is being compiled from a high-level language to a machine code object program, the compiler generates error diagnostics indicating the type of error in the various instructions — particularly syntax errors. Such errors must be corrected before progressing with program testing. Interactive compilers produce error diagnostics after every statement or instruction, whereas batch compilers list the errors at the completion of the compilation run.

38. Execution time errors. These may be defined in two different ways.

(a) *Program error.* Microcomputers programmed in BASIC have interpreters, in ROM chips, for converting BASIC statements into machine code at execution time, i.e. at the time the program is run. It is only then that syntax and other types of error — logical errors — are signalled. This can be very frustrating as it can delay the running of the program. Errors should be detected and corrected during program testing prior to running the program on live data. The unexpected error may still arise at the most inopportune moment.

(b) *Data errors.* Data errors are detected when a program is run. These may be detected interactively when using a microcomputer, from validation checks built into the program. The computer automatically indicates if the incorrect type of data is being input, i.e. whether numeric data instead of alphabetic characters, or vice versa. When batch processing on a mainframe computer, the initial run is for validation purposes to detect errors before the data is subjected to processing (*see* 13: 30).

Closed and open shop programming

39. Closed shop programming. This is a restriction whereby programmers are not themselves allowed to test programs on the computer but must allow the computer operations staff to do this on their behalf and provide the test results. The reason for this restriction is to minimise the time the computer is occupied on program testing and to avoid disrupting routine processing schedules.

40. Open shop programming. This is a facility provided to programmers for program testing, which allows them to use the computer themselves, providing they are suitably experienced. This provides flexibility in program testing and does not rely on the good offices of operations staff to get the job done. If on-line programming facilities are available there need not be any disruption to routine processing.

Closed and open sub-routines

41. Open sub-routine. An open sub-routine is inserted into the main sequence of instructions, rather than transferring control to a sub-routine, in a specific part of a program when it is required. If the sub-routine is repeated a number of times in the program, then the following considerations need to be taken into account:

(a) the frequency with which the sub-routine is repeated;

(b) the need to increase internal memory capacity to cater for repetition of the sub-routine;

(c) the saving of processing time by not having to branch to the sub-routine each time it is required.

42. Closed sub-routine. A closed sub-routine is one which is inserted in the program once and is referred to when required by a GOSUB or CALL instruction. After execution of the sub-routine, control is returned to a specific part of the program automatically. A 'stack' keeps control of sub-routine operations and a branch back to the main routine is accomplished by a RETURN instruction, which automatically returns control to the instruction following the GOSUB instruction last executed.

43. Sub-routine library. Sub-routines can be stored in backing storage in a sub-routine library, and can then be accessed by a CALL command when required for execution at a specific stage of processing the main program.

44. Link editing. The process of link editing can be applied for combining both external sub-routines — those stored in a sub-routine library on disc — and those specifically prepared for a particular application by the programmer. The input/output routines and other routines when combined form a complete suite of programs for a particular application. Consolidated programs can then be stored on disc ready for loading and execution at the appropriate time, i.e. run time.

Program maintenance

45. Volatile systems. Business systems are volatile as they are continuously being affected by external environmental influences of a random nature. Such influences may be due to changes in technology, competition or legislation. It is therefore necessary for business systems to be dynamic and respond to such influences appropriately.

46. Maintenance programmer. Programs are modified by a maintenance programmer who not only modifies them, for the reasons already indicated, but also keeps them up to date to accord with internal system changes for improving administrative efficiency. Systems may be integrated whereby separately structured systems are combined for improving their productivity.

In addition, programs may be modified to provide for changes in company policy: for example, changes in the payroll program to facilitate amendments to long-service increments.

Decision tables

47. Use and construction. Decision tables are used in the process of analysing the factors involved in a problem, which necessitates defining the conditions specific to the problem and the actions to be taken when the various conditions arise.

A computer program written for a specific application must provide for branching to appropriate parts of the program when specified conditions in data are discovered after testing.

A decision table enables the branching requirements of a program to be precisely specified.

Decision tables may be used to assist the preparation of a complicated flowchart to ensure that all conditions and actions have been catered for and that cause and effect relationships are clearly visible.

48. Limited entry decision table. This type of table is divided into four parts:

(*a*) condition stub
(*b*) condition entries   condition statement
(*c*) action stub
(*d*) action entries   action statement

The condition stub and condition entries define the conditions to be tested.

The action stub and action entries define the actions to be taken dependent upon the outcome of the testing.

The 'rules' consist of a set of outcomes of conditions tests, together with the related actions.

A decision table may be prepared from a procedure narrative by underlining all conditions present with a solid line and all actions with a broken line. The conditions and actions are then recorded on the decision table.

The features of a decision table are as follows.

(*a*) Each condition and action stub contains a limited entry, that is to say an entry complete in itself.

(*b*) The entry part of the table in respect of the condition stub indicates if a particular rule satisfies the condition.

(*c*) The entry part of the table in respect of the action stub indicates the action required in respect of the condition entry.

(*d*) Three symbols are used in the condition entry part of the table.

    (*i*)   Y (yes) if the condition is satisfied.

    (*ii*) N (no) if the condition is not satisfied.

    (*iii*) - (hyphen), if the condition is not relevant to the rule.

(*e*) In the action entry part of the table x is recorded to signify a required action. If no action is required the column is left blank.

49. Extended entry decision table. An extended entry decision table only partly records conditions and actions in the stub. The remaining details are recorded in the entry sections. This type of table is more compact and less complex to understand than a limited entry decision table but is less easy to check for completeness. Compare Fig. 18.9 with 18.10 for an indication of the difference between a limited entry and extended entry table.

	RULES			
	1	2	3	4
CONDITION STUB	CONDITION ENTRY			
SALES REGION CODE ≥ £50	Y	Y	N	N
INVOICE AMOUNT ≥ £1000	Y	N	Y	N
ACTION STUB	ACTION ENTRY			
DELIVERY CHARGES				
ADD £15 TO INVOICE TOTAL			X	
ADD £20 TO INVOICE TOTAL	X			
ADD £30 TO INVOICE TOTAL				X
ADD £40 TO INVOICE TOTAL		X		

Figure 18.9 *Limited entry decision table.*

SALES REGION CODE	≥ 50	≥ 50	< 50	< 50
INVOICE AMOUNT	≥ 1000	< 1000	≥ 1000	< 1000
DELIVERY CHARGES	£20	£40	£15	£30

Figure 18.10 *Extended entry decision table.*

50. When to prepare and use a decision table. A decision table may be used to assist the preparation of a program flowchart when the detailed logic involves a number of complex decisions. This ensures that all possible combinations and actions are met. The program flowchart is then prepared on the basis of one rule at a time working through the decision table. Decision tables may be used when programmer time is limited and the available software permits the direct input of decision tables.

Decision tables and program flowcharts

51. Decision table and flowchart exercise 1. This is a CIMA question.

Stockists Limited calculates discounts allowed to customers on the following basis:

Order quantity	% Normal discount
1–99	5
100–199	7
200–499	9
500 and over	10

These discounts apply only if the customer's account balance is below £500 and does not include any item older than three months. If the account is outside both of these limits, the above discounts are reduced by 2 per cent. If only one condition is violated, the discounts are reduced by 1 per cent. If a customer has been trading with Stockists Limited for over five years and

CONDITION STUB	RULES																			
	1	2	3	4	5	6	7	8	9	10	11	12	13	14	15	16	17	18	19	20
	CONDITION ENTRIES																			
ORDER QUANTITY 1 – 99	Y	Y	Y	Y	Y															
ORDER QUANTITY 100 – 199						Y	Y	Y	Y	Y										
ORDER QUANTITY 200 – 499											Y	Y	Y	Y	Y					
ORDER QUANTITY 500 AND OVER																Y	Y	Y	Y	Y
ACCOUNT BALANCE < £500	N	N	Y	Y	Y	N	N	Y	Y	Y	N	N	Y	Y	Y	N	N	Y	Y	Y
ANY ITEM OLDER THAN 3 MONTHS	Y	N	Y	N	N	Y	N	Y	N	N	Y	N	Y	N	N	Y	N	Y	N	N
TRADING FOR OVER 5 YEARS	–	–	–	Y	N	–	–	–	Y	N	–	–	–	Y	N	–	–	–	Y	N
ACTION SUB	ACTION ENTRIES																			
NORMAL DISCOUNT 5%	X	X	X	X	X															
NORMAL DISCOUNT 7%						X	X	X	X	X										
NORMAL DISCOUNT 9%											X	X	X	X	X					
NORMAL DISCOUNT 10%																X	X	X	X	X
NORMAL DISCOUNT –2%			X	X	X			X	X	X			X	X	X			X	X	X
NORMAL DISCOUNT –1%	X		X			X		X			X		X			X		X		
NORMAL DISCOUNT +1%				X					X					X					X	

Figure 18.11 *Decision table and flowchart exercise 1: decision table.*

conforms to both of the above credit checks then he is allowed an additional 1 per cent discount.

You are required to:

(*a*) construct a limited entry decision table illustrating the above situation; and
(*b*) draw a flowchart illustrating the above situation.

SOLUTION
The solution to this question is illustrated in Figs. 18.11 and 18.12.

52. Decision table and flowchart exercise 2. For additional practice in the preparation of decision tables and flowcharts the reader may wish to attempt the following question set by the former IAS, now the AAT.

A soft drinks manufacturer sells to three sales outlets,

(*a*) supermarkets and large departmental stores
(*b*) retailers
(*c*) hotels and catering establishments.

Dependent upon the sales outlet and the value of sales, the following chart indicates the discounts allowed to customers.

Supermarkets and large departmental stores:	*Discount allowed %*
For orders less than £50	5
For orders £50 and over but less than £100	8
For orders £100 and over	10

Retailers:	*Discount allowed %*
For orders less than £50	3
For orders £50 and over but less than £100	7
For orders £100 and over	10

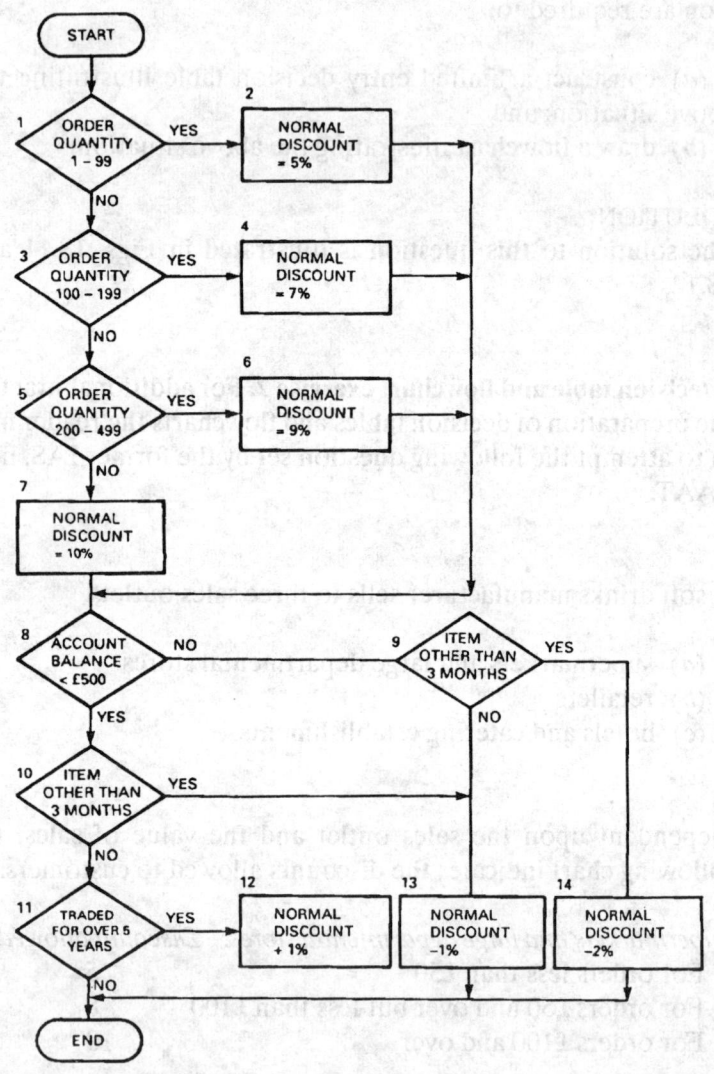

Figure 18.12 *Decision table and flowchart exercise 1: flowchart*

Hotels and catering establishments: *Discount allowed %*
  For orders less than £50   4
  For orders £50 and over but less than £100 $7\frac{1}{2}$
  For orders £100 and over   10

CONDITION STUB	1	2	3	4	5	6	7
	CONDITION ENTRY						
ORDER > £100	N	N	N	N	N	N	Y
RETAILER	Y	Y	N	N	N	N	–
HOTEL & CATERING	–	–	Y	Y	N	N	–
S & L	–	–	–	–	Y	Y	–
ORDER < £50	Y	N	Y	N	Y	N	–
ACTION STUB	ACTION ENTRY						
DISCOUNT							
3%	X						
4%			X				
5%						X	
7%			X				
7¹/₂%					X		
8%							X
10%							X

Figure 18.13 *Decision table and flowchart exercise 2: decision table.*

(*a*) From the information given, construct a 'limited entry' decision table and flowchart.

(*b*) What advantages are there from the use of decision tables?

NOTE: The question has been slightly amended.

SOLUTION
The solution to the question is outlined in Figs. 18.13 and 18.14.

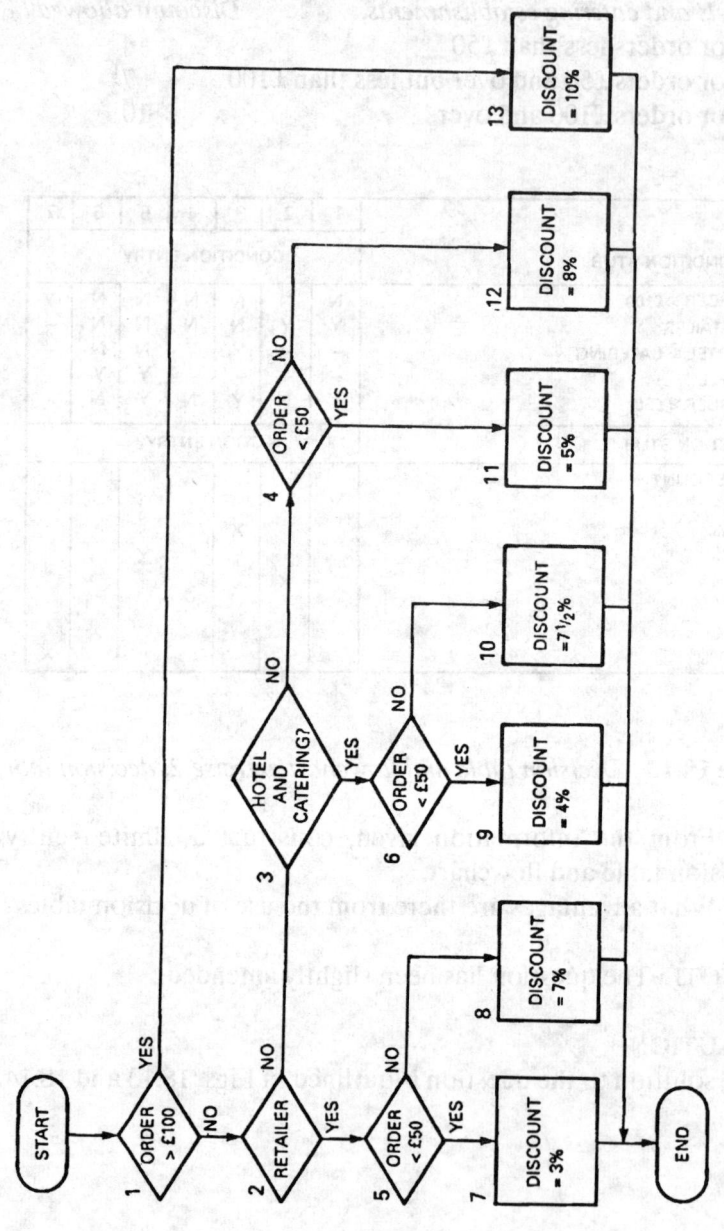

Figure 18.14 *Decision table and flowchart exercise 2: flowchart.*

Progress test 18

1. What is a program?   **(1)**
2. Distinguish between a source program and an object program. **(1)**
3. What is the function of a program instruction?   **(2)**
4. List the stages of the program development cycle.   **(3, 4)**
5. Define the primary structure of a program.   **(5–7)**
6. State the characteristics and purpose of structured programming.   **(8–18)**
7. State the importance of program documentation and programming standards.   **(19, 20)**
8. State the nature of a high-level language.   **(21)**
9. What is the purpose of program portability?   **(22)**
10. Contrast procedural and non-procedural languages. **(23–27)**
11. What is a 4GL?   **(28–31)**
12. What are program generators?   **(32–34)**
13. What is the purpose of a program dump?   **(35)**
14. What is the purpose of checkpoint/restart routines?   **(36)**
15. Distinguish between compile time errors and execution time errors.   **(37, 38)**
16. Contrast the terms 'closed shop programming' and 'open shop programming'.   **(39, 40)**
17. Define the terms 'open sub-routine', 'closed sub-routine', 'sub-routine library' and 'link editor'.   **(41–44)**
18. Why is program maintenance necessary?   **(45, 46)**
19. What is the purpose of decision tables?   **(47)**
20. Distinguish between a limited entry decision table and an extended entry decision table.   **(48, 49)**

19
Applications software

General aspects of software

1. Software defined. The term 'software' relates to all the different types of program used on computer systems, complementing the hardware, i.e. the processor and its peripherals without which it is inanimate and unable to function. To become operational a computer must have software, known as an operating system, resident within its memory. This is 'control software', which is the subject of Chapter 20. This chapter is concerned with the software required for processing specific business applications including payroll, stock control, invoicing, sales ledger, integrated order processing and integrated accounting.

2. Package defined. Packages are pre-written computer programs which are widely used for common applications in order to avoid unnecessary duplication of similar programs by many users. It is a means of rationalising programming effort but this does not imply that the same type of package is not available from more than one source. They are sometimes provided to suit the needs of different models of computer and sometimes in competition. The need to shop around is no less than with competing sources of supply of other commodities and products.

A package consists of a suite of programs, sometimes on the same storage media, for the different routines required to achieve the purpose of the specific application. It consists of documentation in the form of a program/systems manual, containing details of how to set up the program and run it on the computer. The package also includes the relevant medium on which the program is stored. This is usually disc.

3. Package compatibility. Whether a package is suitable for a particular model of computer depends on a number of factors. Packages for a specific make of computer are designed to run on the model with a defined memory capacity, and will not therefore run on machines with less than the specified capacity. Compatibility also depends on the operating system being used, e.g. MS-DOS or PC-DOS, UNIX or XENIX in respect of small business computers. Standard operating systems have available a wide range of packages which can run on any machine using that particular operating system, regardless of the make of machine.

When manufacturers of the larger mainframe computers launch a new model they normally provide for a migration path from one machine to another by making software compatible for the older model and the later model.

4. International Directory of Software. This is a publication by Computing Publications Ltd, which assists the selection of software packages. The products contained in the directory include accounting, administration and banking, communications, CAD/CAM, data management, development aids, distribution, insurance, microprocessor systems, modelling and statistics, production and utilities.

5. Source of packages. Packages are available from a number of sources depending upon the type of computer. Programs for microcomputers, for instance, are available from mail order sources as advertised in computer magazines; or over the counter from retail shops and stores. Packages are also available from dealers in microcomputers, who provide hardware and software, and directly from the computer manufacturer in some instances.

Software for larger computers, i.e. mainframes, is available from a number of sources including the manufacturer of the hardware who also develops the software, from specialist organisations known as software houses, and from private organisations who have developed programs for their own use which they make available to other users for an appropriate fee. Packages are also available from a number of computer bureaux which have expanded their activities.

6. Cost of software. Sometimes a minimum of software is supplied free of charge when the hardware is purchased. Referred to as being 'bundled', this would include the operating system, utilities and applications software. Other software has to be purchased as required on an 'unbundled' basis; it is charged separately.

Microcomputer manufacturers often have a sales promotion policy of providing extensive software with the machine at no extra cost, in order to generate sales of the hardware. This depends on the economic circumstances which prevail at the time and whether a new model is to be launched or new software is becoming available, etc.

Vertical market applications software

Applications software is dedicated to specific industries and types of business. Vertical software is particularly important for the operations of smaller businesses.

7. Accountancy practices. Many suppliers provide facilities for accounting practices, allowing them to computerise the preparation and production of accounts for clients. Some of the facilities required include time and fee recording, foreign currency accounting, work-in-progress scheduling, and the normal range of accounting routines including nominal ledger, fixed asset accounting, profit and loss account and balance sheet, VAT schedule and the production of an audit trail. Apart from the accounting software a database is ideally suited to the storage and retrieval of client information. Word processing software would also benefit the preparation and storage of standard letters, which may be used in conjunction with mailmerge software for selective mail shots.

8. Estate agents. Estate agents need to prepare and store details of many properties coming on to the market, and delete them when a property is sold. A database can be used for this purpose and for maintaining records of clients' property requirements. The searching facilities of a database would greatly increase the productivity and efficiency of this primary task.

Software is available from many suppliers to allow estate agencies to computerise their operations, and provides for the needs of specialist agencies dealing with, for example, commercial, shop and residential properties. Packages should ideally have facilities for producing property advertisements, computing commission on property sales, mortgage services, accounting, valuations and auctions. Electronic diary facilities could be used to advantage for maintaining a record of viewing appointments and other critical time-based activities. Estate agents need to be aware of their exact needs to ensure the selected package(s) covers these requirements.

9. Solicitors. Packages for the legal profession cover conveyancing, litigation support, wills and deeds registers, archiving, time recording, debt collection and trust accounting. Routine accounting procedures are also catered for, including bank reconciliation and cheque writing. The profession also benefits from word processing software due to the numerous types of standard letters to be processed.

10. Stockbrokers. The advent of information technology and de-regulation of the financial services industry have emphasised the fact that efficiency is the keynote to success, and the only effective way to achieve this and obtain a competitive advantage is to computerise operations. Apart from routine accounting applications stockbrokers can apply to advantage computers for accessing current share prices from various databases. Packages should offer modules for share dealings and settlements, etc.

11. Insurance brokers. Packages for this type of business should provide modules for motor vehicles, fire and accident, property and holiday insurance cover, etc. Administrative routines provided should include policy documentation and administration, billing, enquiries, claims administration and provision for processing renewals including instalment plans.

Accounting packages

12. Characteristics and benefits. Efficient accounting systems are imperative for any business, and accounting packages designed to achieve these are available from many sources. Accounting packages can provide valuable information on business performance at the time it is wanted, and provide inbuilt checking facilities to prevent costly errors during computations and when posting transactions to ledgers. Accounting routines to be performed at different frequencies — daily, weekly, monthly and annually — are catered for by appropriate packages and formal reports are usually produced at the month-end.

13. Checklist for selecting accounting packages.

(*a*) What computer and operating system is the software designed for?

(*b*) Is the package for single or multi-user environments? Can single user software be upgraded to multi-user?

(*c*) Can the package be integrated with software from other suppliers?

(*d*) What memory capacity is required?

(*e*) What security facilities does it possess, i.e. access control via passwords and automatic back-up facilities for file security?

(*f*) What is the purchase cost?

(*g*) What are the terms for multiple copies for internal use at different sites?

(*h*) Is software maintenance provided and at what cost?

(*i*) Does the software have a reliable history of use in similar types of business?

(*j*) Does the package contain the latest leading edge technology?

(*k*) Could the package be adapted to meet specific internal requirements and at what cost?

14. Understanding accounting packages. Accounting packages automate accounting routines, providing increased productivity and accuracy of processing, faster reporting and the facility for updating master files on a transaction basis as they occur. Many packages use a mouse to point to the icon of the application (*see* 14: **25–26**), to 'open' and to point to and select the data represented on the screen. Pull-down menus (*see* 2: **10–12**) are used to select and control the functions performed by the package.

The first major consideration before attempting to run any accounting package is to study the manual and set up the system accordingly. The section relating to the nominal ledger (*see* **23–26**) provides information on how this is done. The decision when to change the system over from manual to computer must be made. Usually this is best done at the beginning of a financial year, as balances need to be brought forward in respect of debtors, creditors and fixed assets, etc. New accounts are also opened for sales and expenses at this time. If the system is changed over during a financial year any comparisons with previous years require the figures from the previous system to be added to those produced by the computer — a very tedious process. A year-end date, once established, must be used consistently. Accounting packages are generally user friendly, guiding the user through each processing stage by means of prompts. Some packages are designed to run on a single user basis but others are designed as multi-user or multi-user/ multi-company systems. Some packages provide for account enquiries during data entry activities and the screen displays relevant account details and a print-out is provided if required.

The nature of integrated accounting packages

15. Suite of interrelated programs. An integrated accounting package is a suite of interrelated programs, often in modular form. Each module is designed to run on its own or as part of the package. Integrated accounting packages streamline the accounting routines by allowing the transfer of common information or data relating to business transactions from one application module to another either directly or through a batch file. Typically this relates to the transfer of transaction details from sales and purchasing modules to the nominal ledger. Integrated packages usually include modules covering the following applications:

(*a*) sales, purchase and nominal ledger;

(*b*) invoicing;
(*c*) stock control;
(*d*) payroll and costing;
(*e*) data analysis.

16. Chart of accounts. All accounting systems *must* have a well-structured and effective coding system. Coding structures are specified in a 'chart of accounts', which lists expense, customer, supplier, nominal ledger and departmental (cost centre) codes which facilitate data transfers and postings between ledgers. Customers and suppliers are typically allocated a six-digit code, i.e. a code consisting of six alphanumeric characters, A12345 for instance. Nominal ledger accounts may be structured on the basis of a three- or four-digit nominal code followed by a two-digit department code, A10001 for instance, of which the nominal ledger code is A100 and the departmental code is 01 (up to 99). Some systems have pre-set account names and numbers which are common to many smaller businesses. Some packages allow for unsuitable codes to be deleted and additions incorporated using a nominal ledger maintenance program.

17. Program back-up. When initially setting up a system it is imperative to take copies of the master programs by copying them to other discs. This is a safeguard against the risk of damage to the discs as a result of a malfunction or a disc being corrupted by inadvertent overwriting. Program discs can be very expensive to replace.

18. File back-up. Prior to becoming operational copies of the converted master files, sales, purchase, fixed assets, stock, payroll and cost ledgers should be taken as a security measure against loss or corruption.

19. Defining parameters. A specific application must be tailored to suit the needs of a specific business, requiring parameters to be redefined, such as those indicated in Fig. 19.3. Initially the parameters are defined as a standard set based on typical business characteristics.

20. Audit trail. For purposes of generating an audit trail most packages print out details of transactions, including the value and number of invoices; value and number of credits; cash transactions, amendments, deletions, additions and schedules of updated ledger accounts including the sales ledger and purchase ledger, etc.

21. File security: completion of processing. Typical packages also provide for the creation of back-up files for file security as part of the end of posting routine. Prompts inform the user when to load the discs for copying purposes.

22. Reports. Most packages provide for a variety of reports, details of which can be stored on a predefined spooling file, which allows print runs to be accomplished as one task at a suitable time after the period-end processing is completed.

Nominal ledger packages

23. Details of financial transactions. The nominal ledger package described below is based on information supplied by Apple Computer (UK) Ltd, and the operational details are relevant to the Apple Macintosh with a minimum of 512 Kbytes of memory and a hard disc.

The nominal ledger collects details relating to a business's financial transactions. It is structured to classify transactions according to their nature, i.e. sales, purchases and expenses — including wages, salaries, establishment charges, and administrative, selling and distribution expenses — and to compute gross and net profit for the profit and loss account. Details of fixed and current assets including plant and machinery acquisitions, disposals and depreciation; liabilities including creditors, VAT and corporation tax; and the various types of capital account are recorded in a balance sheet, which shows the financial standing of the business as at a defined date. Nominal ledgers can be integrated with sales and purchase ledger packages and the sales invoicing and stock control packages or be used independently. A coding system is used to identify different types of record and to facilitate the analysis of income and expenditure enabling reports to be produced from several points of view.

24. Setting up a nominal ledger. When a nominal ledger is being set up for the first time the program discs have to be established. The 'file' option is then selected from the menu bar by clicking the mouse, causing a screen to be displayed which prompts for the name of the company to be entered. A disc is then selected for storing the data files, which can be labelled by clicking the mouse on 'save'. A company name icon will now be displayed at the bottom of the screen whenever the file is opened. The 'Data entry' choice on the menu bar is then accessible (*see* Fig. 19.1). When the mouse is clicked at 'Data entry' on the menu bar it is then moved to 'configuration' and clicked, which causes a screen for configuring the nominal ledger to be displayed. The information entered into this window is used to map out or reserve internal memory for the nominal ledger data files. The screen for nominal ledger configuration is shown in Fig. 19.2, which displays the number of ledger account records that will require to be stored and the average number of transactions to be maintained on file for each nominal ledger account. This will vary according both to the nature of the business and whether open-item or balance forward accounts are to be implemented. The number of standing orders to be provided for comes next. The screen finally displays the storage space required and available.

25. Parameters. It is then necessary to select parameters from the 'data entry' menu. The nominal ledger parameter screen is shown in Fig. 19.3, which illustrates the details to be input, including:

(*a*) Company name and address — up to five lines are allowed.

(*b*) Number of periods per year — if accounts are prepared by calendar months the number of periods is 12. If every four weeks, the number of periods is 13.

(*c*) Last month of financial year — this is the calendar month or period number of your year-end. If the year-end is December it is necessary to enter; 12; if March, enter 3.

(*d*) Current NL period/month number — this is the month or period the system is to commence being processed by computer. If the financial year runs from April to March, month 1 is April.

(*e*) Accounting years — these are used as headings on financial reports which are updated by the system.

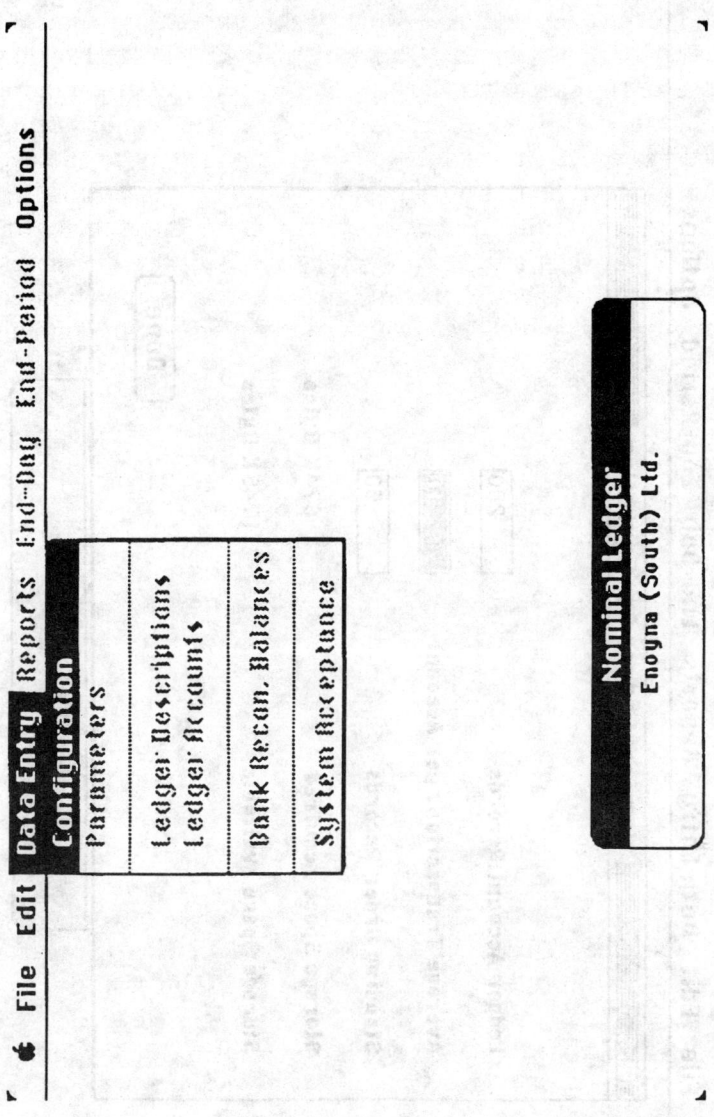

Figure 19.1   *Nominal ledger: configuration (courtesy Soft Numbers Limited).*

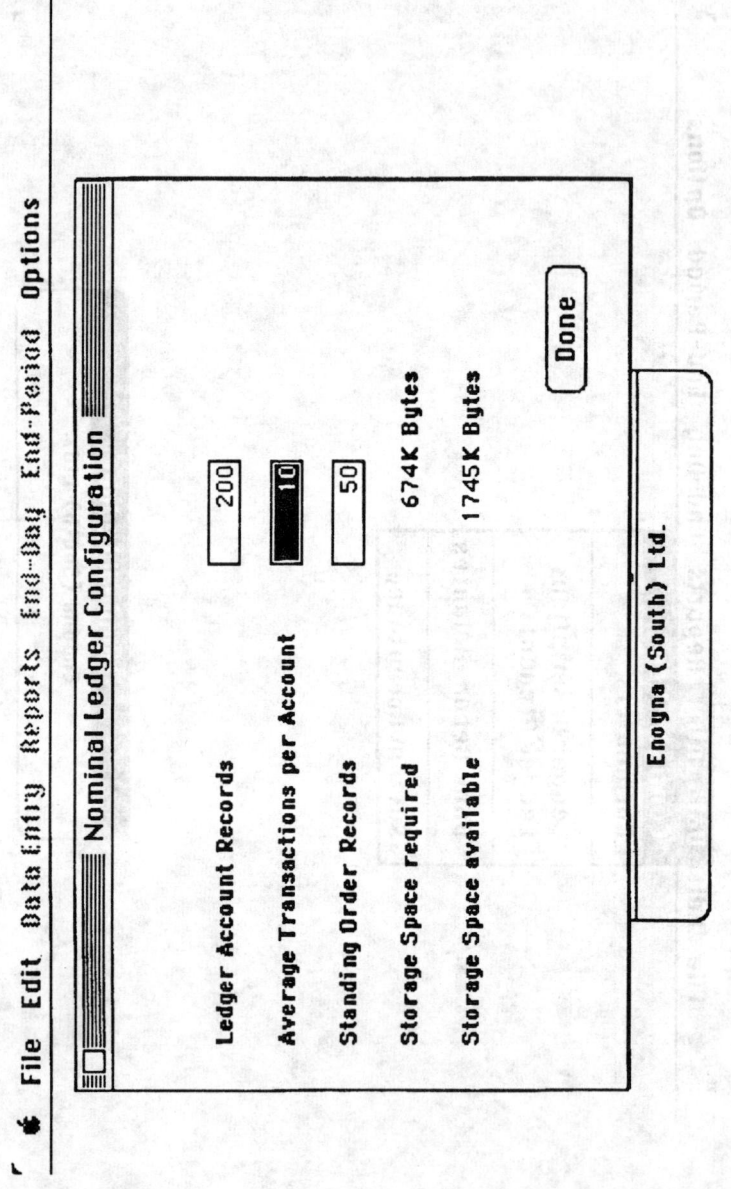

Figure 19.2 *Nominal ledger: configuration (courtesy Soft Numbers Limited).*

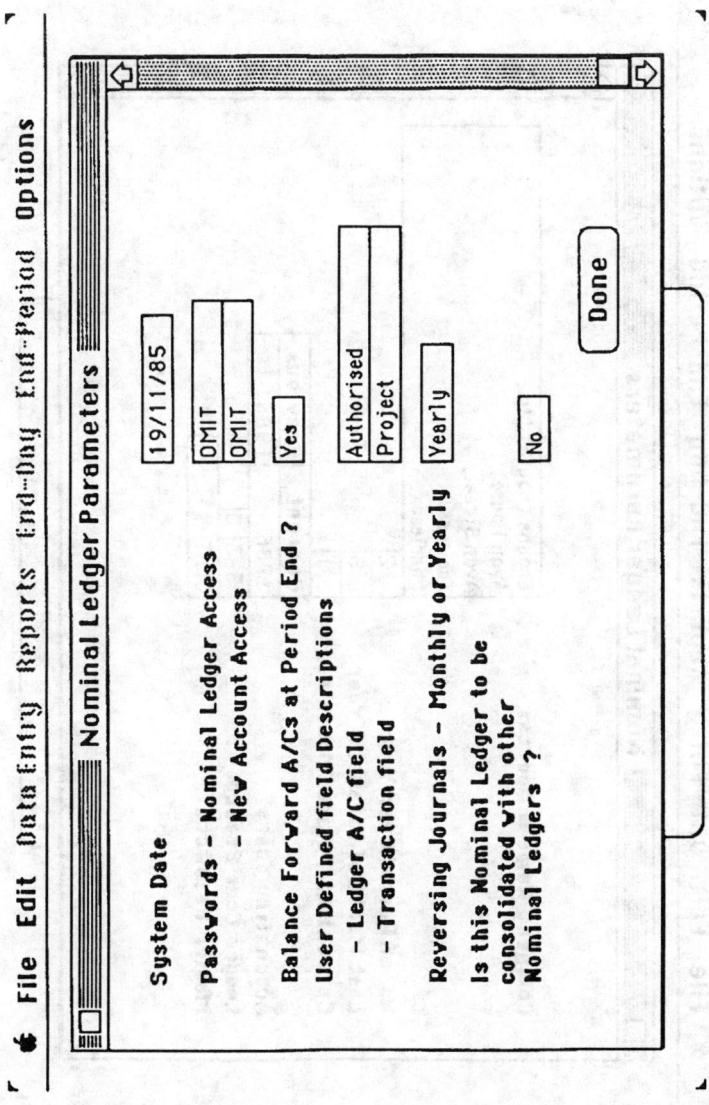

Figure 19.3 *Nominal ledger: parameters screen (courtesy Soft Numbers Limited).*

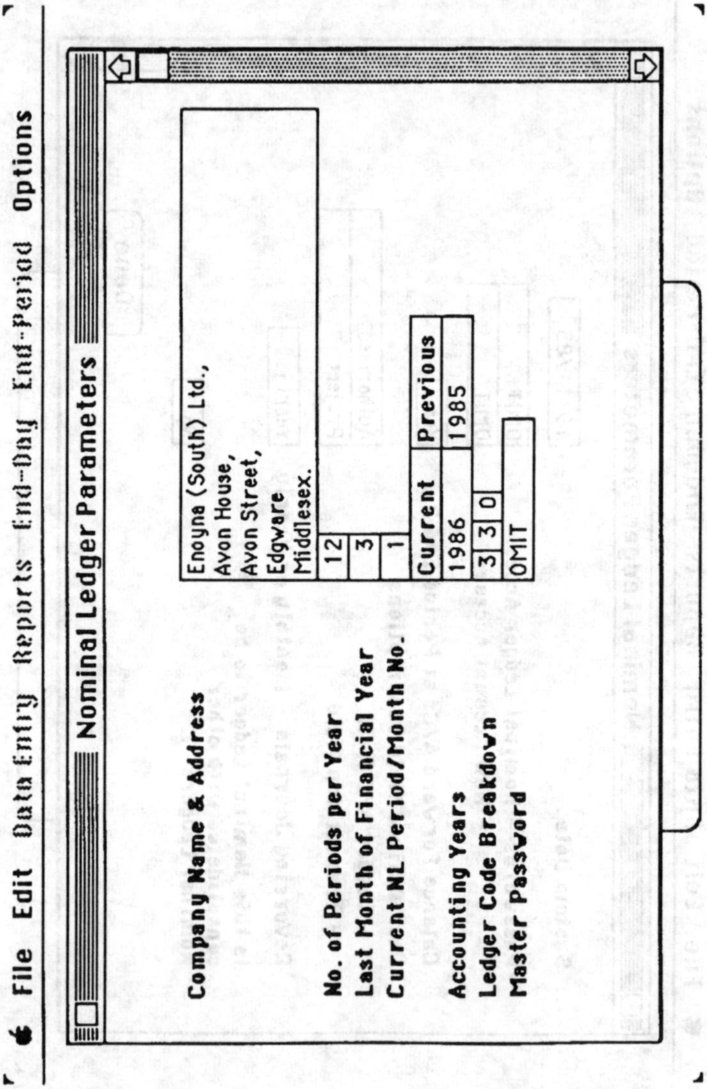

Figure 19.4 *Nominal ledger: parameters screen (courtesy Soft Numbers Limited).*

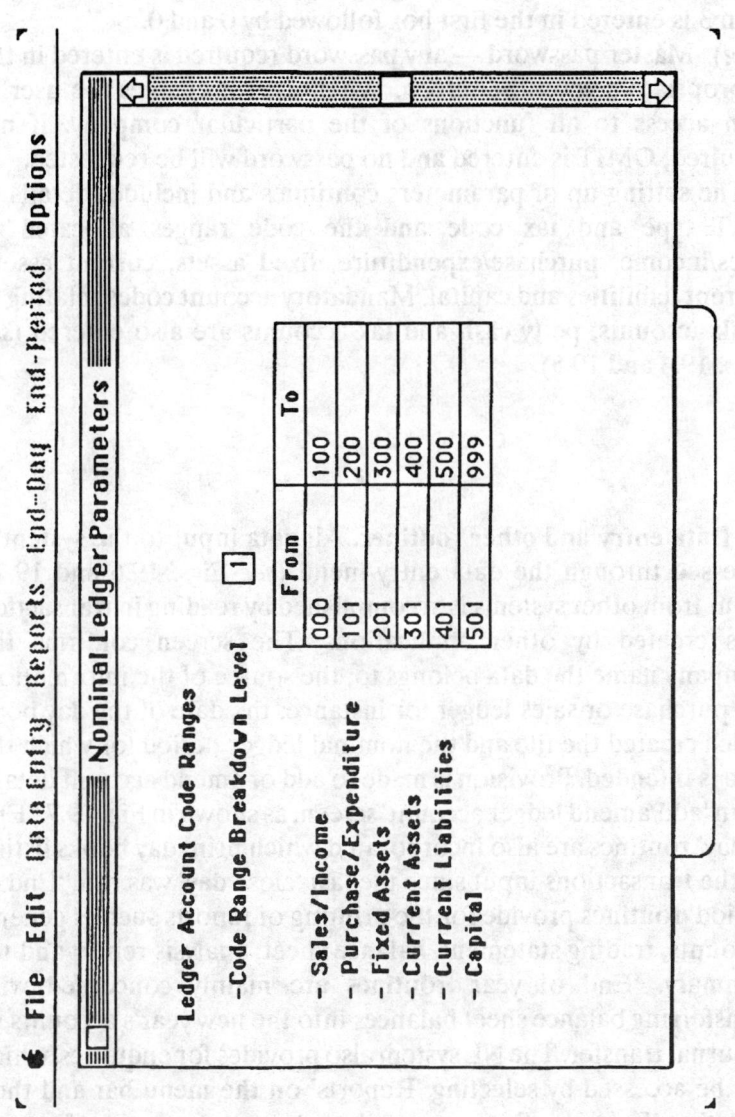

Figure 19.5 *Nominal ledger: parameters; accounts and codes (courtesy Soft Numbers Limited).*

(f) Ledger code breakdown — refer to Fig. 19.5. If only a simple one-level code is required, ranging from 0 to 999, i.e. three digits, then 3 is entered in the first box followed by 0 and 0.

(g) Master password — any password required is entered in the appropriate box on the screen. When used it enables the user to gain access to all functions of the particular company. If not required, OMIT is entered and no password will be requested.

The setting up of parameters continues and includes details of VAT type and tax code and the code ranges allocated to sales/income, purchase/expenditure, fixed assets, current assets, current liabilities and capital. Mandatory account codes relating to bank accounts, petty cash and tax accounts are also entered (*see* Figs. 19.4 and 19.5).

26. Data entry and other routines. All data input to the system is accessed through the data entry menu (*see* Figs. 19.6 and 19.7). Input from other systems is accomplished by reading in transaction files created by other applications. The screen confirms the company name the data belongs to; the source of the information, the purchase or sales ledger for instance; the date of the day book which created the file and the nominal ledger period for which the data is intended. Provision is made to add or amend account details by an 'add/amend ledger account' screen, as shown in Fig. 19.7. 'End of day' routines are also incorporated which print day books listing all the transactions input since the last 'close day' was run. 'End of period' routines provide for the printing of reports such as general accounts, trading statement, balance sheet, analysis report and tax summary. 'End of year' routines are mainly concerned with transferring balance sheet balances into the new year's accounts by a journal transfer. The NL system also provides for enquiries, which can be accessed by selecting 'Reports' on the menu bar and then selecting 'Enquiry'. Reports may be selected at any time for such requirements as a transaction list, account details, account balances, trial balance, standing order list, budget listing, ledger code description, systems parameters report, general accounts chart and analysis report.

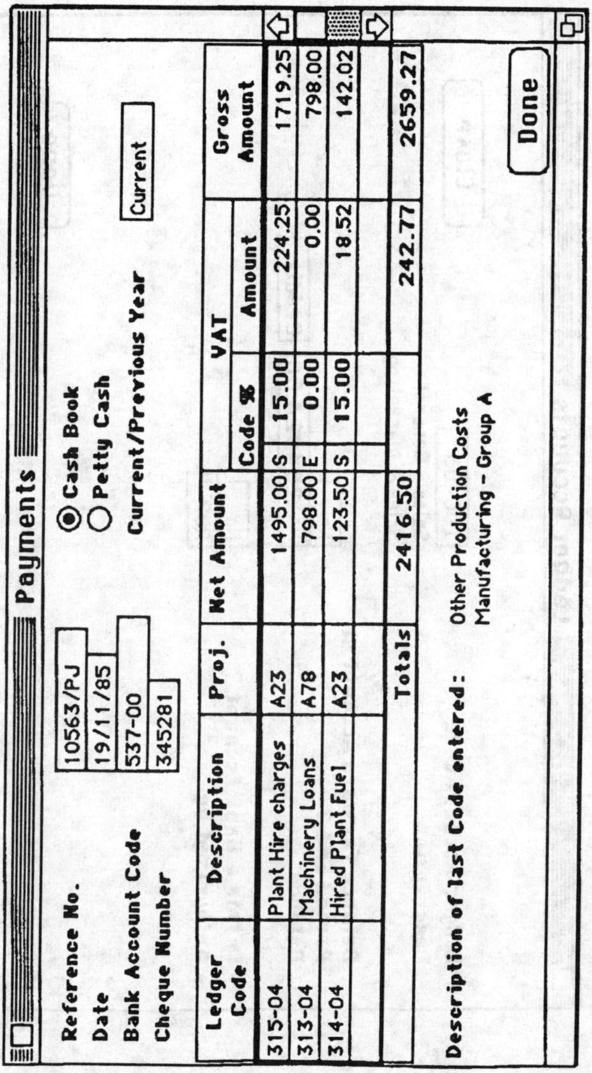

Payments

Reference No.   10563/PJ
Date   19/11/85
Bank Account Code 537-00
Cheque Number   345281

◉ Cash Book
○ Petty Cash
Current/Previous Year   [Current]

Ledger Code	Description	Proj.	Net Amount	VAT Code %	VAT Amount	Gross Amount
315-04	Plant Hire charges	A23	1495.00	S 15.00	224.25	1719.25
313-04	Machinery Loans	A78	798.00	E 0.00	0.00	798.00
314-04	Hired Plant Fuel	A23	123.50	S 15.00	18.52	142.02
	Totals		2416.50		242.77	2659.27

Description of last Code entered: Other Production Costs
                                    Manufacturing – Group A

[Done]

Figure 19.6 *Nominal ledger: payments screen (courtesy Soft Numbers Limited).*

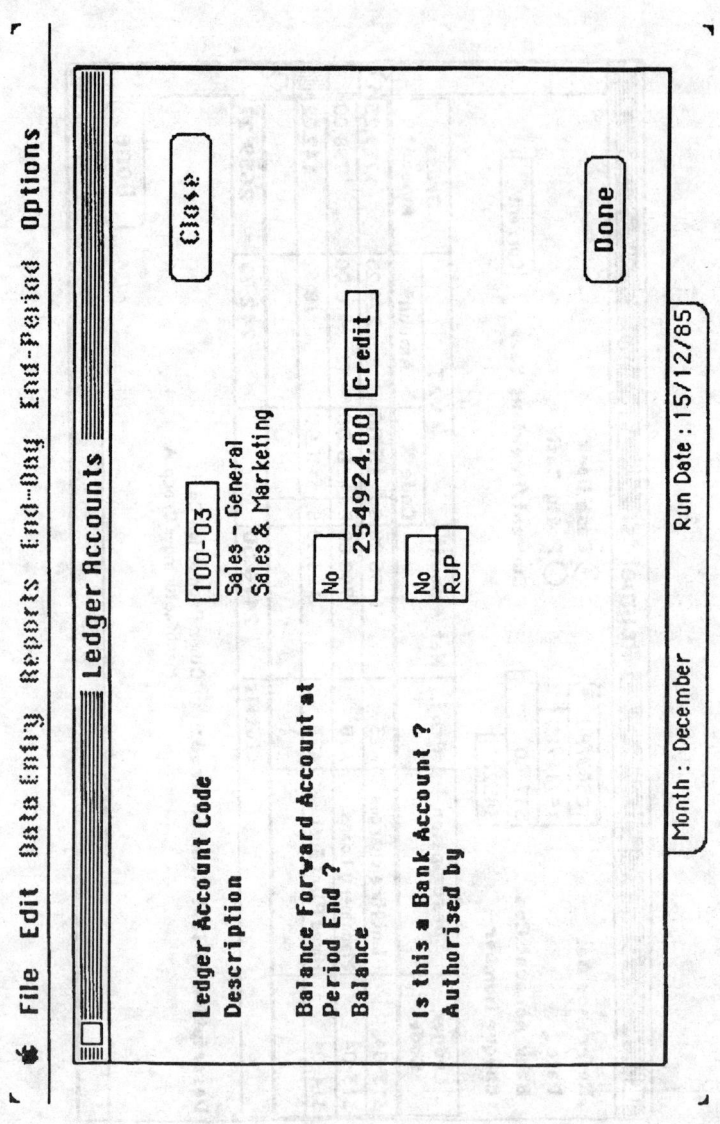

Figure 19.7 *Nominal ledger: accounts screen (courtesy Soft Numbers Limited).*

The sales and purchase ledgers

Of necessity the following details are restricted to those which provide an overall appreciation of the features of sales and purchase ledger application packages, due to the amount of detail involved — which can be seen by referring to the relevant software manual.

The sales ledger

27. Customer transactions. The sales ledger is concerned with maintaining records of transactions with customers, in order to furnish the status of each customer's account. In effect, it controls accounts receivable by showing how much is owed by each customer and for how long. The sales ledger can be used in conjunction with the nominal ledger package or on a stand-alone independent basis. The application is set up in a similar way to that outlined for the nominal ledger. After the initial set-up of the application the package can be used operationally by selecting 'open' from the pull-down menu. A window then appears displaying the sales ledger icon, which is selected (opened) by pointing and clicking the mouse. All data is input by the data entry menu as shown in Fig 19.8. The routine operation of the system includes the daily input of batches of customers' invoices (*see* Fig. 19.9) together with credit notes, remittances and adjustments. New customer records are added as and when required. An 'end of day' procedure ensures that all payments have been correctly allocated to customer accounts, a day book is produced listing the transactions. When the sales ledger is integrated with the nominal ledger the day's sales ledger transaction data is transferred to the respective nominal ledger accounts. The customer account input window, as shown in Fig. 19.10, is accessed by selecting 'Customer account' from the data entry menu. Using the scroll bar displays a second window of information relating to the customer record, as shown in Fig. 19.11. Scrolling to a third window displays customer account data, as shown in Fig. 19.12. At the end of each accounting period the user selects from the menu and prints the required management reports, as shown in Fig. 19.14. The user then selects 'close period', which deletes the unwanted data from the sales ledger files and moves the accounting period on

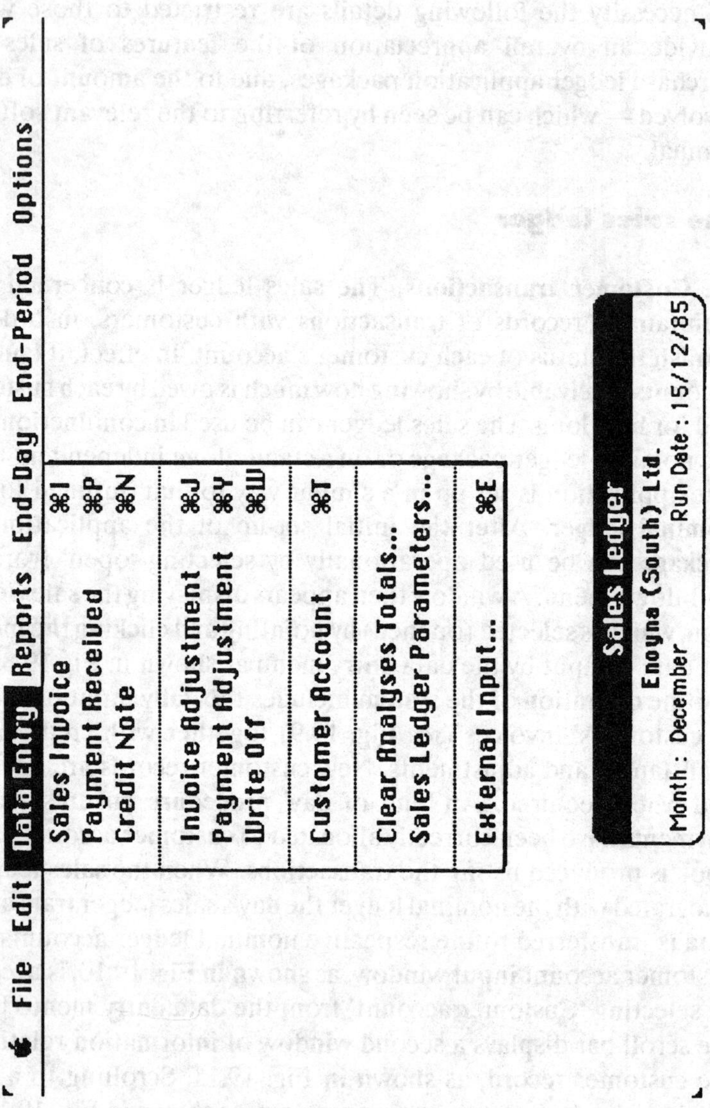

File **Edit** **Data Entry** **Reports** **End-Day** **End-Period** **Options**

Data Entry	
Sales Invoice	⌘I
Payment Received	⌘P
Credit Note	⌘N
Invoice Adjustment	⌘J
Payment Adjustment	⌘Y
Write Off	⌘W
Customer Account	⌘T
Clear Analyses Totals...	
Sales Ledger Parameters...	
External Input...	⌘E

Sales Ledger
Enoyna (South) Ltd.
Month : December   Run Date : 15/12/85

Figure 19.8 *Data entry menu screen (courtesy Soft Numbers Limited).*

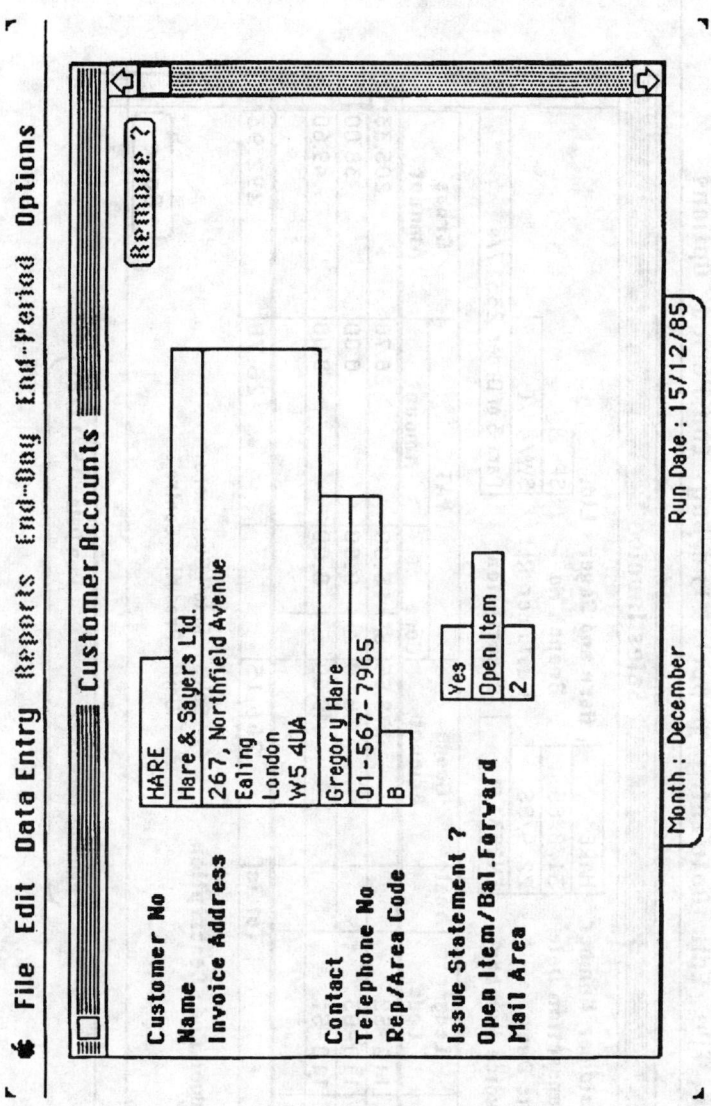

Figure 19.9 *Sales ledger: customer account screen (courtesy Soft Numbers Limited).*

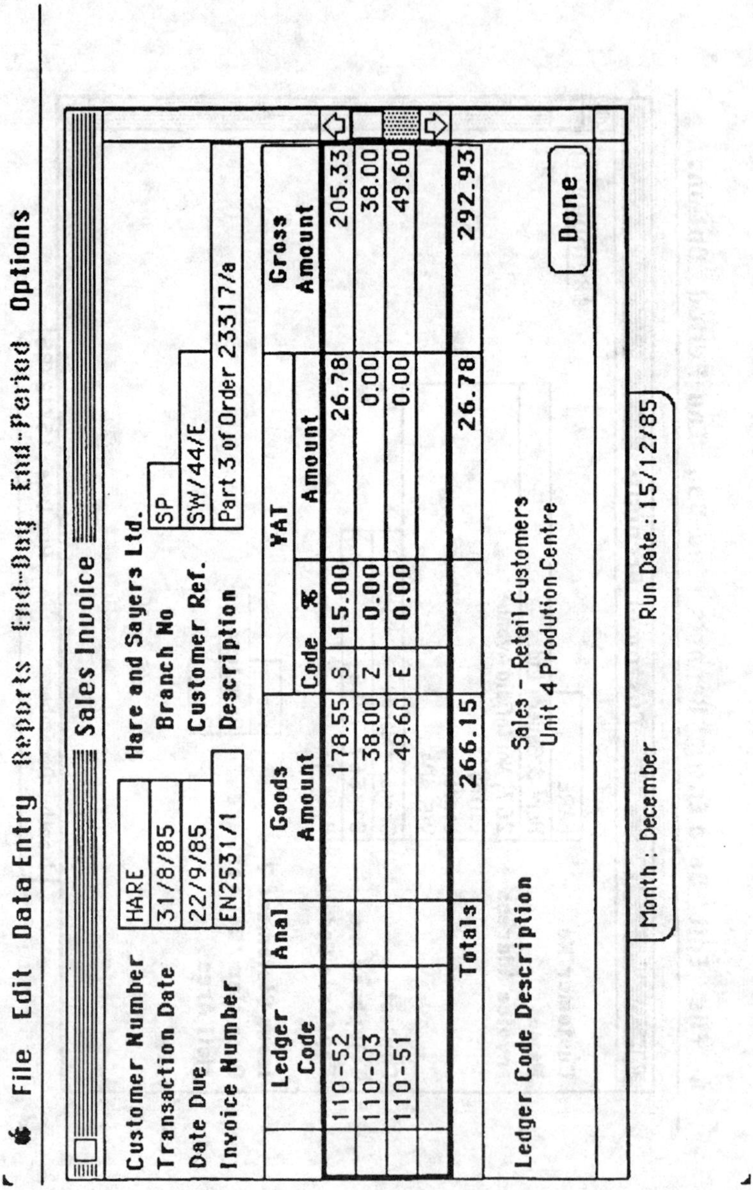

 File Edit Data Entry Reports End-Day End-Period Options

Sales Invoice

Customer Number	HARE	Hare and Sayers Ltd.
Transaction Date	31/8/85	Branch No SP
Date Due	22/9/85	Customer Ref. SW/44/E
Invoice Number	EN2531/1	Description Part 3 of Order 23317/a

Ledger Code	Anal	Goods Amount	VAT Code	%	VAT Amount	Gross Amount
110–52		178.55	S	15.00	26.78	205.33
110–03		38.00	Z	0.00	0.00	38.00
110–51		49.60	E	0.00	0.00	49.60
Totals		266.15			26.78	292.93

Ledger Code Description   Sales – Retail Customers
Unit 4 Prodution Centre

Month : December   Run Date : 15/12/85

Done

Figure 19.10 *Sales ledger: customer account sales invoice screen (courtesy Soft Numbers Limited).*

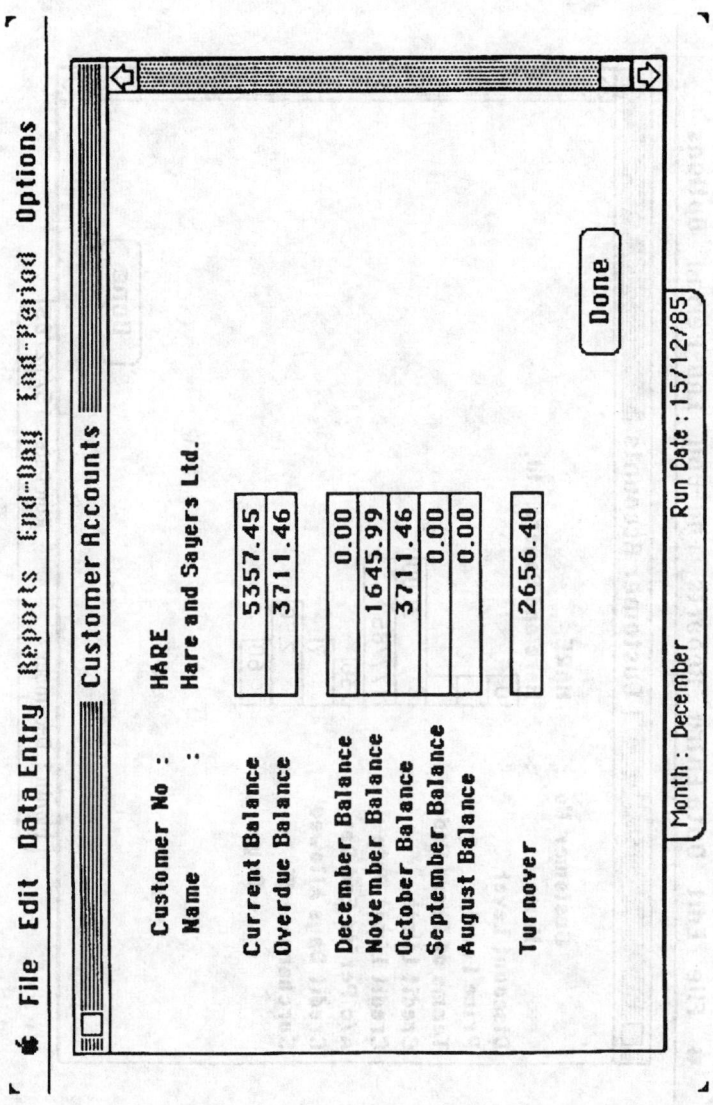

File   Edit   Data Entry   Reports   End-Day   End-Period   Options

Customer Accounts

Customer No :	HARE
Name :	Hare and Sayers Ltd.

Current Balance	5357.45
Overdue Balance	3711.46
December Balance	0.00
November Balance	1645.99
October Balance	3711.46
September Balance	0.00
August Balance	0.00
Turnover	2656.40

Done

Month : December   Run Date : 15/12/85

Figure 19.11 *Sales   ledger: credit control screen (courtesy Soft Numbers Limited).*

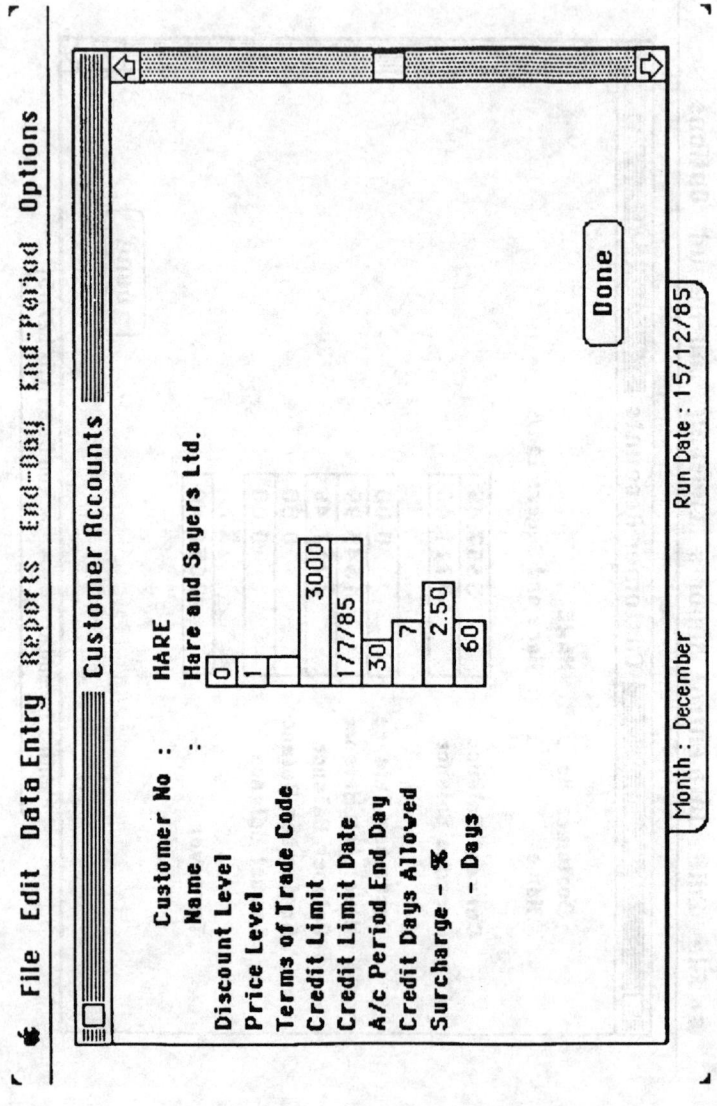

Figure 19.12 *Sales ledger:customer accounts status (courtesy Soft Numbers Limited).*

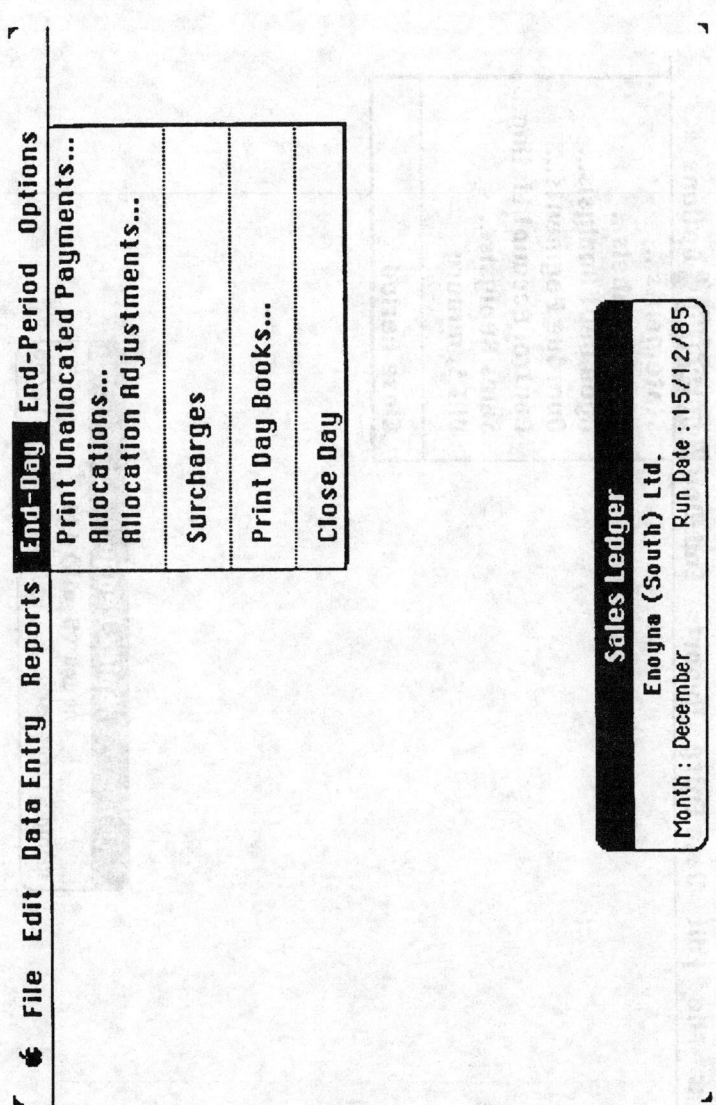

Figure 19.13   *Sales ledger: end of day screen (courtesy Soft Numbers Limited).*

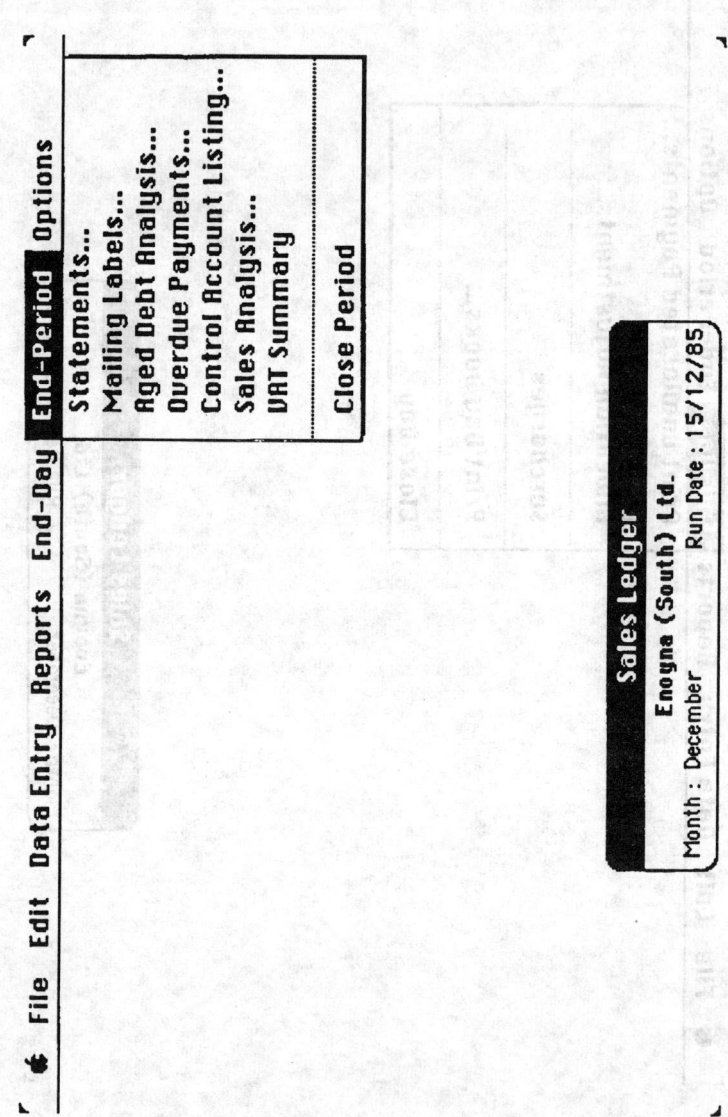

Figure 19.14 *Sales ledger: report selection screen (courtesy Soft Numbers Limited).*

to the next. Back-up copies of files are made on to a different set of discs by selecting the utilities icon, which displays a screen for generating a security copy.

28. Open-item. In this system of record keeping each invoice is recorded on a customer's account and each remittance received is linked to a specific invoice. Paid invoices and the payment transactions associated with them are automatically deleted after the periodic statement is printed. In this way only the outstanding invoices (the 'open items') are maintained on the files.

29. Balance forward. Invoices are recorded during the accounting period together with remittances received from customers. At the end of the accounting period after statements of account have been printed all transactions are deleted and replaced by one figure — the carried forward balance ('balance forward'). This becomes the brought forward balance at the start of the next period.

30. Benefits of using a sales ledger package. The benefits of a computerised package include better management of cash flows by the earlier production of statements of account and greater control of outstanding balances; increased accuracy of records and quicker response to customer enquiries, so improving customer relations; the provision of management information; improved productivity of the accounting functions — a greater level of output with fewer staff and so on.

The purchase ledger

31. Supplier transactions. The purchase ledger records transactions relating to a business's suppliers and maintains the status of each supplier's account. It can be used in conjunction with the nominal ledger package or used on a stand-alone basis. Purchase ledgers can be maintained for a number of companies by a multi-company facility and accounts may be maintained on an open-item or balance forward basis. After the initial configuration of the system, as shown in Figs. 19.15 and 19.16, and definitions of parameters, normal operations commence by selecting the 'open' icon from the file menu. A window is then displayed containing the

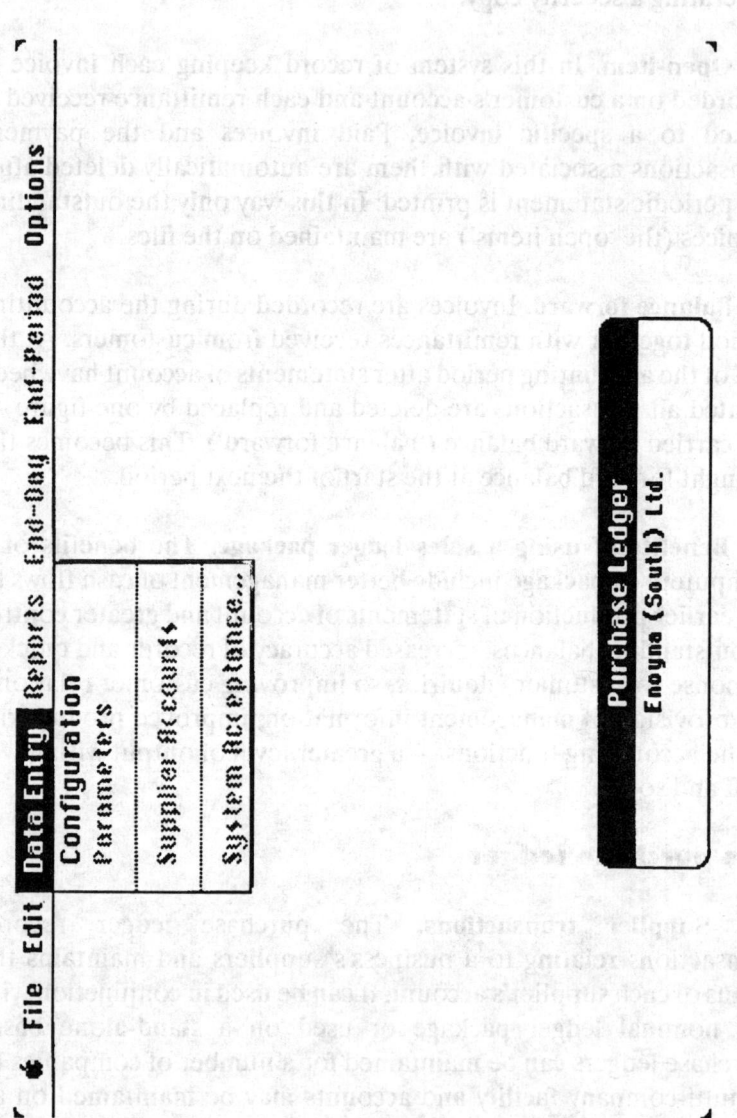

Figure 19.15 *Purchase ledger: data entry selection (courtesy Soft Numbers Limited).*

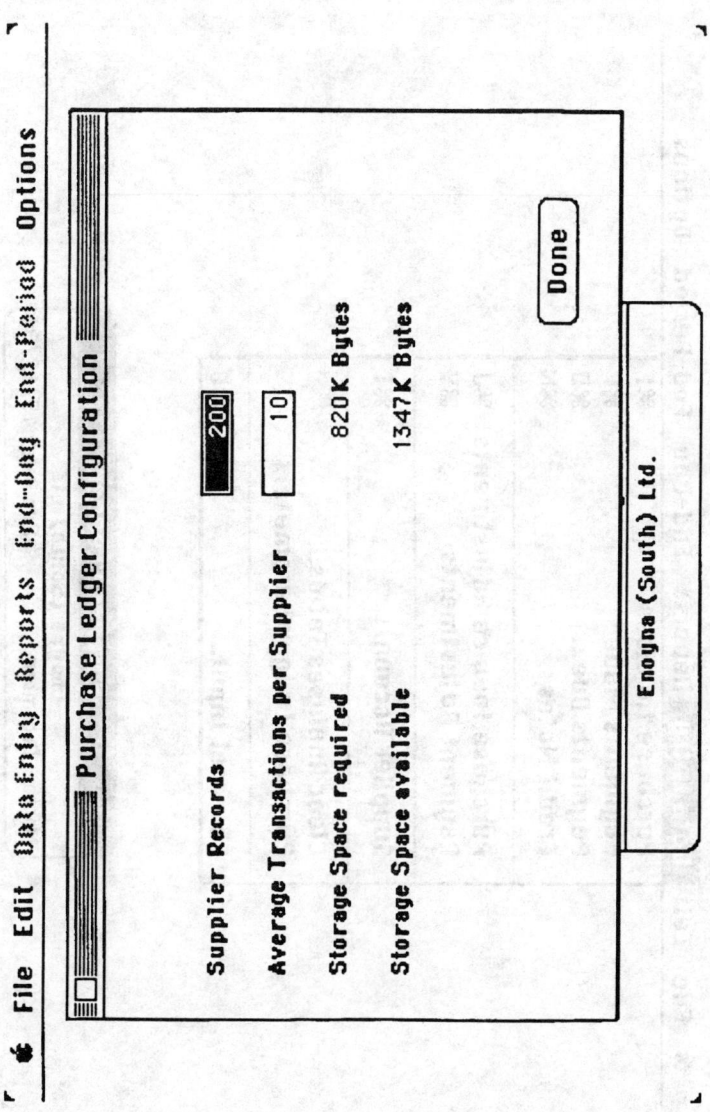

Figure 19.16 *Purchase ledger: configuration screen (courtesy Soft Numbers Limited).*

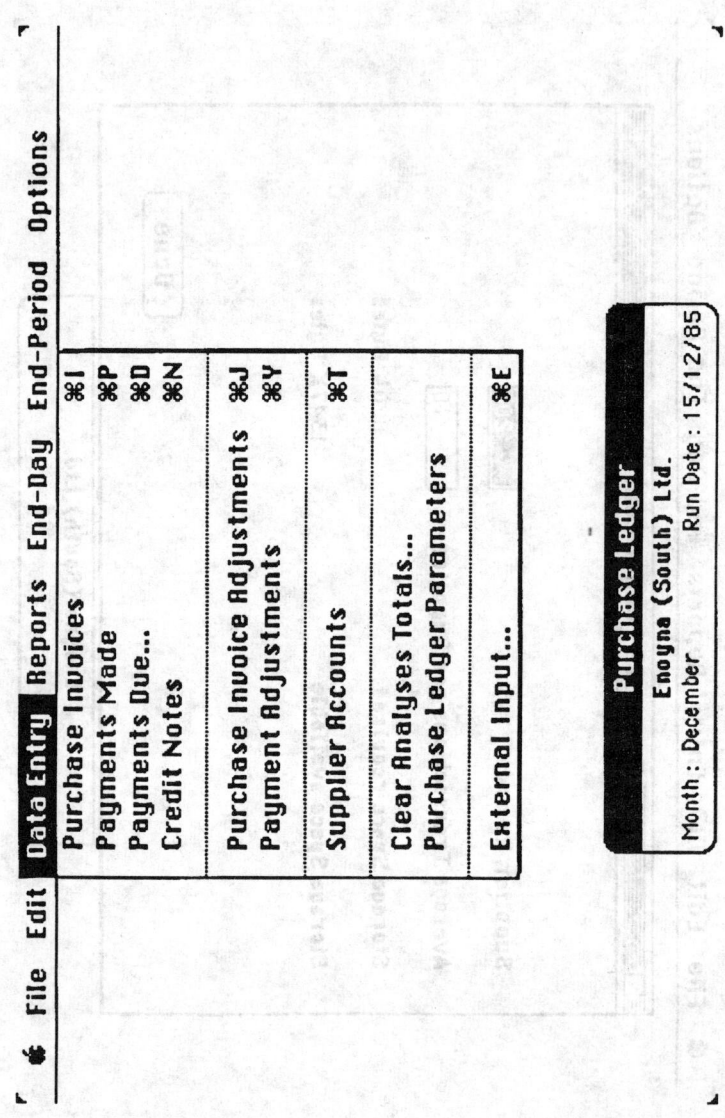

Figure 19.17 *Purchase ledger: data entry menu (courtesy Soft Numbers Limited).*

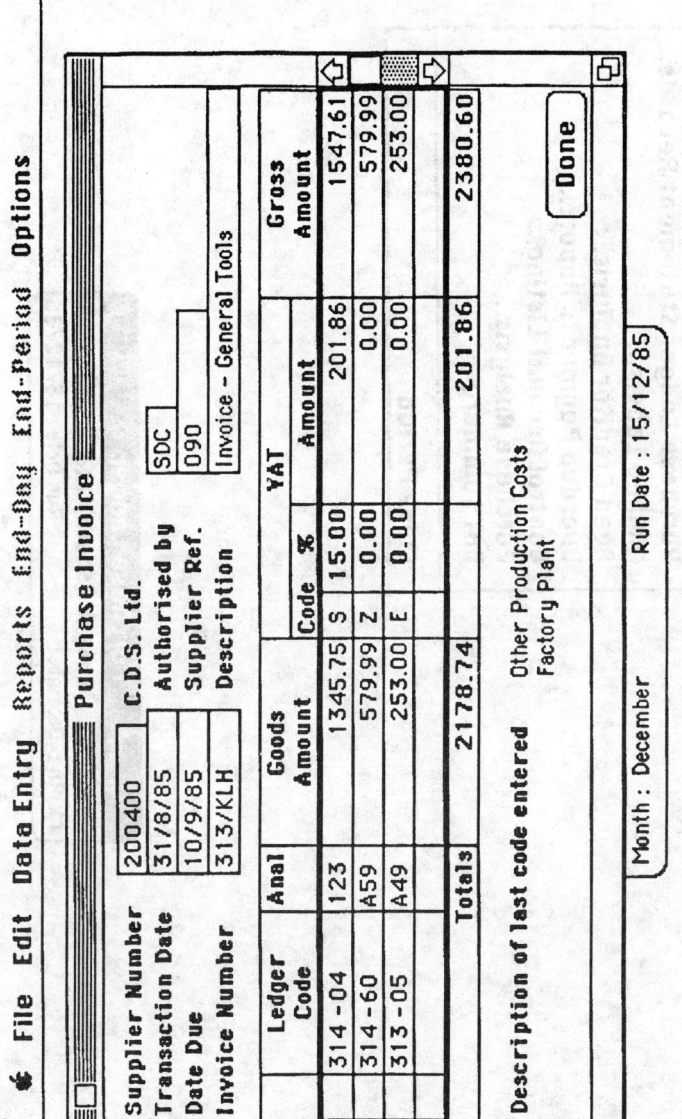

Figure 19.18 *Purchase ledger: purchase invoice screen (courtesy Soft Numbers Limited).*

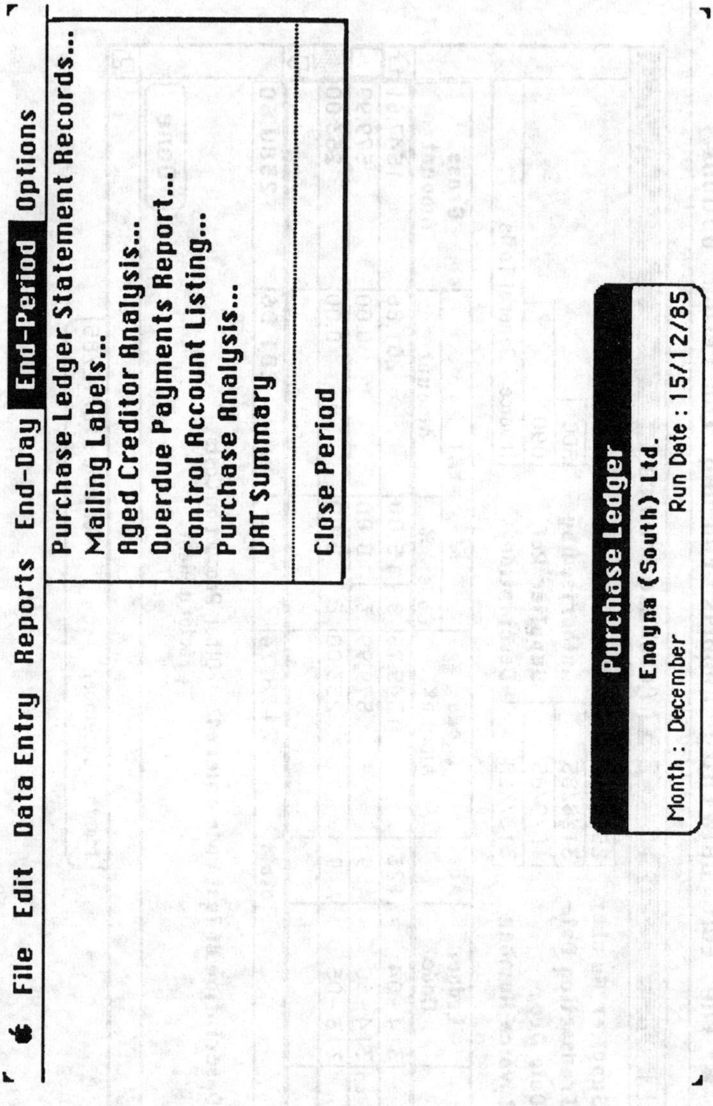

Figure 19.19   *Purchase ledger: report selection screen (courtesy Soft Numbers Limited).*

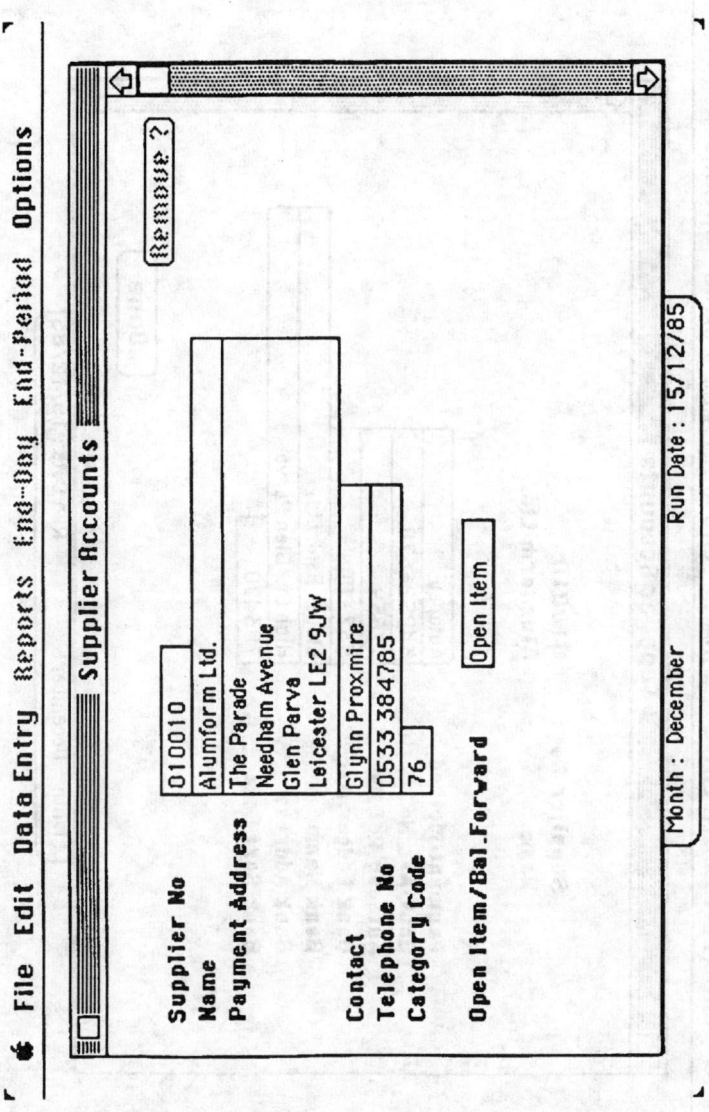

Figure 19.20 *Supplier account details screen 1 (courtesy Soft Numbers Limited).*

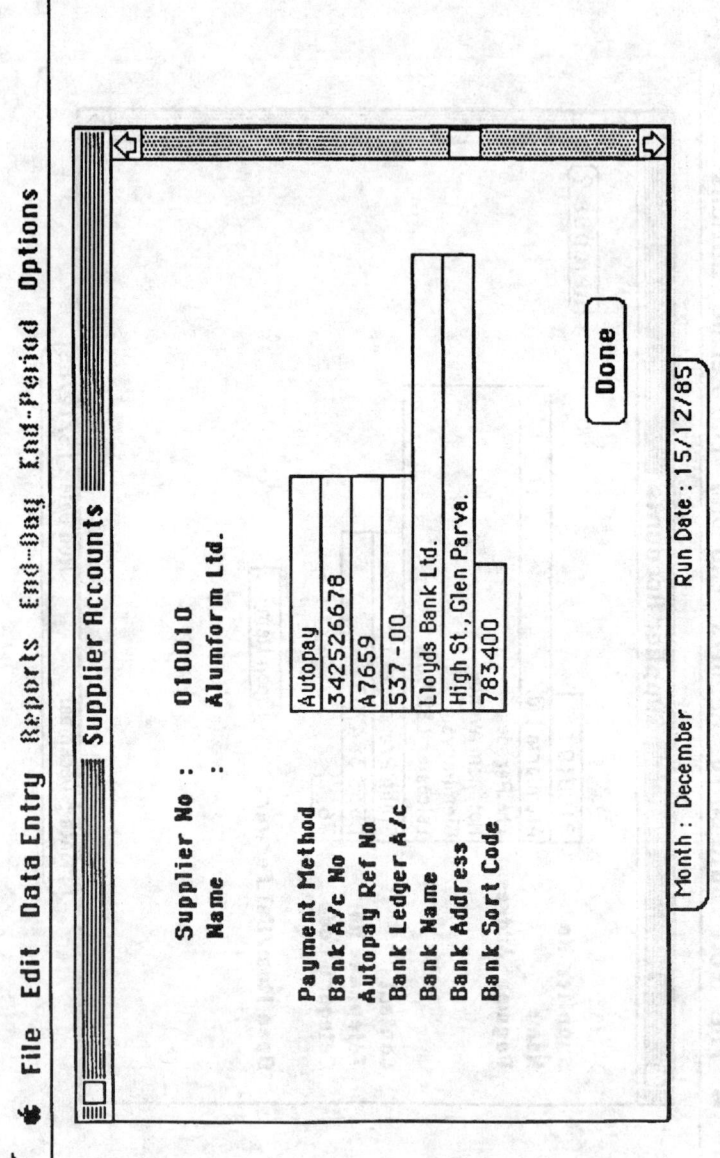

Figure 19.21 *Supplier account details screen 2 (courtesy Soft Numbers Limited).*

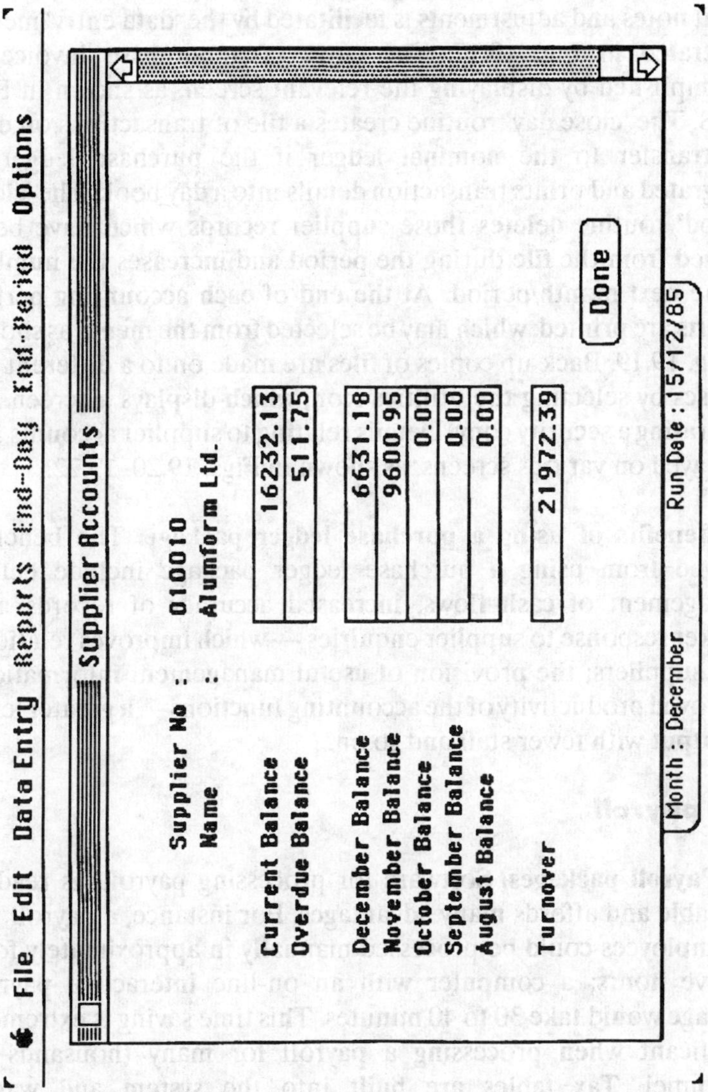

Figure 19.22 *Supplier account details screen 3 (courtesy Soft Numbers Limited).*

purchase ledger icon, which is selected by pointing and clicking the mouse. All data input relating to purchase invoices, remittances, credit notes and adjustments is facilitated by the 'data entry' menu, illustrated in Fig. 19.17. The entry of a purchase invoice is accomplished by displaying the relevant screen, as shown in Fig. 19.18. The 'close day' routine creates a file of transactions on disc for transfer to the nominal ledger if the purchase ledger is integrated and prints transaction details into a day book. The 'close period' routine deletes those supplier records which have been deleted from the file during the period and increases the number of the next month/period. At the end of each accounting period reports are printed, which may be selected from the menu, as shown in Fig. 19.19. Back-up copies of files are made on to a different set of discs by selecting the utilities icon, which displays a screen for generating a security copy. Details relating to supplier accounts are displayed on various screens, as shown in Figs. 19.20–19.22.

32. Benefits of using a purchase ledger package. The benefits derived from using a purchase ledger package include better management of cash flows, increased accuracy of records and quicker response to supplier enquiries — which improves relations with suppliers; the provision of useful management information; improved productivity of the accounting functions — a greater level of output with fewer staff and so on.

The payroll

33. Payroll packages. Software for processing payrolls is readily available and affords many advantages. For instance, a payroll for 30 employees could be processed manually in approximately four to five hours; a computer with an on-line interactive payroll package would take 30 to 40 minutes. This time saving is extremely significant when processing a payroll for many thousands of personnel. Tax tables are built into the system and wages computations and the printing of payrolls and other documentation are performed at a very high speed. The number of personnel engaged on payroll processing is greatly reduced in larger companies, providing cost savings; reduced processing time; increased accuracy of processed results and a reduction in fatigue as the process is largely automated. The operator need input only hours worked or the number of units produced — most other activities are then performed by payroll software.

Payroll packages provide for all the ramifications of payroll preparation, including computation of gross wages, tax calculations, National Insurance deductions, statutory sick pay (SSP) and statutory maternity pay (SMP); printing pay advices, payrolls, lists of deductions, payroll reconciliation, bank transfer list, cheques, giros and/or note and coin analysis, etc. When setting up a payroll package it is necessary to record all employee details on a payroll file stored on magnetic disc. Screen displays are provided for entering configuration details and parameters and for displaying employee records for data entry purposes. The package also provides for deleting, adding or amending records to allow for personnel changes.

34. Payroll procedure. There now follows a general outline of payroll processing procedure which would be provided for in typical payroll packages. When preparing a payroll for the current pay period, the payroll department obtains details relating to each employee from the payroll file. The file contains details of tax code, NHI contribution rate, and other deductions such as savings, loan repayments and pension payments where appropriate; it also contains details of earnings, tax deducted from earnings and NHI contributions to date.

What follows relates to the computation of wages rather than salaries. The current gross wages of employees are computed on the basis of attended hours or payment by results schemes, including bonus earnings. Gross wages for the current week are added to the earnings of the year to date up to the previous week, and the tax payable to date is then computed. The difference between tax payable to date and tax previously paid is either a refund or deduction for the current week depending on the level of gross wages earned. Details are recorded on a pay advice slip, which informs the employee of his or her earnings, tax and other deductions for the current week. The payroll records are updated with the current details to provide the latest 'year to date' status of the records. A summary of all details relating to each employee is recorded on a payroll, which is used for accounting and auditing purposes. Deductions are credited to appropriate accounts in the nominal ledger, including NHI contributions for both employee and employer, standard deductions and tax deducted/refunded. Net wages are credited in the bank account and gross wages are debited to the wages account in the nominal ledger. Other statutory requirements are the preparation of P60s at the end of the tax year on 5 April. The P60 is a certificate of pay, income tax and National Insurance contributions. A listing is produced of the P60s; P45s are provided to employees leaving the company, stating their 'year to date' earnings and tax in the current employment. A list of bank transfers or cheques is produced or a note and coin analysis as appropriate to the method of payment adopted (BACS (*see* 35) perhaps?). An audit trail control list is also produced.

When evaluating a payroll package, general points to consider are those shown in the checklist (*see* 13).

35. Bankers' automated clearing services. In practice, when systems are computerised the BACS system of payment may be used for making payments to employees and suppliers and for receiving remittances from customers. Bankers' automated clearing services (BACS) is the clearing banks' computerised system for making payments on behalf of customers. It provides a means of making payments without recourse to cash, cheques or giro credits. Users' data is submitted on magnetic media such as 8-inch or 5-inch diskettes and is delivered to BACS City Reception, Bread Street, London or to the Edgware reception. Delivery may be by means of user's messenger, security transport, the normal postal service or Datapost. Input from users via telecommunications is received at the Edgware centre.

Arguments for and against the use of packages

36. Arguments for the use of packages. These are summarised as follows:

(*a*) Programmers are able to concentrate their efforts on applications for which no suitable packages exist due to the special nature of a particular task.

(*b*) It is unnecessary to employ specialist programmers,

particularly when using microcomputers, as packages are available for most requirements.

(c) Applications can be up and running (operational) much more quickly than would be the case when developing one's own computer systems, including the writing of programs.

(d) Expertise is *built in* when using packages which, in effect, deskills the use of computers, particularly the use of micros.

37. Arguments against the use of packages. These may be summarised as follows:

(a) Package programs may take longer to run than specially written programs, but this depends on the relative skill of programmers and whether machine code is used rather than high-level languages. Compiled programs usually take longer to run because they contain more instructions than machine code requires to achieve a specific task.

(b) It may be necessary to modify a package, as it may not be compatible with system requirements in all instances and this fact will increase the cost of the package.

(c) Purchased programs may cost more than internally written programs but this is dependent on the expected volume of sales of the package since the larger the sales volume the lower the cost to the ultimate user, as the development costs are spread over a greater volume of sales.

Progress test 19

1. What is a software package? (1, 2)
2. From what sources are packages available? (5)
3. Indicate the nature and purpose of vertical market applications software. Specify the software requirements of: (a) accountancy practices; (b) estate agents; (c) solicitors; (d) stockbrokers; (e) insurance brokers. (7–11)
4. What points would you check about software before making a selection? (13)
5. What advantages do accounting packages provide? (14)
6. Specify the nature and purpose of integrated accounting packages. (15–22)

7. What is a chart of accounts? **(16)**

8. Outline the features of the following packages: (*a*) nominal ledger; (*b*) sales ledger; (*c*) purchase ledger. **(23–32)**

9. State the facilities provided by payroll packages. **(33, 34)**

10. What are the arguments for and against the use of packages? **(36, 37)**

20

Control software and utilities

General aspects of control software

1. Control software. The most important element of control software is the *operating system*; without it a computer system cannot function. An operating system is a master control program which controls the functions of the computer system as a whole and the running of application programs. Many computers operate under the control of different operating systems, making it imperative to assess the operating system used on a particular model before initial commitment. Some operating systems are adopted as 'industry standards', and these should be evaluated because they normally have a good software base. The reason for this is that software houses are willing to expend resources on developing application packages for machines functioning under the control of an operating system which is widely used. The cost of software is likely to be lower in such circumstances as the development costs are spread over a greater number of users.

2. Utility software. Utility software consists of programs which assist processing activities generally irrespective of the application being processed. They are in effect supporting programs designed to streamline and perform specific tasks to aid in achieving high levels of processing productivity. Precise details are included in the text (*see* **8–13**).

Operating systems

3. General features. Mainframe computers usually process several application programs concurrently, switching from one to another, for the purpose of increasing processing productivity. This is known as 'multi-programming' (multi-tasking in the context of microcomputers), and requires a powerful operating system (OS) incorporating work scheduling facilities to control the switching between programs. This entails reading in data for one program while the processor is performing computations on another and printing out results on yet another.

In multi-user environments (*see* 14: **15–16**) an operating system is required to control terminal operations on a shared access basis as only one user can access the system at any moment of time. The operating system allocates control to each terminal in turn. Such systems also require a system for record locking and unlocking to prevent one user attempting to read a record while another is updating it, for instance. The first user is allocated control to write to a record (or a file in some instances) and other users are denied access until the record is updated and unlocked.

Some environments operate in concurrent batch and real-time mode. This means that a 'background' job deals with routine batch processing while the 'foreground' job deals with real-time operations such as airline seat reservations, on-line booking of hotel accommodation or control of warehouse stocks, etc. The real-time operation has priority and the operating system interrupts batch processing operations to deal with real-time enquiries or file updates. The stage of batch processing attained at the time of the interrupt is temporarily transferred to backing storage. After the real-time operation has been dealt with the interrupted program is transferred back to internal memory from backing storage and processing recommences from a 'restart' point. The operating system also copies to disc backing storage the state of the real-time system every few minutes (periodic check points) to provide a means of 'recovering' the system in the event of a malfunction.

An operating system is stored on disc and has to be 'booted' into the internal memory (RAM) where it must reside throughout processing so that commands are instantly available. The operating system commands may exceed the internal memory capacity of the computer in which case only that portion of the OS which is frequently used is retained internally, other modules being read in from disc as required.

Many disc-based microcomputers function under the control of a disc operating system, known as DOS. An operating system performs many important tasks, which assists the activities of programmer and operator alike as many data handling and file organisation tasks are performed automatically by the operating system. The location of records, files or programs stored on disc is maintained by a disc operating system which, in respect of many microcomputers, is MicroSoft Disc Operating System (MS-DOS) or Personal Computer Disc Operating System (PC-DOS). The operating system calculates on which tracks of a disc to store records, files and programs and maintains a directory by file or program name. Disc directories are usually situated on tracks in the centre of the disc. The operating system stores text, records or programs wherever there is an unused sector. When a sector is filled the operating system searches for a free sector and continues recording at that location. When a file is stored on disc a track/sector index is compiled by means of a pair of bytes assigned to each file for specifying the index. One byte defines the track reference and the other the sector location. The first three tracks on a disc are often used for storing the operating system, which also controls the copying of files from one disc to another for file security purposes.

4. Typical tasks performed by an operating system.

(a) Execute and monitor input and output operations.

(b) Monitor the status of hardware devices.

(c) Monitor and process hardware interrupts.

(d) Format new discs.

(e) Maintain disc directories

(f) Execute disc reading and writing operations.

(g) Diagnose disc errors.

(h) Execute disc commands relating to the deletion, copying, renaming and dumping of files.

(i) Report on the status of disc usage and bytes available.

(*j*)   Read-only file protection.

(*k*)   Dynamic allocation of internal memory to software.

(*l*)   Loading programs, chaining between programs and passing parameters.

(*m*) Receive, interpret and execute commands from the operator.

(*n*) Assigning logical input/output devices to the various input/output ports.

(*o*)   Implementing the use of passwords.

(*p*)   Provision of debugging aids.

5. Typical minicomputer and microcomputer operating systems.

(*a*)   *MS-DOS.* An abbreviation for MicroSoft Disc Operating System, MS-DOS has a large software base and is a popular system.

This operating system is known as PC-DOS on the IBM PC. Concurrent DOS is used for multi-tasking machines.

(*b*)   *UNIX and XENIX.* UNIX was initially designed for minicomputers but is now being used on more powerful microcomputers. It supports multi-tasking as well as multiple terminals connected to a single system. It is widely accepted as the main multi-user system available. XENIX is a multi-user system based on UNIX.

(*c*)   *OS/2.* This is the new IBM microcomputer operating system for use on the IBM PS/2 range of computers. It is to supersede PC-DOS. OS/2 was written by MicroSoft by and with IBM and, as with DOS, there will be a version marketed by IBM called IBM Operating System/2, and one from MicroSoft called MicroSoft OS/2. It is an advanced operating system that offers a micro the software facilities normally available only with a UNIX-based workstation. It has multi-tasking abilities and provides methods by which multiple tasks can communicate.

(*d*)   *Apple DOS.* This operating system is used on the Apple series of computers and is an eight-bit system. It has a large software base as many programs were written to run on Apple machines. It occupies relatively little memory compared with other operating systems as it is not so sophisticated.

(*e*)   *IBM Operating System/400.* This operating system runs the

IBM AS/400 family of minicomputers and has powerful facilities. In addition to normal operating system functions, changes made to data may be recorded automatically by a built-in 'journalling' process, keeping track of what is happening to data on the system at all times. Should there be a failure while a transaction is being processed that results in it not being completed, it is restored when the system restarts to the state it was in before the transaction.

6. Mainframe operating systems. A number of operating systems exist for use on mainframe computers including VMS, VME, VAX.

7. Typical operating system commands. The commands listed below are a selection relating to MS-DOS.

(*a*) *CHKDSK.* This command enables details to be obtained relating to disc usage and available capacity in terms of bytes for a specific floppy disc which is displayed on the screen. It also displays the number of files on each disc.

(*b*) *COPY.* The COPY command enables a file stored on disc to be copied, as distinct from copying the whole of the contents of a disc, from one disc to another. The format of the command to accomplish this is: A>COPY CALC C:\ CALC.

If the file has an extension, e.g. .COM or .SYS, this must be typed in. A space must not be inserted, however, between the file name and the extension. A period (.) must precede the extension, otherwise a message will be displayed on the screen that the file is not found. The /S informs DOS that the system configuration has only one disc drive. The screen display is as follows:

```
Loading program ...
Single DISK COPY
Insert Source Disk <CR>
Single Disk Copy
Insert Dest. Disk <CR>
Single Disk Copy
    1 File(s) copied
Strike a key to return to activities.
```

Note: CR means CARRIAGE RETURN or ENTER.

(c) *DIR.* Typing DIR and then pressing the ENTER key will produce a listing of all files on the disc showing their size and the date and time when they were last updated. If the disc contains a substantial number of files, they will zoom up the screen faster than the eye can read them. The scrolling is stopped by the STOP key.

The command is A>DIR

The screen goes blank and a message appears:

Loading program ...
Volume in drive A is Apricot
Directory of A:

COMMAND	COM	16437	7/09/85	10:16a
CONFIG	SYS	128	13/09/85	11:40a
AUTOEXEC	BAT	128	20/04/85	7:24p

After stopping and restarting SCROLLING by the STOP key the screen display continues:

B-W	EXE	10752	13/01/85	6:21p

57 File(s) 122880 bytes free
Strike a key to return to activities

(d) *DIR/P.* This command will fill up the screen with file details and then stop automatically. A message is provided at the bottom of the screen telling the user to 'Press any key' to resume for the purpose of viewing other file details. When the complete directory has been listed a message is displayed indicating the number of files on the disc and the available capacity on the disc for storing more files.

(e) *DIR/W.* Produces an abbreviated list of the directory with the file names only.

(f) *CLS.* Clears the screen except for the A or C prompt.

(g) *REN.* An abbreviation for RENAME, which allows the user to change the name of a file. The command takes the form: REN (old name) (new name). If the file has an extension, e.g. .COM or .SYS, this must be typed in. If a file already exists with the new name on the disc a message on the screen will state this and will not rename the file.

(h) *TYPE.* Allows a text file to be displayed on the screen. TYPE will print text on the screen until the whole of the file is displayed but the process can be stopped with pressing the STOP key. Once stopped the process can be aborted by depressing the Control key and C, i.e. Control-C.

   (*i*) *DELETE*. Deletes files from a disc.

   (*j*) *DISKCOPY*. Makes back-up copies of contents of one disc to another.

   (*k*) *DIR: SORT*. Lists alphabetically sorted disc directory.

   (*l*) *FIND*. Searches for a specific string of text in a file.

Utility programs

8. General features. Utility programs are also referred to as 'service' or 'general-purpose' programs, as they are used for applications in general regardless of the nature of specific application programs. All processing activities require the support of utility programs to facilitate the activities required to attain a high level of performance in processing business information and in the development of business systems. This type of processing requires operations of a routine nature such as sort/merge for the purpose of arranging transactions into the sequence of the master file to which they relate prior to file updating; the conversion of data from one medium to another, e.g. the conversion of data in floppy discs to magnetic tape or high speed discs after being validated. This arrangement enables data to be processed faster; copying of files for security purposes usually applies only to disc files which are copied to magnetic tape; reorganising disc files periodically to eliminate overflow conditions on the tracks; housekeeping routines including such tasks as the writing of header labels on magnetic files, the blocking and deblocking of records and zeroing memory locations to ensure garbage is eliminated.

   It must be appreciated that many of the utilities are contained within the operating system for copying files from one disc to another; copying the complete content of discs to tape streamers or other discs; writing file details to directories and reorganising disc files; formatting discs; tracing routines which enable programs to be checked for errors by monitoring each step in a program as it is run; sub-routines for performing common series of instructions applicable to several applications, and so on.

9. Summary of utility programs. A number of programs falling into this category have been outlined above. Those and others are listed below:

   (a) sort/merge routines;
   (b) conversion of data from one medium to another;
   (c) copying of files;
   (d) reorganising disc files periodically;
   (e) writing of header labels on magnetic files;
   (f) blocking and deblocking of records;
   (g) zeroing memory locations to remove unwanted remnants of data from previous processing runs;
   (h) trace routines for debugging;
   (i) compilers (see 11);
   (j) interpreters (see 12);
   (k) assemblers (see 10);
   (l) program generators (see Chapter 18).

10. Assemblers. These are programs which translate a source program, written in an assembly or programming language, into a machine code object program (see 18: 1). The translation process is performed by the computer itself, and this is known as 'automatic programming'. The purpose is to simplify and speed up the task of programming by enabling the programmer to write programs in a language much simpler than machine code. Instead of writing a program which is immediately compatible to the computer, a program is written which is more compatible to the programmer for solving the problem. The computer is then used for the conversion of this program to machine code.

The assembler translates symbolic or mnemonic function codes into the equivalent machine codes and symbolic addresses into actual internal store locations. Each mnemonic instruction is normally converted into a machine code instruction on a one-for-one basis, but it is possible to use the technique of macro-coding, which enables a complete sub-routine to be incorporated into the object program by means of writing a single 'macro-instruction'. Once again, the objective is to simplify the task of programming.

The term 'object program' is used to define the program which is generated by the translation process and which is then used for processing the data of a specific application. The term 'source program' is self-explanatory, as it is the original program written for processing the data of a specific application but which is not directly usable by the computer. After translation, the object program is retained either in magnetic tape or magnetic disc. In addition, a print-out is produced by the line-printer of both the source and the object program instructions, for comparison and error checking. It is also possible to have a print-out of diagnostics as an aid to error checking (*see* 4:**8–10** and Figs. 4.1 and 4.2).

11. Compilers. These are programs which translate a source program, written in a high-level language, into a machine code object program. A compiler performs the task of assembling the object program, but is generally more complex than an assembler because each source program instruction in a high-level language such as COBOL generates a number of machine code instructions, i.e. a macro-instruction generates a number of micro-instructions.

As a result of the increased complexity, the compiler is larger in terms of the translation instructions it contains, and this produces a problem of internal storage capacity, as a large amount of storage is required to accommodate the compiler during the compilation run. It is sometimes necessary to compile a program on a different computer from that on which the compiled program will be run on account of this factor. As a matter of interest, this is the reason for stating the source computer and object computer in a COBOL program. Compiling is performed for similar reasons to assembling — to reduce the complexity and time involved in writing programs.

To give some idea of the amount of storage required for both assembling and compiling, it must be appreciated that during translation the internal store must hold the source program, the compiler or assembler and the resulting object program.

12. Interpreters. Interpreters are usually used by personal or small business computers, whereas mainframes utilise compilers. Interpreters and compilers are translation programs which, in respect of small computers, convert statements written in BASIC into machine code. When the command RUN is keyed in, each statement in the program is interpreted and if any statement does not conform to the rules or grammar (known as syntax) of the language then a syntax error is displayed on the screen. This can be a disadvantage as it slows down the execution of the program until the errors are removed. In addition, each statement is interpreted each time the program is executed and this also tends to slow down its execution.

Many small computers now have compilers available, which means it is necessary to translate the program only once, during the compilation run, and the compiled program is then stored on tape or disc backing storage until the relevant application is to be run. As each statement does not have to be translated at *run time* the program runs faster than an interpreted program. An interpreter is more 'firmware' than software as it is stored on a ROM (read only memory) chip.

13. Job control language. The purpose of job control language (JCL) is to control the running of jobs on a computer. Often on a large computer several jobs are run concurrently in multi-programming mode. The JCL enables the names of jobs, the files to be used, the peripherals required, priorities of the various jobs and interrupt procedures to be specified. It enables a computer operator to communicate with the operating system by means of the keyboard/VDU for the purpose of controlling the processing of the various jobs.

Table 20A *Job control commands*

Mainframe computers	BASIC for use with microcomputers	Timesharing systems
Compile	Run	Login
Execute	Load	Logout
Delete	Save	EOJ (End of Job)
Start	Verify	
Sort	Clr	
Dump	List	
Edit	New	

Job control commands are written in a job control language. In batch processing applications the job commands are usually predefined and input with a source or object program with the relevant data, or are stored in a 'command file'. Special symbols distinguish commands from program instructions. Examples of job control commands are listed in Table 20A.

Progress test 20

1. State the nature and purpose of an operating system.   (3)
2. List typical tasks performed by an operating system.   (4)
3. Provide six examples of typical operating system commands. (7)
4. State the nature and purpose of utility programs.   (8)
5. Define the difference between an assembler, compiler and interpreter.   (10–12)

Appendix 1
Examination technique

Examination questions in respect of data processing and management information systems are often descriptive and aim to test the candidates' knowledge of how well-defined principles are applied to business situations or problems.

The subject is very wide and practical, candidates should always take care to demonstrate fully the wider implications of what may appear to be very narrow questions.

The examination candidate is recommended to observe the following points.

1. Read each question thoroughly before attempting an answer, in order to avoid any initial misunderstanding of the requirements of the question. A good answer to the wrong question does not score marks.

2. Allocate sufficient time to answer each question. It is fatal to omit an answer to a question through spending too much time on other questions. It is much better to have a fairly complete answer on all the questions rather than no answer at all on some of them.

3. Having determined the requirements of each question, the first one to be attempted should be selected. It is good practice before committing yourself to the answer paper to jot down main headings or topics to be covered on a scrap pad. By this means, initial thoughts may be clarified and the full scope of the question appreciated.

4. The answer may then be written on the answer paper, observing the following points.

(*a*) Write legibly to enable the examiner to interpret your answer easily.

(*b*) Show a good command of English, sentence structure and grammar.

(*c*) Outline the answer on the basis of topic or subject headings sub-analysed as appropriate as follows:

(*a*)
  (*i*)
  (*ii*)
(*b*)
(*c*)
  (*i*)
  (*ii*)
  (*iii*)

By this means the examiner can easily assess the points being made and can more readily appreciate their relevance and award marks accordingly.

(*d*) Keep to the subject and be as concise as possible without unnecessary padding — you either know the subject or you do not. Make sure you do before sitting the examination, even if only to save examination fees.

5. Allow sufficient time to read the answers before handing-in the paper so that corrections can be effected.

6. Answer questions from your own experience whenever possible, as this shows the examiner that you are conversant with the subject in question.

7. Some answers require the presentation of a flowchart or other recording technique, and it is important to use drawing aids in their construction, i.e. charting symbol templates, coins (for circles), and a rule (for straight lines). Neatness of presentation is very important if maximum marks are to be gained. It is also essential to determine the type of flowchart required, e.g. procedure chart, system flowchart (run chart), or program flowchart, or data flow diagram.

Appendix 2
Case study: car hire company

The following case study is based on a question set by the City and Guilds of London Institute in the 747 paper. The question has been slightly modified.

1. System description. A car hire firm operates a self-drive service from 30 offices throughout the UK, most of them being at airports or main railway stations. Customers may pick up a car at one office and return it to the company at a different office.

At the company's London headquarters is a large computer supporting terminals in each of the offices. Each office terminal consists of a VDU, keyboard and hard-copy printer.

Customers may book cars for hire by telephone, by letter or by calling in person. These booking requests should be addressed at least three days in advance to the office where the customer wishes to pick up the car. Since cars may be hired from one office and returned to another, the computer must keep track of the location of each car and what bookings are arranged for it. A minimum of eight hours is required between bookings for any one car for maintenance. Each car is serviced every 5,000 miles, so the computer must keep details of mileages for each car. If an office does not have enough cars at a particular time to cover its bookings then customers are turned away.

You are to design a system to run on this computer configuration to satisfy the following requirements:

(a) *Inputs* (via the keyboard) at each office are:

(i)   *Bookings.* The clerk inputs date and time of collection, date, time and place of returning, size of car required.

(ii)   *Collection.* Hirers pay a deposit on collecting the car. The clerk inputs details of this and confirms to the system that the car is now out on hire.

(iii)   *Return.* Hirers pay the balance of the hire charge on return. The clerk inputs details of this and the car mileage.

(b) *Outputs* required at each office are:

(i)   A twice daily print-out showing the bookings so far recorded for that office for the next 72 hours (details of which cars are booked and which cars are due for service).

(ii)   Details of each car can be displayed on the VDU on request, showing current bookings on file, present location, mileage since last service.

(iii)   Computer-printed confirmation of booking is produced and posted first-class to telephone or postal customers and handed to personal callers.

2. **Tasks.** The overall requirements of the question is to design a system to satisfy the details provided. A number of tasks are necessary, which are outlined below:

(a) As a means of communicating the structure of the proposed system to management, compile a systems flowchart of the system which will be implemented in each of the 30 offices. The interaction of customers, the office and the computer must be clearly shown.

(b) Show by means of a block diagram the computer configuration you think would be in use at the London headquarters, indicating how it is connected to each of the 30 offices.

(c) Prepare a computer run chart, clearly indicating the input, processing, use of master files, and output at each stage of processing.

(d) Define the master files you need to support the system specifying the data elements (fields), data type and the size of each element of data.

3. Solution. *See* Fig. A1.

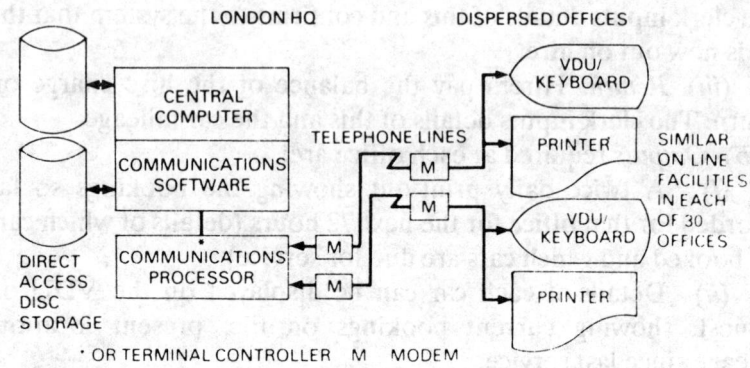

(a) Block diagram of computer configuration.

Figure A1 *Case study solution.*

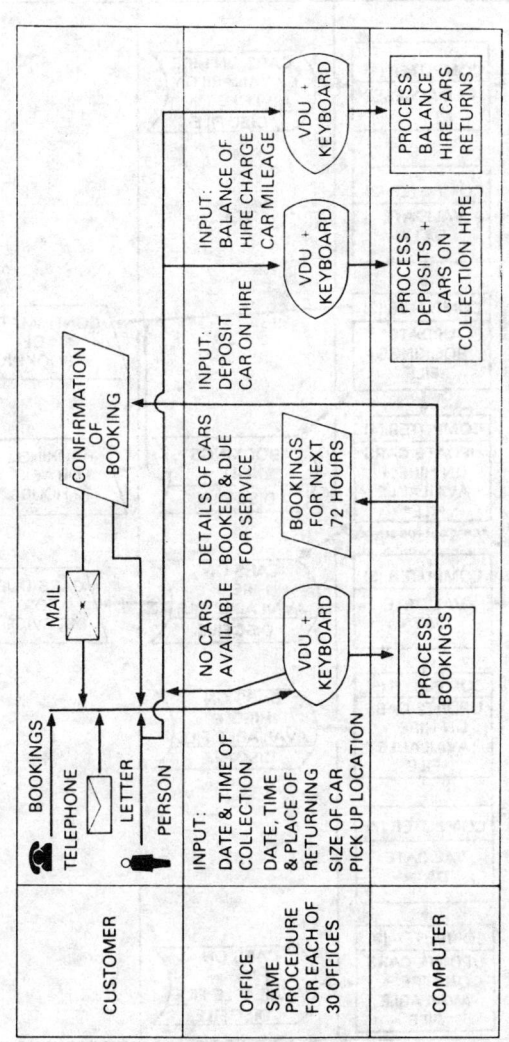

(b) System flowchart.

Figure A1   *Case study solution.*

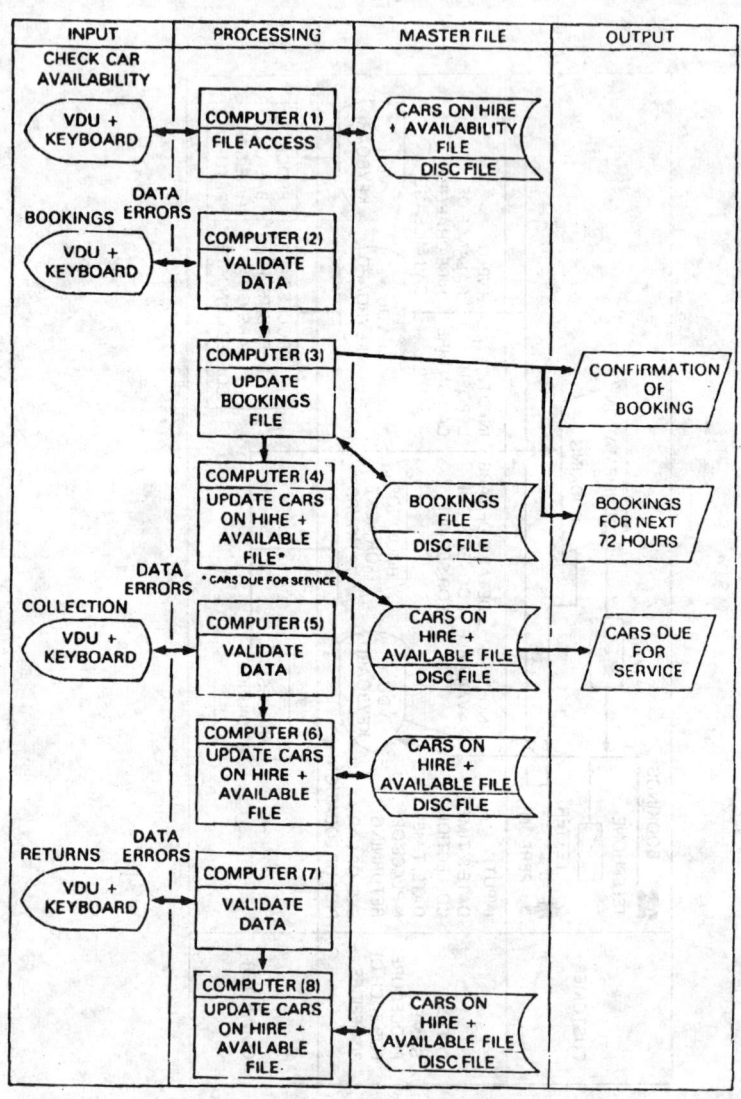

(c) *Computer run chart.*

Figure A1 *Case study solution.*

(*d*) *Content and structure of master files*

Data element	Data type	Data size
Bookings file		
Customer name	X	20
Pick up location (office no.)	N	2
Date of collection	N	8 (25/06/85)
Time of collection	N	4 (24 hour clock)
Date of returning	N	8
Time of returning	N	4
Place of returning (office no.)	N	2
Booking indicator	N	2 (-1, for instance)*
Cars on hire and available file		
Type of car	X	1 (e.g. S for saloon)
Size of car:		
No. of seats	N	1
Engine capacity	N	4 (e.g. 1600 = 1600cc)
Registration no.	X/N	7 (*see* Note below)
Mileage this hiring	N	4
Mileage since last service	N	4
(increased by mileage this hiring)		
Service indicator if mileage	N	2 (+1, for instance)*
=> 5000 miles		
On hire indicator	N	1 (0, for instance)
Deposit paid	X/N	7 (£XX.XX)
Balance of hire charge	X/N	6
(eliminated when paid)		

Notes

X = Alphabetic character;   N = Numeric character

Registration numbers of cars in the UK consist of seven characters, e.g. G443 MFD

*2 characters including sign

Figure A.1 *Case study solution.*

Index

accountancy practice software, 352
accounting packages, 354, 355
accumulator, 41, 42, 49
acoustic coupler, 90, 182
address bus, 48
address generation, 123–5
address register, 44, 48
administrative controls, 212, 213
advantages, direct access storage, 180
Algol, 328
algorithm, 319
algorithmic address generation, *see* address generation
allophones, *see* speech synthesis
ALU, *see* arithmetic logic unit
Amstrad, 33
analogue (digital) input, 98
analogue signals, 90, 182
AND, 41, 145
AND gate, 52
ANSI, 327
Apple, 33
AppleDOS, 392
Apple Macintosh, 33
application software, 350–87
architecture, 20, 21, 29, 39

archiving, 136
arithmetic logic unit (ALU), 19, 40, 41
arithmetic operations, *see* computing
article numbering, 94
ASCII, 18, 96, 184
assembler, 396, 397
assembly code, *see* assembly language
assembly language, 42
attribute, 157
AU, *see* arithmetic logic unit
audit packages, 223
audit trail, 223, 357
auditing, 221–4
auto teller terminal, 94, 95
automatic decision making, 50, 51

backing storage, 29, 34, 167–80
back-up, 241, 244, 246, 356
balance forward, 375
bar code, 94
barrel printer, 103, 104
baseband network, 199
BASIC, 328
BASIC interpreter, *see* interpreter

batch control, 220, 221
batch control slip, 237
batch processing, 237–43
batch processing configuration,
    see configuration
benchmark tests, 299
benefits of using a computer, *see*
    computer benefits
binary chop, 118
binary code, 7
bits, 7, 18
blocking of records, 137
Boolean algebra, 41, 52
broadband network 199
bubble memory, 58, 59
bucket, 122, 123
bus network, 202
buses, 48, 49
byte, 7

C programming language,
    330
cache memory, 59
CAD (computer aided design),
    107
capacity, storage, *see* storage
    capacity
CBASIC compiler, 328
CCITT (Consultative
    Committee for International
    Telegraph and Telephone),
    22
central processing unit, 20,
    39–60
centralised processing, 248,
    253
Centronics parallel interface, 22,
    23
chain printer, 103, 104

changes file, 34
channels, 48
character printer, 101
character set, 7
check digit, 7, 227
check digit verification, 227
check-out scanning, 94
checks and controls, 209–35
chief programmer, 64
chief systems analyst, 62, 63
clock speed, 49
close-coupled network, 202,
    203
closed shop programming, 339
closed subroutine, 340
co-axial cable, 196, 197
COBOL, 329
COM (computer output on
    microfilm), 106, 107
commands, 393–5
communication analysis, 285
company policy, 285
Compaq, 33
compile time errors, 338
compiler, 397
computations, *see* computing
computer aided design, *see*
    CAD
computer benefits, 16, 17
computer bureaux, 259–63
computer input, *see* input
computer literacy, 12–14
computer logic, *see* logic
    functions
computer output, *see* output
computer run, 237, 238
computer run chart, 238
computer, social aspects of,
    14, 15

computer system, nature of, 18–20
computing, 10
computing services, 262, 263
conditional branch, 314
confidentiality, information, 218–20
configuration, 32, 242, 245, 246
consultancy, 263
Consultative Committee International Telephone and Telegraphs, see CCITT
control bus, 49
control unit, 20, 41–7
Coral, 331
correction of errors, 240, 241
cost, software, 352
counter, 314
courting, 165
CPU, see central processing unit
CSMA/CD (Carrier Sense Multiple Access with Collision Detect), 202
cursor, 91
customer file, 138, 141
customer record, 8
customer sales history file, 140
cycles per second, 49
cylinder, 119
cylinder index, 119

daisy wheel printer, 103
data, 7
data analysis, 285, 286
data bus, 49
data capture, see data collection
data channel, 49
data collection, 92–6

data communication, 182–94
data dictionary, 151, 154, 163
data modelling, 162
data path, 49
data preparation, see keyboard encoding
data processing, 3–6
data processing manager, 61, 62
data processing model, 10–12
data processing operations, 9, 10
data processing staff, 272, 273
data processing standards, 232–5
data processing system, 3, 6
Data Protection Act 1984, 219, 220
data storage, 109–46
data transfer, 314
data transmission, see data communication
data validation, 224–7
data verification, 76, 77
database access and security, 151
database administrator, 65
database applications, 153
Database Management System (DBMS), 149, 151, 161
database query system, 151
databases, 148–66, 210
Datakey, 229, 230
Datel, 187–90
Datel network control system, see DNCS
DBMS, see Database Management System

DEC (Digital Equipment Corporation), 32
decision tables, 341–7
decrementing a counter, 321–3
demodulator, 184
dependencies, 165
design philosophy, 222
development of computer applications, 267–89
dialogue, 24
dictionary, *see* data dictionary
digital PABX telephone exchange, 90, 191
digital transmission, 90
disc drives, 168–74
disc operating system (DOS), 25, 174, 175
disc sector, *see* sectors
disc security, 175, 176
diskettes, *see* floppy discs
distributed processing, 95, 248, 253–5
DNX 2000, 191–3
DOS, *see* disc operating system
dot matrix printer, *see* matrix printer
dump/restart, 247
dumping, 217
duties, systems analyst, 280

EAN, *see* European Article Number
earth station, 193
EBCDIC, 18, 184
ECMA, 327
economic feasibility, 274
EDS, *see* exchangeable disc storage

education and training programme, 269
electronic document storage and retrieval, 144
electronic filing, 144, 145
electronic funds transfer, 205
electronic mail, 205
electronic retrieval, 145, 146
electronic technology, 7
elements of a computer system, 19, 20
elements of a data processing system, 10–12
elements of a processor, 40
employee record, *see* payroll record
encoding, *see* keyboard encoding
entity, 157
environmental controls, 213
EPROM, 58
error checking, 187
error reports, *see* invalid items report
errors, 315
European Article Number (EAN), 94, 251
European Computer Manufacturers' Association, *see* ECMA
exception principle, *see* exception reporting
exception reporting, 51
exchangeable disc storage (EDS), 170–2
execution time errors, 338, 339
Extended Binary Coded Decimal Interchange Code, *see* EBCDIC

extended entry decision table, 342
external storage,   167–80
E13B,   80

facilities management,   262
facsimile document transmission, *see* FAX
fact finding,   281–6
factory terminal,   92, 93
fast card,   34
father tape,   216, 217
FAX,   33, 205
feasibility study,   270–3
fetch-execute cycle,   44
fibre optic transmission lines, 184
field,   8, 114, 115
file activity (hit rate),   130
file amendments,   130–3
file conversion,   125, 126, 304
file copying,   217
file creation, *see* file conversion
file organisation,   116–25
file relationships,   133–5
file security,   126
file specification,   297
file updating,   126–30
first normal form,   164
fixed discs, *see* Winchester discs
fixed length field and records, 115
flat records,   115
floppy discs,   172–4
flowcharts,   238, 239, 242
folders,   109
form design,   292–5
formatting,   136, 176
Forth,   331

Fortran,   331
fourth generation language (4GL), 25, 152–4, 333–5
free text,   145
front-end processor,   186
full index,   122
function register,   44
functional decomposition,   277

GEC,   32
GEM interface,   25
generation technique,   217
gigabytes,   29
grandfather tape,   216, 217
graph plotter,   35, 106
graphics tablet,   99

handprint data entry terminal, 95, 96
hard copy,   35
hard discs,   168–72
hard sectoring, *see* formatting
hardware, *see* configuration
hardware controls,   215
Hewlett Packard,   32
hierarchical structure,   157
high level language,   327–31
hit rate, *see* file activity
holographic memory,   59
home record,   124

IAS, *see* immediate access storage
IBM,   32, 33
IBM AS/400,   39
IBM PC,   33, 34
IBM PS/2,   34
ICL,   32
icons (ikons),   26, 27, 255

immediate access storage (IAS), *see* internal memory
incrementing a register, 321–4
indexed sequential, 118–21
information, 3
ink jet printer, 105
input, 12, 73–99
input controls, 214
input device, 20
input specification, 296
inspection, 284
instructions, 314
integrated accounting packages, 355–7
integrated discs, 180
Integrated Digital Network, *see* IDN
Integrated Services Digital Network, *see* ISDN
Intel, 39, 40
intelligent terminals, 92
interactive processing, 244
interactive videotex, 205
inter-block gap, 139, 173
interfacing, 21–7
interfacing devices, 21, 22
internal check, 221, 222
internal memory, 29, 32, 33, 55–9
internal storage, *see* internal memory
internally stored program, *see* internal memory
International Datel Services, 189
International Directory of Software, 351
International Organisation for Standardisation, *see* ISO

interpreter, 397
interviewing, 283
invalid items report, 241
inverted files, 21
inverter, 41
ISDN (Integrated Services Digital Network), 184, 205
ISO, 327
iteration, 320

JCL, *see* job control language
job control language, 398

key, *see* key field
key field, 115, 119, 122, 123, 163
key-to-disc, 77, 78
key-to-diskette, 78
key words, 153
keyboard encoding, 76, 77
keypad, 25
kilostream, 189
Kimball tags, 76

LAN, *see* local area network
lap-top portable computer, 35
laser printer, 104
laser scanner, *see* checkout scanning
ledger cards, 126
light pen, 98, 99
limited entry decision table, 341
line printer, 163
link editing, 340
Lisp, 331, 332
list processing, *see* Lisp
local area network, 196–202
logic circuit, 41, 52

logic functions,   41
logic gate,   41, 52
logic operators,   41
logical data relationships,   154
logical records,   136–8
logical view,   276, 277
LOGO,   330
loop,   44
low-level language,   42

machine code,   396
machine-orientated language,
    327
magnetic ink characters,   80–2
magnetic tape,   167
magnetically encoded,   105
main memory, *see* internal
    memory
mainframe computer,   28–32
maintenance,   308
maintenance programmer,
    340, 341
management services manager,
    68, 70
master file,   133, 134
matrix printer,   102, 103
megabyte,   29
megahertz,   *see* MHz
megastream,   189, 190
member,   155
memory address,   49
memory capacity, *see* storage
    capacity
memory, internal, *see* internal
    memory
menu,   23, 24
Mercury communications,   194
MHz,   39, 49

Michael Jackson structured
    programming,   337
microcomputer,   33–6
microprocessor,   49
Microsoft windows,   249
minicomputer,   32
mnemonic function code,   396
modem,   90, 182–4
modifications,   298, 299
modulus,   227
monitoring,   307
mouse,   256
MS–DOS,   351, 391, 392
multi-tasking,   29, 35, 249, 250
multi-user applications,   247–9
multiplexor,   186
multipoint circuits,   189
multiprogramming,   29

NAND (Not AND),   41
National Computing Centre
    (NCC),   327
natural language,   151
network, *see* local area network
network facilities,   198
network planning,   301–3
network structure,   154–6
next pointer,   156
NLQ,   103
nominal ledger, accounts screen,
    366
nominal ledger, configuration
    screen,   359, 360
nominal ledger, package,
    357–66
nominal ledger, parameter
    screen,   361, 363
nominal ledger, payments screen,
    365

non-procedural language, 332, 333
NOR, 41
NOR gate, 54
normalisation, 163
NOT, 41, 145
NOT gate, 53

object program, 313, 315
observation, 283, 284
OCR, *see* optical characters
OCR–A, 83
OCR–B, 83
off-line data transmission, 186
OMR, *see* optical marks
on-line data transmission, 184–6
on-line order processing, 250–3
on-line processing, 243, 244
open item, 375
open shop programming, 339
open subroutine, 339
operand, 41, 42, 48
operating costs, 284
operating system, 249, 390–2
operating system commands, 393
operating systems, mainframes, 393
operating systems, microcomputers, 392–3
operation standards, 233, 234
operational controls, 214–18
operational data, 284
operations manager, 64, 65
operator, 41, 42
optical character recognition, *see* optical characters

optical characters, 82–4
optical disc, 178, 179
optical fibre cable, 197
optical marks, 85
optical memory, *see* holographic memory
OR (inclusive OR), 41, 145, 146
OR gate, 54
organisation by activity, 61, 63
organisation by purpose, 66, 67
organisation, data processing department, 61–7
organisation, management services department, 67, 68
organisational controls, 211, 212
organisational data, 284
OS/2 operating system, 392
output, 12, 101–7
output device, 20
output specification, 297
overflow address, 119
overflow area, 117
overflow record, 117
owner, 155

PABX, *see* digital PABX telephone exchange
package, *see* package programs
package compatibility, 351
package programs, 350
package sources, 351
packet switching, 190, 191
pages, 32, 135
parallel running, 305, 306
parameters, 356, 358
partial indexing, 122
Pascal, 329, 330

password, 218
payroll application, 12
payroll file, 138
payroll package, 384–6
payroll record, 8, 9
PC, *see* microcomputer
PC–DOS, 391, 392
performance standards, 234
peripheral channel, 49
personal number, 94
physical records, 136–8
pilot scheme, 306
PL/1, 330
planning techniques, 300
plant register file, 142
point-of-sale terminals
  (check-out scanning), 251–3
pointers, 114, 155, 256
pointers, absolute, 114
pointers, relative, 114
pop-up menu, 24
port, 47, 49
portability, 331
preliminary appraisal, 268
Prestel, 205
printers, 101–5
prior pointer, 156
problem-orientated language,
  327
procedural languages, 331,
  332
procedure chart, 286, 288, 289
procedure chart symbols, 287
processing techniques, 237–57
processor, *see* central processing
  unit
processor clock, 49
processor structure, 40
product file, 140

program development cycle,
  314–17
Program Development Facility
  (PDF), 337
program diagnostic routine,
  315
program documentation, 326,
  327
program dump, 337, 338
program flowchart, 343, 346,
  348
program generators, 335–7
program instructions, 43
program specification, 275, 315
programmable read only
  memory, *see* PROM
programming, 313–26
programming standards, 327
project control, *see* project
  management
project life cycle, 300
project management, 299
Prolog, 332
PROM, 58
PROM programmer, 58
prototyping, 278, 279
pull-down menu, 24
purchase ledger, account details
  screen, 381–3
purchase ledger, configuration
  screen, 377
purchase ledger, data entry menu
  screen, 378
purchase ledger, data entry
  selection screen, 376
purchase ledger, invoice screen
  379
purchase ledger, package,
  375–84

purchase ledger, report
    selection screen, 380
quartz crystal, 49
query by example, 160
query language, 25, 152
questionnaire, 283

RAM, 57, 178
random access memory, *see*
    RAM
random enquiries, 244
random file organisation,
    121
read-only memory, *see* ROM
real-time systems, 210, 211,
    246, 247
record key, *see* key field
record locking, 248
record unlocking, 248
recording techniques, 286–9
records, 8
reference file, 134
reference key, *see* key field
relational structure, 157
remote batch processing, 242
remote batch terminal, 95
remote job entry, *see* remote
    batch processing
REPEAT–UNTIL, 320
reports, 357
resources, 284
retraining, 308
ring network, 199–201
ROM, 58
RS–232C, interface, 22

sales accounting, 12
sales ledger, account screen,
    369

sales ledger, credit control
    screen, 371
sales ledger, customer accounts
    screen, 372
sales ledger, customer accounts
    status screen, 372
sales ledger, data entry menu
    screen, 368
sales ledger, end of day screen,
    373
sales ledger, package, 367–75
sales ledger, report selection
    screen, 374
sales ledger, invoice screen, 370
satellite transmission, 193
searching, 153
sectors, 173
security, *see* checks and controls
seek area, 119
self-checking number, *see* check
    digit verification
self-indexing, 122, 123
semiconductor memory, 57
semiconductor storage, 176–8
semiconductor technology, 57
sequence, 320
sequential access, 117
sequential control register, 44
sequential file, 117
serial access, 117
serial file, 117
serial organisation, *see* serial file
silicon chip, 49
silicon wafer, 50
single-address computer, 42
sixteen-bit processor, 39
smart card, 230
social aspects of computers,
    14–16

sociological controls, 214
soft discs, *see* floppy discs
soft sectoring, *see* formatting
software, 350–87
software, accounting practice, 352
software, costs, 352
software, estate agents, 352, 353
software, insurance brokers, 353
software portability, *see* portability
software, solicitors, 353
software, stockbrokers, 353
son tape, 216, 217
source of packages, 351
source program, 313, 315
speech synthesis, 97, 98
spreadsheets, 35
stand-by facilities, 261
standards officer, 234
star network, 201
steering committee, 267
stock control, 12
stock file, 140, 143
storage capacity, 48, 57
storage cartridge, 34
storage device, 20
store and forward, 203
structured files, 148
structured programming, 318, 319
structured systems development, 276–8
subroutine library, 340
symbolic addresses, 396
symbolic code, 396
synonyms, 124, 146, 154

System C, 335–7
system changeover, 297, 305–7
system continuity, 233
system description, 296
system development controls, 231, 232
system documentation, 222, 232, 233
system implementation, *see* systems installation
system life cycle, 274–6
system maintenance, 308
system modifications, 298, 299
system monitoring, 307
system objectives, 296
system specification, 295–8
system testing, 223, 297
System X, 190
System/400 operating system, 393
systems analysis, 280–9
systems analysis team, 281
systems analyst, 280, 281
systems design, 291–308
systems installation, 304–8

tape streamer, 37, 168
technical feasibility, 274
technological controls, 213, 214
telecommunications, *see* data communication
teletype, 89
telex, 90
telex network, 90
terminals, 88–92
test data, 307
text files, 35
thermal printer, 104, 105

third normal form, 165
thirty-two bit processor, 39
time sharing, 218, 260
token ring network, 200
top management support, 268
track reference, 175
transaction file, 134
transmission speed, 187
transposed digits, 227
truth table, 41, 52
tuple, 159
turnkey services, 263
twisted pair wires, 196

unconditional branch, 314
units of storage, 56
UNIX operating system, 392
unstructured documents, 144
user interface, 23, 24
utility software, 389, 395

validation, see data validation
value-added network, 203
VAN, see value-added network
variable length records and fields,
115, 116
VDU, see visual display unit

very large scale integration
(VLSI), 29
video screen, see visual display
unit
virtual storage, 135, 178
visual display unit (VDU), 19,
90-2, 106
vocabulary, see speech synthesis
voice grade telephone lines, 90
voice modulation, 182
volatile, 178, 340
volume, 135

wages computations, see payroll
application
WHILE, 319
WHILE DO, 320
WHILE WEND, 320
wide area network, 203, 205
Winchester discs, 70, 169
windows, 35, 91, 255
word processing, 35
workstations, 96, 97

X–OR (exclusive OR), 41
X–OR gate, 54
Xenix operating system, 392